Happiness

Happiness

Classic and Contemporary Readings in Philosophy

Edited by

Steven M. Cahn
Graduate Center, City University of New York

Christine Vitrano
Brooklyn College, City University of New York

New York   Oxford
OXFORD UNIVERSITY PRESS
2008

Oxford University Press, Inc., publishes works that further Oxford University's
objective of excellence in research, scholarship, and education.

Oxford New York
Auckland Cape Town Dar es Salaam Hong Kong Karachi
Kuala Lumpur Madrid Melbourne Mexico City Nairobi
New Delhi Shanghai Taipei Toronto

With offices in
Argentina Austria Brazil Chile Czech Republic France Greece
Guatemala Hungary Italy Japan Poland Portugal Singapore
South Korea Switzerland Thailand Turkey Ukraine Vietnam

Published by Oxford University Press, Inc.
198 Madison Avenue, New York, New York 10016
http://www.oup.com

Oxford is a registered trademark of Oxford University Press

Library of Congress Cataloging-in-Publication Data

Happiness: classic and contemporary readings in philosophy / edited by Steven M. Cahn
  and Christine Vitrano.
    p. cm.
  ISBN-13: 978-0-19-532140-1
  1. Happiness. I. Cahn, Steven M. II. Vitrano, Christine.

  BJ1481.H37 2007
  170—dc22

                                                                2006050736

Printed in the United States of America
on acid-free paper

CONTENTS

PREFACE

Happiness—its nature, source, and value—has been a central topic in moral philosophy from the time of the ancient Greeks until our own day. Most anthologies, however, treat the subject only in passing, thereby downplaying its importance. This volume is designed to demonstrate how the history of ethics can be viewed as a set of variations on the theme of happiness and how the concept continues to be a key to contemporary debates about utility, welfare, and well-being. The book can thus serve as an engaging introduction both to the major theories of ethics and to some ongoing moral controversies.

The book explores such provocative questions as: What, after all, is happiness? Is it necessary for a worthwhile life? Is it sufficient? Does happiness depend on one's state of mind, one's circumstances, or both? Can a person be immoral yet happy? Many who begin the study of philosophy assume that such matters will be a focus of discussion and are disappointed to learn otherwise. But students can be offered a serious course in ethics that does justice to the subject's complexity and fulfills their original expectations. We hope this book will encourage instructors to try such an approach.

We are grateful to our executive editor, Robert Miller, for his support and guidance, and to his associate editor, Sarah Calabi, for her generous help. We also wish to thank the staff of Oxford University Press for its kind assistance throughout the stages of production.

INTRODUCTION

DANIEL NETTLE

Daniel Nettle is a lecturer in psychology at the University of Newcastle.

"We hold these truths to be self-evident," wrote Thomas Jefferson in the Declaration of Independence in 1776, "that all men are created equal, that they are endowed by their Creator with certain unalienable Rights, that among these are Life, Liberty, and the pursuit of Happiness." Of these three, it is the third that seems most able to imbue our lives with purpose. . . . Jefferson's rights one and two wake the horse up and open the stable door, but only number three—the pursuit of happiness—is going to make it go anywhere.

The idea that happiness is central to the point of the human experience goes back to the ancients. The Greek philosopher Aristippus argued in the fourth century B.C. that the goal of life is to maximize the totality of one's pleasures. If this is true, which is more debatable than it might seem, then happiness becomes . . . the most urgent of personal questions for any human being to solve. More than this, happiness also moves to the center of political and economic decisions. If maximizing happiness is the point of individual lives, then the point of systems of government and economy should be to maximize collective or aggregate happiness. This position is a pure form of the doctrine of utilitarianism, which was made famous by moral philosopher Jeremy Bentham, but foreshadowed in the thought of Francis Hutcheson, who claimed, "That action is best, which procures the greatest Happiness for the greatest Numbers." . . .

The notion of happiness . . . shows up in culture after culture. Many languages draw the distinction between something very immediate like *joy* or *pleasure*, and something more lasting and considered, like *satisfaction* or *contentment* (e.g., Italian *gioa* versus *felicita*). Note that whilst there might be quite a lot of *gioa* involved in a state of *felicita*, you would not have to be joyful all the time for the longer state to count as a happy one. In some languages, there is a specific lexical link between *happiness* and *good luck* (German *Gluck/glucklich* happy/lucky; *good hap* in English originally meant good luck). This suggests . . . something . . . to do with things turning out better than it was reasonable to

From *Happiness: The Science Behind Your Smile*, Oxford University Press, 2005. Used by permission of the publisher.

expect. Thus, being happy might not always be an absolute state, but contains implicit comparison with an expectation or with what other people have.

These observations are sufficient to allow us to begin to sketch the semantic terrain of happiness. Most usages of the term can be classified into one of three increasingly inclusive senses. The most immediate and direct senses of happiness involve an emotion or feeling, something like joy or pleasure. These feelings are transient and have an unmistakable and particular phenomenology—that is to say, paraphrasing Thomas Nagel, there is something which joy feels like. The feeling is brought on by a desired state being (perhaps unexpectedly) attained, and there is not much cognition involved, beyond the recognition that the desired thing has happened. . . . [W]e will henceforth call this sense of happiness "level one happiness."

When people say that they are happy with their lives, they do not usually mean that they are literally joyful, or experiencing pleasure, all of the time. They mean that upon reflection on the balance sheet of pleasures and pains, they feel the balance to be reasonably positive over the long term. This is happiness in the sense usually studied by psychologists. It concerns not so much feelings, as judgments about the balance of feelings. Thus it is a hybrid of emotion, and judgment about emotion. Its synonyms are things like contentment and life satisfaction. This is "level two happiness." It is clear that when Bentham talked about the greatest happiness to the greatest number being the foundation of morals and legislation, he meant happiness in a level two sense: the long-term balance of positive and negative emotions across time and individuals.

Level two happiness, though, is not calculated by a simple summing up of all the positive moments and a subtraction of the negative ones. It also involves more complex, cognitive processes, such as comparison with alternative possible outcomes. Thus I could say, "I am happy about how the first draft of my book came out," in the full knowledge that the first draft is dreadful. If I always write dreadful first drafts, but find it easier to revise them into good shape than I do to get the text down onto the page initially, then this makes perfect sense. I could be happy relative to my expectation that it would be awful, and my belief that the hard work is done by that point. Or, to take another example, if I usually cut myself shaving twice a day, then I could be happy to have cut myself just once today. However, it is unlikely that I took pleasure from the cut. The cut was a painful event which made me swear; the happiness stems from the subsequent processes that compared the pain I went through with the pain I expected or had experienced yesterday.

There are yet broader senses of happiness. Aristotle's ideal of the good life, *eudaimonia*, is sometimes translated as "happiness." However, what is meant by *eudaimonia* is a life in which the person flourishes, or fulfills true potential. Though such a life *could* include many positive emotional experiences, it is not actually part of its definition that it need do so. Contemporary psychologists and philosophers have sometimes talked of happiness when they really mean the good life or *eudaimonia*. When they do so, we shall call this usage a level three sense of the term happiness. Note that "level three happiness" has no characteristic phenomenology since it is not an emotional state. There is no single thing that it feels like to achieve *eudaimonia*, since everyone's potential is different. Indeed, one of the problems of *eudaimonia* and related constructs is that it is not clear who is to be the judge of what one's full potential is. . . .

In addition to the three levels of the ordinary meaning of happiness, some scholars have used the term simply to mean the attainment of whatever it is that people want. This is particularly evident in economics. Jeremy Bentham and the classical economists hypothesized that people make their choices in life so as to maximize their happiness, or, as it was called, utility. By utility, they meant happiness in a level two sense. That is, they believed that if you had a pleasure-measuring device, then you would be able to show that the choices people made were the ones that maximized the balance of pleasurable feelings over painful ones. However, the lack of any practical way of measuring happiness or utility meant that, over time, economists took the utility of an outcome simply to mean the propensity of people to choose it. For example, if people prefer to spend money on cars rather than boats, then economists say that having a car gives greater utility than having boats. This is not a psychological hypothesis. Indeed, it is not an explanatory claim at all. The greater utility of cars cannot explain why people choose them, since the greater utility of cars is *defined* as the propensity of people to choose them. The concept is therefore merely a shorthand for a device for predicting people's behavior when allocating scarce resources.

Sometimes, then, you will find arguments that take the following form: if people choose, for example, a higher income over more leisure time, it follows that a higher income must make people happier than more leisure time, otherwise they would not have chosen it. Here "happiness" is being used to mean behavioral preference, It says nothing about the actual emotional content of the two outcomes. It merely describes people's propensity to choose one or the other. This usage is quite different from that of ordinary language. There are all kinds of reasons that people might choose A over B without A making them happier than B (for example, because they wrongly estimate how much they will enjoy A, because they feel morally obligated, because everyone else around them is choosing A, and so on).

Which definition of happiness we adopt makes a real difference to what we can do and what we conclude. For one thing, the different levels of definitions are more or less amenable to scientific study. Level one happiness can, in principle, be measured objectively. We might well discover a physiological mechanism or brain region that is dedicated to pleasure, and be able to measure its activity. At the very least, in level one terms, people's subjective report of their happiness is king. If they say they are experiencing joy, then we have to take it that they are, and we can record this response as a data point. The same is true to a lesser extent with level two happiness. Here, the different standards of comparison that different individuals employ in their judgments could become a confounding factor, but people's self-reports of happiness are still the primary and proper data points for a scientific study.

Happiness level three is not something that can be so easily measured. As we have seen, assessing it involves making a judgment about what the good life consists of and the extent to which one's life fulfills it. . . .

[W]e intuitively feel that there is something called happiness, something unitary but not trivial, concrete enough to strive for yet broad enough to be worth striving for. The pursuit of this familiar, obscure, paradoxical object of desire is the theme of this book.

Part One

HISTORICAL SOURCES

THE REPUBLIC

PLATO

Plato (c. 428–347 B.C.), the famed Athenian philosopher, wrote a series of dialogues, most of which feature his teacher Socrates (469–399 B.C.). In these excerpts from *The Republic*, Plato's greatest work, Socrates is challenged to defend his belief that a life of injustice leads to unhappiness, while living justly results in happiness.

BOOK II

Glaucon, with that eminent courage which he displays on all occasions, . . . 357 began thus: Socrates, do you wish really to convince us that it is on every account better to be just than to be unjust, or only to seem to have convinced us? b

If it were up to me, I replied, I should prefer convincing you really.

Then, he proceeded, you are not doing what you wish. Let me ask you, Is there, in your opinion, a class of good things of such a kind that we are glad to possess them, not because we desire their consequences, but simply welcoming them for their own sake? Take, for example, the feelings of enjoyment and all those pleasures that are harmless, and that are followed by no consequences, beyond simple enjoyment in their possession.

Yes, I certainly think there is a class of this description.

Well, is there another class, do you think, of those which we value, both c for their own sake and for their results? Such as intelligence, and sight, and health—all of which we surely welcome on both accounts.

Yes.

And do you further recognize a third class of good things, which would include gymnastics training, and submission to medical treatment in illness, as well as the practice of medicine, and all other means of making money? Things like these we should describe as irksome, and yet beneficial to us; and while we should reject them viewed simply in themselves, we accept them for the sake of the rewards, and of the other consequences which result from them. d

Yes, undoubtedly there is such a third class also; but what then?

In which of these classes do you place justice?

From *The Republic*, translated by John Llewelyn Davies and David James Vaughan, revised by Andrea Tschemplik, Rowman & Littlefield Publishers, 2005. Used by permission of the publisher. The notes are provided by Andrea Tschemplik.

358   I should say in the highest—that is, among the good things which will be valued by one who is in the pursuit of true happiness, alike for their own sake and for their consequences.

Then your opinion is not that of the many, by whom justice is ranked in the irksome class, as a thing which in itself, and for its own sake, is disagreeable and repulsive, but which it is well to practice for the advantages to be had from it, with an eye to rewards and to a good name.

I know it is so . . .

b   Listen to my proposal then, and tell me whether you agree to it. . . . I am not satisfied as yet with the exposition that has been given of justice and injustice; for I long to be told what they respectively are, and what force they exert,
c   taken simply by themselves, when residing in the soul, dismissing the consideration of their rewards and other consequences. This shall be my plan then, if you do not object. I will . . . first state the common view respecting what kind of thing justice is and how it came to be; in the second place, I will maintain that all who practice it do so against their will, because it is indispensable, not because it is a good thing; and thirdly, that they act reasonably in so doing, because the life of the unjust man is, as men say, far better than that of the just. Not that I think so myself, Socrates; only my ears are ringing so with what
d   I hear . . . that I am puzzled. Now I have never heard the argument for the superiority of justice over injustice maintained to my satisfaction; for I should like to hear it praised, considered simply in itself; and from you if from anyone, I should expect such a treatment of the subject. Therefore I will speak as forcibly as I can in praise of an unjust life, and I shall thus display the manner in which I wish to hear you afterwards blame injustice and praise justice. See whether you approve of my plan.

Indeed I do, for on what other subject could a sensible man like better to talk and to hear others talk, again and again?

e   Most beautifully spoken! So now listen to me while I speak on my first theme, what kind of thing justice is and how it came to be.

To commit injustice is, they say, in its nature, a good thing, and to suffer it a bad thing; but the bad of suffering injustice exceeds the good of doing injus-
359 tice; and so, after the two-fold experience of both doing and suffering injustice, those who cannot avoid the latter and choose the former find it expedient to make a contract of neither doing nor suffering injustice. Hence arose legislation and contracts between man and man, and hence it became the custom to call that which the law enjoined just, as well as lawful. Such, they tell us, is justice, and so it came into being; and it stands midway between that which is best, to commit injustice with impunity, and that which is worst, to suffer injustice without any power of retaliating. And being a mean between these two extremes, the just is cared for, not as good in itself, but is honored because
b   of the inability to commit injustice; for they say that one who had it in his power to be unjust, and who deserved the name of a man, would never be so weak as to contract with anyone neither to commit injustice nor to suffer it. Such is the current account, Socrates, of the nature of justice, and of the circumstances in which it originated.

Even those men who practice justice do so unwillingly, because they lack the power to violate it, will be most readily perceived, if we use the following reasoning. Let us give full liberty to the just man and to the unjust alike, to do c whatever they please, and then let us follow them, and see whither the inclination of each will lead him. In that case we shall surprise the just man in the act of traveling in the same direction as the unjust, owing to that desire to gain more, the gratification of which every creature naturally pursues as a good, only that it is forced out of its path by law, and constrained to respect the principle of equality. That full liberty of action would, perhaps, be most effectively realized if they were invested with a power which they say was in old times possessed by the ancestor of Gyges the Lydian. He was a shepherd, so the d story runs, in the service of the reigning sovereign of Lydia, when one day a violent storm of rain fell, the ground was rent asunder by an earthquake, and a yawning gulf appeared on the spot where he was feeding his flocks. Seeing what had happened, and wondering at it, he went down into the gulf, and among other marvelous objects he saw, as the legend relates, a hollow bronze horse, with windows in its sides, through which he looked, and beheld in the interior a corpse, apparently of superhuman size; from which he took the only thing remaining, a golden ring on the hand, and therewith made his way out. e Now when the usual meeting of the shepherds occurred, for the purpose of sending to the king their monthly report of the state of his flocks, this shepherd came with the rest, wearing the ring. And, as he was seated with the company, he happened to turn the hoop of the ring round towards himself, until it came to the inside of his hand. Whereupon he became invisible to his neighbors, who 360 were talking about him as if he were gone away. While he was marveling at this, he again began playing with the ring, and turned the hoop to the outside, upon which he became once more visible. Having noticed this effect, he made experiments with the ring, to see whether it possessed this power. And so it was, that when he turned the hoop inwards he became invisible, and when he turned it outwards he was again visible. After this discovery, he immediately contrived to be appointed one of the messengers to carry the report to the king; and upon his arrival he seduced the queen, and conspiring with her, slew the b king, and took possession of the throne.

If then there were two such rings in existence, and if the just and the unjust man were each to put on one, it is to be thought that no one would be so steeled against temptation as to abide in the practice of justice, and resolutely to abstain from touching the property of his neighbors, when he had it in his power to help himself without fear to anything he pleased in the market, or to go into private houses and have intercourse with whom he would, or to kill c and release from prison according to his own pleasure, and in everything else to act among men with the power of a god. And in thus following out his desires the just man will be doing precisely what the unjust man would do; and so they would both be pursuing the same path. Surely this will be allowed to be strong evidence that none are just willingly, but only by compulsion, because to be just is not a good to the individual; for all violate justice whenever they imagine that there is nothing to hinder them. And they do so because everyone thinks that, in the individual case, injustice is much more profitable than justice; and they are right in so thinking, as the speaker of this speech will d maintain. For if anyone having this license within his grasp were to refuse to do any injustice, or to touch the property of others, all who were aware of it would think him a most pitiful and irrational creature, though they would praise him before each other's faces, deceiving one another, through their fear of suffering injustice. And so much for this topic.

e   But in actually deciding between the lives of the two persons in question, we shall be enabled to arrive at a correct conclusion, by contrasting together the thoroughly just and the thoroughly unjust man, and only by so doing. Well then, how are we to contrast them? In this way. Let us take nothing away from the injustice of the unjust or from the justice of the just, but let us suppose each to be perfect in his own line of conduct. First of all then, the unjust man must act as clever craftsmen do. For a first-rate pilot or physician perceives the difference between what is possible and what is impossible in his art; and while

361   he attempts the former, he leaves the latter alone; and moreover, should he happen to make a false step, he is able to recover himself. In the same way, if we are to form a conception of a consummately unjust man, we must suppose that he makes no mistake in the prosecution of his unjust enterprises, and that he escapes detection. But if he be found out, we must look upon him as a bungler, for it is the perfection of injustice to seem just without really being so. We must therefore grant to the perfectly unjust man, without taking anything away, the most perfect injustice; and we must concede to him, that while com-

b   mitting the grossest acts of injustice he has won himself the highest reputation for justice; and that should he make a false step, he is able to recover himself, partly by a talent for speaking with effect in case he be called in question for any of his misdeeds, and partly because his courage and strength, and his command of friends and money, enable him to employ force with success, whenever force is required. Such being our unjust man, let us, in speech, place the just man by his side, a man of true simplicity and nobleness, resolved, as Aeschylus says, not to seem, but to be, good. We must certainly take away the seeming, for if he be thought to be a just man, he will have honors and gifts

c   on the strength of this reputation, so that it will be uncertain whether it is for justice's sake, or for the sake of the gifts and honors, that he is what he is. Yes, we must strip him bare of everything but justice, and make his whole case the reverse of the former. Without being guilty of one unjust act, let him have the worst reputation for injustice, so that his justice may be thoroughly tested, and shown to be proof against infamy and all its consequences; and let him go on until the day of his death, steadfast in his justice, but with a lifelong reputation

d   for injustice, in order that, having brought both the men to the utmost limits of justice and of injustice respectively, we may then give judgment as to which of the two is the happier.

Good heavens! my dear Glaucon, said I, how vigorously you work, scouring the two characters clean for our judgment, like a pair of statues.

I do it as well as I can, he said. And after describing the men as we have done, there will be no further difficulty, I imagine, in proceeding to sketch the

e   kind of life which awaits them respectively. Let me therefore describe it. And if the description be somewhat coarse, do not regard it as mine, Socrates, but as coming from those who commend injustice above justice. They will say

362   that in such a situation the just man will be scourged, racked, fettered, will have his eyes burnt out, and at last, after suffering every kind of torture, will be crucified; and thus learn that it is best to resolve, not to be, but to seem, just.

Indeed those words of Aeschylus are far more applicable to the unjust man than to the just. For it is in fact the unjust man, they will maintain, inasmuch as he devotes himself to a course which is allied to reality, and does not live with an eye to appearances, who "is resolved not to seem, but to be," unjust,

> Reaping a harvest of wise purposes,
> Sown in the fruitful furrows of his mind.[1]   b

First of all he rules in the city through his reputation for justice, and in the next place he chooses a wife wherever he will, and marries his children into whatever family he pleases. He enters into contracts and joins in partnership with anyone he likes, and besides all this, he enriches himself by large profits, because he is not too nice to commit a fraud. Therefore, whenever he engages in a contest, whether public or private, he defeats and over-reaches his enemies, and by so doing grows rich, and is enabled to benefit his friends and injure his enemies, and to offer sacrifices and dedicate gifts to the gods in magnificent abundance. And thus having greatly the advantage over the just   c man to do service to the gods, as well as to such men as he chooses, he is also more likely than the just man to be dearer to the gods. And therefore they affirm, Socrates, that a better provision is made both by gods and men for the life of the unjust, than for the life of the just.

When Glaucon had said this, before I could make the reply I had in mind,   d his brother Adeimantus exclaimed, You surely do not suppose, Socrates, that the argument has been satisfactorily expounded.

Why not? said I.

The very point which was most needed has been omitted.

Well then, according to the proverb, "May a brother be present to help one," it is for you to supply his deficiencies, if there are any, by your assistance. But indeed, for my part, what Glaucon has said is enough to bring me to my knees, and puts it beyond my power to come to the rescue of justice.

You are not in earnest, he said. Listen to the following argument also; for   e we must now go through those representations which, reversing the declarations of Glaucon, commend justice and disparage injustice, in order to bring out more clearly what I take to be his meaning. Now, surely, fathers tell their sons, as do all those who have someone in their care, that one must be just. But when they impress this upon their children, they do not praise justice in itself,   363 but only the respectability which it gives—their object being that a reputation for justice may be gained, and that this reputation may bring the offices, marriages, and the other good things which, as Glaucon has just told us, are secured to the just man by his high character. And these persons carry the advantages of a good name still further; for, by introducing the good opinion of the gods, they are enabled to describe innumerable blessings which the gods, they say, grant to the pious, as the excellent Hesiod tells us, and Homer too—the former saying, that the gods cause the oak-trees of the just

> On their tops to bear acorns, and swarms of bees in the middle;   b
> Also their wool-laden sheep sink under the weight of their
>   fleeces,[2]

with many other good things of the same sort; while the latter, in a similar passage, speaks of one,

Like to a blameless king, who, godlike in virtue and wisdom,

c Justice ever maintains; whose rich land fruitfully yields him
Harvests of barley and wheat, and his orchards are heavy with fruit;
Strong are the young of his flocks; and the sea gives him fish in
abundance.[3]

But the blessings which Musaeus[4] and his son represent the gods as
bestowing upon the just, are still more delectable than these; for they bring

d them to the abode of Hades, and describe them as reclining on couches at a
banquet of the pious, and with garlands on their heads spending all time in
wine-bibbing, the fairest reward of virtue being, in their estimation, an ever-
lasting drunken party. Others, again, do not stop even here in their enumera-
tion of the rewards bestowed by the gods; for they tell us that the man who
is pious and true to his oath leaves children's children and a posterity to
follow him. Such, among others, are the commendations which they lavish
upon justice. The ungodly, on the other hand, and the unjust, they plunge into
a swamp in Hades, and condemn them to carry water in a sieve; and while

e they are still alive, they bring them into ill repute, and inflict upon the unjust
precisely those punishments, which Glaucon enumerated as the lot of the just
who are reputed to be unjust; more they cannot say. Such is their method of
praising the one character and condemning the other.

Once more, Socrates, take into consideration another and a different mode
of speaking with regard to justice and injustice, which we meet with both in

364 common life and in the poets. All as with one mouth proclaim, that to be moderate and just is an admirable thing certainly, but at the same time a hard and
an irksome one; while moderation and injustice are pleasant things and of
easy acquisition, and only rendered shameful by law and public opinion. But
they say that justice is in general less profitable than injustice, and they do not
hesitate to call wicked men happy, and to honor them both in public and in
private, when they are rich or possess other sources of power, and on the other

b hand to treat with dishonor and disdain those who are in any way feeble or
poor, even while they admit that the latter are better men than the former. But
of all their statements the most wonderful are those which relate to the gods
and to virtue; according to which even the gods allot to many good men a
calamitous and bad life, and to men of the opposite character an opposite portion. And there are quacks and soothsayers who flock to the rich man's doors,
and try to persuade him that they have a power procured from the gods, which
enables them, by sacrifices and incantations performed amid feasting and

c indulgence, to make amends for any crime committed either by the individual
himself or by his ancestors; and that, should he desire to do a mischief to anyone, it may be done at a trifling expense, whether the object of his hostility be
a just or an unjust man. They profess that by certain invocations and spells they
can prevail upon the gods to do their bidding. And in support of all these
assertions they produce the evidence of poets—some, to exhibit the facilities of
vice, quoting the words

d Whoever seeks wickedness, may even in abundance obtain it
Easily. Smooth is the way, and short, for near is her dwelling.
Virtue, Heav'n has ordained, shall be reached by the sweat of the
forehead,
and by a long and up-hill road,[5]

while others, to prove that the gods may be turned from their purpose by men, adduce the testimony of Homer, who has said:

> Yea, even the gods do yield to entreaty; e
> Therefore to them men offer both victims and meek supplications,
> Incense and melting fat, and turn them from anger to mercy;
> Sending up sorrowful prayers, when trespass and error is committed[6]

And they produce a host of books written by Musaeus and Orpheus, children, as they say, of Selene and of the Muses, which form their ritual, persuading not individuals merely, but whole cities also, that men may be absolved and 365 purified from crimes, both while they are still alive and even after their death, by means of certain sacrifices and pleasurable amusements which they call initiations—which deliver us from the torments of the other world, while the neglect of them is punished by an awful doom.

When views like these, he continued, my dear Socrates, are proclaimed and repeated with so much variety, concerning the honors in which virtue and vice are respectively held by gods and men, what can we suppose is the effect produced on the minds of all those good-natured young men, who are able, after skimming like birds, as it were, over all that they hear, to draw conclusions from it as to what sort of man one must be, and the path in which he must b walk, in order to live the best possible life? In all probability a young man would say to himself in the words of Pindar, "Shall I by justice or by crooked wiles climb to a loftier stronghold, and, having thus fenced myself in, live my life?" For common opinion declares that to be just without being also thought just, is no advantage to me, but only entails manifest trouble and loss; whereas if I am unjust and get myself a name for justice, an unspeakably marvelous life is promised me. Very well then, since the appearance, as the wise inform me, c overpowers the truth, and is the sovereign dispenser of happiness, to this I must of course wholly devote myself; I must draw round about me a picture of virtue to serve as an exterior front, but behind me I must keep the fox with its cunning and shiftiness—of which that most clever Archilochus tells us.[7] Yes but, it will be objected, it is not an easy matter always to conceal one's wicked- d ness. No, we shall reply, nor yet is anything else easy that is great; neverthe-less, if happiness is to be our goal, this must be our path, as the steps of the argument indicate. To assist in keeping up the deception, we will form secret societies and clubs. There are, moreover, teachers of persuasion, who impart skill in popular and court oratory; and so by persuasion or by force, we shall gain our ends, and carry on our dishonest proceedings with impunity. But, it is urged, neither evasion nor violence can succeed with the gods. Well, but if they either do not exist, or do not concern themselves with the affairs of men, why need *we* concern ourselves to evade their observation? But if they do e exist, and do pay attention to us, we know nothing and have heard nothing of them from any other quarter than the current traditions and the genealogies of poets; and these very authorities state that the gods are beings who may be persuaded and diverted from their purpose by sacrifices and meek supplica-tions and votive offerings. Therefore we must believe them in both statements or in neither. If we are to believe them, we will act unjustly, and offer sacrifices 366 from the proceeds of our crimes. For if we are just, we shall, it is true, escape

punishment at the hands of the gods, but we renounce the profits which accrue
from injustice; but if we are unjust, we shall not only make these gains, but also
by putting up prayers when we overstep and make mistakes, we shall prevail
upon the gods to let us go unscathed. But then, it is again objected, in Hades
we shall pay the just penalty for the crimes committed here, either in our own
persons or in those of our children's children. But my friend, the champion of
b   the argument will continue, the mystic rites, again, are very powerful, and the
absolving gods, as we are told by the mightiest cities, and by the sons of the
gods who have appeared as poets and inspired prophets, who inform us that
these things are so.

What consideration, therefore, remains which should induce us to prefer
justice to the greatest injustice? Since if we combine injustice with a spurious
decorum, we shall fare to our liking with the gods and with men, in this life
and the next, according to the most numerous and the highest authorities.
c   Considering all that has been said, by what device, Socrates, can a man who
has any advantages, either of high talent, or wealth, or personal appearance,
or birth, bring himself to honor justice, instead of smiling when he hears it
praised? Indeed, if there is anyone who is able to show the falsity of what we
have said, and who is fully convinced that justice is best, far from being angry
with the unjust, he doubtless makes great allowance for them, knowing that,
with the exception of those who may possibly refrain from injustice through
the disgust of a godlike nature or from the acquisition of knowledge, there is
d   certainly no one else who is willingly just; but it is from cowardice, or age, or
some other infirmity, that men condemn injustice, simply because they lack the
power to commit it. And the truth of this is proved by the fact, that the first of
these people who comes to power is the first to commit injustice, to the extent
of his ability. And the cause of all this is simply that fact, which my brother and
I both stated at the very beginning of this whole argument, Socrates, saying:
e   With all due respect, to you who profess to be admirers of justice—beginning
with the heroes of old, of whom accounts have descended to the present generation—have every one of you, without exception, made the praise of justice
and condemnation of injustice turn solely upon the reputation and honor and
gifts resulting from them; but what each is in itself, by its own peculiar force as
it resides in the soul of its possessor, unseen either by gods or men, has never,
in poetry or in prose, been adequately discussed, so as to show that injustice is
the greatest curse that a soul can receive into itself, and justice the greatest
367 blessing. Had this been the language used by all of you from the start, and had
you tried to persuade us of this from our childhood, we should not be on the
watch to check one another in the commission of injustice, because everyone
would be his own watchman, fearful lest by committing injustice he might
attach to himself the greatest of evils.

All this, Socrates, and perhaps still more than this, would be put forward respecting justice and injustice, . . . thus vulgarly, in my opinion, turning
b   around the power of each. For my own part, I confess—for I do not want to
hide anything from you—that I have a great desire to hear you defend the
opposite view, and therefore I have exerted myself to speak as forcefully as I
can. So do not limit your argument to the proposition that justice is stronger
than injustice, but show us what is that influence exerted by each of them on

its possessor, whereby the one is in itself a blessing, and the other a curse; and take away the estimation in which the two are held, as Glaucon urged you to do. For if you omit to withdraw from each quality its true reputation and to add the false, we shall declare that you are praising, not the reality, but the appearance of justice, and blaming, not the reality, but the semblance of c injustice; that your advice, in fact, is to be unjust without being found out, and that you hold . . . that justice is another man's good, being for the advantage of the stronger; injustice a man's own interest and advantage, but against the interest of the weaker. Since then you have allowed that justice is one of the greatest goods, the possession of which is valuable, both for the sake of their results, and also in a higher degree for their own sake, such as sight, hearing, understanding, health, and everything else which is genuinely good in its d own nature and not merely reputed to be good. Select for commendation this particular feature of justice, I mean the benefit which in itself it confers on its possessor, in contrast with the harm which injustice inflicts. The rewards and reputations leave to others to praise; because in others I can tolerate this mode of praising justice and condemning injustice, which consists in eulogizing or reviling the reputations and the rewards which are connected with them; but in you I cannot, unless you require it, because you have spent your whole e life in investigating such questions, and such only. Therefore do not content yourself with proving to us that justice is better than injustice; but show us what is that influence exerted by each on its possessor, by which, whether gods and men see it or not, the one is in itself a good, and the other a detriment. . . .

BOOK IV

. . . [T]he soul of a thirsty man, in so far as he is thirsty, has no other wish than 439 to drink; but this it desires, and towards this it is impelled. b

Clearly so.

Therefore, whenever anything pulls back a soul that is under the influence of thirst, it will be something in the soul distinct from the principle which thirsts, and which drives it like a beast to drink. For we hold it to be impossible that the same thing should, at the same time, with the same part of itself, in reference to the same object, be doing two opposite things.

Certainly it is.

Just as, I imagine, it would not be right to say of the bowman, that his hands are at the same time drawing the bow towards him, and pushing it from him—the fact being, that one of his hands pushes it from him, and the other pulls it to him.

Precisely so.

Now, can we say that people sometimes are thirsty, and yet do not wish to c drink?

Yes, certainly; it often happens to many people.

What then can one say of them, except that their soul contains one principle which commands, and another which forbids them to drink, the latter being distinct from and stronger than the former?

That is my opinion.

Whenever the authority which forbids such indulgences grows up in the
d   soul, is it not engendered there by calculation; while the powers which lead
and draw the soul towards them, owe their presence to passive and diseased
states?

It would appear so.

Then we shall have reasonable grounds for assuming that these are two
principles distinct one from the other, and for giving to that part of the soul
with which it reasons the title of the rational principle, and to that part with
which it loves and hungers and thirsts, and experiences the flutter of the other
desires, the title of the irrational and appetitive principle, the ally of sundry
indulgences and pleasures.

e   Yes, he replied; it will not be unreasonable to think so.

Let us consider it settled, then, that these two specific forms exist in the
soul. But now, will spirit, or that by which we feel spirited, constitute a third
distinct part? If not, which of the former two has the same nature?

Perhaps with the appetitive principle.

But I was once told a story, which I trust, to the effect, that Leontius, the
son of Aglaion, as he was walking up from the Piraeus, and approaching the
northern wall from the outside, observed some dead bodies on the ground,
and the executioner standing by them. He immediately felt a desire to look at
440 them, but at the same time loathing the thought he tried to divert himself from
it. For some time he struggled with himself, and covered his eyes, until at
length, over-powered by the desire, he opened his eyes wide with his fingers,
and running up to the bodies, exclaimed, "There, you wretches! Gaze your fill
at the beautiful spectacle!"

I have heard this too.

This story, however, indicates that anger sometimes fights against the
desires, which implies that they are two distinct principles.

True, it does indicate that.

And do we not often observe in other cases that when a man is over-
b   powered by the desires against the dictates of his reason, he reviles himself,
and resents the violence thus exerted within him, and that, in this struggle of
contending parties, the spirited sides with the rational? But that it should make
common cause with the desires, when reason pronounces that they ought not
to act against itself, is a thing which I suppose you will not profess to have
experienced yourself, nor yet, I imagine, to have ever noticed in anyone else.

No, by Zeus, I have not.

c   Well, and when anyone thinks he is doing an injustice, is he not, in proportion to the nobleness of his character, so much the less able to be angry at
being made to suffer hunger or cold or any similar pain at the hands of him
who he thinks does so justly? Will not his spirit, as I describe it, refuse to be
roused against the one punishing him?

True.

On the other hand, when anyone thinks he is suffering an injustice, does
he not instantly boil and chafe, and enlist himself on the side of what he thinks
to be justice; and whatever extremities of hunger and cold and the like he may
d   have to suffer, does he not endure until he conquers, never ceasing from his
noble efforts, until he has either succeeded, or perished in the attempt, or been

recalled and calmed by the voice of reason within, as a dog is called off by a shepherd?

Yes, he replied, the case answers very closely to your description. . . .

But try whether you also apprehend my next observation.

What is it?   e

That our recent view of the spirited principle is exactly reversed. Then we thought it had something of the appetitive character, but now we say that, far from this being the case, it much more readily takes arms on the side of the rational principle in the conflict of the soul.

Decidedly it does.

Is it then distinct from this principle also; or is it only a modification of it, thus making two instead of three distinct principles in the soul, namely, the rational and the appetitive? Or ought we to say that . . . in the soul the spirited   441 principle constitutes a third element, the natural ally of the rational principle, if it be not corrupted by bad training?

It must be a third, he replied.

Yes, I continued; if it shall appear to be distinct, from the rational principle, as we found it different from the appetitive.

That will easily appear. For even in little children anyone may see this, that from their very birth they have plenty of spirit, whereas reason is a principle to which most men only attain after many years, and some, in my opinion, never.   b

Well said, by Zeus. In beasts also one may see what you describe exemplified. And besides, that passage in Homer, which we quoted on a former occasion, will support our view:

Smiting his breast, to his heart thus spake he in accents of chiding.[8]

For in this line Homer has distinctly made a difference between the two prin-   c ciples, representing that which had calculated the good or the bad of the action as rebuking that which was irrationally spirited.

You are perfectly right.

Here then, I proceeded, after a hard swim, we have, though with difficulty, reached the land; and we are pretty well satisfied that there are corresponding divisions, equal in number, . . . in the soul of every individual.

True. . . .

Is it not then essentially the domain of the rational principle to command,   e inasmuch as it is wise, and has to exercise forethought on behalf of the entire soul, and the domain of the spirited principle to be its subject and ally?

Yes, certainly. . . .

And so these two . . . will exercise control over the appetitive principle,   442 which in every man forms the largest portion of the soul, and is by nature most insatiable. And they will watch it narrowly, that it may not be filled with what are called the pleasures of the body, as to grow large and strong, and forthwith refuse to mind its own business, and even aspire to subjugate and dominate   b over that which it has no right to rule by virtue of its class, thus totally upsetting the life of all.

Certainly they will.

And would not these two principles be the best qualified to guard the entire soul and body against enemies from without—the one taking counsel, and the other fighting its battles, in obedience to the ruling power, carrying out its order with courage?

True.

c   In like manner, I think, we call an individual courageous in virtue of the spirited element of his nature, when this part of him holds fast, through pain and pleasure, the instructions of the reason as to what is to be feared, and what is not.

Yes, and rightly.

And we call him wise, in virtue of that small part which reigns within him, and issues these instructions, and which also in its turn contains within itself knowledge of what is advantageous for the whole community composed of these three parts, and for each member of it.

Exactly so.

Again, do we not call a man moderate, in virtue of the friendship and harmony of these same principles, that is to say, when the two that are governed

d   agree with that which governs in regarding the rational principle as the part that ought to rule, and set up no opposition to its authority?

Certainly, he replied; moderation is nothing else than this . . .

Lastly, a man will be just, in the way and by the means which we have repeatedly described.

Unquestionably he will. . . .

443   So that the just man will not permit each part within him to do anything but mind its own business, nor allow the three classes in his soul to meddle with each other, but will really set his house in order; and having gained the mastery over himself, will so regulate his own character as to be on good terms with himself, and to set those three parts in tune together, as if they were truly three chords of a harmony, a highest and a lowest and a middle, and whatever may lie between these. And after he has bound all these together, and reduced

e   the many elements of his nature to a real unity, as a moderate and harmonized man, he will then at length proceed to do whatever he may have to do, whether it involve a business transaction, or the care of his body, a political matter or a private contract. In all of these actions he will believe and profess that the just and fair course is that which preserves and assists in creating the aforesaid con-

444   dition, and that the genuine knowledge which presides over such conduct is wisdom; while on the other hand, he will hold that an unjust action is one which tends to destroy this habit, and that the mere opinion which presides over unjust conduct, is folly.

What you say is thoroughly true, Socrates.

Very good; if we were to say we have discovered the just man . . . , and what justice is . . . , it would not be thought, I imagine, to be a complete lie.

No, by Zeus. It would not.

Shall we say so then?

We will.

Be it so, I continued. In the next place we have to investigate, I imagine, what injustice is.

Evidently we have.

b   Must it not then, as the reverse of justice, be a state of strife between the three parts, and the disposition to meddle and interfere, and the insurrection of a part of the soul against the whole, this part aspiring to the supreme power within the soul, to which it has no right, its proper place and destination being, on the contrary, to do service to any member of the rightfully ruling part? Such doings as these, I imagine, and the confusion and bewilderment of the aforesaid parts, will, in our opinion, constitute injustice, and licentiousness, and cowardice, and folly, and, in one word, all vice.

Yes, precisely so.

And is it not now quite clear to us what it is to act unjustly, and to be c unjust, and, on the other hand, what it is to act justly, knowing as we do the nature of justice and injustice?

How so?

Because there happens to be no difference with regard to the health and disease of the body and the soul.

In what way?

The conditions of health, I presume, produce health, and those of disease engender disease.

Yes.

In the same way, does not the practice of justice beget the habit of justice, d and the practice of injustice the habit of injustice?

Inevitably.

Now to produce health is so to constitute the bodily forces that they shall master and be mastered by one another in accordance with nature; and to produce disease is to make them govern and be governed by one another in a way which violates nature.

True.

Similarly, will it not be true that to beget justice is so to constitute the parts of the soul that they shall master and be mastered by one another in accordance with nature, and that to beget injustice is to make them rule and be ruled by one another in a way which violates nature?

Quite so.

Then virtue, it appears, will be a kind of health and beauty, and good habit of the soul; and vice will be a disease, and deformity, and sickness of it.   e

True.

And may we not add, that all fair practices tend to the acquisition of virtue, and all foul practices to that of vice?

Undoubtedly they do.

What now remains for us, apparently, is to inquire whether it is also profitable to act justly, and to pursue fair aims, and to be just, whether a man 445 be known to be such or not, or to act unjustly, and to be unjust, if one suffer no punishment, and be not made a better man by paying the penalty.

But, Socrates, this appears to be ridiculous by now, seeing that each one has come to light as we described. If life does not seem livable, when the nature of body is ruined, though we may have at our disposal all food and drink, and b wealth and every sort of power, will it then be livable if the nature of that very thing by which we live is corrupted and ruined—even if a man does what he wishes except the one thing which will release him from bad and injustice and which will acquire him justice and virtue?

Yes, it is ludicrous, I replied. . . .

BOOK IX

588
b

[N]ow that we have arrived at this stage of the argument, let us resume that first discussion which brought us here. It was stated, I believe, that injustice is profitable to the man who is perfectly unjust, while he is reputed to be just. Or am I wrong about the statement?

No, you are right.

This is the moment for arguing with the speaker of this remark. . . .

How must we proceed?

We must fashion in speech an image of the soul, in order that the speaker may perceive what his remark amounts to.

c

What kind of image is it to be?

We must imagine, I replied, a creature like one of those which, according to the legend, existed in old times, such as Chimera, and Scylla, and Cerberus, not to mention a host of other monsters, in the case of which we are told that several ideas have naturally grown together and coalesced into one.[9]

True, we do hear such stories.

Well, mold in the first place the idea of a motley many-headed monster, furnished with a ring of heads of tame and wild animals, which he can produce by turns in every instance out of himself.

d

It requires a cunning molder to do so; nevertheless, since speech is more pliable than wax, consider it done.

Now proceed, secondly, to mold the idea of a lion, and, thirdly, the idea of a man. But let the first be the greatest by far of the three, and the second next to it.

That is easier. It is done.

Now combine the three into one, so as to make them grow naturally together to a certain extent.

I have done so.

Lastly, invest them externally with the image of one, namely, the man, so that the person who cannot see inside, and only notices the outside skin, may think that it is one single animal, to wit, a human being.

e

I have molded the form.

And now to the person who asserts that it is profitable for this human being to do injustice, and that it is not for his interest to do justice, let us reply that his assertion amounts to this, that it is profitable for him to feast and strengthen the multifarious monster and the lion and its members, and to starve and enfeeble the man to such an extent as to leave him at the mercy of the guidance of either of the other two, without making any attempt to habituate or make them friends with one another, but leaving them together to bite and struggle and devour each other.

589

True, he replied, the person who praises injustice will certainly in effect say this.

On the other hand, will not the advocate of the profitableness of justice assert that actions and words ought to be such as will enable the inward man to have the firmest control over the entire man, and, with the lion for his ally, to cultivate, like a farmer, the many-headed beast, nursing and rearing the tame parts of it, and checking the growth of the wild; and thus to pursue his

b

training on the principle of concerning himself for all jointly, and making them friends with one another and to himself?

Yes, these again are precisely the assertions of the person who praises justice.

Then in every way the one who praises justice will speak the truth, while the one who praises injustice will lie. For whether you look at pleasure, at c reputation, or at advantage, the one who praises the just man speaks truth, whereas all the criticisms of his enemy are unsound and ignorant.

I am entirely of that opinion, said he.

Let us therefore persuade him mildly—for his mistake is involuntary—and let us put this question to him: My good friend, may we not assert that the practices which are held by law to be beautiful or ugly are beautiful or ugly d according as they either subjugate the brutal parts of our nature to the man—perhaps I should rather say, to the divine part—or make the tame part the servant and slave of the wild? Will he say, yes? Or how will he reply?

He will say yes, if he will take my advice.

Then according to this argument, I proceeded, can it be profitable for anyone to take gold unjustly, since the consequence is, that, in the moment of taking the gold, he is enslaving the best part of him to the most vile? Or, if he e had taken gold to sell a son or a daughter into slavery, and a slavery among wild and wicked masters, could it have done him no good to receive even an immense sum for such a purpose? And will it be argued that, if he ruthlessly enslaves the most divine part of himself to the most ungodly and accursed, that he is not a miserable man? And will he not accept golden bribes for a far more awful destruction than Eriphyle,[10] when she took the necklace as the price of 590 her husband's soul?

I will reply in his behalf, said Glaucon. It is indeed much more awful.

And do you not think that immoderation again, has been blamed for a long time for reasons of that kind, that, during its outbreaks, that great and multiform beast, which is so terrible, receives more liberty than it ought to have?

Obviously, you are right.

And are not stubbornness and discontent blamed whenever the lion-like and serpentine parts are exalted and strengthened inharmoniously?   b

Exactly so.

Again, are not luxury and softness blamed because they relax and unnerve this same part by begetting cowardice in him?

Undoubtedly they are.

And are not the reproachful names of flattery and servility bestowed, whenever a person subjugates this same spirited part to the turbulent monster, and, to gratify the latter's insatiable craving for money, trains the former from youth on, by a long course of insult, to become an ape instead of a lion?

Certainly you are right.   c

And why, let me ask you, are the mechanical and manual arts discredited? May we not assert that these terms imply that the most excellent form in the person to whom they are attributed, is naturally weak, so that instead of being able to govern the creatures within him, he pays them court, and can only learn how to flatter them?

Apparently so, he replied.

Then, in order that such a person may be governed by an authority similar to that by which the best man is governed, do we not maintain that he ought
d   to be made the servant of that best man, in whom the divine element is supreme? We do not indeed imagine that the servant ought to be governed to his own detriment . . . ; on the contrary, we believe it to be better for everyone to be governed by a prudent and divine power, which ought, if possible, to be seated in the man's own heart, the only alternative being to impose it from without; in order that we may be all alike, as far as possible, and all mutual friends, due to the fact that we are steered by the same pilot.

Yes, that is quite right.

e   And this, I continued, is plainly the intention of law, that common friend of all the members of a city, and also of the supervising of children, which consists in withholding their freedom, until the time when we have formed a constitution in them, as we should in a city, and until, by cultivating the best part
591 of their nature, we have established in them a guardian and a sovereign, the very counterpart of our own—from which time forward we let them go free.

Yes that is plain.

On what principle then, Glaucon, and by what line of argument, can we maintain that it is profitable for a man to be unjust, or immoderate, or to commit any disgraceful act, which will sink him deeper in vice, though he may increase his wealth thereby, or acquire additional power?

We cannot maintain this in any way.

And by what argument can we uphold the advantages of disguising the
b   doing of injustice, and escaping the penalties of it? Am I not right in supposing that the man who thus escapes detection, grows still more vicious than before; whereas if he is found out and punished, the brute part of him is put to sleep and tamed, and the tame part is liberated, and the whole soul is molded to its best nature, and thus, through the acquisition of moderation and justice combined with prudence, attains to a condition which is more worthy of honor than that attained by a body endowed with strength and beauty and health, in the exact proportion in which the soul is more honorable than the body?

Yes, indeed, you are right.

NOTES

1. Aeschylus, *Seven Against Thebes* 1.592–94.

2. Hesiod, *Works and Days* 232–33.

3. Homer, *Odyssey* 19.109.

4. Musaeus was a singer and poet of myth and legend.

5. Hesiod, *Works and Days* 287–89.

6. Homer, *Iliad* 9.497–501.

7. Archilochus (675?–635? B.C.E.) was a poet from Paros.

8. Homer, *Odyssey* 20.17.

9. In the ancient understanding, monsters were unnaturally combined creatures, such as the chimera, which had a lion's head, a goat's body, and a serpent's tail.

10. Cf. Homer, *Odyssey* 11.326–27.

THE NICOMACHEAN ETHICS

Aristotle

Aristotle (384–322 B.C.), a student of Plato, made extraordinary contributions not only in virtually every area of philosophical inquiry, but
also in biology, psychology, zoology, meteorology, and astronomy. In
The Nicomachean Ethics, one of the most subtle of all works in the history
of ethics, he develops the view that happiness, *eudaimonia* in Greek, is a
life of activity in accord with virtue and focused on the contemplation of
scientific and philosophical truths.

BOOK I

1. Every art and every inquiry, and similarly every action and pursuit, is
thought to aim at some good; and for this reason the good has rightly been
declared to be that at which all things aim. . . .

2. If, then, there is some end of the things we do, which we desire for its
own sake (everything else being desired for the sake of this), and if we do not
choose everything for the sake of something else (for at that rate the process
would go on to infinity, so that our desire would be empty and vain), clearly
this must be the good and the chief good. Will not the knowledge of it, then,
have a great influence on life? Shall we not, like archers who have a mark to
aim at, be more likely to hit upon what is right? If so, we must try, in outline
at least, to determine what it is . . .

4. Let us resume our inquiry and state, in view of the fact that all knowledge and every pursuit aims at some good, what . . . is the highest of all goods
achievable by action. Verbally there is very general agreement; for both the
general run of men and people of superior refinement say that it is happiness,
and identify living well and faring well with being happy; but with regard to
what happiness is they differ, and the many do not give the same account as
the wise. For the former think it is some plain and obvious thing, like pleasure,
wealth, or honour; they differ, however, from one another—and often even the
same man identifies it with different things, with health when he is ill, with
wealth when he is poor; but, conscious of their ignorance, they admire those
who proclaim some great thing that is above their comprehension. . . .

5. . . . To judge from the lives that men lead, most men, and the men of the
most vulgar type, seem (not without some ground) to identify the good, or
happiness, with pleasure; which is the reason why they love the life of enjoyment. For there are, we may say, three prominent types of life—that just mentioned, the political, and thirdly the contemplative life. Now the mass of
mankind are evidently quite slavish in their tastes, preferring a life suitable to

From *The Nicomachean Ethics*, translated by David Ross, revised by J. L. Ackrill and J. O. Urmson,
Oxford University Press, 1980. Used by permission of the publisher.

beasts. . . . A consideration of the prominent types of life shows that people of superior refinement and of active disposition identify happiness with honour; for this is, roughly speaking, the end of the political life. But it seems too superficial to be what we are looking for, since it is thought to depend on those who bestow honour rather than on him who receives it, but the good we divine to be something of one's own and not easily taken from one. Further, men seem to pursue honour in order that they may be assured of their merit; at least it is by men of practical wisdom that they seek to be honoured, and among those who know them, and on the ground of their virtue; clearly, then, according to them, at any rate, virtue is better. And perhaps one might even suppose this to be, rather than honour, the end of the political life. But even this appears somewhat incomplete; for possession of virtue seems actually compatible with being asleep, or with lifelong inactivity, and, further, with the greatest sufferings and misfortunes; but a man who was living so no one would call happy, unless he were maintaining a thesis at all costs. But enough of this; for the subject has been sufficiently treated even in the popular discussions. Third comes the contemplative life, which we shall consider later.

The life of money-making is one undertaken under compulsion, and wealth is evidently not the good we are seeking; for it is merely useful and for the sake of something else. And so one might rather take the aforenamed objects to be ends; for they are loved for themselves. But it is evident that not even these are ends; yet many arguments have been wasted on the support of them. Let us leave this subject, then.

7. Let us again return to the good we are seeking, and ask what it can be. It seems different in different actions and arts; it is different in medicine, in strategy, and in the other arts likewise. What then is the good of each? Surely that for whose sake everything else is done. In medicine this is health, in strategy victory, in architecture a house, in any other sphere something else, and in every action and pursuit the end; for it is for the sake of this that all men do whatever else they do. Therefore, if there is an end for all that we do, this will be the good achievable by action, and if there are more than one, these will be the goods achievable by action.

So the argument has by a different course reached the same point; but we must try to state this even more clearly. Since there are evidently more than one end, and we choose some of these (e.g. wealth, flutes, and in general instruments) for the sake of something else, clearly not all ends are final ends; but the chief good is evidently something final. Therefore, if there is only one final end, this will be what we are seeking, and if there are more than one, the most final of these will be what we are seeking. Now we call that which is in itself worthy of pursuit more final than that which is worthy of pursuit for the sake of something else, and that which is never desirable for the sake of something else more final than the things that are desirable both in themselves and for the sake of that other thing, and therefore we call final without qualification that which is always desirable in itself and never for the sake of something else.

Now such a thing happiness, above all else, is held to be; for this we choose always for itself and never for the sake of something else, but honour, pleasure, reason, and every virtue we choose indeed for themselves (for if nothing resulted from them we should still choose each of them), but we choose them also for the sake of happiness, judging that through them we shall be happy. Happiness, on the other hand, no one chooses for the sake of these, nor, in general, for anything other than itself.

From the point of view of self-sufficiency the same result seems to follow; for the final good is thought to be self-sufficient. Now by self-sufficient we do not mean that which is sufficient for a man by himself, for one who lives a solitary life, but also for parents, children, wife, and in general for his friends and fellow citizens, since man is born for citizenship. But some limit must be set to this; for if we extend our requirement to ancestors and descendants and friends' friends we are in for an infinite series. Let us examine this question, however, on another occasion; the self-sufficient we now define as that which when isolated makes life desirable and lacking in nothing; and such we think happiness to be; and further we think it most desirable of all things, not a thing counted as one good thing among others—if it were so counted it would clearly be made more desirable by the addition of even the least of goods; for that which is added becomes an excess of goods, and of goods the greater is always more desirable. Happiness, then, is something final and self-sufficient, and is the end of action.

Presumably, however, to say that happiness is the chief good seems a platitude, and a clearer account of what is is still desired. This might perhaps be given, if we could first ascertain the function of man. For just as for a flute-player, a sculptor, or any artist, and, in general, for all things that have a function or activity, the good and the "well" is thought to reside in the function, so would it seem to be for man, if he has a function. Have the carpenter, then, and the tanner certain functions or activities, and has man none? Is he born without a function? Or as eye, hand, foot, and in general each of the parts evidently has a function, may one lay it down that man similarly has a function apart from all these? What then can this be? Life seems to belong even to plants, but we are seeking what is peculiar to man. Let us exclude, therefore, the life of nutrition and growth. Next there would be a life of perception, but *it* also seems to be shared even by the horse, the ox, and every animal. There remains then, an active life of the element that has a rational principle; of this, one part has such a principle in the sense of being obedient to one, the other in the sense of possessing one and exercising thought. And, as "life of the rational element" also has two meanings, we must state that life in the sense of activity is what we mean; for this seems to be the more proper sense of the term. Now if the function of man is an activity of soul which follows or implies a rational principle, and if we say "a so-and-so" and "a good so-and-so" have a function which is the same in kind, e.g., a lyre-player and a good lyre-player, and so without qualification in all cases, eminence in respect of goodness being added to the name of the function (for the function of a lyre-player is to play the lyre, and that of a good lyre-player is to do so well): if this is the case and we state the function of man to be a certain kind of life, and this to be an activity or actions of the soul implying a rational principle, and the function of a good man to be the good and noble performance of these, and if any action is well performed when it is performed in accordance with the appropriate excellence: if this is the case, human good turns out to be activity of soul exhibiting excellence, and if there are more than one excellence, in accordance with the best and most complete.

But we must add "in a complete life." For one swallow does not make a summer, nor does one day; and so too one day, or a short time, does not make a man blessed and happy.

Let this serve as an outline of the good. . . .

10. Must no one at all, then, be called happy while he lives; must we, as Solon says, see the end? Even if we are to lay down this doctrine, is it also the case that a man *is* happy when he is *dead*? Or is not this quite absurd, especially for us who say that happiness is an activity? But if we do not call the dead man happy, and if Solon does not mean this, but that one can then safely *call* a man blessed, as being at last beyond evils and misfortunes, this also affords matter for discussion; for both evil and good are thought to exist for a dead man, as much as for one who is alive but not aware of them; e.g., honours and dishonours and the good or bad fortunes of children, and in general of descendants. And this also presents a problem; for though a man has lived blessedly until old age and has had a death worthy of his life, many reverses may befall his descendants—some of them may be good and attain the life they deserve, while with others the opposite may be the case; and clearly too the degrees of relationship between them and their ancestors may vary indefinitely. It would be odd, then, if the dead man were to share in these changes and become at one time happy, at another wretched; while it would also be odd if the fortunes of the descendants did not for *some* time have *some* effect on the happiness of their ancestors.

But we must return to our first difficulty; for perhaps by a consideration of it our present problem might be solved. Now if we must see the end and only then call a man blessed, not as being blessed but as having been so before, surely this is a paradox, that when he is happy the attribute that belongs to him is not to be truly predicated of him because we do not wish to call living men happy, on account of the changes that may befall them, and because we have assumed happiness to be something permanent and by no means easily changed, while a single man may suffer many turns of fortune's wheel. For clearly if we were to follow his fortunes, we should often call the same man happy and again wretched, making the happy man out to be "a chameleon, and insecurely based." Or is this following his fortunes quite wrong? Success or failure in life does not depend on these, but human life, as we said, needs these as well, while virtuous activities or their opposites are what determine happiness or the reverse.

The question we have now discussed confirms our definition. For no function of man has so much permanence as virtuous activities (these are thought to be more durable even than knowledge of the sciences), and of these themselves the most valuable are more durable because those who are blessed spend their life most readily and most continuously in these; for this seems to be the reason why we do not forget them. The attribute in question, then, will belong to the happy man, and he will be happy throughout his life; for always, or by preference to everything else, he will do and contemplate what is excellent, and he will bear the chances of life most nobly and altogether decorously, if he is "truly good" and "foursquare beyond reproach."

Now many events happen by chance, and events differing in importance; small pieces of good fortune or of its opposite clearly do not weigh down the scales of life one way or the other, but a multitude of great events if they turn out well will make life more blessed (for not only are they themselves such as to add beauty to life, but the way a man deals with them may be noble and good), while if they turn out ill they crush and maim blessedness; for they both bring pain with them and hinder many activities. Yet even in these nobility shines through, when a man bears with resignation many great misfortunes, not through insensibility to pain but through nobility and greatness of soul.

If activities are, as we said, what determines the character of life, no blessed man can become miserable; for he will never do the acts that are hateful and mean. For the man who is truly good and wise, we think, bears all the chances of life becomingly and always makes the best of circumstances, as a good general makes the best military use of the army at his command, and a good shoemaker makes the best shoes out of the hides that are given him; and so with all other craftsmen. And if this is the case, the happy man can never become miserable—though he will not reach *blessedness*, if he meet with fortunes like those of Priam.

Nor, again, is he many-coloured and changeable; for neither will he be moved from his happy state easily or by any ordinary misadventures, but only by many great ones, nor, if he has had many great misadventures, will he recover his happiness in a short time, but if at all, only in a long and complete one in which he has attained many splendid successes.

Why then should we not say that he is happy who is active in accordance with complete virtue and is sufficiently equipped with external goods, not for some chance period but throughout a complete life? Or must we add "and who is destined to live thus and die as befits his life"? Certainly the future is obscure to us, while happiness, we claim, is an end and something in every way final. If so, we shall call blessed those among living men in whom these conditions are, and are to be, fulfilled—but blessed *men*. So much for these questions.

BOOK II

1. Virtue, then, being of two kinds, intellectual and moral, intellectual virtue in the main owes both its birth, and its growth to teaching (for which reason it requires experience and time), while moral virtue comes about as a result of habit. . . . From this it is also plain that none of the moral virtues arises in us by nature; for nothing that exists by nature can form a habit contrary to its nature. For instance the stone which by nature moves downwards cannot be habituated to move upwards, not even if one tries to train it by throwing it up ten thousand times; nor can fire be habituated to move downwards, nor can anything else that by nature behaves in one way be trained to behave in another. Neither by nature, then, nor contrary to nature do the virtues arise in us; rather we are adapted by nature to receive them, and are made perfect by habit.

Again, of all the things that come to us by nature we first acquire the potentiality and later exhibit the activity (this is plain in the case of the senses; for it was not by often seeing or often hearing that we got these senses, but on the contrary we had them before we used them, and did not come to have them by using them); but the virtues we get by first exercising them, as also happens in the case of the arts as well. For the things we have to learn before we can do them, we learn by doing them, e.g., men become builders by building and lyre-players by playing the lyre; so too we become just by doing just acts, temperate by doing temperate acts, brave by doing brave acts.

This is confirmed by what happens in states; for legislators make the citizens good by forming habits in them, and this is the wish of every legislator, and those who do not effect it miss their mark, and it is in this that a good constitution differs from a bad one.

Again, it is from the same causes and by the same means that every virtue is both produced and destroyed, and similarly every art; for it is from playing the lyre that both good and bad lyre-players are produced. And the corresponding statement is true of builders and of all the rest; men will be good or bad builders as a result of building well or badly. For if this were not so, there would have been no need of a teacher, but all men would have been born good or bad at their craft. This, then, is the case with the virtues also; by doing the acts that we do in our transactions with other men we become just or unjust, and by doing the acts that we do in the presence of danger, and by being habituated to feel fear or confidence, we become brave or cowardly. The same is true of appetites and feelings of anger; some men become temperate and good-tempered, others self-indulgent and irascible, by behaving in one way or the other in the appropriate circumstances. Thus, in one word, states of character arise out of like activities. This is why the activities we exhibit must be of a certain kind; it is because the states of character correspond to the differences between these. It makes no small difference, then, whether we form habits of one kind or of another from our very youth; it makes a very great difference, or rather *all* the difference. . . .

3. We must take as a sign of states of character the pleasure or pain that supervenes upon acts; for the man who abstains from bodily pleasures and delights in this very fact is temperate, while the man who is annoyed at it is self-indulgent, and he who stands his ground against things that are terrible and delights in this or at least is not pained is brave, while the man who is pained is a coward. For moral excellence is concerned with pleasures and pains; it is on account of the pleasure that we do bad things, and on account of the pain that we abstain from noble ones. . . .

The following facts also may show us that virtue and vice are concerned with these same things. There being three objects of choice and three of avoidance, the noble, the advantageous, the pleasant, and their contraries, the base, the injurious, the painful, about all of these the good man tends to go right and the bad man to go wrong, and especially about pleasure; for this is common to the animals, and also it accompanies all objects of choice; for even the noble and the advantageous appear pleasant. . . .

4. The question might be asked, what we mean by saying that we must become just by doing just acts, and temperate by doing temperate acts; for if men do just and temperate acts, they are already just and temperate, exactly as, if they do what is in accordance with the laws of grammar and of music, they are grammarians and musicians.

Or is this not true even of the arts? It is possible to do something that is in accordance with the laws of grammar, either by chance or under the guidance of another. A man will be a grammarian, then, only when he has both said something grammatical and said it grammatically; and this means doing it in accordance with the grammatical knowledge in himself.

Again, the case of the arts and that of the virtues are not similar; for the products of the arts have their goodness in themselves, so that it is enough that they should have a certain character, but if the arts that are in accordance with the virtues have themselves a certain character it does not follow that they are done justly or temperately. The agent also must be in a certain condition when he does them; in the first place he must have knowledge, secondly he must choose the acts, and choose them for their own sakes, and thirdly his action must proceed from a firm and unchangeable character. . . .

Actions, then, are called just and temperate when they are such as the just or the temperate man would do; but it is not the man who does those that is just and temperate, but the man who also does them as just and temperate men do them. It is well said, then, that it is by doing just acts that the just man is produced, and by doing temperate acts the temperate man; without doing these no one would have even a prospect of becoming good. . . .

5. Next we must consider what virtue is. Since things that are found in the soul are of three kinds—passions, faculties, states of character—virtue must be one of these. By passions I mean appetite, anger, fear, confidence, envy, joy, friendly feeling, hatred, longing, emulation, pity, and in general the feelings that are accompanied by pleasure or pain; by faculties the things in virtue of which we are said to be capable of feeling these, e.g., of becoming angry or being pained or feeling pity; by states of character the things in virtue of which we stand well or badly with reference to the passions, e.g., with reference to anger we stand badly if we feel it violently or too weakly, and well if we feel it moderately: and similarly with reference to the other passions.

Now neither the virtues nor the vices are *passions*, because we are not called good or bad on the ground of our passions, but are so called on the ground of our virtues and our vices, and because we are neither praised nor blamed for our passions (for the man who feels fear or anger is not praised, nor is the man who simply feels anger blamed, but the man who feels it in a certain way), but for our virtues and our vices we *are* praised or blamed.

Again, we feel anger and fear without choice, but the virtues are modes of choice or involve choice. Further, in respect of the passions we are said to be moved, but in respect of the virtues and the vices we are said not to be moved but to be disposed in a particular way.

For these reasons also they are not *faculties*; for we are neither called good or bad, nor praised or blamed, for the simple capacity of feeling the passions; again, we have the faculties by nature, but we are not made good or bad by nature; we have spoken of this before.

If, then, the virtues are neither passions nor faculties, all that remains is that they should be *states of character*.

Thus we have stated what virtue is in respect of its genus.

6. We must, however, not only describe virtue as a state of character, but also say what sort of state it is. We may remark, then, that every virtue or

excellence both brings into good condition the thing of which it is the excellence and makes the work of that thing be done well; e.g., the excellence of the eye makes both the eye and its work good; for it is by the excellence of the eye that we see well. Similarly the excellence of the horse makes a horse both good in itself and good at running and at carrying its rider and at awaiting the attack of the enemy. Therefore, if this is true in every case, the virtue of man also will be the state of character which makes a man good and which makes him do his own work well.

How this is to happen we have stated already, but it will be made plain also by the following consideration of the specific nature of virtue. In everything that is continuous and divisible it is possible to take more, less, or an equal amount, and that either in terms of the thing itself or relatively to us; and the equal is an intermediate between excess and defect. By the intermediate in the object I mean that which is equidistant from each of the extremes, which is one and the same for all men; by the intermediate relatively to us that which is neither too much nor too little—and this is not one, nor the same for all. For instance, if ten is many and two is few, six is the intermediate, taken in terms of the object; for it exceeds and is exceeded by an equal amount; this is intermediate according to arithmetical proportion. But the intermediate relatively to us is not to be taken so; if ten pounds are too much for a particular person to eat and two too little, it does not follow that the trainer will order six pounds; for this also is perhaps too much for the person who is to take it, or too little—too little for Milo, too much for the beginner in athletic exercises. The same is true of running and wrestling. Thus a master of any art avoids excess and defect, but seeks the intermediate and chooses this—the intermediate not in the object but relatively to us.

If it is thus, then, that every art does its work well—by looking to the intermediate and judging its works by this standard (so that we often say of good works of art that it is not possible either to take away or to add anything, implying that excess and defect destroy the goodness of works of art, while the mean preserves it; and good artists, as we say, look to this in their work), and if, further, virtue is more exact and better than any art, as nature also is, then virtue must have the quality of aiming at the intermediate. I mean moral virtue; for it is this that is concerned with passions and actions, and in these there is excess, defect, and the intermediate. For instance, both fear and confidence and appetite and anger and pity and in general pleasure and pain may be felt both too much and too little, and in both cases not well; but to feel them at the right times, with reference to the right objects, towards the right people, with the right motive, and in the right way, is what is both intermediate and best, and this is characteristic of virtue. Similarly with regard to actions also there is excess, defect, and the intermediate. Now virtue is concerned with passions and actions, in which excess is a form of failure, and so is defect, while the intermediate is praised and is a form of success; and being praised and being successful are both characteristics of virtue. Therefore virtue is a kind of mean, since, as we have seen, it aims at what is intermediate.

Again, it is possible to fail in many ways (for evil belongs to the class of the unlimited, as the Pythagoreans conjectured, and good to that of the limited), while to succeed is possible only in one way (for which reason also one is easy and the other difficult—to miss the mark easy, to hit it difficult); for these reasons also, then, excess and defect are characteristic of vice, and the mean of virtue.

For men are good in but one way, but bad in many.

Virtue, then, is a state of character concerned with choice, lying in a mean, i.e., the mean relative to us, this being determined by a rational principle, and by that principle by which the man of practical wisdom would determine it. Now it is a mean between two vices, that which depends on excess and that which depends on defect; and again it is a mean because the vices respectively fall short of or exceed what is right in both passions and actions, while virtue both finds and chooses that which is intermediate. Hence in respect of what it is, i.e., the definition which states its essence, virtue is a mean, with regard to what is best and right it is an extreme.

But not every action nor every passion admits of a mean; for some have names that already imply badness, e.g., spite, shamelessness, envy, and in the case of actions adultery, theft, murder; for all of these and suchlike things imply by their names that they are themselves bad, and not the excesses or deficiencies of them. It is not possible, then, ever to be right with regard to them; one must always be wrong. Nor does goodness or badness with regard to such things depend on committing adultery with the right woman, at the right time, and in the right way, but simply to do any of them is to go wrong. It would be equally absurd, then, to expect that in unjust, cowardly, and voluptuous action there should be a mean, an excess, and a deficiency; for at that rate there would be a mean of excess and of deficiency, an excess of excess, and a deficiency of deficiency. But as there is no excess and deficiency of temperance and courage because what is intermediate is in a sense an extreme, so too of the actions we have mentioned there is no mean nor any excess and deficiency, but however they are done they are wrong; for in general there is neither a mean of excess and deficiency, nor excess and deficiency of a mean.

7. . . . With regard to feelings of fear and confidence courage is the mean; of the people who exceed, he who exceeds in fearlessness has no name (many of the states have no name), while the man who exceeds in confidence is rash, and he who exceeds in fear and falls short in confidence is a coward. With regard to pleasures and pains—not all of them, and not so much with regard to the pains—the mean is temperance, the excess self-indulgence. Persons deficient with regard to the pleasures are not often found; hence such persons also have received no name. But let us call them "insensible."

With regard to giving and taking of money the mean is liberality, the excess and the defect prodigality and meanness. In these actions people exceed and fall short in contrary ways; the prodigal exceeds in spending and falls short in taking, while the mean man exceeds in taking and falls short in spending. (At present we are giving a mere outline or summary, and are satisfied with this; later these states will be more exactly determined.) With regard to money there are also other dispositions—a mean, magnificence (for the magnificent man differs from the liberal man; the former deals with large sums, the latter with small ones), an excess, tastelessness and vulgarity, and a deficiency, niggardliness; these differ from the states opposed to liberality, and the mode of their difference will be stated later.

With regard to honour and dishonour the mean is proper pride, the excess is known as a sort of "empty vanity", and the deficiency is undue humility; and as we said liberality was related to magnificence, differing from it by dealing with small sums, so there is a state similarly related to proper pride, being concerned with small honours while that is concerned with great. For it is possible to desire honour as one ought, and more than one ought, and less, and the man who exceeds in his desires is called ambitious, the man who falls short unambitious, while the intermediate person has no name. The dispositions also are nameless, except that that of the ambitious man is called ambition. Hence the people who are at the extremes lay claim to the middle place; and we ourselves sometimes call the intermediate person ambitious and sometimes unambitious, and sometimes praise the ambitious man and sometimes the unambitious. The reason of our doing this will be stated in what follows; but now let us speak of the remaining states according to the method which has been indicated.

With regard to anger also there is an excess, a deficiency, and a mean. Although they can scarcely be said to have names, yet since we call the intermediate person good-tempered let us call the mean good temper; of the persons at the extremes let the one who exceeds be called irascible, and his vice irascibility, and the man who falls short an unirascible sort of person, and the deficiency unirascibility.

There are also three other means, which have a certain likeness to one another, but differ from one another: for they are all concerned with intercourse in words and actions, but differ in that one is concerned with truth in this sphere, the other two with pleasantness; and of this one kind is exhibited in giving amusement, the other in all the circumstances of life. We must therefore speak of these too, that we may the better see that in all things the mean is praiseworthy, and the extremes neither praiseworthy nor right, but worthy of blame. Now most of these states also have no names, but we must try, as in the other cases, to invent names ourselves so that we may be clear and easy to follow. With regard to truth, then, the intermediate is a truthful sort of person and the mean may be called truthfulness, while the pretence which exaggerates is boastfulness and the person characterized by it a boaster, and that which understates is mock modesty and the person characterized by it mock-modest. With regard to pleasantness in the giving of amusement the intermediate person is ready-witted and the disposition ready wit, the excess is buffoonery and the person characterized by it a buffoon, while the man who falls short is a sort of boor and his state is boorishness. With regard to the remaining kind of pleasantness, that which is exhibited in life in general, the man who is pleasant in the right way is friendly and the mean is friendliness, while the man who exceeds is an obsequious person if he has no end in view, a flatterer if he is aiming at his own advantage, and the man who falls short and is unpleasant in all circumstances is a quarrel-some and surly sort of person. . . .

There are also means in the passions and concerned with the passions; since shame is not a virtue, and yet praise is extended to the modest man. For even in these matters one man is said to be intermediate, and another to exceed, as for instance the bashful man who is ashamed of everything; while he who falls short or is not ashamed of anything at all is shameless, and the intermediate person is modest. Righteous indignation is a mean between envy and spite, and these states are concerned with the pain and pleasure that are felt at the fortunes of our neighbours; the man who is characterized by righteous indignation is pained at undeserved good fortune, the envious man, going beyond him, is pained at all good fortune, and the spiteful man falls so far short of being pained that he even rejoices. But these states there will be an opportunity of describing elsewhere; with regard to justice, since it has not one simple meaning, we shall, after describing the other states, distinguish its two kinds and say how each of them is a mean; and similarly we shall treat also of the rational virtues.

8. There are three kinds of disposition, then, two of them vices, involving excess and deficiency respectively, and one a virtue, viz. the mean. . . .

To the mean in some cases the deficiency, in some the excess, is more opposed; e.g., it is not rashness, which is an excess, but cowardice, which is a deficiency, that is more opposed to courage, and not insensibility, which is a deficiency, but self-indulgence, which is an excess, that is more opposed to temperance. This happens from two reasons, one being drawn from the thing itself; for because one extreme is nearer and liker to the intermediate, we oppose not this but rather its contrary to the intermediate. E.g., since rashness is thought liker and nearer to courage, and cowardice more unlike, we oppose rather the latter to courage; for things that are further from the intermediate are thought more contrary to it. This, then, is one cause, drawn from the thing itself; another is drawn from ourselves; for the things to which we ourselves more naturally tend seem more contrary to the intermediate. For instance, we ourselves tend more naturally to pleasures, and hence are more easily carried away towards self-indulgence than towards propriety. We describe as contrary to the mean, then, rather the directions in which we more often go to great lengths; and therefore self-indulgence, which is an excess, is the more contrary to temperance.

9. . . . [I]t is no easy task to be good. For in everything it is no easy task to find the middle, e.g., to find the middle of a circle is not for everyone but for him who knows; so, too, anyone can get angry—that is easy—or give or spend money; but to do this to the right person, to the right extent, at the right time, with the right motive, and in the right way, *that* is not for everyone, nor is it easy; wherefore goodness is both rare and laudable and noble. . . .

Now in everything the pleasant or pleasure is most to be guarded against; for we do not judge it impartially. . . .

[T]o hit the mean . . . is no doubt difficult, and especially in individual cases; for it is not easy to determine both how and with whom and on what provocation and how long one should be angry, for we too sometimes praise those who fall short and call them good-tempered, but sometimes we praise those who get angry and call them manly. The man, however, who deviates little from goodness is not blamed, whether he do so in the direction of the more or of the less, but only the man who deviates more widely; for *he* does not fail to be noticed. But up to what point and to what extent a man must deviate before he becomes blameworthy it is not easy to determine by reasoning, any more than anything else that is perceived by the senses; such things depend on particular facts, and the decision rests with perception. So much, then, is plain, that the intermediate state is in all things to be praised, but that we must incline sometimes towards the excess, sometimes towards the deficiency; for so shall we most easily hit the mean and what is right.

BOOK X

6. Now that we have spoken of the virtues . . . what remains is to discuss in outline the nature of happiness, since this is what we state the end of human affairs to be. Our discussion will be the more concise if we first sum up what we have said already. We said, then, that it is not a state; for if it were it might belong to someone who was asleep throughout his life, living the life of a plant, or, again, to someone who was suffering the greatest misfortunes. If these implications are unacceptable, and we must rather class happiness as an activity, as we have said before, and if some activities are necessary, and desirable for the sake of something else, while others are so in themselves, evidently happiness must be placed among those desirable in themselves, not among those desirable for the sake of something else; for happiness does not lack anything, but is self-sufficient. Now those activities are desirable in themselves from which nothing is sought beyond the activity. And of this nature virtuous actions are thought to be; for to do noble and good deeds is a thing desirable for its own sake.

Pleasant amusements also are thought to be of this nature: we choose them not for the sake of other things; for we are injured rather than benefited by them, since we are led to neglect our bodies and our property. But most of the people who are deemed happy take refuge in such pastimes, which is the reason why those who are ready-witted at them are highly esteemed at the courts of tyrants; they make themselves pleasant companions in the tyrants' favourite pursuits, and that is the sort of man they want. Now these things are thought to be of the nature of happiness because people in despotic positions spend their leisure in them, but perhaps such people prove nothing; for virtue and reason, from which good activities flow, do not depend on despotic position; nor, if these people, who have never tasted pure and generous pleasure, take refuge in the bodily pleasures, should these for that reason be thought more desirable; for boys, too, think the things that are valued among themselves are the best. It is to be expected, then, that, as different things seem valuable to boys and to men, so they should to bad men and to good. Now, as we have often maintained, those things are both valuable and pleasant which are such to the good man; and to each man the activity in accordance with his own state is most desirable, and therefore to the good man that which is in accordance with virtue. Happiness, therefore, does not lie in amusement; it would, indeed, be strange if the end were amusement, and one were to take trouble and suffer hardship all one's life in order to amuse oneself. For, in a word, everything that we choose we choose for the sake of something else—except happiness, which is an end. Now to exert oneself and work for the sake of amusement seems silly and utterly childish. But to amuse oneself in order that one may exert oneself, as Anacharsis puts it, seems right; for amusement is a sort of relaxation, and we need relaxation because we cannot work continuously. Relaxation, then, is not an end; for it is taken for the sake of activity.

The happy life is thought to be virtuous; now a virtuous life requires exertion, and does not consist in amusement. And we say that serious things are better than laughable things and those connected with amusement, and that the activity of the better of any two things—whether it be two elements of our being or two men—is the more serious; but the activity of the better is ipso facto superior and more of the nature of happiness. And any chance person—even a slave—can enjoy the bodily pleasures no less than the best man; but no one assigns to a slave a share in happiness—unless he assigns to him also a share in human life. For happiness does not lie in such occupations, but, as we have said before, in virtuous activities.

7. If happiness is activity in accordance with virtue, it is reasonable that it should be in accordance with the highest virtue; and this will be that of the best thing in us. Whether it be reason or something else that is this element which is thought to be our natural ruler and guide and to take thought of things noble and divine, whether it be itself also divine or only the most divine element in us, the activity of this in accordance with its proper virtue will be perfect happiness. That this activity is contemplative we have already said.

Now this would seem to be in agreement both with what we said before and with the truth. For, firstly, this activity is the best (since not only is reason the best thing in us, but the objects of reason are the best of knowable objects); and, secondly, it is the most continuous, since we can contemplate truth more continuously than we can *do* anything. And we think happiness ought to have pleasure mingled with it, but the activity of philosophic wisdom is admittedly the pleasantest of virtuous activities; at all events the pursuit of it is thought to offer pleasures marvellous for their purity and their enduringness, and it is to be expected that those who know will pass their time more pleasantly than those who inquire. And the self-sufficiency that is spoken of must belong most to the contemplative activity. For while a philosopher, as well as a just man or one possessing any other virtue, needs the necessaries of life, when they are sufficiently equipped with things of that sort the just man needs people towards whom and with whom he shall act justly, and the temperate man, the brave man, and each of the others is in the same case, but the philosopher, even when by himself, can contemplate truth, and the better the wiser he is; he can perhaps do so better if he has fellow workers, but still he is the most self-sufficient. And this activity alone would seem to be loved for its own sake; for nothing arises from it apart from the contemplating, while from practical activities we gain more or less apart from the action. And happiness is thought to depend on leisure; for we are busy that we may have leisure, and make war that we may live in peace. Now the activity of the practical virtues is exhibited in political or military affairs, but the actions concerned with these seem to be unleisurely. Warlike actions are completely so (for no one chooses to be at war, or provokes war, for the sake of being at war; anyone would seem absolutely murderous if he were to make enemies of his friends in order to bring about battle and slaughter); but the action of the statesman also is unleisurely, and aims—beyond the political action itself—at despotic power and honours, or at all events happiness, for him and his fellow citizens—a happiness different from political action, and evidently sought as being different. So if among virtuous actions political and military actions are distinguished by nobility and greatness, and these are unleisurely and aim at an end and are not desirable for their own sake, but the activity of reason, which is contemplative, seems both to be superior in serious worth and to aim at no end beyond itself, and to have its pleasure proper to itself (and this augments the activity), and the self-sufficiency, leisureliness, unweariedness (so far as this is possible for man), and all the other attributes ascribed to the supremely happy man are evidently those connected with this activity, it follows that this will be the complete happiness of man, if it be allowed a complete term of life (for none of the attributes of happiness is *in*complete).

But such a life would be too high for man; for it is not in so far as he is man that he will live so, but in so far as something divine is present in him; and by so much as this is superior to our composite nature is its activity superior to that which is the exercise of the other kind of virtue. If reason is divine, then, in comparison with man, the life according to it is divine in comparison with human life. But we must not follow those who advise us, being men, to think of human things, and, being mortal, of mortal things, but must, so far as we can, make ourselves immortal, and strain every nerve to live in accordance with the best thing in us; for even if it be small in bulk, much more does it in power and worth surpass everything. And this would seem actually to *be* each man, since it is the authoritative and better part of him. It would be strange, then, if he were to choose not the life of himself but that of something else. And what we said before will apply now: that which is proper to each thing is by nature best and most pleasant for each thing; for man, therefore, the life according to reason is best and pleasantest, since reason more than anything else *is* man. This life therefore is also the happiest.

8. But in a secondary degree the life in accordance with the other kind of virtue is happy; for the activities in accordance with this befit our human estate. Just and brave acts, and other virtuous acts, we do in relation to each other, observing our respective duties with regard to contracts and services and all manner of actions and with regard to passions; and all of these seem to be typically human. Some of them seem even to arise from the body, and virtue of character to be in many ways bound up with the passions. Practical wisdom, too, is linked to virtue of character, and this to practical wisdom, since the principles of practical wisdom are in accordance with the moral virtues and rightness in morals is in accordance with practical wisdom. Being connected with the passions also, the moral virtues must belong to our composite nature; and the virtues of our composite nature are human; so, therefore, are the life and the happiness which correspond to these. The excellence of the reason is a thing apart: we must be content to say this much about it, for to describe it precisely is a task greater than our purpose requires. It would seem, however, also to need external equipment but little, or less than moral virtue does. Grant that both need the necessaries, and do so equally, even if the statesman's work is the more concerned with the body and things of that sort; for there will be little difference there; but in what they need for the exercise of their activities there will be much difference. The liberal man will need money for the doing of his liberal deeds, and the just man too will need it for the returning of services (for wishes are hard to discern, and even people who are not just *pretend* to wish to act justly); and the brave man will need power if he is to accomplish any of the acts that correspond to his virtue, and the temperate man will need

opportunity; for how else is either he or any of the others to be recognized? It is debated, too, whether the will or the deed is more essential to virtue, which is assumed to involve both; it is surely clear that its perfection involves both; but for deeds many things are needed, and more, the greater and nobler the deeds are. But the man who is contemplating the truth needs no such thing, at least with a view to the exercise of his activity; indeed they are, one may say, even hindrances, at all events to his contemplation; but in so far as he is a man and lives with a number of people, he chooses to do virtuous acts; he will therefore need such aids to living a human life.

But that perfect happiness is a contemplative activity will appear from the following consideration as well. We assume the gods to be above all other beings blessed and happy; but what sort of actions must we assign to them? Acts of justice? Will not the gods seem absurd if they make contracts and return deposits, and so on? Acts of a brave man, then, confronting dangers and running risks because it is noble to do so? Or liberal acts? To whom will they give? It will be strange if they are really to have money or anything of the kind. And what would their temperate acts be? Is not such praise tasteless, since they have no bad appetites? If we were to run through them all, the circumstances of action would be found trivial and unworthy of gods. Still, everyone supposes that they *live* and therefore that they are active; we cannot suppose them to sleep like Endymion. Now if you take away from a living being action, and still more production, what is left but contemplation? Therefore the activity of God, which surpasses all others in blessedness, must be contemplative; and of human activities, therefore, that which is most akin to this must be most of the nature of happiness.

This is indicated, too, by the fact that the other animals have no share in happiness, being completely deprived of such activity. For while the whole life of the gods is blessed, and that of men too in so far as some likeness of such activity belongs to them, none of the other animals is happy, since they in no way share in contemplation. Happiness extends, then, just so far as contemplation does, and those to whom contemplation more fully belongs are more truly happy, not as a mere concomitant but in virtue of the contemplation; for this is in itself precious. Happiness, therefore, must be some form of contemplation.

But, being a man, one will also need external prosperity; for our nature is not self-sufficient for the purpose of contemplation, but our body also must be healthy and must have food and other attention. Still, we must not think that the man who is to be happy will need many things or great things, merely because he cannot be supremely happy without external goods; for self-sufficiency and action do not involve excess, and we can do noble acts without ruling earth and sea; for even with moderate advantages one can act virtuously (this is manifest enough; for private persons are thought to do worthy acts no less than despots—indeed even more); and it is enough that we should have so much as that; for the life of the man who is active in accordance with virtue will be happy. Solon, too, was perhaps sketching well the happy man when he described him as moderately furnished with externals but as having done (as Solon thought) the noblest acts, and lived temperately; for one can with but moderate possessions do what one ought. Anaxagoras also seems to have supposed the happy man not to be rich nor a despot, when he said that he would not be surprised if the happy man were to seem to most people a strange person; for they judge by externals, since these are all they perceive. The opinions of the wise seem, then, to harmonize with our arguments. But while even such things carry some conviction, the truth in practical matters is discerned from the facts of life; for these are the decisive factor. We must therefore survey what we have already said, bringing it to the test of the facts of life, and if it harmonizes with the facts we must accept it, but if it clashes with them we must suppose it to be mere theory. Now he who exercises his reason and cultivates it seems to be both in the best state of mind and most dear to the gods. For if the gods have any care for human affairs, as they are thought to have, it would be reasonable both that they should delight in that which was best and most akin to them (i.e., reason) and that they should reward those who love and honour this most, as caring for the things that are dear to them and acting both rightly and nobly. And that all these attributes belong most of all to the philosopher is manifest. He, therefore, is the dearest to the gods. And he who is that will presumably be also the happiest; so that in this way too the philosopher will more than any other be happy.

LETTER TO MENOECEUS

Epicurus

Epicurus (341–271 B.C.) was a citizen of Athens, where he established his school, the Garden, and wrote voluminously, although only a few short works survive. He developed an ethical theory according to which happiness can be achieved by ridding ourselves of unnecessary desires, achieving self-sufficiency, and not fearing death.

Let no one when young delay to study philosophy, nor when he is old grow weary of his study. For no one can come too early or too late to secure the health of his soul. And the man who says that the age for philosophy has either not yet come or has gone by is like the man who says that the age for happiness is not yet come to him, or has passed away. Wherefore both when young and old a man must study philosophy, that as he grows old he may be young in blessings through the grateful recollection of what has been, and that in youth he may be old as well, since he will know no fear of what is to come. We must then meditate on the things that make our happiness, seeing that when that is with us we have all, but when it is absent we do all to win it.

From *Epicurus: The Extant Remains*, translated by Cyril Bailey, Oxford University Press, 1926. Reprinted by permission of the publisher.

The things which I used unceasingly to commend to you, these do and practice, considering them to be the first principles of the good life. First of all believe that god is a being immortal and blessed, even as the common idea of a god is engraved on men's minds, and do not assign to him anything alien to his immortality or ill-suited to his blessedness: but believe about him everything that can uphold his blessedness and immortality. For gods there are, since the knowledge of them is by clear vision. But they are not such as the many believe them to be: for indeed they do not consistently represent them as they believe them to be. And the impious man is not he who denies the gods of the many, but he who attaches to the gods the beliefs of the many. For the statements of the many about the gods are not conceptions derived from sensation, but false suppositions, according to which the greatest misfortunes befall the wicked and the greatest blessings the good by the gift of the gods. For men being accustomed always to their own virtues welcome those like themselves, but regard all that is not of their nature as alien.

Become accustomed to the belief that death is nothing to us. For all good and evil consists in sensation, but death is deprivation of sensation. And therefore a right understanding that death is nothing to us makes the mortality of life enjoyable, not because it adds to it an infinite span of time, but because it takes away the craving for immortality. For there is nothing terrible in life for the man who has truly comprehended that there is nothing terrible in not living. So that the man speaks but idly who says that he fears death not because it will be painful when it comes, but because it is painful in anticipation. For that which gives no trouble when it comes, is but an empty pain in anticipation. So death, the most terrifying of ills, is nothing to us, since so long as we exist, death is not with us; but when death comes, then we do not exist. It does not then concern either the living or the dead, since for the former it is not, and the latter are no more.

But the many at one moment shun death as the greatest of evils, at another yearn for it as a respite from the evils in life. But the wise man neither seeks to escape life nor fears the cessation of life, for neither does life offend him nor does the absence of life seem to be any evil. And just as with food he does not seek simply the larger share and nothing else, but rather the most pleasant, so he seeks to enjoy not the longest period of time, but the most pleasant.

And he who counsels the young man to live well, but the old man to make a good end, is foolish, not merely because of the desirability of life, but also because it is the same training which teaches to live well and to die well. Yet much worse still is the man who says it is good not to be born, but

"once born make haste to pass the gates of Death."

For if he says this from conviction why does he not pass away out of life? For it is open to him to do so, if he had firmly made up his mind to this. But if he speaks in jest, his words are idle among men who cannot receive them.

We must then bear in mind that the future is neither ours, nor yet wholly not ours, so that we may not altogether expect it as sure to come, nor abandon hope of it, as if it will certainly not come.

We must consider that of desires some are natural, others vain, and of the natural some are necessary and others merely natural; and of the necessary some are necessary for happiness, others for the repose of the body, and others for very life. The right understanding of these facts enables us to refer all choice and avoidance to the health of the body and the soul's freedom from disturbance, since this is the aim of the life of blessedness. For it is to obtain this end that we always act, namely, to avoid pain and fear. And when this is once secured for us, all the tempest of the soul is dispersed, since the living creature has not to wander as though in search of something that is missing, and to look for some other thing by which he can fulfil the good of the soul and the good of the body. For it is then that we have need of pleasure, when we feel pain owing to the absence of pleasure; but when we do not feel pain, we no longer need pleasure. And for this cause we call pleasure the beginning and end of the blessed life. For we recognize pleasure as the first good innate in us, and from pleasure we begin every act of choice and avoidance, and to pleasure we return again, using the feeling as the standard by which we judge every good.

And since pleasure is the first good and natural to us, for this very reason we do not choose every pleasure, but sometimes we pass over many pleasures, when greater discomfort accrues to us as the result of them: and similarly we think many pains better than pleasures, since a greater pleasure comes to us when we have endured pains for a long time. Every pleasure then because of its natural kinship to us is good, yet not every pleasure is to be chosen: even as every pain also is an evil, yet not all are always of a nature to be avoided. Yet by a scale of comparison and by the consideration of advantages and disadvantages we must form our judgement on all these matters. For the good on certain occasions we treat as bad, and conversely the bad as good.

And again independence of desire we think a great good—not that we may at all times enjoy but a few things, but that, if we do not possess many, we may enjoy the few in the genuine persuasion that those have the sweetest pleasure in luxury who least need it, and that all that is natural is easy to be obtained, but that which is superfluous is hard. And so plain savours bring us a pleasure equal to a luxurious diet, when all the pain due to want is removed; and bread and water produce the highest pleasure, when one who needs them puts them to his lips. To grow accustomed therefore to a simple and not luxurious diet gives us health to the full, and makes a man alert for the needful employments of life, and when after long intervals we approach luxuries disposes us better towards them, and fits us to be fearless of fortune.

When, therefore, we maintain that pleasure is the end, we do not mean the pleasures of profligates and those that consist in sensuality, as is supposed by some who are either ignorant or disagree with us or do not understand, but freedom from pain in the body and from trouble in the mind. For it is not continuous drinkings and revellings, nor the satisfaction of lusts, nor the enjoyment of fish and other luxuries of the wealthy table, which produce a pleasant life, but sober reasoning, searching out the motives for all choice and avoidance, and banishing mere opinions, to which are due the greatest disturbance of the spirit.

Of all this the beginning and the greatest good is prudence. Wherefore prudence is a more precious thing even than philosophy: for from prudence are sprung all the other virtues, and it teaches us that it is not possible to live pleasantly without living prudently and honourably and justly, nor, again, to live a life of prudence, honour, and justice without living pleasantly. For the virtues are by nature bound up with the pleasant life, and the pleasant life is inseparable from them. For indeed who, think you, is a better man than he who holds reverent opinions concerning the gods, and is at all times free from fear of death, and has reasoned out the end ordained by nature? He understands that the limit of good things is easy to fulfil and easy to attain, whereas the course of ills is either short in time or slight in pain: he laughs at destiny, whom some have introduced as the mistress of all things. He thinks that with us lies the chief power in determining events, some of which happen by necessity and some by chance, and some are within our control; for while necessity cannot be called to account, he sees that chance is inconstant, but that which is in our control is subject to no master, and to it are naturally attached praise and blame. For, indeed, it were better to follow the myths about the gods than to become a slave to the destiny of the natural philosophers: for the former suggests a hope of placating the gods by worship, whereas the latter involves a necessity which knows no placation. As to chance, he does not regard it as a god as most men do (for in a god's acts there is no disorder), nor as an uncertain cause of all things: for he does not believe that good and evil are given by chance to man for the framing of a blessed life, but that opportunities for great good and great evil are afforded by it. He therefore thinks it better to be unfortunate in reasonable action than to prosper in unreason. For it is better in a man's actions that what is well chosen should fail, rather than that what is ill chosen should be successful owing to chance.

Meditate therefore on these things and things akin to them night and day by yourself, and with a companion like to yourself, and never shall you be disturbed waking or asleep, but you shall live like a god among men. For a man who lives among immortal blessings is not like to a mortal being.

LEADING DOCTRINES

EPICURUS

I. The blessed and immortal nature knows no trouble itself nor causes trouble to any other, so that it is never constrained by anger or favour. For all such things exist only in the weak.

II. Death is nothing to us: for that which is dissolved is without sensation; and that which lacks sensation is nothing to us.

III. The limit of quantity in pleasures is the removal of all that is painful. Wherever pleasure is present, as long as it is there, there is neither pain of body nor of mind, nor of both at once.

From *Epicurus: The Extant Remains*, translated by Cyril Bailey, Oxford University Press, 1926. Reprinted by permission of the publisher.

IV. Pain does not last continuously in the flesh, but the acutest pain is there for a very short time, and even that which just exceeds the pleasure in the flesh does not continue for many days at once. But chronic illnesses permit a predominance of pleasure over pain in the flesh.

V. It is not possible to live pleasantly without living prudently and honourably and justly [nor again to live a life of prudence, honour, and justice], without living pleasantly. And the man who does not possess the pleasant life, is not living prudently and honourably and justly, and the man who does not possess the virtuous life, cannot possibly live pleasantly.

VI. To secure protection from men anything is a natural good, by which you may be able to attain this end.

VII. Some men wished to become famous and conspicuous, thinking that they would thus win for themselves safety from other men. Wherefore if the life of such men is safe, they have obtained the good which nature craves; but if it is not safe, they do not possess that for which they strove at first by the instinct of nature.

VIII. No pleasure is a bad thing in itself: but the means which produce some pleasures bring with them disturbances many times greater than the pleasures.

IX. If every pleasure could be intensified so that it lasted and influenced the whole organism or the most essential parts of our nature, pleasures would never differ from one another.

X. If the things that produce the pleasures of profligates could dispel the fears of the mind about the phenomena of the sky and death and its pains, and also teach the limits of desires and of pains, we should never have cause to blame them: for they would be filling themselves full with pleasures from every source and never have pain of body or mind, which is the evil of life.

XI. If we were not troubled by our suspicions of the phenomena of the sky and about death, fearing that it concerns us, and also by our failure to grasp the limits of pains and desires, we should have no need of natural science.

XII. A man cannot dispel his fear about the most important matters if he does not know what is the nature of the universe but suspects the truth of some mythical story. So that without natural science it is not possible to attain our pleasures unalloyed.

XIII. There is no profit in securing protection in relation to men, if things above and things beneath the earth and indeed all in the boundless universe remain matters of suspicion.

XIV. The most unalloyed source of protection from men, which is secured to some extent by a certain force of expulsion, is in fact the immunity which results from a quiet life and the retirement from the world.

XV. The wealth demanded by nature is both limited and easily procured; that demanded by idle imaginings stretches on to infinity.

XVI. In but few things chance hinders a wise man, but the greatest and most important matters reason has ordained and throughout the whole period of life does and will ordain.

XVII. The just man is most free from trouble, the unjust most full of trouble.

XVIII. The pleasure in the flesh is not increased, when once the pain due to want is removed, but is only varied: and the limit as regards pleasure in the mind is begotten by the reasoned understanding of these very pleasures and of the emotions akin to them, which used to cause the greatest fear to the mind.

XIX. Infinite time contains no greater pleasure than limited time, if one measures by reason the limits of pleasure.

XX. The flesh perceives the limits of pleasure as unlimited and unlimited time is required to supply it. But the mind, having attained a reasoned understanding of the ultimate good of the flesh and its limits and having dissipated the fears concerning the time to come, supplies us with the complete life, and we have no further need of infinite time: but neither does the mind shun pleasure, nor, when circumstances begin to bring about the departure from life, does it approach its end as though it fell short in any way of the best life.

XXI. He who has learned the limits of life knows that that which removes the pain due to want and makes the whole of life complete is easy to obtain; so that there is no need of actions which involve competition.

XXII. We must consider both the real purpose and all the evidence of direct perception, to which we always refer the conclusions of opinion; otherwise, all will be full of doubt and confusion.

XXIII. If you fight against all sensations, you will have no standard by which to judge even those of them which you say are false.

XXIV. If you reject any single sensation and fail to distinguish between the conclusion of opinion as to the appearance awaiting confirmation and that which is actually given by the sensation or feeling, or each intuitive apprehension of the mind, you will confound all other sensations as well with the same groundless opinion, so that you will reject every standard of judgement. And if among the mental images created by your opinion you affirm both that which awaits confirmation and that which does not, you will not escape error, since you will have preserved the whole cause of doubt in every judgement between what is right and what is wrong.

XXV. If on each occasion instead of referring your actions to the end of nature, you turn to some other nearer standard when you are making a choice or an avoidance, your actions will not be consistent with your principles.

XXVI. Of desires, all that do not lead to a sense of pain, if they are not satisfied, are not necessary, but involve a craving which is easily dispelled, when the object is hard to procure or they seem likely to produce harm.

XXVII. Of all the things which wisdom acquires to produce the blessedness of the complete life, far the greatest is the possession of friendship.

XXVIII. The same conviction which has given us confidence that there is nothing terrible that lasts for ever or even for long, has also seen the protection of friendship most fully completed in the limited evils of this life.

XXIX. Among desires some are natural and necessary, some natural but not necessary, and others neither natural nor necessary, but due to idle imagination.

XXX. Wherever in the case of desires which are physical, but do not lead to a sense of pain, if they are not fulfilled, the effort is intense, such pleasures are due to idle imagination, and it is not owing to their own nature that they fail to be dispelled, but owing to the empty imaginings of the man.

XXXI. The justice which arises from nature is a pledge of mutual advantage to restrain men from harming one another and save them from being harmed.

XXXII. For all living things which have not been able to make compacts not to harm one another or be harmed, nothing ever is either just or unjust; and likewise too for all tribes of men which have been unable or unwilling to make compacts not to harm or be harmed.

XXXIII. Justice never is anything in itself, but in the dealings of men with one another in any place whatever and at any time it is a kind of compact not to harm or be harmed.

XXXIV. Injustice is not an evil in itself, but only in consequence of the fear which attaches to the apprehension of being unable to escape those appointed to punish such actions.

XXXV. It is not possible for one who acts in secret contravention of the terms of the compact not to harm or be harmed, to be confident that he will escape detection, even if at present he escapes a thousand times. For up to the time of death it cannot be certain that he will indeed escape.

XXXVI. In its general aspect justice is the same for all, for it is a kind of mutual advantage in the dealings of men with one another: but with reference to the individual peculiarities of a country or any other circumstances the same thing does not turn out to be just for all.

XXXVII. Among actions which are sanctioned as just by law, that which is proved on examination to be of advantage in the requirements of men's dealings with one another, has the guarantee of justice, whether it is the same for all or not. But if a man makes a law and it does not turn out to lead to advantage in men's dealings with each other, then it no longer has the essential nature of justice. And even if the advantage in the matter of justice shifts from one side to the other, but for a while accords with the general concept, it is none the less just for that period in the eyes of those who do not confound themselves with empty sounds but look to the actual facts.

XXXVIII. Where, provided the circumstances have not been altered, actions which were considered just, have been shown not to accord with the general concept in actual practice, then they are not just. But where, when circumstances have changed, the same actions which were sanctioned as just no longer lead to advantage, there they were just at the time when they were of advantage for the dealings of fellow-citizens with one another; but subsequently they are no longer just, when no longer of advantage.

XXXIX. The man who has best ordered the element of disquiet arising from external circumstances has made those things that he could akin to himself and the rest at least not alien: but with all to which he could not do even this, he has refrained from mixing, and has expelled from his life all which it was of advantage to treat thus.

XL. As many as possess the power to procure complete immunity from their neighbours, these also live most pleasantly with one another, since they have the most certain pledge of security, and after they have enjoyed the fullest intimacy, they do not lament the previous departure of a dead friend, as though he were to be pitied.

ON THE HAPPY LIFE

Seneca

Lucius Annaeus Seneca (c. 3 B.C.–A.D. 65), born in Spain, was a Roman philosopher, dramatist, and statesman, who served as a teacher and influential adviser to Nero but was later accused of conspiracy against the emperor and forced to commit suicide, an act performed with remarkable equanimity. Seneca was an early advocate of Stoicism, according to which happiness requires living in accord with reason, putting aside desires and fears, accepting with tranquility whatever may be the outcome of events, and willingly doing one's duty.

To live happily, my brother Gallio, is the desire of all men, but their minds are blinded to a clear vision of just what it is that makes life happy; and so far from its being easy to attain the happy life, the more eagerly a man strives to reach it, the farther he recedes from it if he has made a mistake in the road; for when it leads in the opposite direction, his very speed will increase the distance that separates him.

First, therefore, we must seek what it is that we are aiming at; then we must look about for the road by which we can reach it most quickly, and on the journey itself, if only we are on the right path, we shall discover how much of the distance we overcome each day, and how much nearer we are to the goal toward which we are urged by a natural desire. But so long as we wander aimlessly, having no guide, and following only the noise and discordant cries of those who call us in different directions, life will be consumed in making mistakes—life that is brief even if we should strive day and night for sound wisdom. Let us, therefore, decide both upon the goal and upon the way, and not fail to find some experienced guide who has explored the region towards which we are advancing; for the conditions of this journey are different from those of most travel. On most journeys some well-recognized road and inquiries made of the inhabitants of the region prevent you from going astray; but on this one all the best beaten and the most frequented paths are the most deceptive. Nothing, therefore, needs to be more emphasized than the warning that we should not, like sheep, follow the lead of the throng in front of us, travelling, thus, the way that all go and not the way that we ought to go. Yet nothing involves us in greater trouble than the fact that we adapt ourselves to common report in the belief that the best things are those that have met with great approval,—the fact that, having so many to follow, we live after the rule, not of reason, but of imitation. The result of this is that people are piled high, one above another, as they rush to destruction. And just as it happens that in a great crush of humanity, when the people push against each other, no one can

From *On the Happy Life*, Loeb Classical Library® vol. 254, translated by J. W. Basore, Harvard University Press and Heinemann, 1932. Reprinted by permission of the publishers.

fall down without drawing along another, and those that are in front cause destruction to those behind—this same thing you may see happening everywhere in life. No man can go wrong to his own hurt only, but he will be both the cause and the sponsor of another's wrongdoing. For it is dangerous to attach one's self to the crowd in front, and so long as each one of us is more willing to trust another than to judge for himself, we never show any judgement in the matter of living, but always a blind trust, and a mistake that has been passed on from hand to hand finally involves us and works our destruction. It is the example of other people that is our undoing; let us merely separate ourselves from the crowd, and we shall be made whole. But as it is, the populace, defending its own iniquity, pits itself against reason. And so we see the same thing happening that happens at the elections, where, when the fickle breeze of popular favour has shifted, the very same persons who chose the praetors wonder that those praetors were chosen. The same thing has one moment our favour, the next our disfavour; this is the outcome of every decision that follows the choice of the majority.

When the happy life is under debate, there will be no use for you to reply to me, as if it were a matter of votes: "This side seems to be in a majority." For that is just the reason it is the worse side. Human affairs are not so happily ordered that the majority prefer the better things; a proof of the worst choice is the crowd. Therefore let us find out what is best to do, not what is most commonly done—what will establish our claim to lasting happiness, not what finds favour with the rabble, who are the worst possible exponents of the truth. But by the rabble I mean no less the servants of the court than the servants of the kitchen; for I do not regard the colour of the garments that clothe the body. In rating a man I do not rely upon eyesight; I have a better and surer light, by which I may distinguish the false from the true. Let the soul discover the good of the soul. If the soul ever has leisure to draw breath and to retire within itself—ah! to what self-torture will it come, and how, if it confesses the truth to itself, it will say: "All that I have done hitherto, I would were undone; when I think of all that I have said, I envy the dumb; of all that I have prayed for, I rate my prayers as the curses of my enemies; of all that I have feared—ye gods! how much lighter it would have been than the load of what I have coveted! With many I have been at enmity, and, laying aside hatred, have been restored to friendship with them—if only there can be any friendship between the wicked; with myself I have not yet entered into friendship. I have made every effort to remove myself from the multitude and to make myself noteworthy by reason of some endowment. What have I accomplished save to expose myself to the darts of malice and show it where it can sting me? See you those who praise your eloquence, who trail upon your wealth, who court your favour, who exalt your power? All these are either now your enemies, or—it amounts to the same thing—can become such. To know how many are jealous of you, count your admirers. Why do I not rather seek some real good—one which I could feel, not one which I could display? These things that draw the eyes of men, before which they halt, which they show to one another in wonder, outwardly glitter, but are worthless within."

Let us seek something that is a good in more than appearance—something that is solid, constant, and more beautiful in its more hidden part; for this let us delve. And it is placed not far off; you will find it—you need only to know where to stretch out your hand. As it is, just as if we groped in darkness, we pass by things near at hand, stumbling over the very objects we desire.

Not to bore you, however, with tortuous details, I shall pass over in silence the opinions of other philosophers, for it would be tedious to enumerate and refute them all. Do you listen to ours. But when I say "ours," I do not bind myself to some particular one of the Stoic masters; I, too, have the right to form an opinion. Accordingly, I shall follow so-and-so, I shall request so-and-so to divide the question; perhaps, too, when called upon after all the rest, I shall impugn none of my predecessors' opinions, and shall say: "I simply have this much to add." Meantime, I follow the guidance of Nature—a doctrine upon which all Stoics are agreed. Not to stray from Nature and to mould ourselves according to her law and pattern—this is true wisdom.

The happy life, therefore, is a life that is in harmony with its own nature, and it can be attained in only one way. First of all, we must have a sound mind and one that is in constant possession of its sanity; second, it must be courageous and energetic, and, too, capable of the noblest fortitude, ready for every emergency, careful of the body and of all that concerns it, but without anxiety; lastly, it must be attentive to all the advantages that adorn life, but with overmuch love for none—the user, but not the slave, of the gifts of Fortune. You understand, even if I do not say more, that, when once we have driven away all that excites or affrights us, there ensues unbroken tranquillity and enduring freedom; for when pleasures and fears have been banished, then, in place of all that is trivial and fragile and harmful just because of the evil it works, there comes upon us first a boundless joy that is firm and unalterable, then peace and harmony of the soul and true greatness coupled with kindliness; for all ferocity is born from weakness.

It is possible also to define this good of ours in other terms—that is, the same idea may be expressed in different language. Just as an army remains the same, though at one time it deploys with a longer line, now is massed into a narrow space and either stands with hollowed centre and wings curved forward, or extends a straightened front, and, no matter what its formation may be, will keep the selfsame spirit and the same resolve to stand in defence of the selfsame cause,—so the definition of the highest good may at one time be given in prolix and lengthy form, and at another be restrained and concise. So it will come to the same thing if I say: "The highest good is a mind that scorns the happenings of chance, and rejoices only in virtue," or say: "It is the power of the mind to be unconquerable, wise from experience, calm in action, showing the while much courtesy and consideration in intercourse with others." It may also be defined in the statement that the happy man is he who recognizes no good and evil other than a good and an evil mind—one who cherishes honour, is content with virtue, who is neither puffed up, nor crushed, by the happenings of chance, who knows of no greater good than that which he alone is able to bestow upon himself, for whom true pleasure will be the scorn of pleasures. It is possible, too, if one chooses to be discursive, to transfer the same idea to various other forms of expression without injuring or weakening its meaning. For what prevents us from saying that the happy life is to have a mind that is free, lofty, fearless and steadfast—a mind that is placed beyond the reach of fear, beyond the reach of desire, that counts virtue the only good, baseness the only evil, and all else but a worthless mass of things, which come and go without increasing or diminishing the highest good, and neither subtract any part from the happy life nor add any part to it?

A man thus grounded must, whether he wills or not, necessarily be attended by constant cheerfulness and a joy that is deep and issues from deep within, since he finds delight in his own resources, and desires no joys greater than his inner joys. Should not such joys as these be rightly matched against the paltry and trivial and fleeting sensations of the wretched body? The day a man becomes superior to pleasure, he will also be superior to pain; but you see in what wretched and baneful bondage he must linger whom pleasures and pains, those most capricious and tyrannical of masters, shall in turn enslave. Therefore we must make our escape to freedom. But the only means of procuring this is through indifference to Fortune. Then will be born the one inestimable blessing, the peace and exaltation of a mind now safely anchored, and, when all error is banished, the great and stable joy that comes from the discovery of truth, along with kindliness and cheerfulness of mind; and the source of a man's pleasure in all of these will not be that they are good, but that they spring from a good that is his own.

Seeing that I am employing some freedom in treating my subject, I may say that the happy man is one who is freed from both fear and desire because of the gift of reason; since even rocks are free from fear and sorrow, and no less are the beasts of the field, yet for all that no one could say that these things are "blissful," when they have no comprehension of bliss. Put in the same class those people whose dullness of nature and ignorance of themselves have reduced them to the level of beasts of the field and of inanimate things. There is no difference between the one and the other, since in one case they are things without reason, and in the other their reason is warped, and works their own hurt, being active in the wrong direction; for no man can be said to be happy if he has been thrust outside the pale of truth. Therefore the life that is happy has been founded on correct and trustworthy judgement, and is unalterable. Then, truly, is the mind unclouded and freed from every ill, since it knows how to escape not only deep wounds, but even scratches, and, resolved to hold to the end whatever stand it has taken, it will defend its position even against the assaults of an angry Fortune. For so far as sensual pleasure is concerned, though it flows about us on every side, steals in through every opening, softens the mind with its blandishments, and employs one resource after another in order to seduce us in whole or in part, yet who of mortals, if he has left in him one trace of a human being, would choose to have his senses tickled night and day, and, forsaking the mind, devote his attention wholly to the body?

"But the mind also," it will be said, "has its own pleasures." Let it have them, in sooth, and let it pose as a judge of luxury and pleasures; let it gorge itself with all the things that are wont to delight the senses, then let it look back upon the past, and, recalling faded pleasures, let it intoxicate itself with former experiences and be eager now for those to come, and let it lay its plans, and, while the body lies helpless from present cramming, let it direct its thoughts to that to come—yet from all this, it seems to me, the mind will be more wretched than ever, since it is madness to choose evils instead of goods. But no man can be happy unless he is sane, and no man can be sane who searches for what will injure him in place of what is best. The happy man, therefore, is one who has right judgement; the happy man is content with his present lot, no matter what it is, and is reconciled to his circumstances; the happy man is he who allows reason to fix the value of every condition of existence.

Even those who declare that the highest good is in the belly see in what a dishonourable position they have placed it. And so they say that it is not possible to separate pleasure from virtue, and they aver that no one can live virtuously without also living pleasantly, nor pleasantly without also living virtuously. But I do not see how things so different can be cast in the same mould. What reason is there, I beg of you, why pleasure cannot be separated from virtue? Do you mean, since all goods have their origin in virtue, even the things that you love and desire must spring from its roots? But if the two were inseparable, we should not see certain things pleasant, but not honourable, and certain things truly most honourable, but painful and capable of being accomplished only through suffering. Then, too, we see that pleasure enters into even the basest life, but, on the other hand, virtue does not permit life to be evil, and there are people who are unhappy not without pleasure—nay, are so on account of pleasure itself—and this could not happen if pleasure were indissolubly joined to virtue; virtue often lacks pleasure, and never needs it. Why do you couple things that are unlike, nay, even opposites? Virtue is something lofty, exalted and regal, unconquerable, and unwearied; pleasure is something lowly, servile, weak, and perishable, whose haunt and abode are the brothel and the tavern. Virtue you will find in the temple, in the forum, in the senate-house—you will find her standing in front of the city walls, dusty and stained, and with calloused hands; pleasure you will more often find lurking out of sight, and in search of darkness, around the public baths and the sweating-rooms and the places that fear the police—soft, enervated, reeking with wine and perfume, and pallid, or else painted and made up with cosmetics like a corpse. The highest good is immortal, it knows no ending, it permits neither surfeit nor regret; for the right-thinking mind never alters, it neither is filled with self-loathing nor suffers any change in its life, that is ever the best. But pleasure is extinguished just when it is most enjoyed; it has but small space, and thus quickly fills it—it grows weary and is soon spent after its first assault. Nor is anything certain whose nature consists in movement. So it is not even possible that there should be any substance in that which comes and goes most swiftly and will perish in the very exercise of its power; for it struggles to reach a point at which it may cease, and it looks to the end while it is beginning.

What, further, is to be said of the fact that pleasure belongs alike to the good and the evil, and that the base delight no less in their disgrace than do the honourable in fair repute? And therefore the ancients have enjoined us to follow, not the most pleasant, but the best life, in order that pleasure should be, not the leader, but the companion of a right and proper desire. For we must use Nature as our guide; she it is that Reason heeds, it is of her that it takes counsel. Therefore to live happily is the same thing as to live according to Nature. What this is, I shall proceed to make clear. If we shall guard the endowments of the body and the needs of Nature with care and fearlessness, in the thought that they have been given but for a day and are fleeting, if we shall not be their slaves, nor allow these alien things to become our masters, if we shall count that the gratifications of the body, unessential as they are, have a place like to that of the auxiliaries and light-armed troops in camp—if we let them serve, not command—thus and thus only will these things be profitable to the mind. Let a man not be corrupted by external things, let him be unconquerable and admire only himself, courageous in spirit and ready for any fate, let him be the moulder of his own life; let not his confidence be without knowledge, nor his knowledge without firmness; let his decisions once made abide, and let not his decrees be altered by any erasure. It will be understood, even without my adding it, that such a man will be poised and well ordered, and will show majesty mingled with courtesy in all his actions. Let reason search into external things at the instigation of the senses, and, while it derives from them its first knowledge—for it has no other base from which it may operate, or begin its assault upon truth—yet let it fall back upon itself. For God also, the all-embracing world and the ruler of the universe, reaches forth into outward things, yet, withdrawing from all sides, returns into himself. And our mind should do the same; when, having followed the senses that serve it, it has through them reached to things without, let it be the master both of them and of itself. In this way will be born an energy that is united, a power that is at harmony with itself, and that dependable reason which is not divided against itself, nor uncertain either in its opinions, or its perceptions, or in its convictions; and this reason, when it has regulated itself, and established harmony between all its parts, and, so to speak, is in tune, has attained the highest good. For no crookedness, no slipperiness is left to it, nothing that will cause it to stumble or fall. It will do everything under its own authority and nothing unexpected will befall it, but whatever it does will turn out a good, and that, too, easily and readily and without subterfuge on the part of the doer; for reluctance and hesitation are an indication of conflict and instability. Wherefore you may boldly declare that the highest good is harmony of the soul; for where concord and unity are, there must the virtues be. Discord accompanies the vices.

"But even you," it is retorted, "cultivate virtue for no other reason than because you hope for some pleasure from it." But, in the first place, even though virtue is sure to bestow pleasure, it is not for this reason that virtue is sought; for it is not this, but something more than this that she bestows, nor does she labour for this, but her labour, while directed toward something else, achieves this also. As in a ploughed field, which has been broken up for corn, some flowers will spring up here and there, yet it was not for these poor little plants, although they may please the eye, that so much toil was expended—the sower had a different purpose, these were superadded—just so pleasure is neither the cause nor the reward of virtue, but its by-product, and we do not accept virtue because she delights us, but if we accept her, she also delights us. The highest good lies in the very choice of it, and the very attitude of a mind made perfect, and when the mind has completed its course and fortified itself within its own bounds, the highest good has now been perfected, and nothing further is desired; for there can no more be anything outside of the whole than there can be some point beyond the end. Therefore you blunder when you ask what it is that makes me seek virtue; you are looking for something beyond the supreme. Do you ask what it is that I seek in virtue? Only herself. For she offers nothing better—she herself is her own reward. Or does this seem to you too small a thing? When I say to you, "The highest good is the inflexibility of an unyielding mind, its foresight, its sublimity, its soundness, its freedom, its harmony, its beauty," do you require of me something still greater to which these blessings may be ascribed? Why do you mention to me pleasure? It is the good of man that I am searching for, not that of his belly—the belly of cattle and wild beasts is more roomy!

"You are misrepresenting what I say," you retort; "for I admit that no man can live pleasantly without at the same time living virtuously as well, and this is patently impossible for dumb beasts and for those who measure their good by mere food. Distinctly, I say, and openly I testify that the life that I denominate pleasant is impossible without the addition of virtue." Yet who does not know that those who are most apt to be filled with your sort of pleasure are all the greatest fools, and that wickedness abounds in enjoyments, and that the mind itself supplies many kinds of pleasure that are vicious? Foremost are haughtiness, a too high opinion of one's self and a puffed-up superiority to others, a blind and unthinking devotion to one's own interests, dissolute luxury, extravagant joy springing from very small and childish causes, and, besides a biting tongue and the arrogance that takes pleasure in insults, sloth, and the degeneracy of a sluggish mind that falls asleep over itself. All these things Virtue tosses aside, and she plucks the ear, and appraises pleasures before she permits them, and those that she approves she sets no great store by, or even just permits them, and it is not her use of them, but her temperance that gives her joy. Since, however, temperance reduces our pleasures, injury results to your highest good. You embrace pleasure, I enchain her; you enjoy pleasure, I use it; you think it the highest good, I do not think it even a good; you do everything for the sake of pleasure, I, nothing.

When I say that "I" do nothing for the sake of pleasure, I am speaking of the ideal wise man, to whom alone you are willing to concede pleasure. But I do not call him a wise man who is dominated by anything, still less by pleasure. And yet if he is engrossed by this, how will he withstand toil and danger and want and all the threatening ills that clamour about the life of man? How will he endure the sight of death, how grief, how the crashes of the universe and all the fierce foes that face him, if he has been subdued by so soft an adversary? You say: "He will do whatever pleasure advises." But come, do you not see how many things it will be able to advise? "It will not be able to advise anything base," you say, "because it is linked with virtue." But once more, do you not see what sort of thing that highest good must be if it needs a guardian in order to become a good? And how shall Virtue guide Pleasure if she follows her, since it is the part of one who obeys to follow, of one who commands to guide? Do you station in the rear the one that commands? Truly a fine office that you assign to Virtue—to be the foretaster of your pleasures! We shall see later whether to those who have treated virtue so contemptuously she still remains virtue; for she cannot keep her name if she yields her place. Meanwhile—for this is the point here—I shall show that there are many who are besieged by pleasures, upon whom Fortune has showered all her gifts, and yet, as you must needs admit, are wicked men. Look at Nomentanus and Apicius, digesting, as they say, the blessings of land and sea, and reviewing the creations of every nation arrayed upon their board! See them, too, upon a heap of roses, gloating over their rich cookery, while their ears are delighted by the sound of music, their eyes by spectacles, their palates by savours; soft and soothing stuffs caress with their warmth the length of their bodies, and, that the nostrils may not meanwhile be idle, the room itself, where sacrifice is being made to Luxury, reeks with varied perfumes. You will recognize that these are living in the midst of pleasures, and yet it will not be well with them, because what they delight in is not a good.

"It will be ill with them," you say, "because many things will intrude that perturb the soul, and opinions, conflicting with one another, will disquiet the mind." That this is so I grant; but none the less these very men, foolish as they are and inconsistent and subject to the pangs of remorse, will have experience of very great pleasures, so that you must admit that, while in that state they lack all pain, they no less lack a sound mind, and, as is the case with very many others, that they make merry in madness and laugh while they rave. But, on the other hand, the pleasures of the wise man are calm, moderate, almost listless and subdued, and scarcely noticeable inasmuch as they come unsummoned, and, although they approach of their own accord, are not held in high esteem and are received without joy on the part of those who experience them; for they only let them mingle now and then with life as we do amusements and jests with serious affairs.

Let them cease, therefore, to join irreconcilable things and to link pleasure with virtue—a vicious procedure which flatters the worst class of men. The man who has plunged into pleasures, in the midst of his constant belching and drunkenness, because he knows that he is living with pleasure, believes that he is living with virtue as well; for he hears first that pleasure cannot be separated from virtue, then dubs his vices wisdom, and parades what ought to be concealed. And so it is not Epicurus who has driven them to debauchery, but they, having surrendered themselves to vice, hide their debauchery in the lap of philosophy and flock to the place where they may hear the praise of pleasure, and they do not consider how sober and abstemious the "pleasure" of Epicurus really is—for so, in all truth, I think it—but they fly to a mere name seeking some justification and screen for their lusts. And thus they lose the sole good that remained to them in their wickedness—shame for wrongdoing. For they now praise the things that used to make them blush, and they glory in vice; and therefore they cannot even recover their youth, when once an honourable name has given warrant to their shameful laxity. The reason why your praise of pleasure is pernicious is that what is honourable in your teaching lies hid within, what corrupts is plainly visible.

Personally I hold the opinion—I shall express it though the members of our school may protest—that the teachings of Epicurus are upright and holy and, if you consider them closely, austere; for his famous doctrine of pleasure is reduced to small and narrow proportions, and the rule that we Stoics lay down for virtue, this same rule he lays down for pleasure—he bids that it obey Nature. But it takes a very little luxury to satisfy Nature! What then is the case?

Whoever applies the term "happiness" to slothful idleness and the alternate indulgence in gluttony and lust, looks for a good sponsor for his evil course, and when, led on by an attractive name, he has found this one, the pleasure he pursues is not the form that he is taught, but the form that he has brought, and when he begins to think that his vices accord with the teacher's maxims, he indulges in them no longer timidly, and riots in them, not now covertly, but from this time on in broad daylight. And so I shall not say, as do most of our sect, that the school of Epicurus is an academy of vice, but this is what I say— it has a bad name, is of ill repute, and yet undeservedly. How can anyone know this who has not been admitted to the inner shrine? Its mere outside gives ground for scandal and incites to evil hopes. The case is like that of a strong man dressed up in a woman's garb; you maintain your chastity, your virility is unimpaired, your body is free from base submission—but in your hand is a tambourine! Therefore you should choose some honourable super-scription and a motto that in itself appeals to the mind; the one that stands has attracted only the vices.

Whosoever has gone over to the side of virtue, has given proof of a noble nature; he who follows pleasure is seen to be weakly, broken, losing his man-hood, and on the sure path to baseness unless someone shall establish for him some distinction between pleasures, so that he may know which of them lie within the bounds of natural desire, which sweep headlong onward and are unbounded and are the more insatiable the more they are satisfied. Come then! let virtue lead the way, and every step will be safe. Then, too, it is the excess of pleasure that harms; but in the case of virtue there need be no fear of any excess, for in virtue itself resides moderation. That cannot be a good that suffers from its own magnitude. Besides, to creatures endowed with a rational nature what better guide can be offered than reason? Even if that com-bination pleases you, if you are pleased to proceed toward the happy life in such company, let virtue lead the way, let pleasure attend her—let it hover about the body like its shadow. To hand over virtue, the loftiest of mistresses, to be the handmaid of pleasure is the part of a man who has nothing great in his soul.

Let virtue go first, let her bear the standard. We shall none the less have pleasure, but we shall be the master and control her; at times we shall yield to her entreaty, never to her constraint. But those who surrender the leadership to pleasure, lack both; for they lose virtue, and yet do not possess pleasure, but are possessed by it, and they are either tortured by the lack of it or strangled by its excess—wretched if it deserts them, more wretched if it overwhelms them—they are like sailors who have been caught in the waters around the Syrtes, and now are left on the dry shore, and again are tossed by the seething waves. But this results from a complete lack of self-control and blind love for an object; for, if one seeks evils instead of goods, success becomes dangerous. As the hunt for wild beasts is fraught with hardship and danger, and even those that are captured are an anxious possession—for many a time they rend their masters—so it is as regards great pleasures; for they turn out to be a great misfortune, and captured pleasures become now the captors. And the more and the greater the pleasures are, the more inferior will that man be whom the crowd calls happy, and the more masters will he have to serve. I wish to dwell still further upon this comparison. Just as the man who tracks wild animals to their lairs, and counts it a great delight

With noose the savage beasts to snare,

and

Around the spreading woods to fling a line of hounds,

in order that he may follow upon their tracks, leaves things that are more worth while and forsakes many duties, so he who pursues pleasures makes everything else secondary, and first of all gives up liberty, and he pays this price at the command of his belly; nor does he buy pleasures for himself, but he sells himself to pleasures.

"Nevertheless," someone asks, "what is there to prevent the blending of virtue and pleasure into one, and constituting the highest good in such a way that the honourable and the agreeable may be the same thing?" The answer is that the honourable can have no part that is not honourable, nor will the highest good preserve its integrity if it sees in itself something that is different from its better part. Even the joy that springs from virtue, although it is a good, is not nevertheless a part of the absolute good, any more than are cheerfulness and tranquillity, although they spring from the noblest origins; for goods they are, yet they only attend on the highest good but do not consummate it. But whoever forms an alliance between virtue and pleasure—and that too, not an equal one—by the frailty of one good dulls whatever power the other may have, and sends beneath the yoke that liberty which remains unconquered only so long as it finds nothing more precious than itself. For it begins to need the help of Fortune, and this is the depth of servitude; there follows a life of anxiety, suspicion, and alarm, a dread of mishap and worry over the changes time brings. You do not give to virtue a foundation solid and immovable, but bid her stand on unstable ground; yet what is so unstable as trust in the hazards of chance and the vicissitudes of the body and the things that affect the body? How is such a man able to obey God and to receive in cheerful spirit whatever happens, and, interpreting his mishaps indulgently, never to complain of Fate, if he is agitated by the petty prickings of pleasure and pain? But he is not even a good guardian or avenger of his country, nor a defender of his friends if he has a leaning toward pleasures. Therefore let the highest good mount to a place from which no force can drag it down, where neither pain nor hope nor fear finds access, nor does any other thing that can lower the authority of the highest good; but Virtue alone is able to mount to that height. We must follow her footsteps to find that ascent easy; bravely will she stand, and she will endure whatever happens, not only patiently, but even gladly; she will know that every hardship that time brings comes by a law of Nature, and like a good soldier she will submit to wounds, she will count her scars, and, pierced by darts, as she dies she will love him for whose sake she falls—her commander; she will keep in mind that old injunction, "Follow God!" But whoever complains and weeps and moans, is compelled by force to obey commands, and, even though he is unwilling, is rushed none the less to the bidden tasks. But what madness to prefer to be dragged rather than to follow! As much so, in all faith, as it is great folly and ignorance of one's lot to grieve because of some lack or some rather bitter happening, and in like manner to be surprised or indignant at those ills that befall the good no less than the bad—I mean sickness and death and infirmities and all the other unexpected ills that invade human life. All that the very constitution of the universe obliges us to suffer, must be borne with high courage. This is the sacred obligation by which we are bound—to submit to the human lot, and not to be disquieted by those things which we have no power to avoid. We have been born under a monarchy; to obey God is freedom.

Therefore true happiness is founded upon virtue. And what is the counsel this virtue will give to you? That you should not consider anything either a good or an evil that will not be the result of either virtue or vice; then, that you should stand unmoved both in the face of evil and by the enjoyment of good, to the end that—as far as is allowed—you may body forth God. And what does virtue promise you for this enterprise? Mighty privileges and equal to the divine. You shall be bound by no constraint, nothing shall you lack, you shall be free, safe, unhurt; nothing shall you essay in vain, from nothing be debarred; all things shall happen according to your desire, nothing adverse shall befall you, nothing contrary to your expectations and wish. "What! does virtue alone suffice for living happily?" Perfect and divine as it is, why should it not suffice—nay, suffice to overflowing? For if a man has been placed beyond the reach of any desire, what can he possibly lack? If a man has gathered into himself all that is his, what need does he have of any outside thing? But the man who is still on the road to virtue, who, even though he has proceeded far, is still struggling in the toils of human affairs, does have need of some indulgence from Fortune until he has loosed that knot and every mortal bond. Where then lies the difference? In that some are closely bound, others fettered—even hand and foot. He who has advanced toward the higher realm and has lifted himself to higher levels drags a loosened chain; he is not yet free, but still is as good as free.

THE HAPPY LIFE

Augustine

Augustine (354–430), born in North Africa, became bishop of Hippo and a Christian church father. Strongly influenced by Platonism, his voluminous writings played a crucial role in the transition from classical thought to medieval philosophy. He argued that the happy person possesses wisdom, whose source is God.

From *Writings of Saint Augustine, Vol. 1,* translated by Ludwig Schopp, CIMA Publishing Co., 1948.

CHAPTER 1

(6) On the Ides of November fell my birthday. After a breakfast light enough not to impede our powers of thinking, I asked all those of us who, not only that day but every day, were living together to have a congenial session in the bathing quarters, a quiet place fitting for the season. Assembled there— for without hesitation I present them to your kindness, though only by name— were first, our mother, to whose merit, in my opinion, I owe everything that I live; my brother Navigius; Trygetius and Licentius, fellow citizens and my pupils; Lastidianus and Rusticus, relatives of mine, whom I did not wish to be absent, though they are not trained even in grammar, since I believed their common sense was needed for the difficult matter I was undertaking. Also my son, Adeodatus, the youngest of all, was with us, who promises great success, unless my love deceives me. While all these were paying attention, I started in the following manner.

CHAPTER 2

(10) . . . "We wish to be happy, do we not?"
No sooner had I said this, than they agreed, with one voice.
I asked: "In your opinion, is a person happy who does not possesses what he wants?"
They said: "By no means."
"What? Everyone who possesses what he wants is happy?"
At this point our mother said: "If he wishes and possesses good things, he is happy; if he desires evil things—no matter if he possesses them—he is wretched."
I smiled at her and said cheerfully: "Mother, you have really gained the mastery of the very stronghold of philosophy. For, undoubtedly you were wanting the words to express yourself like Tullius, who also has dealt with this matter. In his *Hortensius*, a book written in the praise and defense of philosophy, he said: 'Behold, not the philosophers, but only people who like to argue, state that all are happy who live according to their own will. This, of course, is not true, for, to wish what is not fitting is the worst of wretchedness. But it is not so deplorable to fail of attaining what we desire as it is to wish to attain what is not proper. For, greater evil is brought about through one's wicked will than happiness through fortune.'"
At these words our mother exclaimed in such a way that we, entirely forgetting her sex, thought we had some great man in our midst, while in the meantime I became fully aware whence and from what divine source this flowed.
Then Licentius spoke up: "You must tell us what a person has to wish in order to be happy, and what kind of things he must desire."
"Invite me," I said, "to your birthday party, and I will accept gladly what you serve. In this manner, please, be my guest today and do not ask for something that perhaps is not prepared."

When he felt sorry because of his request, though it was modest and not out of place, I asked: "Do we all now agree that nobody can be happy without possessing what he desires, and that not everyone who has what he wants is happy?"

They all expressed their approval.

(11) "But what about this?" I asked. "Do you grant that everyone who is not happy is wretched?"

They had no doubt about this.

"Everyone, then," I continued, "who does not possess what he wants, is miserable."

All assented.

"But what preparation should a man make to gain happiness?" I asked. "For this, perhaps, is also a question to serve up at our banquet, so that the eagerness of Licentius may not be disregarded. In my opinion, what a man possesses ought to be obtained by him when he wants it."

"That is evident," they said.

"It must be something," I remarked, "that ever remains, and is neither dependent upon fate nor subject to any mishap. For, whatever is mortal and transitory we cannot possess whenever we wish it, and as long as we wish to have it."

All agreed.

But Trygetius said: "Many favorites of fortune possess abundantly and plentifully those things which, though frail and subject to mishaps, are pleasant for this earthly life. And they lack nothing that they desire."

To him I replied: "In your opinion, is a person happy who has fear?"

"It does not seem so," he answered.

"If, then, someone is likely to lose what he loves, can he be without fear?"

"No," he said.

"All those fortuitous things can be lost. No one, then, who possesses and loves them can ever be happy."

He did not refute this.

At this point, however, our mother said: "Even if somebody were certain that he would not lose all those things, he still could not be satisfied with such possessions. Hence, he is miserable because he is ever needy."

"But, in your opinion would not somebody be happy," I asked, "who has all these things in abundance and superfluity, if he is moderate in his desires, and enjoys them with contentment properly and pleasantly?"

"In this case," she replied, "he is not happy through the possession of these things, but through the moderation of his mind."

"Very well expressed," I said. "No better answer to my question could be expected, and no other one from you. Therefore, we do not have the slightest doubt that anyone setting out to be happy must obtain for himself that which always endures and cannot be snatched away through any severe misfortune."

Trygetius said: "We have already agreed to this."

"Is God, in your opinion, eternal and ever remaining?" I asked.

"This, of course, is so certain," replied Licentius, "that the question is unnecessary." All the others agreed with pious devotion.

"Therefore," I concluded, "whoever possesses God is happy."

(12) As they readily and joyfully agreed to this, I continued: "It seems to me, therefore, that we have only to inquire what man really possesses God, for he, certainly, will be happy. It is your opinion about this that I now ask."

Here Licentius remarked: "He who lives an upright life possesses God."

Trygetius continued: "He who does what God wills to be done possesses God."

Lastidianus also agreed to this opinion.

The boy, the youngest of all, said, however: "Whoever has a spirit free from uncleanness has God."

Our mother approved all the answers, especially the last one.

Navigius remained silent. When I asked him what he thought, he replied that he was rather pleased with the last answer.

In order that Rusticus should not appear to be neglected in such an important matter, I asked him for his opinion, for it seemed to me that he kept silence not so much out of deliberation as through bashfulness. He agreed with Trygetius.

(13) Then I said: "Now I know the opinions of all on this most important matter. Beyond this question we have no need to inquire nor can anything be found, if only we continue our investigation, as we began, with the greatest serenity and sincerity. However, this investigation would be tedious today; for the mind also in its feasts may go to excess if it indulges too greedily in the meal—in this way it digests poorly, and the consequent discomfort is no less harmful to the health of the mind than is hunger itself. Therefore, if you do not object, we will rather take up this question tomorrow, when we are hungry again." . . .

CHAPTER 3

(17) When we had convened again in the same room on the following day after breakfast, though a little later than the day before, I began: . . . "Unless I am mistaken, He is the one about whom we all piously and firmly agreed yesterday—that it is He, through His steady presence in men, who makes them happy. For, when our reason had demonstrated that a man who possesses God is happy, and when none of you opposed this conclusion, the question was asked: Who, in your opinion, possessed God."

"If I remember correctly, three opinions were expressed on this point. The first preferred to think that one possesses God who does His will. Others, however, thought that a person who lived an upright life possessed God. Still others saw God in those souls that are free of unclean spirits."

(18) "But perhaps all of you have expressed the same opinion, only in different words. For, if we consider the first two statements—everyone who lives uprightly does what God wills, and everyone who does what God wills lives uprightly—we see that living an upright life is the same as doing what pleases God; unless this seems to you otherwise."

They agreed. . . .

(19) "Now I intend to question you, rather briefly, about this point: whether God desires that man seek Him."

They said: "Yes."

I also asked: "Can we say that one who seeks God leads a bad life?"

"By no means," was their reply.

"Answer me yet a third question: Is an impure spirit able to seek God?"

They said: "No." Navigius, still a little in doubt, at first, finally agreed with the others.

"If, then," I said, "one who seeks God obeys the will of God, he both lives righteously and is without an impure spirit. On the other hand, one who seeks God has not yet found God. Nothing, then, immediately compels our belief that whoever lives an upright life, or does what God wills, or has not an impure spirit, has God."

While the others laughed at the fact that they were misled through their own admissions, our mother, stunned for a while, requested that through an explanation I should loosen and untangle for her the logical knot I had been compelled to present.

After this had been done, she said: "But nobody can attain God without first seeking Him."

"Very well," I replied. "But one who is still seeking has not yet attained God, although he lives an upright life. Therefore, not everyone who lives a good life possesses God."

She then said: "I believe that everyone possesses God, but, if one lives righteously, he has God favorable to him, and, if wrongly, hostile."

"Incorrectly, then," I said, "we conceded yesterday that the one is happy who possesses God, since every man possesses God and yet not every man is happy."

"Therefore, add the word 'favorable,'" she said.

(20) "Are we at least certain about the conclusion, that he is happy who has God favorable to him?" I asked.

"I should like to agree," said Navigius, "but I am afraid about the man who is still searching for God." . . .

"For it is impossible for me to say that God is unfavorable to the man who seeks Him: and, if it is improper to say this, He will be favorable. But, whoever has God favorable to him is happy. The man who seeks is, therefore, happy, although everyone who seeks does not possess what he wants."

"Thus, also, that man is happy who does not possess what he wants, a conclusion that appeared to be absurd to us all yesterday." . . .

(21) At this point, when even our mother had smiled, Trygetius said: "I do not at once concede that God is unfavorable to the one to whom He is not favorable. But I believe there is a middle state."

I then asked him: "Do you believe that such a man, to whom God is neither favorable nor hostile, still possesses God in some way?"

Since he was a little reluctant, our mother said: "To possess God, and not to be without God, are two quite different things."

"Which, then," I asked, "is better: to possess God, or not to be without God?"

"As far as I can see," she replied, "my opinion is this: He who lives righteously possesses God, that is, has Him propitious to him; he who lives a bad life also possesses God, but as hostile to him. But, whoever is still seeking

God, and has not yet found Him, has Him neither as propitious nor as hostile, yet is not without God."

"Is this also your opinion?" I asked the others.

They said: "Yes."

"Kindly tell me," I urged: "In your opinion, is not God more propitious to the one whom He favors?"

They acknowledged that it was so.

"Is God not favorable toward the man who is seeking Him?" I asked again.

"Yes," they replied.

"Consequently, whoever seeks God has God propitious to him. But, everybody who has God propitious to him is happy. On the strength of this, also, one is happy who seeks God. But, whoever is seeking does not yet possess what he wishes to possess. Consequently, he is happy who does not possess what he wants to possess."

Our mother remarked: "According to my view, by no means is one happy who does not possess what he wishes."

"Then," I said, "not everybody is happy who has God propitious to him."

"If reasoning demands this conclusion," she replied, "I cannot deny it."

Then I said: "We, therefore, have to make the following distinction: Everyone is happy who has already found God and has God propitious to him; on the other hand, everyone who is seeking God has God propitious to him, but is not yet happy. Of course, everybody who, through vices and sins, goes astray from God is not only unhappy, but is not even living with God's favor."

(22) When this was approved by all, I continued. "Very well; I am afraid only that you will be vexed through a conclusion already agreed upon, namely, that he is miserable who is not happy; for, thence it logically follows that that man is miserable who [has God propitious to him, since—as we have said—he still seeks God and therefore is not yet happy.] Or, indeed, should we, like Tullius, call the owners of large estates rich, but the possessors of all virtues poor? But consider whether, as it is true that every needy person is miserable, it is also true that every miserable one is needy. In this case, then, it will be correct to say that misery is but poverty, a statement which, after it is made, I now approve as you have heard.

"However, the investigation of this would take too long for today. Thus, that you may not become dismayed, I ask you to meet again tomorrow at the same table."

As soon as all had expressed their eagerness to comply with my request, we rose.

CHAPTER 4

(23) On the third day of our discussion, the morning mist, which was keeping us in the bathing quarters, dispersed, and the weather gave us a very sunny afternoon. So we decided to go down to the little meadow nearby. After we were all seated in what seemed a comfortable spot, the remainder of our colloquy was taken up as follows.

I began: "Almost everything which, in questioning you, I wanted you to concede, I have received and retained. Therefore I believe—since we are finally able to distinguish our session through a certain interval of days—there will be no need for you today to give me any answer or, at least, not many answers. However, our mother has stated that wretchedness is nothing but poverty, and we are all agreed also that all are wretched who are needy. But, whether also all who are wretched are in need is a question which we could not explain yesterday.

"If reason has demonstrated that this is so, then the question 'Who is happy?' is perfectly solved: it will be the one who is not in need. For, everyone who is not miserable is happy. Therefore, happy is the man who is without need, if we are to say that need [*egestas*] is identified with misery [*miseria*]."

(24) "Cannot the conclusion that everyone is happy who is not in need," asked Trygetius, "be drawn from the evident fact that every needy man is miserable? I remember that we agreed upon no middle state between the miserable and the happy."

"In your opinion, does a middle state exist between a dead and a living man?" I asked. "Is not every man either alive or dead?"

"I grant you that here also there is no middle state," he replied. "But to what avail is this?"

"Because," I continued, "I believe that you will also concede that a person is dead who has been buried for a year."

He did not deny it.

"But, does it follow from this that also one is still living who has not been buried for a year?"

"This does not follow," he said.

"Therefore," I continued, "it does not follow, from the supposition that everyone is miserable who is in want, that everyone is happy who is not in want, although a middle state cannot any more be found between the miserable and the happy than between a living man and a dead man." . . .

(26) "But, now consider whether every wretched man is also in want. To admit this is rather difficult in view of the fact that many people live in the midst of fortune's abundant gifts, people for whom everything is pleasant and easy; whatever their passion desires is furnished immediately at their nod. Such a life, of course, is not easy to attain.

"But, let us think of such a man as resembles Tullius' description of Orata.[1] Who could affirm offhand that Orata had been afflicted with want, since he was a man of great riches, luxuries, and delights, not lacking anything in regard to pleasure, influence, dignity, and having a healthy constitution? Immensely rich in estates, and exceptionally blessed with most charming friends, he had in abundance whatever his heart desired, and all these goods in the interest of his physical wellbeing. In a word, all his undertakings and his every wish were crowned with success.

"Perhaps one of you may say that this man desired to have more than he actually had. But this is unknown to us. Since it is enough for our purpose, let us take for granted that he did not desire more than he had already. Do you think that he was in want?"

Licentius answered: "Even if I concede that he did not desire anything further—something hard to believe of a man who is not wise—yet, assuredly, he must have been afraid of losing all his possessions through one sudden mishap, since, as it is said, he was a man of high intelligence. For it was not difficult to comprehend that all such things, no matter how great, were subject to chance."

At this point I smiled and said: "Licentius, you see that the brilliancy of his own mind impeded this man, exceptionally favored by fortune, from enjoying a happy life. Through the greater sharpness of his mind he gained a deeper realization of the contingency of his possessions. Therefore he was bent down by fear, and expressed this sufficiently by a common saying: The man without faith is prudent in his own folly."

(27) When he and the others had smiled, I said: "Let us consider this a little more carefully, since he [Orata], though imbued with fear, was not in want; from which point rises our question. For, to be in want consists in not possessing, not in fearing the loss of your possessions. He was miserable because of fear, not because of want. Consequently, not everybody is in want who is miserable."

With all the others, my mother also, whose opinion I was defending, approved of this. Still a little in doubt, she said: "I do not yet quite understand how misery can be separated from want, and want from misery. Although he had great riches and abundance and—according to your own statement—desired nothing more, he still was in want of wisdom, since he entertained the fear of losing these things. Are we going to consider him in want, if he be without silver and money, and not if he should lack wisdom?"

When, at this point, all had expressed their admiration, and I myself was filled with joy and delight because it was she who had uttered that truth which, as gleaned from the books of the philosophers, I had intended to bring forward as an imposing final argument, I said: "Do you all see now that a great difference exists between many and varied doctrines and a soul that is devoted to God? For from what other source flow these words that we admire?"

Licentius joyfully exclaimed: "Verily, no truer or more divine words could have been spoken. For, there is no greater and more pitiable want than the want of wisdom. Whoever does not lack wisdom cannot lack anything."

(28) "Consequently, the want of the soul is nothing but foolishness," I said. "It is the opposite of wisdom, as death is the opposite of life, or a happy life is the opposite of a miserable one, that is, without a middle state. For, just as every man who is not happy is miserable, and every man who is not dead is alive, so, manifestly, every man who is not foolish is wise.

"From this we may rightly conclude that Sergius Orata was miserable, not merely because he feared losing those gifts of fortune, but because he was unwise. Of course, he would have been more miserable if he had been quite without fear for those unsteady and changeable things which he regarded as good. In this case he would have found an added security, not through a watch kept by courage but through a mental lethargy, and his deeper folly would have sunk him deeper into misery. Therefore, if everybody without wisdom suffers from a great want, it follows that foolishness is nothing but want. Just as every fool is miserable, so every miserable man is a fool. Thus, evidently, just as all want is identical with misery, so all misery is identical with want." . . .

(30) All agreed to this conclusion, and I said: "Now we have to inquire who it is that is not in want, for it is he who will be wise and happy. Now, foolishness is want and a term of want, while this word 'want' usually signifies a sort of sterility and lack." . . .

"You now agree that every fool is in want, and that every person in want is a fool. And I think you also concede that a foolish soul is faulty, and that all faults of the mind can be included in that one term foolishness. . . .

"Of what, then, do we conceive as the opposite of 'want,' about which we are speaking?"

While the others hesitated, Trygetius said: "If I speak of wealth, I see that poverty is its opposite."

"This is almost right," I answered. "For poverty and want are usually understood in the same sense. But, another word has to be found so that the commendable side may not lack a term. Otherwise, the one side would have two terms [poverty and want], confronted on the other side by the one term [wealth]. For, nothing could be more absurd than to lack a word where one is needed in opposition to 'want.'"

Licentius said: "If we may say so, the word 'fullness' [*plenitudo*] seems to me to be the proper opposite of 'want.'"

(31) . . . "I accept your 'fullness.' . . . 'Fullness' and 'want,' then, are opposites." . . .

"If 'want' is identical with 'foolishness,' 'fullness' will be 'wisdom.' And, quite correctly, many have called frugality the mother of all virtues. Tullius also agrees with them, when, in one of his popular orations, he says:[2] 'Whatever may be others' opinion, I think that frugality, that is, moderation and restraint, is the greatest virtue.' This is very learnedly and becomingly said. . . . But, because of the common manner of speech, according to which 'frugality' means the same as 'thriftiness,' he illustrates what he has in mind by adding 'moderation' and 'restraint.' Let us now consider these two words more closely."

(32) "The word *modestia* [moderation] is derived from *modus* [measure], and the word *temperantia* [restraint] from *temperies* [proper mixture]. Wherever measure and proper mixture are, there is nothing either too much or too little. Here, then, we have the precise sense of 'fullness' [*plenitudo*], which is the word we chose as the opposite of 'want' [*egestas*]. . . .

"But the measure of the soul is wisdom. Wisdom, however, is undeniably the opposite of foolishness, and foolishness is want, but fullness is the opposite of want. Therefore, wisdom is fullness. Yet, in fullness is measure. Hence, the measure of the soul is in wisdom. Hence, the very famous proverb rightly known as the most useful principle in life: 'Not anything too much.'"[3]

(33) "At the beginning of our discussion today we intended to call that man happy who is not in want, in case we should find misery identical with want. This is now found to be so. Therefore, 'to be happy' means nothing else than 'not to be in want,' that is, 'to be wise.'

"If now you ask what wisdom is—our reason has also explained and developed this as far as was at present possible—the answer is that wisdom is nothing but the measure of the soul, that is, that through which the soul keeps its equilibrium so that it neither runs over into too much nor remains short of its fullness. It runs over into luxuries, despotism, pride, and other things of this kind, through which the souls of immoderate and miserable men believe they get joy and might. But it is narrowed down by meanness, fear, grief, passion, and many other things through which miserable men make acknowledgement of their misery.

"However, when it [the soul] beholds the wisdom found and ... devotes itself to it, ... it then fears no immoderateness, and therefore no want and hence no misery. Thus, whoever is happy possesses his measure, that is, wisdom."

(34) "But what wisdom should be so called, if not the wisdom of God? We have also heard through divine authority that the Son of God is nothing but the wisdom of God, and the Son of God is truly God. Thus, everyone having God is happy—a statement already acclaimed by everyone at the beginning of our symposium. . . .

(35) . . . "But, as long as we are still seeking, and not yet satiated by . . . fullness [*plenitudo*]—we must confess that we have not yet reached our measure; therefore, notwithstanding the help of God, we are not yet wise and happy."

NOTES

1. C. Sergius Orata, wealthy epicure, was a contemporary of Cicero, who writes of his estates in *De officiis* 2:16.—L.S.

2. Cicero, *Pro Deiotaro* 9:26.

3. Terence, *Andria*, Act I, Scene I.

SUMMA CONTRA GENTILES

Thomas Aquinas

Saint Thomas Aquinas (1225–1274), born near Naples, was the most influential philosopher of the medieval period. His system, which synthesized Aristotelianism and Christianity, was given official approval six centuries later by the Catholic Church. Aquinas maintained that the greatest happiness is not to be found in bodily pleasures, honors, riches, power, glory, or even moral actions but, rather, in the contemplation of God.

From *On the Truth of the Catholic Faith*, translated by Vernon J. Bourke, Hanover House, 1956.

BOOK THREE: PROVIDENCE

Chapter 27

That Human Felicity Does Not Consist in Pleasures of the Flesh

[1] Now, it is clear . . . that it is impossible for human felicity to consist in bodily pleasures, the chief of which are those of food and sex. . . .

[4] . . . [F]elicity is a certain kind of good, appropriate to man. Indeed, brute animals cannot be deemed happy, unless we stretch the meaning of the term. But these pleasures that we are talking about are common to men and brutes. So, felicity should not be attributed to them.

[5] Moreover, the ultimate end is the noblest appurtenance of a thing; in fact, the term means the best. But these pleasures are not agreeable to man by virtue of what is noblest in him, namely, his understanding, but by virtue of his sense capacity. So, felicity should not be located in pleasures of this kind.

[6] Furthermore, the highest perfection of man cannot lie in a union with things inferior to himself, but, rather, in a union with some reality of a higher character, for the end is better than that which is for the sake of the end. Now, the aforementioned pleasures consist in this fact: that man is, through his senses, united with some things that are his inferiors, that is, with certain sensible objects. So, felicity is not to be located in pleasures of this sort.

[7] Again, something which is not good unless it be moderated is not good of itself; rather, it receives goodness from the source of the moderation. Now, the enjoyment of the aforementioned pleasures is not good for man unless it be moderated; otherwise, these pleasures will interfere with each other. So, these pleasures are not of themselves the good for man. But that which is the highest good is good of itself, because what is good of itself is better than what depends on something else. Therefore, such pleasures are not the highest good for man, that is, felicity.

[8] Besides, in the case of all things that are predicated per se, an absolute variation is directly accompanied by a similar variation in the degree of intensification. Thus, if a hot thing heats, then a hotter thing heats more, and the hottest thing will heat the most. So, if the aforementioned pleasures were goods of themselves, the maximum enjoyment of them should be the best. But this is clearly false, for excessive enjoyment of them is considered vicious, and is also harmful to the body, and it prevents the enjoyment of similar pleasures. Therefore, they are not of themselves the good for man. So, human felicity does not consist in them.

[9] Moreover, virtuous acts are praiseworthy because they are ordered to felicity. So, if human felicity consisted in the aforementioned pleasures, a virtuous act would be more praiseworthy when it involved the enjoyment of these pleasures than when it required abstention from them. However, it is clear that this is false, for the act of temperance is given most praise when it involves abstaining from pleasures; as a result, it gets its name from this fact. Therefore, man's felicity does not lie in the aforesaid pleasures.

[10] Furthermore, the ultimate end of everything is God. . . . So, we should consider the ultimate end of man to be that whereby he most closely approaches God. But, through the aforesaid pleasures, man is kept away from a close

approach to God, for this approach is effected through contemplation, and the aforementioned pleasures are the chief impediment to contemplation, since they plunge man very deep into sensible things, consequently distracting him from intelligible objects. Therefore, human felicity must not be located in bodily pleasures.

[11] Through this conclusion we are refuting the error of the Epicureans, who placed man's felicity in these enjoyments. . . .

Chapter 28

That Felicity Does Not Consist in Honors

[1] It is also clear from the foregoing that the highest good for man, that is felicity, does not lie in honors. . . .

[3] . . . [T]hat, which is good and desirable on account of something else is not the ultimate end. But honor is of this sort. A person is not rightly honored unless it be because of some other good that is present in him. And this is why men seek to be honored, desiring, as it were, to have a witness to some good feature present in them. Hence, men take greater joy in being honored by important and wise people. So, man's felicity is not to be identified with honors.

[4] Besides, the attainment of felicity is accomplished through virtue. Now, virtuous operations are voluntary; otherwise, they would not merit praise. So, felicity ought to be some good which man may attain by his own will. But the gaining of honor is not within the power of any man; rather, it is in the power of the one who gives the honor. Therefore, human felicity is not to be identified with honors.

[5] Moreover, to be worthy of honor can only be an attribute of good men. But it is possible for even evil men to be honored. So, it is better to become worthy of honor than to be honored. Therefore, honor is not the highest good for man.

[6] Furthermore, the highest good is the perfect good. But the perfect good is completely exclusive of evil. Now, that in which there can be no evil cannot itself be evil. Therefore, that which is in possession of the highest good cannot be evil. But it is possible for a bad man to attain honor. So, honor is not the highest good for man.

Chapter 29

That Man's Felicity Does Not Consist in Glory

[1] From this it is also apparent that the highest good for man does not consist in glory, which means a widely recognized reputation.

[2] Now, according to Tully, glory is "widespread repute accompanied by praise of a person." And according to Ambrose, it is "an illustrious reputation accompanied by praise." Now, men desire to become known in connection with some sort of praise and renown, for the purpose of being honored by those who know them. So, glory is sought for the sake of honor. Hence, if honor is not the highest good, much less is glory. . . .

[4] Besides, to know is more noble than to be known; only the more noble things know, but the lowest things are known. So, the highest good for man cannot be glory, for it consists in the fact that a person is well known.

[5] Moreover, a person desires to be known only for good things; where bad things are concerned, he seeks concealment. So, to be known is a good and desirable thing, because of the good things that are known about a person. And so, these good things are better than being widely known. Therefore, glory is not the highest good, for it consists in a person being widely known.

[6] Furthermore, the highest good should be perfect, for it should satisfy the appetite. Now, the knowledge associated with fame, in which human glory consists, is imperfect, for it is possessed of the greatest uncertainty and error. Therefore, such glory cannot be the highest good.

[7] Again, the highest good for man should be what is most enduring among human affairs, for an endless duration of the good is naturally desired. Now, glory, in the sense of fame, is the least permanent of things; in fact, nothing is more variable than opinion and human praise. Therefore, such glory is not the highest good for man.

Chapter 30

That Man's Felicity Does Not Consist in Riches

[1] From this, moreover, it is also clear that riches are not the highest good for man.

[2] Indeed, riches are only desired for the sake of something else; they provide no good of themselves but only when we use them, either for the maintenance of the body or some such use. Now, that which is the highest good is desired for its own sake and not for the sake of something else. Therefore, riches are not the highest good for man.

[3] Again, man's highest good cannot lie in the possession or keeping of things that chiefly benefit man through being spent. Now, riches are chiefly valuable because they can be expended, for this is their use. So, the possession of riches cannot be the highest good for man.

[4] Besides, an act of virtue is praiseworthy in so far as it comes closer to felicity. Now, acts of liberality and magnificence, which have to do with money, are more praiseworthy in a situation in which money is spent than in one in which it is saved. So, it is from this fact that the names of these virtues are derived. Therefore, the felicity of man does not consist in the possession of riches.

[5] Moreover, that object in whose attainment man's highest good lies must be better than man. But man is better than riches, for they are but things subordinated to man's use. Therefore, the highest good for man does not lie in riches.

[6] Furthermore, man's highest good is not subject to fortune, for things subject to fortune come about independently of rational effort. But it must be through reason that man will achieve his proper end. Of course, fortune occupies an important place in the attainment of riches. Therefore, human felicity is not founded on riches.

[7] Again, this becomes evident in the fact that riches are lost in an involuntary manner, and also that they may accrue to evil men who must fail to achieve the highest good, and also that riches are unstable—and for other reasons of this kind which may be gathered from the preceding arguments.

Chapter 31

That Felicity Does Not Consist in Worldly Power

[1] Similarly, neither can worldly power be man's highest good, since in its attainment, also, fortune can play a most important part. It is also unstable; nor is it subject to man's will; oftentimes it comes to bad men—and these characteristics are incompatible with the highest good, as was evident in the foregoing arguments.

[2] Again, man is deemed good chiefly in terms of his attainment of the highest good. Now, he is not called good, or bad, simply because he has power, for not everyone who can do good things is a good man, nor is a person bad because he is able to do evil things. Therefore, the highest good does not consist in the fact of being powerful.

[3] Besides, all power is relative to some other thing. But the highest good is not relative to something else. Therefore, power is not man's highest good.

[4] Moreover, a thing that one can use both for good and for evil cannot be man's highest good, for that is better which no one can use in a bad way. Now, one can use power well or badly, "for rational powers are capable of contrary effects." Therefore, man's highest good does not consist in human power.

[5] Furthermore, if any sort of power is the highest good, it ought to be the most perfect. But human power is most imperfect, since it is rooted in the wills and the opinions of men, in which there is the greatest inconstancy. And the more important the power is considered to be, the more does it depend on large numbers of people, which fact also contributes to its frailty, since what depends on many can be destroyed in many ways. Therefore, man's highest good does not lie in worldly power.

[6] Man's felicity, then, consists in no exterior good, since all exterior goods, the ones that are called "goods of fortune," are contained under the preceding headings.

Chapter 32

That Felicity Does Not Consist in Goods of the Body

[1] Moreover, that man's highest good does not lie in goods of the body, such as health, beauty, and strength, is clearly evident from similar considerations. For these things are possessed in common by both good and bad men; they are also unstable; moreover, they are not subject to the will.

[2] Again, the soul is better than the body, which is not alive, and which does not possess the aforementioned goods except by means of the soul. So, a good of the soul, like understanding and that sort of thing, is better than a good of the body. Therefore, the good of the body is not man's highest good.

[3] Besides, these goods are common to men and other animals. But felicity is the proper good of man. Therefore, man's felicity does not lie in the aforesaid goods.

[4] Moreover, many animals are better endowed than men, as far as the goods of the body go; for some are faster than man, some are stronger, and so on. If, then, man's highest good lay in these things, man would not be the most excellent of animals; which is obviously false. Therefore, human felicity does not consist in goods of the body.

Chapter 33

That Human Felicity Does Not Lie in the Senses

[1] In the same way, it is also apparent that man's highest good does not lie in the goods of his sensitive part. For these goods, too, are common to men and other animals.

[2] Again, intellect is better than sense. So, the good of the intellect is better than the good of the senses. Therefore, man's highest good does not lie in sense.

[3] Besides, the greatest pleasures in the sense order have to do with food and sexual activities; and so, the highest good ought to lie in these areas, if it were in sense. But it is not found in these things. Therefore, man's highest good does not lie in the senses.

[4] Moreover, the senses are treasured because of their usefulness, and also because of their knowledge. Now, the entire utility of the senses has reference to the goods of the body. But sense cognition is subordinated to intellectual cognition; thus, animals devoid of understanding take no pleasure in sensing, except in regard to some benefit pertaining to the body, according as they obtain food or sexual satisfaction through sense knowledge. Therefore, man's highest good, his felicity, does not lie in his sensitive part.

Chapter 34

That Man's Ultimate Felicity Does Not Lie in Acts of the Moral Virtues

[1] It is clear, too, that the ultimate felicity of man does not consist in moral actions.

[2] In fact, human felicity is incapable of being ordered to a further end, if it is ultimate. But all moral operations can be ordered to something else. This is evident from the most important instances of these actions. The operations of fortitude, which are concerned with warlike activities, are ordered to victory and to peace. Indeed, it would be foolish to make war merely for its own sake. Likewise, the operations of justice are ordered to the preservation of peace among men, by means of each man having his own possessions undisturbed. And the same thing is evident for all the other virtues. Therefore, man's ultimate felicity does not lie in moral operations.

[3] Again, the moral virtues have this purpose: through them the mean is preserved in the internal passions and in regard to external things. Now, it is not possible for such a measuring of passions, or of external things, to be the ultimate end of human life, since these passions and exterior things are

capable of being ordered to something else. Therefore, it is not possible for man's ultimate felicity to lie in acts of the moral virtues.

[4] Besides, since man is man by virtue of his possession of reason, his proper good which is felicity should be in accord with what is appropriate to reason. Now, that is more appropriate to reason which reason has within itself than which it produces in another thing. So, since the good of moral virtue is something produced by reason in things other than itself, it could not be that which is best for man; namely, felicity. Rather would felicity seem to be a good situated in reason itself.

[5] Moreover, it was shown above that the ultimate end of all things is to become like unto God. So, that whereby man is made most like God will be his felicity. Now, this is not a function of moral acts, since such acts cannot be attributed to God, except metaphorically. Indeed, it does not befit God to have passions, or the like, with which moral acts are concerned. Therefore, man's ultimate felicity, that is, his ultimate end, does not consist in moral actions.

[6] Furthermore, felicity is the proper good for man. So, that which is most proper among all human goods, for man in contrast to the other animals, is the good in which his ultimate felicity is to be sought. Now, an act of moral virtue is not of this sort, for some animals share somewhat, either in liberality or in fortitude, but an animal does not participate at all in intellectual action. Therefore, man's ultimate felicity does not lie in moral acts.

Chapter 35

That Ultimate Felicity Does Not Lie in the Act of Prudence

[1] From this it is also apparent that man's ultimate felicity does not lie in an act of prudence.

[2] For the act of prudence is only concerned with things that pertain to the moral virtues. Now, man's ultimate felicity does not lie in acts of the moral virtues, nor, then, in the act of prudence.

[3] Again, man's ultimate felicity consists in the best operation of man. Now, the best operation of man, according to what is proper to man, lies in a relationship to the most perfect object. But the operation of prudence is not concerned with the most perfect object of understanding or reason; indeed, it does not deal with necessary objects, but with contingent problems of action. Therefore, man's ultimate felicity does not lie in this operation.

[4] Besides, that which is ordered to another thing as an end is not the ultimate felicity for man. But the operation of prudence is ordered to something else as an end: both because all practical knowledge, in which category prudence is included, is ordered to action, and because prudence makes a man well disposed in regard to things that are to be chosen for the sake of the end, as is clear from Aristotle, in *Ethics* vi. Therefore, man's ultimate felicity does not lie in the operation of prudence.

[5] Moreover, irrational animals do not participate in felicity, as Aristotle proves in *Ethics* i. However, some of them do participate somewhat in prudence, as appears in the same writer, in *Metaphysics* i. Therefore, felicity does not consist in the operation of prudence.

Chapter 36

That Felicity Does Not Consist in the Operation of Art

[1] It is also clear that it does not lie in the operation of art.

[2] For the knowledge that pertains to art is also practical knowledge. And so, it is ordered to an end, and is not itself the ultimate end.

[3] Again, the ends of art operations are artifacts. These cannot be the ultimate end of human life, for we ourselves are, rather, the ends for all artificial things. Indeed, they are all made for man's use. Therefore, ultimate felicity cannot lie in the operation of art.

Chapter 37

That the Ultimate Felicity of Man Consists in the Contemplation of God

[1] So, if the ultimate felicity of man does not consist in external things which are called the goods of fortune, nor in the goods of the body, nor in the goods of the soul according to its sensitive part, nor as regards the intellective part according to the activity of the moral virtues, nor according to the intellectual virtues that are concerned with action, that is, art and prudence—we are left with the conclusion that the ultimate felicity of man lies in the contemplation of truth.

[2] Indeed, this is the only operation of man which is proper to him, and in it he shares nothing in common with the other animals.

[3] So, too, this is ordered to nothing else as an end, for the contemplation of truth is sought for its own sake.

[4] Also, through this operation man is united by way of likeness with beings superior to him, since this alone of human operations is found also in God and in separate substances.

[5] Indeed, in this operation he gets in touch with these higher beings by knowing them in some way.

[6] Also, for this operation man is rather sufficient unto himself, in the sense that for it he needs little help from external things.

[7] In fact, all other human operations seem to be ordered to this one, as to an end. For, there is needed for the perfection of contemplation a soundness of body, to which all the products of art that are necessary for life are directed. Also required are freedom from the disturbances of the passions—this is achieved through the moral virtues and prudence—and freedom from external disorders, to which the whole program of government in civil life is directed. And so, if they are rightly considered, all human functions may be seen to subserve the contemplation of truth.

[8] However, it is not possible for man's ultimate felicity to consist in the contemplation which depends on the understanding of principles, for that is very imperfect, being most universal, including the potential cognition of things. Also, it is the beginning, not the end, of human enquiry, coming to us from nature and not because of our search for truth. Nor, indeed, does it lie in the area of the sciences which deal with lower things, because felicity should lie in the working of the intellect in relation to the noblest objects of understanding. So, the conclusion remains that man's ultimate felicity

consists in the contemplation of wisdom, based on the considering of divine
matters.

[9] From this, that is also clear by way of induction, which was proved
above by rational arguments, namely, that man's ultimate felicity consists only
in the contemplation of God.

LEVIATHAN

Thomas Hobbes

Thomas Hobbes (1588–1679) is widely regarded as a founding figure in
English moral and political philosophy. He argued that in the absence of
an effective government, individuals, driven by self-interest, would fail
to secure happiness and would be doomed, instead, to lives that he
famously described as "solitary, poor, nasty, brutish, and short."

CHAPTER 6

Of the Interior Beginnings of Voluntary Motions: Commonly Called the Passions; and the Speeches by Which They are Expressed

There be in animals, two sorts of *motions* peculiar to them: one called *vital*;
begun in generation, and continued without interruption through their whole
life; such as are the *course* of the *blood*, the *pulse*, the *breathing*, the *concoction*,
nutrition, excretion, &c.; to which motions there needs no help of imagination:
the other is *animal motion*, otherwise called *voluntary motion*; as to *go*, to *speak*,
to *move* any of our limbs, in such manner as is first fancied in our minds.
That sense is motion in the organs and interior parts of man's body, caused
by the action of the things we see, hear, &c.; and that fancy is but the relics
of the same motion, remaining after sense, has been already said in the first
and second chapters. And because *going, speaking*, and the like voluntary
motions, depend always upon a precedent thought of *whither, which way*, and
what; it is evident, that the imagination is the first internal beginning of all
voluntary motion. And although unstudied men do not conceive any motion
at all to be there, where the thing moved is invisible; or the space it is moved
in, is (for the shortness of it) insensible; yet that doth not hinder, but that
such motions are. For let a space be never so little, that which is moved over a
greater space, whereof that little one is part, must first be moved over that.
These small beginnings of motion, within the body of man, before they appear

From *Leviathan* (1651).

in walking, speaking, striking, and other visible actions, are commonly called ENDEAVOUR.

This endeavour, when it is toward something which causes it, is called APPETITE, or DESIRE; the latter, being the general name; and the other, oftentimes restrained to signify the desire of food, namely *hunger* and *thirst*. And when the endeavour is fromward something, it is generally called AVERSION. These words, *appetite* and *aversion*, we have from the *Latins*; and they both of them signify the motions, one of approaching, the other of retiring. . . .

That which men desire, they are also said to LOVE: and to HATE those things for which they have aversion. So that desire and love are the same thing; save that by desire, we always signify the absence of the object; by love, most commonly the presence of the same. So also by aversion, we signify the absence; and by hate, the presence of the object.

Of appetites and aversions, some are born with men; as appetite of food, appetite of excretion and exoneration, (which may also and more properly be called aversions, from somewhat they feel in their bodies;) and some other appetites, not many. The rest, which are appetites of particular things, proceed from experience, and trial of their effects upon themselves or other men. For of things we know not at all, or believe not to be, we can have no further desire, than to taste and try. But aversion we have for things, not only which we know have hurt us, but also that we do not know whether they will hurt us, or not.

Those things which we neither desire, nor hate, we are said to *contemn*; CONTEMPT being nothing else but an immobility, or contumacy of the heart, in resisting the action of certain things; and proceeding from that the heart is already moved otherwise, by other more potent objects; or from want of experience of them.

And because the constitution of a man's body is in continual mutation, it is impossible that all the same things should always cause in him the same appetites, and aversions: much less can all men consent, in the desire of almost any one and the same object.

But whatsoever is the object of any man's appetite or desire, that is it which he for his part calleth *good*: and the object of his hate and aversion, *evil*; and of his contempt, *vile* and *inconsiderable*. For these words of good, evil, and contemptible, are ever used with relation to the person that useth them: there being nothing simply and absolutely so; nor any common rule of good and evil, to be taken from the nature of the objects themselves; but from the person of the man (where there is no commonwealth;) or, (in a commonwealth,) from the person that representeth it; or from an arbitrator or judge, whom men disagreeing shall by consent set up, and make his sentence the rule thereof. . . .

Continual success in obtaining those things which a man from time to time desireth, that is to say, continual prospering, is that men call FELICITY; I mean the felicity of this life. For there is no such thing as perpetual tranquillity of mind, while we live here; because life itself is but motion, and can never be without desire, nor without fear, no more than without sense. What kind of felicity God hath ordained to them that devoutly honour Him, a man shall no sooner know, than enjoy; being joys, that now are as incomprehensible, as the word of school-men *beatifical vision* is unintelligible.

CHAPTER 11

Of the Difference of Manners

By manners, I mean not here, decency of behaviour; as how one man should salute another, or how a man should wash his mouth, or pick his teeth before company, and such other points of the *small morals*; but those qualities of mankind, that concern their living together in peace, and unity. To which end we are to consider, that the felicity of this life, consisteth not in the repose of a mind satisfied. For there is no such *finus ultimus*, (utmost aim,) nor *summum bonum*, (greatest good,) as is spoken of in the books of the old moral philosophers. Nor can a man any more live, whose desires are at an end, than he, whose senses and imaginations are at a stand. Felicity is a continual progress of the desire, from one object to another; the attaining of the former, being still but the way to the latter. The cause whereof is, that the object of man's desire, is not to enjoy once only, and for one instant of time; but to assure for ever, the way of his future desire. And therefore the voluntary actions, and inclinations of all men, tend, not only to the procuring, but also to the assuring of a contented life; and differ only in the way: which ariseth partly from the diversity of passions, in divers men; and partly from the difference of the knowledge, or opinion each one has of the causes, which produce the effect desired.

So that in the first place, I put for a general inclination of all mankind, a perpetual and restless desire of power after power, that ceaseth only in death. And the cause of this, is not always that a man hopes for a more intensive delight, than he has already attained to; or that he cannot be content with a moderate power: but because he cannot assure the power and means to live well, which he hath present, without the acquisition of more. And from hence it is, that kings, whose power is greatest, turn their endeavors to the assuring it at home by laws, or abroad by wars: and when that is done, there succeedeth a new desire; in some, of fame from new conquest; in others, of ease and sensual pleasure; in others, of admiration, or being flattered for excellence in some art, or other ability of the mind.

Competition of riches, honour, command, or other power, inclineth to contention, enmity, and war: because the way of one competitor, to the attaining of his desire, is to kill, subdue, supplant, or repel the other. Particularly, competition of praise, inclineth to a reverence of antiquity. For men contend with the living, not with the dead; to these ascribing more than due, that they may obscure the glory of the other.

Desire of ease, and sensual delight, disposeth men to obey a common power: because by such desires, a man doth abandon the protection might be hoped for from his own industry, and labour. Fear of death, and wounds, disposeth to the same: and for the same reason. On the contrary, needy men, and hardy, not contented with their present condition; as also, all men that are ambitious of military command, are inclined to continue the causes of war; and to stir up trouble and sedition: for there is no honour military but by war; not any such hope to mend an ill game, as by causing a new shuffle.

Desire of knowledge, and arts of peace, inclineth men to obey a common power: For such desire, containeth a desire of leisure; and consequently protection from some other power than their own.

Desire of praise, disposeth to laudable actions, such as please them whose judgment they value; for of those men whom we contemn, we contemn also the praises. Desire of fame after death does the same. And though after death, there be no sense of the praise given us on earth, as being joys, that are either swallowed up in the unspeakeable joys of Heaven, or extinguished in the extreme torments of hell: yet is not such fame vain; because men have a present delight therein, from the foresight of it, and of the benefit that may redound thereby to their posterity: which though they now see not, yet they imagine; and any thing that is pleasure in the sense, the same also is pleasure in the imagination. . . .

CHAPTER 13

Of the Natural Condition of Mankind as Concerning Their Felicity, and Misery

Nature hath made men so equal, in the faculties of body, and mind; as that though there be found one man sometimes manifestly stronger in body, or of quicker mind than another; yet when all is reckoned together, the difference between man, and man, is not so considerable, as that one man can thereupon claim to himself any benefit, to which another may not pretend, as well as he. For as to the strength of body, the weakest has strength enough to kill the strongest, either by secret machination, or by confederacy with others, that are in the same danger as himself.

And as to the faculties of the mind, (setting aside the arts grounded upon words, and especially that skill of proceeding upon general, and infallible rules, called science; which very few have, and but in few things; as being not a native faculty, born with us; nor attained, (as prudence,) while we look after someone else,) I find yet a greater equality amongst men, than that of strength. For prudence, is but experience; which equal time, equally bestows on all men, in those things they equally apply themselves unto. That which may perhaps make such equality incredible, is but a vain conceit of one's own wisdom, which almost all men think they have in a greater degree, than the vulgar; that is, than all men but themselves, and a few others, whom by fame, or for concurring with themselves, they approve. For such is the nature of men, that howsoever they may acknowledge many others to be more witty, or more eloquent, or more learned; yet they will hardly believe there be many so wise as themselves: For they see their own wit at hand, and other men's at a distance. But this proveth rather that men are in that point equal, than unequal. For there is not ordinarily a greater sign of the equal distribution of any thing, than that every man is contented with his share.

From this equality of ability, ariseth equality of hope in the attaining of our ends. And therefore if any two men desire the same thing, which nevertheless they cannot both enjoy, they become enemies; and in the way to their end, (which is principally their own conservation, and sometimes their delectation only,) endeavour to destroy, or subdue one another. And from hence it comes to pass, that where an invader hath no more to fear, than another man's single power; if one plant, sow, build, or possess a convenient seat, others may probably be expected to come prepared with forces united, to dispossess, and deprive him, not only of the fruit of his labour, but also of his life, or liberty. And the invader again is in the like danger of another.

And from this diffidence of one another, there is no way for any man to secure himself, so reasonable, as anticipation; that is, by force, or wiles, to master the persons of all men he can, so long, till he see no other power great enough to endanger him: and this is no more than his own conservation requireth, and is generally allowed. Also because there be some, that taking pleasure in contemplating their own power in the acts of conquest, which they pursue farther than their security requires; if others, that otherwise would be glad to be at ease within modest bounds, should not by invasion increase their power, they would not be able, long time, by standing only on their defence, to subsist. And by consequence, such augmentation of dominion over men, being necessary to a man's conservation, it ought to be allowed him.

Again, men have no pleasure, (but on the contrary a great deal of grief) in keeping company, where there is no power able to over-awe them all. For every man looketh that his companion should value him, at the same rate he sets upon himself: and upon all signs of contempt, or undervaluing, naturally endeavours, as far as he dares (which amongst them that have no common power to keep them in quiet, is far enough to make them destroy each other,) to extort a greater value from his contemners, by damage; and from others, by the example.

So that in the nature of man, we find three principal causes of quarrel. First, competition; secondly, diffidence; thirdly, glory.

The first, maketh man invade for gain; the second, for safety; and the third, for reputation. The first use violence, to make themselves masters of other men's persons, wives, children, and cattle; the second, to defend them; the third, for trifles, as a word, a smile, a different opinion, and any other sign of undervalue, either direct in their persons, or by reflection in their kindred, their friends, their nation, their profession, or their name.

Hereby it is manifest, that during the time men live without a common power to keep them all in awe, they are in that condition which is called war; and such a war, as is of every man, against every man. For WAR, consisteth not in battle only, or the act of fighting; but in a tract of time, wherein the will to contend by battle is sufficiently known: and therefore the notion of *time*, is to be considered in the nature of war; as it is in the nature of weather. For as the nature of foul weather, lieth not in a shower or two of rain; but in an inclination thereto of many days together: so the nature of war, consisteth not in actual fighting; but in the known disposition thereto, during all the time there is no assurance to the contrary. All other time is PEACE.

Whatsoever therefore is consequent to a time of war, where every man is enemy to every man; the same is consequent to the time, wherein men live without other security, than what their own strength, and their own invention shall furnish them withal. In such condition, there is no place for industry; because the fruit thereof is uncertain: and consequently no culture of the earth; no navigation, nor use of the commodities that may be imported by sea; no commodious building; no instruments of moving, and removing such things as require much force; no knowledge of the face of the earth; no account of time; no arts; no letters; no society; and which is worst of all, continual fear, and danger of violent death; and the life of man, solitary, poor, nasty, brutish, and short.

It may seem strange to some man, that has not well weighed these things; that nature should thus dissociate, and render men apt to invade, and destroy one another: and he may therefore, not trusting to this inference, made from the passions, desire perhaps to have the same confirmed by experience. Let him therefore consider with himself, when taking a journey, he arms himself, and seeks to go well accompanied; when going to sleep, he locks his doors; when even in his house he locks his chests; and this when he knows there be laws, and public officers, armed, to revenge all injuries shall be done him; what opinion he has of his fellow subjects, when he rides armed; of his fellow citizens, when he locks his doors; and of his children, and servants, when he locks his chests. Does he not there as much accuse mankind by his actions, as I do by my words? But neither of us accuse man's nature in it. The desires, and other passions of man, are in themselves no sin. No more are the actions, that proceed from those passions, till they know a law that forbids them: which till laws be made they cannot know: nor can any law be made, till they have agreed upon the person that shall make it.

It may peradventure be thought, there was never such a time, nor condition of war as this; and I believe it was never generally so, over all the world: but there are many places, where they live so now. For the savage people in many places of *America*, except the government of small families, the concord whereof dependeth on natural lust, have no government at all; and live at this day in that brutish manner, as I said before. Howsoever, it may be perceived what manner of life there would be, where there were no common power to fear; by the manner of life, which men that have formerly lived under a peacefull government, use to degenerate into, in a civil war.

But though there had never been any time, wherein particular men were in a condition of war one against another; yet in all times, kings, and persons of sovereign authority, because of their independency, are in continual jealousies, and in the state and posture of gladiators; having their weapons pointing, and their eyes fixed on one another; that is, their forts, garrisons, and guns upon the frontiers of their kingdoms; and continual spies upon their neighbours; which is a posture of war. But because they uphold thereby, the industry of their subjects; there does not follow from it, that misery, which accompanies the liberty of particular men.

To this war of every man against every man, this also is consequent; that nothing can be unjust. The notions of right and wrong, justice and injustice have there no place. Where there is no common power, there is no law: where no law, no injustice. Force, and fraud, are in war the two cardinal virtues. Justice, and injustice are none of the faculties neither of the body, nor mind. If they were, they might be in a man that were alone in the world, as well as his senses, and passions. They are qualities, that relate to men in society, not in solitude. It is consequent also to the same condition, that there be no propriety, no dominion, no *mine* and *thine* distinct; but only that to be every man's, that he can get; and for so long, as he can keep it. And thus much for the ill condition, which many by mere nature is actually placed in; though with a possibility to come out of it, consisting partly in the passions, partly in his reason.

The passions that incline men to peace, are fear of death; desire of such things as are necessary to commodious living; and a hope by their industry to obtain them. And reason suggesteth convenient articles of peace, upon which men may be drawn to agreement. These articles, are they, which otherwise are called the Laws of Nature: whereof I shall speak more particularly, in the two following chapters.

CHAPTER 14

Of the First and Second Natural Laws, and of Contracts

The right of nature, which writers commonly call *jus naturale,* is the liberty each man hath, to use his own power, as he will himself, for the preservation of his own nature; that is to say, of his own life; and consequently, of doing any thing, which in his own judgment, and reason, he shall conceive to be the aptest means thereunto.

By liberty, is understood, according to the proper signification of the word, the absence of external impediments: which impediments, may oft take away part of a man's power to do what he would; but cannot hinder him from using the power left him, according as his judgment, and reason shall dictate to him.

A law of nature, (*lex naturalis,*) is a precept, or general rule, found out by reason, by which a man is forbidden to do that, which is destructive of his life, or taketh away the means of preserving the same; and to omit that, by which he thinketh it may be best preserved. For though they that speak of this subject, use to confound *jus,* and *lex, right* and *law;* yet they ought to be distinguished; because RIGHT, consisteth in liberty to do, or to forbear; whereas LAW, determineth, and bindeth to one of them: so that law, and right, differ as much, as obligation, and liberty, which in one and the same matter are inconsistent.

And because the condition of man, (as hath been declared in the precedent chapter) is a condition of war of every one against every one; in which case every one is governed by his own reason; and there is nothing he can make use of, that may not be a help unto him, in preserving his life against his enemies, it followeth, that in such a condition, every man has a right to every thing: even to one another's body. And therefore, as long as this natural right of every man to every thing endureth, there can be no security to any man, (how strong or wise soever he be,) of living out the time, which nature ordinarily alloweth men to live. And consequently it is a precept, or general rule of reason, *that every man, ought to endeavour peace, as far as he has hope of obtaining it; and when he cannot obtain it, that he may seek, and use, all helps, and advantages of war.* The first branch of which rule, containeth the first, and fundamental law of nature; which is, *to seek peace, and follow it.* The second, the sum of the right of nature; which is, *by all means we can, to defend ourselves.*

From this fundamental law of nature, by which men are commanded to endeavor peace, is derived this second law; *that a man be willing, when others are so too, as farforth, as for peace, and defence of himself he shall think it necessary, to lay down this right to all things; and be contented with so much liberty against other men, as he would allow other men against himself.* For as long as every man holdeth this right, of doing any thing he liketh; so long are all men in the condition of war. But if other men will not lay down their right, as well as he; then there is no reason for any one, to divest himself of his: for that were to expose himself to prey, (which no man is bound to) rather than to dispose himself to peace. This is that law of the Gospel; *whatsoever you require that others should do for you, that do ye to them.* And that law of all men, *quod tibi fieri non vis, alteri ne feceris. . . .*[1]

CHAPTER 15

Of Other Laws of Nature

From that law of nature, by which we are obliged to transfer to another, such rights, as being retained, hinder the peace of mankind, there followeth a third; which is this, *that men perform their covenants made*: without which, covenants are in vain, and but empty words; and the right of all men to all things remaining, we are still in the condition of war.

And in this law of nature, consisteth the fountain and original of JUSTICE. For where no covenant hath preceded, there hath no right been transferred, and every man has right to every thing; and consequently, no action can be unjust. But when a covenant is made, then to break it is *unjust*; and the definition of INJUSTICE, is no other than *the not performance of covenant.* And whatsoever is not unjust, is *just.*

But because covenants of mutual trust, where there is fear of not performance on either part, (as hath been said in the former chapter,) are invalid; though the original of justice be the making of covenants; yet injustice actually there can be none, till the cause of such fear be taken away; which while men are in the natural condition of war, cannot be done. Therefore before the names of just, and unjust can have place, there must be some coercive power, to compel men equally to the performance of their covenants, by the terror of some punishment, greater than the benefit they expect by the breach of their covenant; and to make good that propriety, which by mutual contract men acquire, in recompense of the universal right they abandon: and such power there is none before the erection of a commonwealth. And this is also to be gathered out of the ordinary definition of justice in the Schools: for they say, that *justice is the constant will of giving to every man his own.* And therefore where there is no *own*, that is, no propriety, there is no injustice; and where there is no coercive power erected, that is, where there is no commonwealth, there is no propriety; all men having right to all things: therefore where there is no commonwealth, there nothing is unjust. So that the nature of justice, consisteth in keeping of valid covenants: but the validity of covenants begins not but with the constitution of a civil power, sufficient to compel men to keep them: and then it is also that propriety begins. . . .

CHAPTER 17

Of the Causes, Generation, and Definition of a Commonwealth

The final cause, end, or design of men, (who naturally love liberty, and dominion over others,) in the introduction of that restraint upon themselves, (in which we see them live in commonwealths,) is the foresight of their own preservation, and of a more contented life thereby; that is to say, of getting themselves out from that miserable condition of war, which is necessarily consequent (as hath been shown), to, the natural passions of men, when there is no visible power to keep them in awe, and tie them by fear of punishment to the performance of their covenants, and observation of those laws of nature set down in the fourteenth and fifteenth chapters.

For the laws of nature (as *justice, equity, modesty, mercy,* and (in sum) *doing to others, as we would be done to,*) of themselves, without the terror of some power, to cause them to be observed, are contrary to our natural passions, that carry us to partiality, pride, revenge, and the like. And covenants, without the sword, are but words, and of no strength to secure a man at all. Therefore notwithstanding the laws of nature, (which every one hath then kept, when he has the will to keep them, when he can do it safely,) if there be no power erected, or not great enough for our security; every man will and may lawfully rely on his own strength and art, for caution against all other men. . . .

The only way to erect such a common power, as may be able to defend them from the invasion of foreigners, and the injuries of one another, and thereby to secure them in such sort, as that by their own industry, and by the fruits of the earth, they may nourish themselves and live contentedly; is, to confer all their power and strength upon one man, or upon one assembly of men, that may reduce all their wills, by plurality of voices, unto one will: which is as much as to say, to appoint one man, or assembly of men, to bear their person; and even one to own, and acknowledge himself to be author of whatsoever he that so beareth their person, shall act, or cause to be acted, in those things which concern the common peace and safety; and therein to submit their wills, every one to his will, and their judgments, to his judgment. This is more than consent, or concord; it is a real unity of them all, in one and the same person, made by covenant of every man with every man, in such manner, as if every man should say to every man, *I authorise and give up my right of governing myself, to this man, or to this assembly of men, on this condition, that thou give up thy right to him, and authorize all his actions in like manner.* This done, the multitude so united in one person, is called a COMMONWEALTH, in Latin CIVITAS. This is the generation of that great LEVIATHAN, or rather (to speak more reverently) of that *mortal god,* to which we owe under the *immortal God,* our peace and defence. For by this authority, given him by every particular man in the commonwealth, he hath the use of so much power and strength conferred on him, that by terror thereof, he is enabled to form the wills of them all, to peace at home, and mutual aid against their enemies abroad. And in him consisteth the essence of the commonwealth; which (to define it,) is *one person, of whose acts a great multitude, by mutual covenants one with another, have made themselves every one the author, to the end he may use the strength and means of them all, as he shall think expedient, for their peace and common defence.*

And he that carrieth this person, is called SOVEREIGN, and said to have sovereign power; and every one besides, his SUBJECT.

NOTE

1. Do not unto others what you would not have done unto you.

UPON THE LOVE OF OUR NEIGHBOUR

Joseph Butler

Joseph Butler (1692–1752) was a graduate of Oxford University who became preacher at the Rolls Chapel in London and eventually bishop of Durham. In his sermons, he developed an influential ethical theory in which he stressed, unlike Hobbes, that benevolence is not contrary to self-interest and happiness.

SERMON XI

Upon the Love of Our Neighbour

And if there be any other commandment, it is briefly comprehended in this saying, namely, Thou shalt love thy neighbour as thyself.—Rom. xiii. 9.

It is commonly observed, that there is a disposition in men to complain of the viciousness and corruption of the age in which they live, as greater than that of former ones; which is usually followed with this further observation, that mankind has been in that respect much the same in all times. Now, not to determine whether this last be not contradicted by the accounts of history; thus much can scarce be doubted, that vice and folly takes different turns, and some particular kinds of it are more open and avowed in some ages than in others; and, I suppose, it may be spoken of as very much the distinction of the present to profess a contracted spirit, and greater regards to self-interest, than appears to have been done formerly. Upon this account it seems worth while to inquire, whether private interest is likely to be promoted in proportion to the degree in which self-love engrosses us, and prevails over all other principles; *or whether the contracted affection may not possibly be so prevalent as to disappoint itself, and even contradict its own end, private good.*

From *Fifteen Sermons Preached at the Rolls Chapel* (1726).

And since, further, there is generally thought to be some peculiar kind of contrariety between self-love and the love of our neighbour, between the pursuit of public and of private good; insomuch that when you are recommending one of these, you are supposed to be speaking against the other; and from hence arises a secret prejudice against, and frequently open scorn of all talk of public spirit, and real good-will to our fellow-creatures; it will be necessary to *inquire what respect benevolence hath to self-love, and the pursuit of private interest to the pursuit of public*: or whether there be any thing of that peculiar inconsistence and contrariety between them, over and above what there is between self-love and other passions and particular affections, and their respective pursuits.

These inquiries, it is hoped, may be favourably attended to: for there shall be all possible concessions made to the favourite passion, which hath so much allowed to it, and whose cause is so universally pleaded: it shall be treated with the utmost tenderness and concern for its interests.

In order to this, as well as to determine the forementioned questions, it will be necessary to *consider the nature, the object, and end of that self-love, as distinguished from other principles or affections in the mind, and their respective objects.*

Every man hath a general desire of his own happiness; and likewise a variety of particular affections, passions, and appetites to particular external objects. The former proceeds from, or is self-love; and seems inseparable from all sensible creatures, who can reflect upon themselves and their own interest or happiness, so as to have that interest an object to their minds: what is to be said of the latter is, that they proceed from, or together make up that particular nature, according to which man is made. The object the former pursues it somewhat internal, our own happiness, enjoyment, satisfaction; whether we have, or have not, a distinct particular perception what it is, or wherein it consists: the objects of the latter are this or that particular external thing, which the affections tend towards, and of which it hath always a particular idea or perception. The principle we call self-love never seeks any thing external for the sake of the thing, but only as a means of happiness or good: particular affections rest in the external things themselves. One belongs to man as a reasonable creature reflecting upon his own interest or happiness. The other, though quite distinct from reason, are as much a part of human nature.

That all particular appetites and passions are towards *external things themselves*, distinct from the *pleasure arising from them*, is manifested from hence; that there could not be this pleasure, were it not for that prior suitableness between the object and the passion: there could be no enjoyment or delight from one thing more than another, from eating food more than from swallowing a stone, if there were not an affection or appetite to one thing more than another.

Every particular affection, even the love of our neighbour, is as really our own affection, as self-love; and the pleasure arising from its gratification is as much my own pleasure, as the pleasure self-love would have, from knowing I myself should be happy some time hence, would be my own pleasure. And if, because every particular affection is a man's own, and the pleasure arising from its gratification his own pleasure, or pleasure to himself, such particular affection must be called self-love; according to this way of speaking, no creature whatever can possibly act but merely from self-love; and every action and every affection whatever is to be resolved up into this one principle. But then this is not the language of mankind: or if it were, we should want words to express the difference, between the principle of an action, proceeding from cool consideration that it will be to my own advantage; and an action, suppose of revenge, or of friendship, by which a man runs upon certain ruin, to do evil or good to another. It is manifest the principles of these actions are totally different, and so want different words to be distinguished by: all that they agree in is, that they both proceed from, and are done to gratify an inclination in a man's self. But the principle or inclination in one case is self-love; in the other, hatred or love of another. There is then a distinction between the cool principle of self-love, or general desire of our own happiness, as one part of our nature, and one principle of action; and the particular affections towards particular external objects, as another part of our nature, and another principle of action. How much soever therefore is to be allowed to self-love, yet it cannot be allowed to be the whole of our inward constitution; because, you see, there are other parts or principles which come into it.

Further, private happiness or good is all which self-love can make us desire, or be concerned about: in having this consists its gratification: it is an affection to ourselves; a regard to our own interest, happiness, and private good: and in the proportion a man hath this, he is interested, or a lover of himself. Let this be kept in mind; because there is commonly, as I shall presently have occasion to observe, another sense put upon these words. On the other hand, particular affections tend towards particular external things: these are their objects: having these is their end: in this consists their gratification: no matter whether it be, or be not, upon the whole, our interest or happiness. An action done from the former of these principles is called an interested action. An action proceeding from any of the latter has its denomination of passionate, ambitious, friendly, revengeful, or any other, from the particular appetite or affection from which it proceeds. Thus self-love as one part of human nature, and the several particular principles as the other part, are, themselves, their objects and ends, stated and shewn.

From hence it will be easy to see, how far, and in what ways, each of these can contribute and be subservient to the private good of the individual. Happiness does not consist in self-love. The desire of happiness is no more the thing itself, than the desire of riches is the possession or enjoyment of them. People may love themselves with the most entire and unbounded affection, and yet be extremely miserable. Neither can self-love any way help them out, but by setting them on work to get rid of the causes of their misery, to gain or make use of those objects which are by nature adapted to afford satisfaction. Happiness or satisfaction consists only in the enjoyment of those objects, which are by nature suited to our several particular appetites, passions, and affections. So that if self-love wholly engrosses us, and leaves no room for any other principle, there can be absolutely no such thing at all as happiness, or enjoyment of any kind whatever; since happiness consists in the gratification of particular passions, which supposes the having of them. Self-love then does not constitute *this* or *that* to be our interest or good; but, our interest or good being constituted by nature and supposed, self-love only puts us upon obtaining and securing it. Therefore, if it be possible, that self-love may prevail and exert itself in a degree or manner which is not subservient to this end; then it will not follow, that our interest will be promoted in proportion to the degree in which that principle engrosses us, and prevails over others. Nay further, the private and contracted affection, when it is not subservient to this end, private good, may, for any thing that appears, have a direct contrary tendency and effect. And if we will consider the matter, we shall see that it often really has. *Disengagement* is absolutely necessary to enjoyment: and a person may have so steady and fixed an eye upon his own interest, whatever he places it in, as may hinder him from *attending* to many gratifications within his reach, which others have their minds *free* and *open* to. Over-fondness for a child is not generally thought to be for its advantage: and, if there be any guess to be made from appearances, surely that character we call selfish is not the most promising for happiness. Such a temper may plainly be, and exert itself in a degree and manner which may give unnecessary and useless solicitude and anxiety, in a degree and manner which may prevent obtaining the means and materials of enjoyment, as well as the making use of them. Immoderate self-love does very ill consult its own interest: and, how much soever a para-dox it may appear, it is certainly true, that even from self-love we should endeavour to get over all inordinate regard to, and consideration of ourselves. Every one of our passions and affections hath its natural stint and bound, which may easily be exceeded; whereas our enjoyments can possibly be but in a determinate measure and degree. Therefore such excess of the affection, since it cannot procure any enjoyment, must in all cases be useless; but is generally attended with inconveniences, and often is downright pain and misery. This holds as much with regard to self-love as to all other affections. The natural degree of it, so far as it sets us on work to gain and make use of the materials of satisfaction, may be to our real advantage; but beyond or besides this, it is in several respects an inconvenience and disadvantage. Thus it appears, that private interest is so far from being likely to be promoted in proportion to the degree in which self-love engrosses us, and prevails over all other principles; that *the contracted affection may be so prevalent as to disappoint itself, and even contradict its own end, private good.*

"But who, except the most sordidly covetous, ever thought there was any rivalship between the love of greatness, honour, power, or between sensual appetites, and self-love? No, there is a perfect harmony between them. It is by means of these particular appetites and affections that self-love is gratified in enjoyment, happiness, and satisfaction. The competition and rivalship is between self-love and the love of our neighbour: that affection which leads us out of ourselves, makes us regardless of our interest, and substitute that of another in its stead." Whether then there be any peculiar competition and con-trariety in this case, shall now be considered.

Self-love and interestedness was stated to consist in or be an affection to ourselves, a regard to our own private good: it is therefore distinct from benevolence, which is an affection to the good of our fellow-creatures. But that benevolence is distinct from, that is, not the same thing with self-love, is no reason for its being looked upon with any peculiar suspicion; because every principle whatever, by means of which self-love is gratified, is distinct from it: and all things which are distinct from each other are equally so. A man has an affection or aversion to another: that one of these tends to, and is gratified by doing good, that the other tends to, and is gratified by doing harm, does not in the least alter the respect which either one or the other of these inward feelings has to self-love. We use the word *property* so as to exclude any other persons having an interest in that of which we say a particular man has the property. And we often use the word *selfish* so as to exclude in the same manner all regards to the good of others. But the cases are not parallel: for though that exclusion is really part of the idea of property; yet such positive exclusion, or bringing this peculiar disregard to the good of others into the idea of self-love, is in reality adding to the idea, or changing it from what it was before stated to consist in, namely, in an affection to ourselves. This being the whole idea of self-love, it can no otherwise exclude good-will or love of others, than merely by not including it, no otherwise, than it excludes love of arts or reputation, or of any thing else. Neither on the other hand does benevolence, any more than love of arts or of reputation, exclude self-love. Love of our neighbour then has just the same respect to, is no more distant from, self-love, than hatred of our neighbour, or than love or hatred of any thing else. Thus the principles, from which men rush upon certain ruin for the destruction of an enemy, and for the preservation of a friend, have the same respect to the private affection, and are equally interested, or equally disinterested: and it is of no avail, whether they are said to be one or the other. Therefore to those who are shocked to hear virtue spoken of as disinterested, it may be allowed that it is indeed absurd to speak thus of it; unless hatred, several particular instances of vice, and all the common affections and aversions in mankind, are acknowledged to be disinterested too. Is there any less inconsistence, between the love of inanimate things, or of creatures merely sensitive, and self-love; than between self-love and the love of our neighbour? Is desire of and delight in the happiness of another any more a diminution of self-love, than desire of and delight in the esteem of another? They are both equally desire of and delight in somewhat external to ourselves: either both or neither are so. The object of self-love is expressed in the term self: and every appetite of sense, and every particular affection of the heart, are equally interested or disinterested, because the objects of them all are equally self or somewhat else. Whatever ridicule therefore the mention of a disinterested principle or action may be supposed to lie open to, must, upon the matter being thus stated, relate to ambition, and every appetite and particular affection, as much as to benevolence. And indeed all the ridicule, and all the grave perplexity, of which this subject hath had its full share, is merely from words. The most intelligible way of speaking of it seems to be this: that self-love and the actions done in consequence of it (for these will presently appear to be the same as to this question) are interested; that particular affections towards external objects, and the actions done in consequence of those affections, are not so. But every one is at liberty to use words as he pleases. All that is here insisted upon is, that ambition, revenge, benevolence, all particular passions whatever, and the actions they produce, are equally interested or disinterested.

Thus it appears that there is no peculiar contrariety between self-love and benevolence; no greater competition between these, than between any other particular affections and self-love. This relates to the affections themselves. Let us now see whether there be any peculiar contrariety between the respective courses of life which these affections lead to; whether there be any greater competition between the pursuit of private and of public good, than between any other particular pursuits and that of private good.

There seems no other reason to suspect that there is any such peculiar contrariety, but only that the course of action which benevolence leads to, has a more direct tendency to promote the good of others, than that course of action which love of reputation, suppose, or any other particular affection leads to. But that any affection tends to the happiness of another, does not hinder its tending to one's own happiness too. That others enjoy the benefit of the air and the light of the sun, does not hinder but that these are as much one's own private advantage now, as they would be if we had the property of them exclusive of all others. So a pursuit which tends to promote the good of another, yet may have as great tendency to promote private interest, as a pursuit which does not tend to the good of another at all, or which is mischievous to him. All particular affections whatever, resentment, benevolence, love of arts, equally lead to a course of action for their own gratification, i.e., the gratification of ourselves; and the gratification of each gives delight: so far then it is manifest they have all the same respect to private interest. Now take into consideration further, concerning these three pursuits, that the end of the first is the harm, of the second, the good of another, of the last, somewhat indifferent; and is there any necessity, that these additional considerations should alter the respect, which we before saw these three pursuits had to private interest; or render any one of them less conducive to it, than any other? Thus one man's affection is to honour as his end; in order to obtain which he thinks no pains too great. Suppose another, with such a singularity of mind, as to have the same affection to public good as his end, which he endeavours with the same labour to obtain. In case of success, surely the man of benevolence hath as great enjoyment as the man of ambition; they both equally having the end their affections, in the same degree, tended to: but in case of disappointment, the benevolent man has clearly the advantage; since endeavouring to do good considered as a virtuous pursuit, is gratified by its own consciousness, i.e. is in a degree its own reward.

And as to these two, or benevolence and any other particular passions whatever, considered in a further view, as forming a general temper, which more or less disposes us for enjoyment of all the common blessings of life, distinct from their own gratification: is benevolence less the temper of tranquillity and freedom than ambition or covetousness? Does the benevolent man appear less easy with himself, from his love to his neighbour? Does he less relish his being? Is there any peculiar gloom seated on his face? Is his mind less open to entertainment, to any particular gratification? Nothing is more manifest, than that being in good humour, which is benevolence whilst it lasts, is itself the temper of satisfaction and enjoyment.

Suppose then a man sitting down to consider how he might become most easy to himself, and attain the greatest pleasure he could; all that which is his real natural happiness. This can only consist in the enjoyment of those objects, which are by nature adapted to our several faculties. These particular enjoyments make up the sum total of our happiness: and they are supposed to arise from riches, honours, and the gratification of sensual appetites: be it so: yet none profess themselves so completely happy in these enjoyments, but that there is room left in the mind for others, if they were presented to them: nay, these, as much as they engage us, are not thought so high, but that human nature is capable even of greater. Now there have been persons in all ages, who have professed that they found satisfaction in the exercise of charity, in the love of their neighbour, in endeavouring to promote the happiness of all they had to do with, and in the pursuit of what is just and right and good, as the general bent of their mind, and end of their life; and that doing an action of baseness or cruelty, would be as great violence to *their* self, as much breaking in upon their nature, as any external force. Persons of this character would add, if they might be heard, that they consider themselves as acting in the view of an infinite Being, who is in a much higher sense the object of reverence and of love, than all the world besides; and therefore they could have no more enjoyment from a wicked action done under his eye, than the persons to whom they are making their apology could, if all mankind were the spectators of it; and that the satisfaction of approving themselves to his unerring judgment, to whom they thus refer all their actions, is a more continued settled satisfaction than any this world can afford; as also that they have, no less than others, a mind free and open to all the common innocent gratifications of it, such as they are. And if we go no further, does there appear any absurdity in this? Will any one take upon him to say, that a man cannot find his account in this general course of life, as much as in the most unbounded ambition, and the excesses of pleasure? Or that such a person has not consulted so well for himself, for the satisfaction and peace of his own mind, as the ambitious or dissolute man? And though the consideration, that God himself will in the end justify their taste, and support their cause, is not formally to be insisted upon here; yet thus much comes in, that all enjoyments whatever are much more clear and unmixed from the assurance that they will end well. Is it certain then that there is nothing in these pretensions to happiness? especially when there are not wanting persons, who have supported themselves with satisfactions of this kind in sickness, poverty, disgrace, and in the very pangs of death; whereas it is manifest all other enjoyments fail in these circumstances. This surely looks suspicious of having somewhat in it. Self-love methinks should be alarmed. May she not possibly pass over greater pleasures, than those she is so wholly taken up with?

The short of the matter is no more than this. Happiness consists in the gratification of certain affections, appetites, passions, with objects which are by nature adapted to them. Self-love may indeed set us on work to gratify these: but happiness or enjoyment has no immediate connection with self-love, but arises from such gratification alone. Love of our neighbour is one of those affections. This, considered as a *virtuous principle*, is gratified by a consciousness of *endeavouring* to promote the good of others; but considered as a natural affection, its gratification consists in the actual accomplishment of this endeavour. Now indulgence or gratification of this affection, whether in that consciousness or this accomplishment, has the same respect to interest, as indulgence of any other affection; they equally proceed from or do not proceed from self-love, they equally include or equally exclude this principle. Thus it appears, that *benevolence and the pursuit of public good hath at least as great respect to self- love and the pursuit of private good, as any other particular passions, and their respective pursuits.*

Neither is covetousness, whether as a temper or pursuit, any exception to this. For if by covetousness is meant the desire and pursuit of riches for their own sake, without any regard to, or consideration of, the uses of them; this hath as little to do with self-love, as benevolence hath. But by this word is usually meant, not such madness and total distraction of mind, but immoderate affection to and pursuit of riches as possessions in order to some further end; namely, satisfaction, interest, or good. This therefore is not a particular affection, or particular pursuit, but it is the general principle of self-love, and the general pursuit of our own interest; for which reason, the word *selfish* is by every one appropriated to this temper and pursuit. Now as it is ridiculous to assert, that self-love and the love of our neighbour are the same; so neither is it asserted, that following these different affections hath the same tendency and respect to our own interest. The comparison is not between self-love and the love of our neighbour; between pursuit of our own interest, and the interest of others; but between the several particular affections in human nature towards external objects, as one part of the comparison; and the one particular affection to the good of our neighbour, as the other part of it: and it has been shewn, that all these have the same respect to self-love and private interest.

There is indeed frequently an inconsistence or interfering between self-love or private interest, and the several particular appetites, passions, affections, or the pursuits they lead to. But this competition or interfering is merely accidental; and happens much oftener between pride, revenge, sensual gratifications, and private interest, than between private interest and benevolence. For nothing is more common, than to see men give themselves up to a passion or an affection to their known prejudice and ruin, and in direct contradiction to manifest and real interest, and the loudest calls of self-love: whereas the seeming competitions and interfering, between benevolence and private interest, relate much more to the materials or means of enjoyment, than to enjoyment itself. There is often an interfering in the former, when there is none in the latter. Thus as to riches: so much money as a man gives away, so much less will remain in his possession. Here is a real interfering. But though a man cannot possibly give without lessening his fortune, yet there are multitudes might give without lessening their own enjoyment; because they may have more than they can turn to any real use or advantage to themselves. Thus, the more thought and time any one employs about the interests and good of others, he must necessarily have less to attend his own; but he may have so ready and large a supply of his own wants, that such thought might be really useless to himself, though of great service and assistance to others.

The general mistake, that there is some greater inconsistence between endeavouring to promote the good of another and self-interest, than between self-interest and pursuing any thing else, seems, as hath already been hinted, to arise from our notions of property; and to be carried on by this property's being supposed to be itself our happiness or good. People are so very much taken up with this one subject, that they seem from it to have formed a general way of thinking, which they apply to other things that they have nothing to do with. Hence, in a confused and slight way, it might well be taken for granted, that another's having no interest in an affection (i.e., his good not being the object of it), renders, as one may speak, the proprietor's interest in it greater; and that if another had an interest in it, this would render his less, or occasion that such affection could not be so friendly to self-love, or conducive to private good, as an affection or pursuit which has not a regard to the good of another. This, I say, might be taken for granted, whilst it was not attended to, that the object of every particular affection is equally somewhat external to ourselves; and whether it be the good of another person, or whether it be any other external thing, makes no alteration with regard to its being one's own affection, and the gratification of it one's own private enjoyment. And so far as it is taken for granted, that barely having the means and materials of enjoyment is what constitutes interest and happiness; that our interest or good consists in possessions themselves, in having the property of riches, houses, lands, gardens, not in the enjoyment of them; so far it will even more strongly be taken for granted, in the way already explained, that an affection's conducing to the good of another, must even necessarily occasion to it conduce less to private good, if not to be positively detrimental to it. For, if property and happiness are one and the same thing, as by increasing the property of another you lessen your own property, so by promoting the happiness of another you must lessen your own happiness. But whatever occasioned the mistake, I hope it has been fully proved to be one; as it has been proved, that there is no peculiar rivalship or competition between self-love and benevolence: that as there may be a competition between these two, so there may also between any particular affection whatever and self-love: that every particular affection, benevolence among the rest, is subservient to self-love by being the instrument of private enjoyment; and that in one respect benevolence contributes more to private interest, i.e., enjoyment or satisfaction, than any other of the particular common affections, as it is in a degree its own gratification.

And to all these things may be added, that religion, from whence arises our strongest obligation to benevolence, is so far from disowning the principle of self-love, that it often addresses itself to that very principle, and always to the mind in that state when reason presides; and there can no access be had to the understanding, but by convincing men, that the course of life we would persuade them to is not contrary to their interest. It may be allowed, without any prejudice to the cause of virtue and religion, that our ideas of happiness and misery are of all our ideas the nearest and most important to us; that they will, nay, if you please, that they ought to prevail over those of order, and beauty, and harmony, and proportion, if there should ever be, as it is impossible there ever should be, any inconsistence between them: though these last too, as expressing the fitness of actions, are real as truth itself. Let it be allowed, though virtue or moral rectitude does indeed consist in affection to and pursuit of what is right and good, as such; yet, that when we sit down in a cool hour, we can neither justify to ourselves this or any other pursuit, till we are convinced that it will be for our happiness, or at least not contrary to it.

Common reason and humanity will have some influence upon mankind, whatever becomes of speculations; but, so far as the interests of virtue depend upon the theory of it being secured from open scorn, so far its very being in the world depends upon its appearing to have no contrariety to private interest and self-love. The foregoing observations, therefore, it is hoped, may have gained a little ground in favour of the precept before us; the particular explanation of which shall be the subject of the next discourse.

THE SCEPTIC

David Hume

The Scotsman David Hume (1711–1776) was a prominent essayist, renowned historian, and one of the most influential of all philosophers. His skepticism about the power of the human mind is displayed in the following essay in which he defends the view that our lives are governed more by chance than by reason and that we should not expect a perfect correlation between virtue and happiness.

I have long entertained a suspicion, with regard to the decisions of philosophers upon all subjects, and found in myself a greater inclination to dispute, than assent to their conclusions. There is one mistake, to which they seem liable, almost without exception; they confine too much their principles, and make no account of that vast variety, which nature has so much affected in all her operations. When a philosopher has once laid hold of a favourite principle, which perhaps accounts for many natural effects, he extends the same principle over the whole creation, and reduces to it every phenomenon, though by the most violent and absurd reasoning. Our own mind being narrow and contracted, we cannot extend our conception to the variety and extent of nature; but imagine, that she is as much bounded in her operations, as we are in our speculation.

But if ever this infirmity of philosophers is to be suspected on any occasion, it is in their reasonings concerning human life, and the methods of attaining happiness. In that case, they are led astray, not only by the narrowness of their understandings, but by that also of their passions. Almost every one has a predominant inclination, to which his other desires and affections submit, and which governs him, though, perhaps, with some intervals, through the whole course of his life. It is difficult for him to apprehend, that any thing, which appears totally indifferent to him, can ever give enjoyment to any person, or can possess charms, which altogether escape his observation. His own pursuits are always, in his account, the most engaging: The objects of his passion, the most valuable: And the road, which he pursues, the only one that leads to happiness.

From *Essays, Moral and Political* (1742). The bracketed notes are by Eugene F. Miller.

But would these prejudiced reasoners reflect a moment, there are many obvious instances and arguments, sufficient to undeceive them, and make them enlarge their maxims and principles. Do they not see the vast variety of inclinations and pursuits among our species; where each man seems fully satisfied with his own course of life, and would esteem it the greatest unhappiness to be confined to that of his neighbour? Do they not feel in themselves, that what pleases at one time, displeases at another, by the change of inclination; and that it is not in their power, by their utmost efforts, to recall that taste or appetite, which formerly bestowed charms on what now appears indifferent or disagreeable? What is the meaning therefore of those general preferences of the town or country life, of a life of action or one of pleasure, of retirement or society; when besides the different inclinations of different men, every one's experience may convince him, that each of these kinds of life is agreeable in its turn, and that their variety or their judicious mixture chiefly contributes to the rendering all of them agreeable.

But shall this business be allowed to go altogether at adventures? And must a man consult only his humour and inclination, in order to determine his course of life, without employing his reason to inform him what road is preferable, and leads most surely to happiness? Is there no difference then between one man's conduct and another?

I answer, there is a great difference. One man, following his inclination, in choosing his course of life, may employ much surer means for succeeding than another, who is led by his inclination into the same course of life, and pursues the same object. *Are riches the chief object of your desires?* Acquire skill in your profession; be diligent in the exercise of it; enlarge the circle of your friends and acquaintance; avoid pleasure and expence; and never be generous, but with a view of gaining more than you could save by frugality. *Would you acquire the public esteem?* Guard equally against the extremes of arrogance and fawning. Let it appear that you set a value upon yourself, but without despising others. If you fall into either of the extremes, you either provoke men's pride by your insolence, or teach them to despise you by your timorous submission, and by the mean opinion which you seem to entertain of yourself.

These, you say, are the maxims of common prudence, and discretion; what every parent inculcates on his child, and what every man of sense pursues in the course of life, which he has chosen.—What is it then you desire more? Do you come to a philosopher as to a *cunning man*, to learn something by magic or witchcraft, beyond what can be known by common prudence and discretion? —Yes; we come to a philosopher to be instructed, how we shall choose our ends, more than the means for attaining these ends: We want to know what desire we shall gratify, what passion we shall comply with, what appetite we shall indulge. As to the rest, we trust to common sense, and the general maxims of the world for our instruction.

I am sorry then, I have pretended to be a philosopher: For I find your questions very perplexing; and am in danger, if my answer be too rigid and severe, of passing for a pedant and scholastic; if it be too easy and free, of being taken for a preacher of vice and immorality. However, to satisfy you, I shall deliver my opinion upon the matter, and shall only desire you to esteem it of as little consequence as I do myself. By that means you will neither think it worthy of your ridicule nor your anger.

If we can depend upon any principle, which we learn from philosophy, this, I think, may be considered as certain and undoubted, that there is nothing, in itself, valuable or despicable, desirable or hateful, beautiful or deformed; but that these attributes arise from the particular constitution and fabric of human sentiment and affection. What seems the most delicious food to one animal, appears loathsome to another: What affects the feeling of one with delight, produces uneasiness in another. This is confessedly the case with regard to all the bodily senses: But if we examine the matter more accurately, we shall find, that the same observation holds even where the mind concurs with the body, and mingles its sentiment with the exterior appetite.

Desire this passionate lover to give you a character of his mistress: He will tell you, that he is at a loss for words to describe her charms, and will ask you very seriously if ever you were acquainted with a goddess or an angel? If you answer that you never were: He will then say, that it is impossible for you to form a conception of such divine beauties as those which his charmer possesses; so complete a shape; such well-proportioned features; so engaging an air; such sweetness of disposition; such gaiety of humour. You can infer nothing, however, from all this discourse, but that the poor man is in love; and that the general appetite between the sexes, which nature has infused into all animals, is in him determined to a particular object by some qualities, which give him pleasure. The same divine creature, not only to a different animal, but also to a different man, appears a mere mortal being, and is beheld with the utmost indifference.

Nature has given all animals a like prejudice in favour of their offspring. As soon as the helpless infant sees the light, though in every other eye it appears a despicable and a miserable creature, it is regarded by its fond parent with the utmost affection, and is preferred to every other object, however perfect and accomplished. The passion alone, arising from the original structure and formation of human nature, bestows a value on the most insignificant object.

We may push the same observation further, and may conclude, that, even when the mind operates alone, and feeling the sentiment of blame or approbation, pronounces one object deformed and odious, another beautiful and amiable; I say, that, even in this case, those qualities are not really in the objects, but belong entirely to the sentiment of that mind which blames or praises. I grant, that it will be more difficult to make this proposition evident, and as it were, palpable, to negligent thinkers; because nature is more uniform in the sentiments of the mind than in most feelings of the body, and produces a nearer resemblance in the inward than in the outward part of human kind. There is something approaching to principles in mental taste; and critics can reason and dispute more plausibly than cooks or perfumers. We may observe, however, that this uniformity among human kind, hinders not, but that there is a considerable diversity in the sentiments of beauty and worth, and that education, custom, prejudice, caprice, and humour, frequently vary our taste of this kind. You will never convince a man, who is not accustomed to Italian music, and has not an ear to follow its intricacies, that a Scotch tune is not preferable. You have not even any single argument, beyond your own taste, which you can employ in your behalf: And to your antagonist, his particular taste will always appear a more convincing argument to the contrary. If you be wise, each of you will allow, that the other may be in the right; and having many other instances of this diversity of taste, you will both confess, that beauty and worth are merely of a relative nature, and consist in an agreeable sentiment, produced by an object in a particular mind, according to the peculiar structure and constitution of that mind.

By this diversity of sentiment, observable in human kind, nature has, perhaps, intended to make us sensible of her authority, and let us see what surprising changes she could produce on the passions and desires of mankind, merely by the change of their inward fabric, without any alteration on the objects. The vulgar may even be convinced by this argument: But men, accustomed to thinking, may draw a more convincing, at least a more general argument, from the very nature of the subject.

In the operation of reasoning, the mind does nothing but run over its objects, as they are supposed to stand in reality, without adding any thing to them, or diminishing any thing from them. If I examine the Ptolomaic and Copernican systems,[1] I endeavour only, by my enquiries, to know the real situation of the planets; that is in other words, I endeavour to give them, in my conception, the same relations, that they bear towards each other in the heavens. To this operation of the mind, therefore, there seems to be always a real, though often an unknown standard, in the nature of things; nor is truth or falsehood variable by the various apprehensions of mankind. Though all human race should for ever conclude, that the sun moves, and the earth remains at rest, the sun stirs not an inch from his place for all these reasonings; and such conclusions are eternally false and erroneous.

But the case is not the same with the qualities of *beautiful and deformed, desirable and odious*, as with truth and falsehood. In the former case, the mind is not content with merely surveying its objects, as they stand in themselves: It also feels a sentiment of delight or uneasiness, approbation or blame, consequent to that survey; and this sentiment determines it to affix the epithet *beautiful or deformed, desirable or odious*. Now, it is evident, that this sentiment must depend upon the particular fabric or structure of the mind, which enables such particular forms to operate in such a particular manner, and produces a sympathy or conformity between the mind and its objects. Vary the structure of the mind or inward organs, the sentiment no longer follows, though the form remains the same. The sentiment being different from the object, and arising from its operation upon the organs of the mind, an alteration upon the latter must vary the effect, nor can the same object, presented to a mind totally different, produce the same sentiment.

This conclusion every one is apt to draw of himself, without much philosophy, where the sentiment is evidently distinguishable from the object. Who is not sensible, that power, and glory, and vengeance, are not desirable of themselves, but derive all their value from the structure of human passions, which begets a desire towards such particular pursuits? But with regard to beauty, either natural or moral, the case is commonly supposed to be different. The agreeable quality is thought to lie in the object, not in the sentiment; and that merely because the sentiment is not so turbulent and violent as to distinguish itself, in an evident manner, from the perception of the object.

But a little reflection suffices to distinguish them. A man may know exactly all the circles and ellipses of the Copernican system, and all the irregular spirals of the Ptolomaic, without perceiving that the former is more beautiful than the latter. Euclid[2] has fully explained every quality of the circle, but has not, in any proposition, said a word of its beauty. The reason is evident. Beauty is not a quality of the circle. It lies not in any part of the line *whose* parts are all equally distant from a common center. It is only the effect, which that figure produces upon a mind, whose particular fabric or structure renders it susceptible of such sentiments. In vain would you look for it in the circle, or seek it, either by your senses, or by mathematical reasonings, in all the properties of that figure.

The mathematician, who took no other pleasure in reading Virgil, but that of examining Aeneas's voyage by the map, might perfectly understand the meaning of every Latin word, employed by that divine author; and consequently, might have a distinct idea of the whole narration. He would even have a more distinct idea of it, than they could attain who had not studied so exactly the geography of the poem. He knew, therefore, every thing in the poem: But he was ignorant of its beauty; because the beauty, properly speaking, lies not in the poem, but in the sentiment or taste of the reader. And where a man has no such delicacy of temper, as to make him feel this sentiment, he must be ignorant of the beauty, though possessed of the science and understanding of an angel.[3]

The inference upon the whole is, that it is not from the value or worth of the object, which any person pursues, that we can determine his enjoyment, but merely from the passion with which he pursues it, and the success which he meets with in his pursuit. Objects have absolutely no worth or value in themselves. They derive their worth merely from the passion. If that be strong, and steady, and successful, the person is happy. It cannot reasonably be doubted, but a little miss, dressed in a new gown for a dancing-school ball, receives as compleat enjoyment as the greatest orator, who triumphs in the spendor of his eloquence, while he governs the passions and resolutions of a numerous assembly.

All the difference, therefore, between one man and another, with regard to life, consists either in the *passion*, or in the *enjoyment*: And these differences are sufficient to produce the wide extremes of happiness and misery.

To be happy, the *passion* must neither be too violent nor too remiss. In the first case, the mind is in a perpetual hurry and tumult; in the second, it sinks into a disagreeable indolence and lethargy.

To be happy, the passion must be benign and social; not rough or fierce. The affections of the latter kind are not near so agreeable to the feeling, as those of the former. Who will compare rancour and animosity, envy and revenge, to friendship, benignity, clemency, and gratitude?

To be happy, the passion must be cheerful and gay, not gloomy and melancholy. A propensity to hope and joy is real riches: One to fear and sorrow, real poverty.

Some passions or inclinations, in the *enjoyment* of their object, are not so steady or constant as others, nor convey such durable pleasure and satisfaction. *Philosophical devotion*, for instance, like the enthusiasm of a poet, is the transitory effect of high spirits, great leisure, a fine genius, and a habit of study and contemplation: But notwithstanding all these circumstances, an abstract, invisible object, like that which *natural* religion alone presents to us, cannot long actuate the mind, or be of any moment in life. To render the passion of continuance, we must find some method of affecting the senses and imagination, and must embrace some *historical*, as well as *philosophical* account of the divinity. Popular superstitions and observances are even found to be of use in this particular.

Though the tempers of men be very different, yet we may safely pronounce in general, that a life of pleasure cannot support itself so long as one of business, but is much more subject to satiety and disgust. The amusements, which are the most durable, have all a mixture of application and attention in them; such as gaming and hunting. And in general, business and action fill up all the great vacancies in human life.

But where the temper is the best disposed for any *enjoyment*, the object is often wanting: And in this respect, the passions, which pursue external objects, contribute not so much to happiness, as those which rest in ourselves; since we are neither so certain of attaining such objects, nor so secure in possessing them. A passion for learning is preferable, with regard to happiness, to one for riches.

Some men are possessed of great strength of mind; and even when they pursue *external* objects, are not much affected by a disappointment, but renew their application and industry with the greatest cheerfulness. Nothing contributes more to happiness than such a turn of mind.

According to this short and imperfect sketch of human life, the happiest disposition of mind is the *virtuous*; or, in other words, that which leads to action and employment, renders us sensible to the social passions, steels the heart against the assaults of fortune, reduces the affections to a just moderation, makes our own thoughts an entertainment to us, and inclines us rather to the pleasures of society and conversation, than to those of the senses. This, in the mean time, must be obvious to the most careless reasoner, that all dispositions of mind are not alike favourable to happiness, and that one passion or humour may be extremely desirable, while another is equally disagreeable. And indeed, all the difference between the conditions of life depends upon the mind; nor is there any one situation of affairs, in itself, preferable to another. Good and ill, both natural and moral, are entirely relative to human sentiment and affection. No man would ever be unhappy, could he alter his feelings. Proteus-like, he would elude all attacks, by the continual alterations of his shape and form.[4]

But of this resource nature has, in a great measure, deprived us. The fabric and constitution of our mind no more depends on our choice, than that of our body. The generality of men have not even the smallest notion, that any alteration in this respect can ever be desirable. As a stream necessarily follows the several inclinations of the ground, on which it runs; so are the ignorant and thoughtless part of mankind actuated by their natural propensities. Such are effectually excluded from all pretensions to philosophy, and the *medicine of the mind*, so much boasted. But even upon the wise and thoughtful, nature has a prodigious influence; nor is it always in a man's power, by the utmost art and industry, to correct his temper, and attain that virtuous character, to which he aspires. The empire of philosophy extends over a few; and with regard to these too, her authority is very weak and limited. Men may well be sensible of the value of virtue, and may desire to attain it; but it is not always certain, that they will be successful in their wishes.

Whoever considers, without prejudice, the course of human actions, will find, that mankind are almost entirely guided by constitution and temper, and that general maxims have little influence, but so far as they affect our taste or sentiment. If a man have a lively sense of honour and virtue, with moderate passions, his conduct will always be conformable to the rules of morality; or if he depart from them, his return will be easy and expeditious. On the other hand, where one is born of so perverse a frame of mind, of so callous and insensible a disposition, as to have no relish for virtue and humanity, no sympathy with his fellow-creatures, no desire of esteem and applause; such a one must be allowed entirely incurable, nor is there any remedy in philosophy. He reaps no satisfaction but from low and sensual objects, or from the indulgence of malignant passions: He feels no remorse to control his vicious inclinations: He has not even that sense or taste, which is requisite to make him desire a better character: For my part, I know not how I should address myself to such a one, or by what arguments I should endeavour to reform him. Should I tell him of the inward satisfaction which results from laudable and humane actions, the delicate pleasure of disinterested love and friendship, the lasting enjoyments of a good name and an established character, he might still reply, that these were, perhaps, pleasures to such as were susceptible of them; but that, for his part, he finds himself of a quite different turn and disposition. I must repeat it; my philosophy affords no remedy in such a case, nor could I do any thing but lament this person's unhappy condition. But then I ask, If any other philosophy can afford a remedy; or if it be possible, by any system, to render all mankind virtuous, however perverse may be their natural frame of mind? Experience will soon convince us of the contrary; and I will venture to affirm, that, perhaps, the chief benefit, which results from philosophy, arises in an indirect manner, and proceeds more from its secret, insensible influence, than from its immediate application.

It is certain, that a serious attention to the sciences and liberal arts softens and humanizes the temper, and cherishes those fine emotions, in which true virtue and honour consists. It rarely, very rarely happens, that a man of taste and learning is not, at least, an honest man, whatever frailties may attend him. The bent of his mind to speculative studies must mortify in him the passions of interest and ambition, and must, at the same time, give him a greater sensibility of all the decencies and duties of life. He feels more fully a moral distinction in characters and manners; nor is his sense of this kind diminished, but, on the contrary, it is much encreased, by speculation.

Besides such insensible changes upon the temper and disposition, it is highly probable, that others may be produced by study and application. The prodigious effects of education may convince us, that the mind is not altogether stubborn and inflexible, but will admit of many alterations from its original make and structure. Let a man propose to himself the model of a character, which he approves: Let him be well acquainted with those particulars, in which his own character deviates from this model: Let him keep a constant watch over himself, and bend his mind, by a continual effort, from the vices, towards the virtues; and I doubt not but, in time, he will find, in his temper, an alteration for the better.

Habit is another powerful means of reforming the mind, and implanting in it good dispositions and inclinations. A man, who continues in a course of sobriety and temperance, will hate riot and disorder: If he engage in business or study, indolence will seem a punishment to him: If he constrain himself to practise beneficence and affability, he will soon abhor all instances of pride and violence. Where one is thoroughly convinced that the virtuous course of life is preferable; if he have but resolution enough, for some time, to impose a violence on himself; his reformation needs not be despaired of. The misfortune is, that this conviction and this resolution never can have place, unless a man be, before-hand, tolerably virtuous.

Here then is the chief triumph of art and philosophy: It insensibly refines the temper, and it points out to us those dispositions which we should endeavour to attain, by a constant *bent* of mind, and by repeated *habit*. Beyond this I cannot acknowledge it to have great influence; and I must entertain doubts concerning all those exhortations and consolations, which are in such vogue among speculative reasoners.

We have already observed, that no objects are, in themselves, desirable or odious, valuable or despicable; but that objects acquire these qualities from the particular character and constitution of the mind, which surveys them. To diminish therefore, or augment any person's value for an object, to excite or moderate his passions, there are no direct arguments or reasons, which can be employed with any force or influence. The catching of flies, like Domitian, if it give more pleasure, is preferable to the hunting of wild beasts, like William Rufus, or conquering of kingdoms, like Alexander.[5]

But though the value of every object can be determined only by the sentiment or passion of every individual, we may observe, that the passion, in pronouncing its verdict, considers not the object simply, as it is in itself, but surveys it with all the circumstances, which attend it. A man transported with joy, on account of his possessing a diamond, confines not his view to the glistering stone before him: He also considers its rarity, and thence chiefly arises his pleasure and exultation. Here therefore a philosopher may step in, and suggest particular views, and considerations, and circumstances, which otherwise would have escaped us; and, by that means, he may either moderate or excite any particular passion.

It may seem unreasonable absolutely to deny the authority of philosophy in this respect: But it must be confessed, that there lies this strong presumption against it, that, if these views be natural and obvious, they would have occurred of themselves, without the assistance of philosophy; if they be not natural, they never can have any influence on the affections. *These* are of a very delicate nature, and cannot be forced or constrained by the utmost art or industry. A consideration, which we seek for on purpose, which we enter into with difficulty, which we cannot retain without care and attention, will never produce those genuine and durable movements of passion, which are the result of nature, and the constitution of the mind. A man may as well pretend to cure himself of love, by viewing his mistress through the *artificial* medium of a microscope or prospect, and beholding there the coarseness of her skin, and monstrous disproportion of her features, as hope to excite or moderate any passion by the *artificial* arguments of a Seneca or an Epictetus.[6] The remembrance of the natural aspect and situation of the object, will, in both cases, still recur upon him. The reflections of philosophy are too subtle and distant to take place in common life, or eradicate any affection. The air is too fine to breathe in, where it is above the winds and clouds of the atmosphere.

Another defect of those refined reflections, which philosophy suggests to us, is, that commonly they cannot diminish or extinguish our vicious passions, without diminishing or extinguishing such as are virtuous, and rendering the mind totally indifferent and unactive. They are, for the most part, general, and are applicable to all our affections. In vain do we hope to direct their influence only to one side. If by incessant study and meditation we have rendered them intimate and present to us, they will operate throughout, and spread an universal insensibility over the mind. When we destroy the nerves, we extinguish the sense of pleasure, together with that of pain, in the human body.

It will be easy, by one glance of the eye, to find one or other of these defects in most of those philosophical reflections, so much celebrated both in ancient and modern times. *Let not the injuries or violence of men*, say the philosophers,[7] *ever discompose you by anger or hatred. Would you be angry at the ape for its malice, or the tiger for its ferocity?* This reflection leads us into a bad opinion of human nature, and must extinguish the social affections. It tends also to prevent all remorse for a man's own crimes; when he considers, that vice is as natural to mankind, as the particular instincts to brute-creatures.

All ills arise from the order of the universe, which is absolutely perfect. Would you wish to disturb so divine an order for the sake of your own particular interest? What if the ills I suffer arise from malice or oppression? *But the vices and imperfections of men are also comprehended in the order of the universe:*

> *If plagues and earthquakes break not heav'n's design,*
> *Why then a* Borgia *or a* Catiline?[8]

Let this be allowed; and my own vices will also be a part of the same order.

To one who said, that none were happy, who were not above opinion, a Spartan replied, *then none are happy but knaves and robbers.*[9]

Man is born to be miserable; and is he surprized at any particular misfortune? And can he give way to sorrow and lamentation upon account of any disaster? Yes: He very reasonably laments, that he should be born to be miserable. Your consolation presents a hundred ills for one, of which you pretend to ease him.

You should always have before your eyes death, disease, poverty, blindness, exile, calumny, and infamy, as ills which are incident to human nature. If any one of these ills falls to your lot, you will bear it the better, when you have reckoned upon it. I answer, if we confine ourselves to a general and distant reflection on the ills of human life, *that* can have no effect to prepare us for them. If by close and intense meditation we render them present and intimate to us, *that* is the true secret for poisoning all our pleasures, and rendering us perpetually miserable.

Your sorrow is fruitless, and will not change the course of destiny. Very true: And for that very reason I am sorry.

Cicero's consolation for deafness is somewhat curious. *How many languages are there*, says he, *which you do not understand? The* Punic, Spanish, Gallic, Egyptian, *&c. With regard to all these, you are as if you were deaf, yet you are indifferent about the matter. Is it then so great a misfortune to be deaf to one language more?*[10]

I like better the repartee of Antipater the Cyreniac, when some women were condoling with him for his blindness: *What!* says he, *Do you think there are no pleasures in the dark?*[11]

Nothing can be more destructive, says Fontenelle,[12] *to ambition, and the passion for conquest, than the true system of astronomy. What a poor thing is even the whole globe in comparison of the infinite extent of nature?* This consideration is evidently too distant ever to have any effect. Or, if it had any, would it not destroy patriotism as well as ambition? The same gallant author adds with some reason, that the bright eyes of the ladies are the only objects, which lose nothing of their lustre or value from the most extensive views of astronomy, but stand proof against every system. Would philosophers advise us to limit our affection to them?

Exile, says Plutarch to a friend in banishment, *is no evil: Mathematicians tell us, that the whole earth is but a point, compared to the heavens. To change one's country then is little more than to remove from one street to another. Man is not a plant, rooted to a certain spot of earth: All soils and all climates are alike suited to him.*[13] These topics are admirable, could they fall only into the hands of banished persons. But what if they come also to the knowledge of those who are employed in public affairs, and destroy all their attachment to their native country? Or will they operate like the quack's medicine, which is equally good for a diabetes and a dropsy?

It is certain, were a superior being thrust into a human body, that the whole of life would to him appear so mean, contemptible, and puerile, that he never could be induced to take part in any thing, and would scarcely give attention to what passes around him. To engage him to such a condescension as to play even the part of a Philip with zeal and alacrity, would be much more difficult, than to constrain the same Philip, after having been a king and a conqueror during fifty years, to mend old shoes with proper care and attention; the occupation which Lucian assigns him in the infernal regions.[14] Now all the same topics of disdain towards human affairs, which could operate on this supposed being, occur also to a philosopher; but being, in some measure, disproportioned to human capacity, and not being fortified by the experience of any thing better, they make not a full impression on him. He sees, but he feels not sufficiently their truth; and is always a sublime philosopher, when he needs not; that is, as long as nothing disturbs him, or rouses his affections. While others play, he wonders at their keenness and ardour; but he no sooner puts in his own stake, than he is commonly transported with the same passions, that he had so much condemned, while he remained a simple spectator.

There are two considerations chiefly, to be met with in books of philosophy, from which any important effect is to be expected, and that because these considerations are drawn from common life, and occur upon the most superficial view of human affairs. When we reflect on the shortness and uncertainty of life, how despicable seem all our pursuits of happiness? And even, if we

would extend our concern beyond our own life, how frivolous appear our
most enlarged and most generous projects; when we consider the incessant
changes and revolutions of human affairs, by which laws and learning, books
and governments are hurried away by time, as by a rapid stream, and are lost
in the immense ocean of matter? Such a reflection certainly tends to mortify all
our passions: But does it not thereby counterwork the artifice of nature, who
has happily deceived us into an opinion, that human life is of some importance? And may not such a reflection be employed with success by voluptuous
reasoners, in order to lead us, from the paths of action and virtue, into the
flowery fields of indolence and pleasure?

We are informed by Thucydides,[15] that, during the famous plague of Athens,
when death seemed present to every one, a dissolute mirth and gaiety pre-
vailed among the people, who exhorted one another to make the most of life as
long as it endured. The same observation is made by Boccaccio with regard to
the plague of Florence.[16] A like principle makes soldiers, during war, be more
addicted to riot and expence, than any other race of men. Present pleasure is
always of importance; and whatever diminishes the importance of all other
objects must bestow on it an additional influence and value.

The *second* philosophical consideration, which may often have an influence
on the affections, is derived from a comparison of our own condition with the
condition of others. This comparison we are continually making, even in common life; but the misfortune is, that we are rather apt to compare our situation
with that of our superiors, than with that of our inferiors. A philosopher corrects this natural infirmity, by turning his view to the other side, in order to
render himself easy in the situation, to which fortune has confined him. There
are few people, who are not susceptible of some consolation from this reflection, though, to a very good-natured man, the view of human miseries should
rather produce sorrow than comfort, and add, to his lamentations for his own
misfortunes, a deep compassion for those of others. Such is the imperfection,
even of the best of these philosophical topics of consolation.[17]

I shall conclude this subject with observing, that, though virtue be
undoubtedly the best choice, when it is attainable; yet such is the disorder and
confusion of human affairs, that no perfect or regular distribution of happiness
and misery is ever, in this life, to be expected. Not only the goods of fortune,
and the endowments of the body (both of which are important), not only these
advantages, I say, are unequally divided between the virtuous and vicious, but
even the mind itself partakes, in some degree, of this disorder, and the most
worthy character, by the very constitution of the passions, enjoys not always
the highest felicity.

It is observable, that, though every bodily pain proceeds from some
disorder in the part or organ, yet the pain is not always proportioned to the
disorder; but is greater or less, according to the greater or less sensibility of
the part, upon which the noxious humours exert their influence. A *toothache*
produces more violent convulsions of pain than a *phthisis* or a *dropsy*. In like
manner, with regard to the economy of the mind, we may observe, that all
vice is indeed pernicious; yet the disturbance or pain is not measured out by
nature with exact proportion to the degree of vice, nor is the man of highest
virtue, even abstracting from external accidents, always the most happy. A

gloomy and melancholy disposition is certainly, *to our sentiments*, a vice or imperfection; but as it may be accompanied with great sense of honour and great integrity, it may be found in very worthy characters; though it is sufficient alone to embitter life, and render the person affected with it completely miserable. On the other hand, a selfish villain may possess a spring and alacrity of temper, a certain *gaiety of heart*, which is indeed a good quality, but which is rewarded much beyond its merit, and when attended with good fortune, will compensate for the uneasiness and remorse arising from all the other vices.

I shall add, as an observation to the same purpose, that, if a man be liable to a vice or imperfection, it may often happen, that a good quality, which he possesses along with it, will render him more miserable, than if he were completely vicious. A person of such imbecility of temper as to be easily broken by affliction, is more unhappy for being endowed with a generous and friendly disposition, which gives him a lively concern for others, and exposes him the more to fortune and accidents. A sense of shame, in an imperfect character, is certainly a virtue; but produces great uneasiness and remorse, from which the abandoned villain is entirely free. A very amorous complexion, with a heart incapable of friendship, is happier than the same excess in love, with a generosity of temper, which transports a man beyond himself, and renders him a total slave to the object of his passion.

In a word, human life is more governed by fortune than by reason; is to be regarded more as a dull pastime than as a serious occupation; and is more influenced by particular humor, than by general principles. Shall we engage ourselves in it with passion and anxiety? It is not worthy of so much concern. Shall we be indifferent about what happens? We lose all the pleasure of the game by our phlegm and carelessness. While we are reasoning concerning life, life is gone; and death, though *perhaps* they receive him differently, yet treats alike the fool and the philosopher. To reduce life to exact rule and method, is commonly a painful, oft a fruitless occupation: And is it not also a proof, that we overvalue the prize for which we contend? Even to reason so carefully concerning it, and to fix with accuracy its just idea, would be overvaluing it, were it not that, to some tempers, this occupation is one of the most amusing, in which life could possibly be employed.

NOTES

1. [Ptolemy (second century A.D.) taught that the earth is at the center of the planetary system and immovable, while Nicholas Copernicus's (1473–1543) heliocentric system holds that the earth moves daily around its own axis and yearly around the sun.]

2. [The Greek mathematician Euclid, who lived from the late fourth century to the early third century B.C., is famous for his textbook on geometry, *The Elements*.]

3. Were I not afraid of appearing too philosophical, I should remind my reader of that famous doctrine, supposed to be fully proved in modern times, "That tastes and colours, and all other sensible qualities, lie not in the bodies, but merely in the senses." The case is the same with beauty and deformity, virtue and vice. This doctrine, however, takes off no more from the reality of the latter qualities, than from that of the former; nor need it give any umbrage either to critics or moralists. Though colours were allowed to lie only in the eye, would dyers or painters ever be less regarded or esteemed? There is a sufficient uniformity in the senses and

feelings of mankind, to make all these qualities the objects of art and reasoning, and to have the greatest influence on life and manners. And as it is certain, that the discovery above-mentioned in natural philosophy, makes no alteration on action and conduct; why should a like discovery in morsl philosophy make any alteration?

4. [According to Greek mythology, the sea god Proteus has the power to change his shape and to prophesy. If grasped hard, he takes his true shape and gives answers to questions.]

5. [Suetonius (*Lives of the Caesars*, Domitian, sec. 3) reports that the emperor Domitian, at the beginning of his reign, used to spend hours in seclusion each day, doing nothing but catching flies and stabbing them with a sharp knife. William Rufus, king of England from 1087 to 1100, engaged in hunting as his sole amusement. He was killed accidentally by the arrow of a fellow hunter (see Hume, *History of England*, chap. 5). Alexander the Great conquered the area from Greece eastward to India.]

6. [Lucius Annaeus Seneca (4? B.C.–A.D. 65) and Epictetus (A.D. 55–135?) were Stoic moral philosophers.]

7. PLUT. *de ira cohibenda*. "On the Control of Anger," in Plutarch's *Moralia*, or ethical writings.

8. [Alexander Pope, *An Essay on Man* 1.155–56. The original reads: "If plagues or earthquakes . . ."]

9. PLUT. *Lacon. Apophtheg.* [*Apophthegmata Laconica* (Sayings of Spartans), sec. 217, in Plutarch's *Moralia*.]

10. TUSC. *Quest.* lib. v. [Cicero, *Tusculan Disputations* 5.40.]

11. [Ibid., 5.38.]

12. [In Fontenelle's *Conversations on the Plurality of Worlds*.]

13. *De exilio.* [Plutarch, *De exilio* (On exile) in the *Moralia*.]

14. [See Lucian, *Menippus, or the Descent into Hades*, sec. 17.]

15. [Thucydides, *The Peloponnesian War* 2.53.]

16. [Giovanni Boccaccio (1313–75), *Decameron*, "Introduction: To the Ladies."]

17. The Sceptic, perhaps, carries the matter too far, when he limits all philosophical topics and reflections to these two. There seem to be others, whose truth is undeniable, and whose natural tendency is to tranquillize and soften all the passions. Philosophy greedily seizes these, studies them, weighs them, commits them to the memory, and familiarizes them to the mind: And their influence on tempers, which are thoughtful, gentle, and moderate, may be considerable. But what is their influence, you will say, if the temper be antecedently disposed after the same manner as that to which they pretend to form it? They may, at least, fortify that temper, and furnish it with views, by which it may entertain and nourish itself. Here are a few examples of such philosophical reflections.

1. Is it not certain, that every condition has concealed ills? Then why envy anybody?

2. Everyone has known ills; and there is a compensation throughout. Why not be contented with the present?

3. Custom deadens the sense both of the good and the ill, and levels everything.

4. Health and humor all. The rest of little consequence, except these be affected.

5. How many other good things have I? Then why be vexed for one ill?

6. How many are happy in the condition of which I complain? How many envy me?

7. Every good must be paid for: Fortune by labour, favour by flattery. Would I keep the price, yet have the commodity?

8. Expect not too great happiness in life. Human nature admits it not.

9. Propose not a happiness too complicated. But does that depend on me? Yes: The first choice does. Life is like a game: One may choose the game: And passion, by degrees, seizes the proper object.

10. Anticipate by your hopes and fancy future consolation, which time infallibly brings to every affliction.

11. I desire to be rich. Why? That I may possess many fine objects; houses, gardens, equipage, &c. How many fine objects does nature offer to every one without expence? If enjoyed, sufficient. If not: See the effect of custom or of temper, which would soon take off the relish of the riches.

12. I desire fame. Let this occur: If I act well, I shall have the esteem of all my acquaintance. And what is all the rest to me?

These reflections are so obvious, that it is a wonder they occur not to every man: So convincing, that it is a wonder they persuade not every man. But perhaps they do occur to and persuade most men; when they consider human life, by a general and calm survey: But where any real, affecting incident happens; when passion is awakened, fancy agitated, example draws, and counsel urges; the philosopher is lost in the man, and he seeks in vain for that persuasion which before seemed so firm and unshaken. What remedy for this inconvenience? Assist yourself by a frequent perusal of the entertaining moralists: Have recourse to the learning of Plutarch, the imagination of Lucian, the eloquence of Cicero, the wit of Seneca, the gaiety of Montaigne, the sublimity of Shaftesbury. Moral precepts, so couched, strike deep, and fortify the mind against the illusions of passion. But trust not altogether to external aid: By habit and study acquire that philosophical temper which both gives force to reflection, and by rendering a great part of your happiness independent, takes off the edge from all disorderly passions, and tranquillizes the mind. Despise not these helps; but confide not too much in them neither; unless nature has been favourable in the temper, with which she has endowed you.

AN INTRODUCTION TO THE PRINCIPLES OF MORALS AND LEGISLATION

Jeremy Bentham

Jeremy Bentham (1748–1822) was an influential British philosopher and social reformer. He developed the ethical system of utilitarianism, according to which actions are to be judged as moral to the extent that they produce the greatest happiness for the greatest number, maximizing pleasure and minimizing pain for all persons counted equally.

CHAPTER I

Of the Principle of Utility

1. Nature has placed mankind under the governance of two sovereign masters, *pain* and *pleasure*. It is for them alone to point out what we ought to do, as well as to determine what we shall do. On the one hand the standard of right and wrong, on the other the chain of causes and effects, are fastened to their throne. They govern us in all we do, in all we say, in all we think: every effort

From *An Introduction to the Principles of Morals and Legislation* (1789).

we can make to throw off our subjection, will serve but to demonstrate and confirm it. In words a man may pretend to abjure their empire: but in reality he will remain subject to it all the while. The *principle of utility* recognises this subjection, and assumes it for the foundation of that system, the object of which is to rear the fabric of felicity by the hands of reason and of law. Systems which attempt to question it, deal in sounds instead of sense, in caprice instead of reason, in darkness instead of light.

But enough of metaphor and declamation: it is not by such means that moral science is to be improved.

2. The principle of utility is the foundation of the present work: it will be proper therefore at the outset to give an explicit and determinate account of what is meant by it. By the principle of utility is meant that principle which approves or disapproves of every action whatsoever, according to the tendency which it appears to have to augment or diminish the happiness of the party whose interest is in question: or, what is the same thing in other words, to promote or to oppose that happiness. I say of every action whatsoever; and therefore not only of every action of a private individual, but of every measure of government.

3. By utility is meant that property in any object, whereby it tends to produce benefit, advantage, pleasure, good, or happiness, (all this in the present case comes to the same thing), or (what comes again to the same thing) to prevent the happening of mischief, pain, evil, or unhappiness to the party whose interest is considered: if that party be the community in general, then the happiness of the community: if a particular individual, then the happiness of that individual.

4. The interest of the community is one of the most general expressions that can occur in the phraseology of morals: no wonder that the meaning of it is often lost. When it has a meaning, it is this. The community is a fictitious *body*, composed of the individual persons who are considered as constituting as it were its *members*. The interest of the community then is, what?—the sum of the interests of the several members who compose it.

5. It is in vain to talk of the interest of the community, without understanding what is the interest of the individual. A thing is said to promote the interest, or to be *for* the interest, of an individual, when it tends to add to the sum total of his pleasures: or, what comes to the same thing, to diminish the sum total of his pains.

6. An action then may be said to be conformable to the principle of utility, or, for shortness sake, to utility, (meaning with respect to the community at large) when the tendency it has to augment the happiness of the community is greater than any it has to diminish it.

7. A measure of government (which is but a particular kind of action, performed by a particular person or persons) may be said to be conformable to or dictated by the principle of utility, when in like manner the tendency which it has to augment the happiness of the community is greater than any which it has to diminish it.

8. When an action, or in particular a measure of government, is supposed by a man to be conformable to the principle of utility, it may be convenient, for the purposes of discourse, to imagine a kind of law or dictate, called a law or

dictate of utility: and to speak of the action in question, as being conformable to such law or dictate.

9. A man may be said to be a partisan of the principle of utility, when the approbation or disapprobation he annexes to any action, or to any measure, is determined by, and proportioned to the tendency which he conceives it to have to augment or to diminish the happiness of the community: or in other words, to its conformity or unconformity to the laws or dictates of utility.

10. Of an action that is conformable to the principle of utility, one may always say either that it is one that ought to be done, or at least that it is not one that ought not to be done. One may say also, that it is right it should be done; at least that it is not wrong it should be done: that it is a right action; at least that it is not a wrong action. When thus interpreted, the words *ought*, and *right* and *wrong*, and others of that stamp, have a meaning: when otherwise, they have none. . . .

CHAPTER IV

Value of a Lot of Pleasure or Pain, How to Be Measured

1. Pleasures then, and the avoidance of pains, are the *ends* which the legislator has in view: it behoves him therefore to understand their *value*. Pleasures and pains are the *instruments* he has to work with: it behoves him therefore to understand their force, which is again, in another point of view their value.

2. To a person considered *by himself*, the value of a pleasure or pain considered *by itself*, will be greater or less, according to the four following circumstances:

1. Its *intensity*.
2. Its *duration*.
3. Its *certainty* or *uncertainty*.
4. Its *propinquity* or *remoteness*.

3. These are the circumstances which are to be considered in estimating a pleasure or a pain considered each of them by itself. But when the value of any pleasure or pain is considered for the purpose of estimating the tendency of any *act* by which it is produced, there are two other circumstances to be taken into the account; these are,

5. Its *fecundity*, or the chance it has of being followed by sensations of the *same* kind: that is, pleasures, if it be a pleasure: pains, if it be a pain.
6. Its *purity*, or the chance it has of *not* being followed by sensations of the *opposite* kind: that is, pains, if it be a pleasure: pleasures, if it be a pain.

These two last, however, are in strictness scarcely to be deemed properties of the pleasure or the pain itself; they are not, therefore, in strictness to be taken into the account of the value of that pleasure or that pain. They are in strictness to be deemed properties only of the act, or other event, by which such pleasure or pain has been produced; and accordingly are only to be taken into the account of the tendency of such act or such event.

4. To a *number* of persons, with reference to each of whom the value of a pleasure or a pain is considered, it will be greater or less, according to seven circumstances: to wit, the six preceding ones; viz.

1. Its *intensity*.
2. Its *duration*.
3. Its *certainty* or *uncertainty*.
4. Its *propinquity* or *remoteness*.
5. Its *fecundity*.
6. Its *purity*.

And one other; to wit;

7. Its *extent*; that is, the number of persons to whom it *extends*; or (in other words) who are affected by it.

5. To take an exact account then of the general tendency of any act, by which the interests of a community are affected, proceed as follows. Begin with any one person of those whose interests seem most immediately to be affected by it: and take an account,

1. Of the value of each distinguishable *pleasure* which appears to be produced by it in the *first* instance.
2. Of the value of each *pain* which appears to be produced by it in the *first* instance.
3. Of the value of each pleasure which appears to be produced by it *after* the first. This constitutes the *fecundity* of the first *pleasure* and the impurity of the first *pain*.
4. Of the value of each *pain* which appears to be produced by it after the first. This constitutes the *fecundity* of the first *pain*, and the *impurity* of the first pleasure.
5. Sum up all the values of all the *pleasures* on the one side, and those of all the *pains* on the other. The balance, if it be on the side of pleasure, will give the *good* tendency of the act upon the whole, with respect to the interests of that *individual* person; if on the side of pain, the *bad* tendency of it upon the whole.
6. Take an account of the *number* of persons whose interests appear to be concerned; and repeat the above process with respect to each. *Sum up* the numbers expressive of the degrees of *good* tendency, which the act has, with respect to each individual, in regard to whom the tendency of it is *good* upon the whole: do this again with respect to each individual, in regard to whom the tendency of it is *good* upon the whole: do this again with respect to each individual, in regard to whom the tendency of it is *bad* upon the whole. Take the *balance*; which, if on the side of *pleasure*, will give the general *good tendency* of the act, with respect to the total number or community of individuals concerned; if on the side of pain, the general *evil tendency*, with respect to the same community.

6. It is not to be expected that this process should be strictly pursued previously to every moral judgment, or to every legislative or judicial operation. It may, however, be always kept in view: and as near as the process actually pursued on these occasions approaches to it, so near will such process approach to the character of an exact one.

7. The same process is alike applicable to pleasure and pain, in whatever shape they appear: and by whatever denomination they are distinguished: to pleasure, whether it be called *good* (which is properly the cause or instrument of pleasure) or *profit* (which is distant pleasure, or the cause or instrument of distant pleasure,) or *convenience*, to *advantage, benefit, emolument, happiness*, and so forth: to pain, whether it be called *evil*, (which corresponds to *good*) or *mischief*, or *inconvenience*, or *disadvantage*, or *loss*, or *unhappiness*, and so forth.

8. Nor is this a novel and unwarranted, any more than it is a useless theory. In all this there is nothing but what the practice of mankind, wheresoever they have a clear view of their own interest, is perfectly conformable to. An article of property, an estate in land, for instance, is valuable, on what account? On account of the pleasures of all kinds which it enables a man to produce, and what comes to the same thing the pains of all kinds which it enables him to avert. But the value of such an article of property is universally understood to rise or fall according to the length or shortness of the time which a man has in it: the certainty or uncertainty of its coming into possession: and the nearness or remoteness of the time at which, if at all, it is to come into possession. As to the *intensity* of the pleasures which a man may derive from it, this is never thought of, because it depends upon the use which each particular person may come to make of it: which cannot be estimated till the particular pleasures he may come to derive from it, or the particular pains he may come to exclude by means of it, are brought to view. For the same reason, neither does he think of the *fecundity* or *purity* of those pleasures.

Thus much for pleasure and pain, happiness and unhappiness, in *general*.

GROUNDWORK OF THE METAPHYSICS OF MORALS

Immanuel Kant

Immanuel Kant (1724–1804), who lived his entire life in the Prussian town of Königsberg, is a preeminent figure in the history of philosophy, having made groundbreaking contributions to virtually every area of the subject. His influential ethical system defends one moral principle, the

From *Groundwork of the Metaphysics of Morals*, translated by Mary Gregor, Cambridge University Press, 1997. Used by permission of the publisher.

categorical imperative, as binding on all rational beings regardless of
their individual desires. In his monumental *Critique of Pure Reason*, Kant
maintained that the existence of God could not be proved but needed
to be postulated in order to ensure a correlation between morality and
happiness.

SECTION I

It is impossible to think of anything at all in the world, or indeed even beyond
it, that could be considered good without limitation except a good will.
Understanding, wit, judgment and the like, whatever such *talents* of mind may
be called, or courage, resolution, and perseverance in one's plans, as qualities
of *temperament*, are undoubtedly good and desirable for many purposes, but
they can also be extremely evil and harmful if the will which is to make use
of these gifts of nature, and whose distinctive constitution is therefore called
character, is not good. It is the same with *gifts of fortune*. Power, riches, honor,
even health and that complete well-being and satisfaction with one's condition
called *happiness*, produce boldness and thereby often arrogance as well unless
a good will is present which corrects the influence of these on the mind and, in
so doing, also corrects the whole principle of action and brings it into conformity with universal ends—not to mention that an impartial rational spectator
can take no delight in seeing the uninterrupted prosperity of a being graced
with no feature of a pure and good will, so that a good will seems to constitute
the indispensable condition even of worthiness to be happy.

Some qualities are even conducive to this good will itself and can make
its work much easier; despite this, however, they have no inner unconditional
worth but always presuppose a good will, which limits the esteem one otherwise rightly has for them and does not permit their being taken as absolutely
good. Moderation in affects and passions, self-control, and calm reflection are
not only good for all sorts of purposes but even seem to constitute a part of the
inner worth of a person; but they lack much that would be required to declare
them good without limitation (however unconditionally they were praised by
the ancients); for, without the basic principles of a good will they can become
extremely evil, and the coolness of a scoundrel makes him not only far more
dangerous but also immediately more abominable in our eyes than we would
have taken him to be without it.

A good will is not good because of what it effects or accomplishes, because
of its fitness to attain some proposed end, but only because of its volition, that is,
it is good in itself and, regarded for itself, is to be valued incomparably higher
than all that could merely be brought about by it in favor of some inclination
and indeed, if you will, of the sum of all inclinations. Even if, by a special dis-
favor of fortune or by the niggardly provision of a stepmotherly nature, this will
should wholly lack the capacity to carry out its purpose—if with its greatest
efforts it should yet achieve nothing and only the good will were left (not, of
course, as a mere wish but as the summoning of all means insofar as they are
in our control)—then, like a jewel, it would still shine by itself, as something that

has its full worth in itself. Usefulness or fruitlessness can neither add anything to this worth nor take anything away from it. Its usefulness would be, as it were, only the setting to enable us to handle it more conveniently in ordinary commerce or to attract to it the attention of those who are not yet expert enough, but not to recommend it to experts or to determine its worth.

There is, however, something so strange in this idea of the absolute worth of a mere will, in the estimation of which no allowance is made for any usefulness, that, despite all the agreement even of common understanding with this idea, a suspicion must yet arise that its covert basis is perhaps mere high-flown fantasy and that we may have misunderstood the purpose of nature in assigning reason to our will as its governor. Hence we shall put this idea to the test from this point of view.

In the natural constitution of an organized being, that is, one constituted purposively for life, we assume as a principle that there will be found in it no instrument for some end other than what is also most appropriate to that end and best adapted to it. Now in a being that has reason and a will, if the proper end of nature were its *preservation*, its *welfare*, in a word its *happiness*, then nature would have hit upon a very bad arrangement in selecting the reason of the creature to carry out this purpose. For all the actions that the creature has to perform for this purpose, and the whole rule of its conduct, would be marked out for it far more accurately by instinct, and that end would have thereby been attained much more surely than it ever can be by reason; and if reason should have been given, over and above, to this favored creature, it must have served it only to contemplate the fortunate constitution of its nature, to admire this, to delight in it, and to be grateful for it to the beneficent cause, but not to submit its faculty of desire to that weak and deceptive guidance and meddle with nature's purpose. In a word, nature would have taken care that reason should not break forth into *practical use* and have the presumption, with its weak insight, to think out for itself a plan for happiness and for the means of attaining it. Nature would have taken upon itself the choice not only of ends but also of means and, with wise foresight, would have entrusted them both simply to instinct.

And, in fact, we find that the more a cultivated reason purposely occupies itself with the enjoyment of life and with happiness, so much the further does one get away from true satisfaction; and from this there arises in many, and indeed in those who have experimented most with this use of reason, if only they are candid enough to admit it, a certain degree of *misology*, that is, hatred of reason; for, after calculating all the advantages they draw—I do not say from the invention of all the arts of common luxury, but even from the sciences (which seem to them to be, at bottom, only a luxury of the understanding)— they find that they have in fact only brought more trouble upon themselves instead of gaining in happiness; and because of this they finally envy rather than despise the more common run of people, who are closer to the guidance of mere natural instinct and do not allow their reason much influence on their behavior. And to this extent we must admit that the judgment of those who greatly moderate, and even reduce below zero, eulogies extolling the advantages that reason is supposed to procure for us with regard to the happiness and satisfaction of life is by no means surly or ungrateful to the goodness of the government of the world; we must admit, instead, that these judgments have as their covert basis the idea of another and far worthier purpose of one's existence, to which therefore, and not to happiness, reason is properly destined, and to which, as supreme condition, the private purpose of the human being must for the most part defer.

Since reason is not sufficiently competent to guide the will surely with regard to its objects and the satisfaction of all our needs (which it to some extent even multiplies)—an end to which an implanted natural instinct would have led much more certainly; and since reason is nevertheless given to us as a practical faculty, that is, as one that is to influence the *will*; then, where nature has everywhere else gone to work purposively in distributing its capacities, the true vocation of reason must be to produce a will that is good, not perhaps *as a means* to other purposes, but *good in itself*, for which reason was absolutely necessary. This will need not, because of this, be the sole and complete good, but it must still be the highest good and the condition of every other, even of all demands for happiness. In this case it is entirely consistent with the wisdom of nature if we perceive that the cultivation of reason, which is requisite to the first and unconditional purpose, limits in many ways—at least in this life—the attainment of the second, namely happiness, which is always conditional; indeed it may reduce it below zero without nature proceeding unpurposively in the matter, because reason, which cognizes its highest practical vocation in the establishment of a good will, in attaining this purpose is capable only of its own kind of satisfaction, namely from fulfilling an end which in turn only reason determines, even if this should be combined with many infringements upon the ends of inclination.

We have, then, to explicate the concept of a will that is to be esteemed in itself and that is good apart from any further purpose, as it already dwells in natural sound understanding and needs not so much to be taught as only to be clarified—this concept that always takes first place in estimating the total worth of our actions and constitutes the condition of all the rest. In order to do so, we shall set before ourselves the concept of duty, which contains that of a good will though under certain subjective limitations and hindrances, which, however, far from concealing it and making it unrecognizable, rather bring it out by contrast and make it shine forth all the more brightly.

I here pass over all actions that are already recognized as contrary to duty, even though they may be useful for this or that purpose; for in their case the question whether they might have been done *from duty* never arises, since they even conflict with it. I also set aside actions that are really in conformity with duty but to which human beings have *no inclination* immediately and which they still perform because they are impelled to do so through another inclination. For in this case it is easy to distinguish whether an action in conformity with duty is done *from duty* or from a self-seeking purpose. It is much more difficult to note this distinction when an action conforms with duty and the subject has, besides, an *immediate* inclination to it. For example, it certainly conforms with duty that a shopkeeper not overcharge an inexperienced customer, and where there is a good deal of trade a prudent merchant does not overcharge but keeps a fixed general price for everyone, so that a child can buy from him as well as everyone else. People are thus served *honestly*; but this is not nearly enough for us to believe that the merchant acted in this way from duty and basic principles of honesty; his advantage required it; it cannot be assumed here that he had, besides, an immediate inclination toward his customers, so as from love, as it were, to give no one preference over another in the matter of price. Thus the action was done neither from duty nor from immediate inclination but merely for purposes of self-interest.

On the other hand, to preserve one's life is a duty, and besides everyone has an immediate inclination to do so. But on this account the often anxious care that most people take of it still has no inner worth and their maxim has no moral content. They look after their lives *in conformity with duty* but not *from duty*. On the other hand, if adversity and hopeless grief have quite taken away the taste for life; if an unfortunate man, strong of soul and more indignant about his fate than despondent or dejected, wishes for death and yet preserves his life without loving it, not from inclination or fear but from duty, then his maxim has moral content.

To be beneficent where one can is a duty, and besides there are many souls so sympathetically attuned that, without any other motive of vanity or self-interest they find an inner satisfaction in spreading joy around them and can take delight in the satisfaction of others so far as it is their own work. But I assert that in such a case an action of this kind, however it may conform with duty and however amiable it may be, has nevertheless no true moral worth but is on the same footing with other inclinations, for example, the inclination to honor, which, if it fortunately lights upon what is in fact in the common interest and in conformity with duty and hence honorable, deserves praise and encouragement but not esteem; for the maxim lacks moral content, namely that of doing such actions not from inclination but *from duty*. Suppose, then, that the mind of this philanthropist were overclouded by his own grief, which extinguished all sympathy with the fate of others, and that while he still had the means to benefit others in distress their troubles did not move him because he had enough to do with his own; and suppose that now, when no longer incited to it by any inclination, he nevertheless tears himself out of this deadly insensibility and does the action without any inclination, simply from duty; then the action first has its genuine moral worth. Still further: if nature had put little sympathy in the heart of this or that man; if (in other respects an honest man) he is by temperament cold and indifferent to the sufferings of others, perhaps because he himself is provided with the special gift of patience and endurance toward his own sufferings and presupposes the same in every other or even requires it; if nature had not properly fashioned such a man (who would in truth not be its worst product) for a philanthropist, would he not still find within himself a source from which to give himself a far higher worth than what a mere good-natured temperament might have? By all means! It is just then that the worth of character comes out, which is moral and incomparably the highest, namely that he is beneficent not from inclination but from duty.

To assure one's own happiness is a duty (at least indirectly); for, want of satisfaction with one's condition, under pressure from many anxieties and amid unsatisfied needs, could easily become a great *temptation to transgression of duty*. But in addition, without looking to duty here, all people have already, of themselves, the strongest and deepest inclination to happiness because it is just in this idea that all inclinations unite in one sum. However, the precept of happiness is often so constituted that it greatly infringes upon some inclinations, and yet one can form no determinate and sure concept of the sum of satisfaction of all inclinations under the name of happiness. Hence it is not to be wondered at that a single inclination, determinate both as to what it promises and as to the time within which it can be satisfied, can often outweigh a fluctuating idea, and that a man—for example, one suffering from gout—can choose to enjoy what he likes and put up with what he can since, according to his calculations, on this occasion at least he has not sacrificed the enjoyment of the present moment to the perhaps groundless expectation of a happiness that is supposed to lie in health. But even in this case, when the general inclination to happiness did not determine his will; when health, at least for him, did not enter as so necessary into this calculation, there is still left over here, as in all other cases, a law, namely to promote his happiness not from inclination but from duty; and it is then that his conduct first has properly moral worth. . . .

SECTION II

. . . Everything in nature works in accordance with laws. Only a rational being has the capacity to act *in accordance with the representation* of laws, that is, in accordance with principles, or has a *will.* . . .

The representation of an objective principle, insofar as it is necessitating for a will, so called a command (of reason), and the formula of the command is called an imperative. . . .

Now, all imperatives command either *hypothetically* or *categorically.* The former represent the practical necessity of a possible action as a means to achieving something else that one wills (or that it is at least possible for one to will). The categorical imperative would be that which represented an action as objectively necessary of itself, without reference to another end. . . .

Now, if the action would be good merely as a means *to something else* the imperative is *hypothetical*; if the action is represented as *in itself* good, hence as necessary in a will in itself conforming to reason, as its principle, *then it is categorical.* . . .

There is, however, *one* end that can be presupposed as actual in the case of all rational beings (insofar as imperatives apply to them, namely as dependent beings), and therefore one purpose that they not merely *could* have but that we can safely presuppose they all actually *do have* by a natural necessity, and that purpose is *happiness*. The hypothetical imperative that represents the practical necessity of an action as a means to the promotion of happiness . . . may be set forth not merely as necessary to some uncertain, merely possible purpose but to a purpose that can be presupposed surely . . . in the case of every human being, because it belongs to his essence. Now, skill in the choice of means to one's own greatest well-being can be called *prudence* in the narrowest sense. Hence the imperative that refers to the choice of means to one's own happiness, that is, the precept of prudence, is still always *hypothetical*; the action is not commanded absolutely but only as a means to another purpose. . . .

But it is a misfortune that the concept of happiness is such an indeterminate concept that, although every human being wishes to attain this, he can still never say determinately and consistently with himself what he really wishes and wills.... Now, it is impossible for the most insightful and at the same time most powerful but still finite being to frame for himself a determinate concept of what he really wills here. If he wills riches, how much anxiety, envy and intrigue might he not bring upon himself in his way! If he wills a great deal of cognition and insight, that might become only an eye all the more acute to show him, as all the more dreadful, ills that are now concealed from him and that cannot be avoided, or to burden his desires, which already give him enough to do, with still more needs. If he wills a long life, who will guarantee him that it would not be a long misery? If he at least wills health, how often has not bodily discomfort kept someone from excesses into which unlimited health would have let him fall, and so forth. In short, he is not capable of any principle by which to determine with complete certainty what would make him truly happy, because for this omniscience would be required. One cannot therefore act on determinate principles for the sake of being happy, but only on empirical counsels, for example, of a regimen, frugality, courtesy, reserve and so forth, which experience teaches are most conducive to well-being on the average. From this it follows that imperatives of prudence cannot, to speak precisely, command at all, that is, present actions objectively as practically *necessary*; that they are to be taken as counsels (*consilia*) rather than as commands (*praecepta*) of reason; that the problem of determining surely and universally which action would promote the happiness of a rational being is completely insoluble, so that there can be no imperative with respect to it that would, in the strict sense, command him to do what would make him happy....

When I think of a *hypothetical* imperative in general I do not know beforehand what it will contain; I do not know this until I am given the condition. But when I think of a *categorical* imperative I know at once what it contains. For, since the imperative contains, beyond the law, only the necessity that the maxim be in conformity with this law, while the law contains no condition to which it would be limited, nothing is left with which the maxim of action is to conform but the universality of a law as such; and this conformity alone is what the imperative properly represents as necessary.

There is, therefore, only a single categorical imperative and it is this: *act only in accordance with that maxim through which you can at the same time will that it become a universal law....*

We shall now enumerate a few duties in accordance with the usual division of them into duties to ourselves and to other human beings....

1) Someone feels sick of life because of a series of troubles that has grown to the point of despair, but is still so far in possession of his reason that he can ask himself whether it would not be contrary to his duty to himself to take his own life. Now he inquires whether the maxim of his action could indeed become a universal law of nature. His maxim, however, is: from self-love I make it my principle to shorten my life when its longer duration threatens more troubles than it promises agreeableness. The only further question is whether this principle of self-love could become a universal law of nature. It is

then seen at once that a nature whose law it would be to destroy life itself by means of the same feeling whose destination is to impel toward the furtherance of life would contradict itself and would therefore not subsist as nature; thus that maxim could not possibly be a law of nature and, accordingly, altogether opposes the supreme principle of all duty.

2) Another finds himself urged by need to borrow money. He well knows that he will not be able to repay it but sees also that nothing will be lent him unless he promises firmly to repay it within a determinate time. He would like to make such a promise, but he still has enough conscience to ask himself: is it not forbidden and contrary to duty to help oneself out of need in such a way? Supposing that he still decided to do so, his maxim of action would go as follows: when I believe myself to be in need of money I shall borrow money and promise to repay it, even though I know that this will never happen. Now this principle of self-love or personal advantage is perhaps quite consistent with my whole future welfare, but the question now is whether it is right. I therefore turn the demand of self-love into a universal law and put the question as follows: how would it be if my maxim became a universal law? I then see at once that it could never hold as a universal law of nature and be consistent with itself, but must necessarily contradict itself. For, the universality of a law that everyone, when he believes himself to be in need, could promise whatever he pleases with the intention of not keeping it would make the promise and the end one might have in it itself impossible, since no one would believe what was promised him but would laugh at all such expressions as vain pretenses.

3) A third finds in himself a talent that by means of some cultivation could make him a human being useful for all sorts of purposes. However, he finds himself in comfortable circumstances and prefers to give himself up to pleasure than to trouble himself with enlarging and improving his fortunate natural predispositions. But he still asks himself whether his maxim of neglecting his natural gifts, besides being consistent with his propensity to amusement, is also consistent with what one calls duty. He now sees that a nature could indeed always subsist with such a universal law, although (as with the South Sea Islanders) the human being should let his talents rust and be concerned with devoting his life merely to idleness, amusement, procreation—in a word, to enjoyment; only he cannot possibly will that this become a universal law or be put in us as such by means of natural instinct. For, as a rational being he necessarily wills that all the capacities in him be developed, since they serve him and are given to him for all sorts of possible purposes.

Yet a *fourth*, for whom things are going well while he sees that others (whom he could very well help) have to contend with great hardships, thinks: what is it to me? let each be as happy as heaven wills or as he can make himself; I shall take nothing from him nor even envy him; only I do not care to contribute anything to his welfare or to his assistance in need! Now, if such a way of thinking were to become a universal law the human race could admittedly very well subsist, no doubt even better than when everyone prates about sympathy and benevolence and even exerts himself to practice them occasionally, but on the other hand also cheats where he can, sells the right of human beings or otherwise infringes upon it. But although it is possible that a universal law of nature could very well subsist in accordance with such a maxim, it is still impossible to will that such a principle hold everywhere as a law of nature. For, a will that decided this would conflict with itself, since many cases could occur in which one would need the love and sympathy of others and in which, by such a law of nature arisen from his own will, he would rob himself of all hope of the assistance he wishes for himself.

These are a few of the many actual duties, or at least of what we take to be such, whose derivation from the one principle cited above is clear. We must *be able to will* that a maxim of our action become a universal law: this is the canon of moral appraisal of action in general. Some actions are so constituted that their maxim cannot even be *thought* without contradiction as a universal law of nature, far less could one *will* that it *should* become such. In the case of others that inner impossibility is indeed not to be found, but it is still impossible to *will* that their maxim be raised to the universality of a law of nature because such a will would contradict itself. . . .

Now I say that the human being and in general every rational being *exists* as an end in itself, *not merely as a means* to be used by this or that will at its discretion; instead he must in all his actions, whether directed to himself or also to other rational beings, always be regarded *at the same time as an end*. All objects of the inclinations have only a conditional worth; for, if there were not inclinations and the needs based on them, their object would be without worth. But the inclinations themselves, as sources of needs, are so far from having an absolute worth, so as to make one wish to have them, that it must instead be the universal wish of every rational being to be altogether free from them. Thus the worth of any object *to be acquired* by our action is always conditional. Beings the existence of which rests not on our will but on nature, if they are beings without reason, still have only a relative worth, as means, and are therefore called *things*, whereas rational beings are called *persons* because their nature already marks them out as an end in itself, that is, as something that may not be used merely as a means, and hence so far limits all choice (and is an object of respect). These, therefore, are not merely subjective ends, the existence of which as an effect of our action has a worth *for us*, but rather *objective ends*, that is, beings the existence of which is in itself an end, and indeed one such that no other end, to which they would serve *merely* as means, can be put in its place, since without it nothing of *absolute worth* would be found anywhere; but if all worth were conditional and therefore contingent, then no supreme practical principle for reason could be found anywhere.

If, then, there is to be a supreme practical principle and, with respect to the human will, a categorical imperative, it must be one such that, from the representation of what is necessarily an end for everyone because it is an *end in itself*, it constitutes an *objective* principle of the will and thus can serve as a universal practical law. The ground of this principle is: *rational nature exists as an end in itself*. The human being necessarily represents his own existence in this way; so far it is thus a *subjective* principle of human actions. But every other rational being also represents his existence in this way consequent on just the same rational ground that also holds for me; thus it is at the same time an *objective* principle from which, as a supreme practical ground, it must be possible to derive all laws of the will. The practical imperative will therefore be the following: *So act that you use humanity, whether in your own person or in the person of any other, always at the same time as an end, never merely as a means.* We shall see whether this can be carried out.

To keep to the preceding examples:

First, as regards the concept of necessary duty to oneself, someone who has suicide in mind will ask himself whether his action can be consistent with the idea of humanity *as an end in itself*. If he destroys himself in order to escape from a trying condition he makes use of a person *merely as a means* to maintain a tolerable condition up to the end of life. A human being, however, is not a thing and hence not something that can be used *merely* as a means, but must in all his actions always be regarded as an end in itself. I cannot, therefore, dispose of a human being in my own person by maiming, damaging or killing him. (I must here pass over a closer determination of this principle that would prevent any misinterpretation, e.g., as to having limbs amputated in order to preserve myself, or putting my life in danger in order to preserve my life, and so forth; that belongs to morals proper.)

Second, as regards necessary duty to others or duty owed them, he who has it in mind to make a false promise to others sees at once that he wants to make use of another human being *merely as a means*, without the other at the same time containing in himself the end. For, he whom I want to use for my purposes by such a promise cannot possibly agree to my way of behaving toward him, and so himself contain the end of this action. This conflict with the principle of other human beings is seen more distinctly if examples of assaults on the freedom and property of others are brought forward. For then it is obvious that he who transgresses the rights of human beings intends to make use of the person of others merely as means, without taking into consideration that, as rational beings, they are always to be valued at the same time as ends, that is, only as beings who must also be able to contain in themselves the end of the very same action.

Third, with respect to contingent (meritorious) duty to oneself, it is not enough that the action does not conflict with humanity in our person as an end in itself; it must also *harmonize with it*. Now there are in humanity predispositions to greater perfection, which belong to the end of nature with respect to humanity in our subject; to neglect these might admittedly be consistent with the *preservation* of humanity as an end in itself but not with the *furtherance* of this end.

Fourth, concerning meritorious duty to others, the natural end that all human beings have is their own happiness. Now, humanity might indeed subsist if no one contributed to the happiness of others but yet did not intentionally withdraw anything from it; but there is still only a negative and not a positive agreement with *humanity as an end in itself* unless everyone also tries, as far as he can, to further the ends of others. For, the ends of a subject who is an end in itself must as far as possible be also *my* ends, if that representation is to have its *full* effect in me.

CRITIQUE OF PURE REASON

IMMANUEL KANT

THE CANON OF PURE REASON

Section II: On the Ideal of the Highest Good . . .

I maintain . . . that everyone has cause to hope for happiness insofar as he has made himself worthy of it in his conduct, and hence to assume that the system of morality is linked inseparably . . . with the system of happiness.

[T]his connection may be hoped for only if a *supreme reason* that commands according to moral laws is also laid at the basis of nature, as nature's cause.

The idea of such an intelligence wherein the morally most perfect will . . . is the cause of all happiness in the world, insofar as this happiness is exactly proportionate to one's morality . . . I call *the ideal of the highest good*. . . . [T]he world of sense does not now offer us such a connection between happiness and morality . . .

Morality in itself amounts to a system; but happiness does not, except insofar as its distribution is exactly commensurate with morality. This, however, is possible only in the intelligible world under a wise originator and ruler. Reason finds itself compelled either to assume such a being, along with life in such a world, which we must regard as a future world; or to regard the moral laws as idle chimeras, because without this presupposition the necessary result that reason connects with these laws would have to vanish. This is, moreover, why everyone regards the moral laws as *commands*; this the moral laws could not be if they did not . . . carry with them *promises* and *threats*. But this again the moral laws cannot do unless they reside in a necessary being that, as the highest good, can alone make such a purposive unity possible. . . .

It is necessary that our entire way of life be subjected to moral maxims. But it is at the same time impossible for this to occur unless reason connects with moral law, which is a mere idea, an efficient cause that determines for all conduct conforming to this law an outcome, whether in this or in another life, that corresponds exactly to our highest purposes. Hence without a God and without a world that is invisible to us now but is hoped for, the splendid ideas of morality are indeed objects of approbation and admiration, but are not incentives for our resolve and for our carrying out these ideas. . . .

Happiness by itself is . . . far from being the complete good. For happiness is not approved by our reason (however much it may be wished for by our inclination) unless this happiness is united with worthiness to be happy, i.e., with morally good conduct. But morality by itself—and with it the mere *worthiness* to be happy—is also far from being the complete good. In order for this good to be completed, the person who in his conduct has not been unworthy of happiness must be able to hope that he will partake of it. . . . [T]he

From *Critique of Pure Reason*, translated by Werner S. Pluhar, Hackett Publishing Co., 1996. Used by permission of the publisher.

two components are linked essentially—although in such a way that it is the moral attitude, as condition, that first makes possible the sharing in happiness, and not, conversely, the prospect of happiness that first makes possible the moral attitude. For in the latter case the attitude would not be moral, and hence would also not be worthy of full happiness. . . .

[H]appiness, in exact balance with the morality of rational beings whereby these beings are worthy of happiness, alone amounts to the highest good of a world into which . . . we must definitely transfer ourselves. That world, to be sure, is only an intelligible one, for the world of sense does not promise to us, as arising from the nature of things, such systematic unity of purposes. Moreover, the reality of that intelligible world cannot be based on anything other than the presupposition of a highest original good.

ON THE VARIETY AND SUFFERING OF LIFE

ARTHUR SCHOPENHAUER

> Arthur Schopenhauer (1788–1860) was an influential German philosopher who maintained that the essence of the world is will, that individuals are embodiments of that will, that the world is without purpose, and that our lives of blind willing are doomed to misery. In his view, we live in the worst of all possible worlds, and all happiness is but an illusion.

Awakened to life out of the night of unconsciousness, the will finds itself an individual, in an endless and boundless world, among innumerable individuals, all striving, suffering, erring; and as if through a troubled dream it hurries back to its old unconsciousness. Yet till then its desires are limitless, its claims inexhaustible, and every satisfied desire gives rise to a new one. No possible satisfaction in the world could suffice to still its longings, set a goal to its infinite cravings, and fill the bottomless abyss of its heart. Then let one consider what as a rule are the satisfactions of any kind that a man obtains. For the most part, nothing more than the bare maintenance of this existence itself, extorted day by day with unceasing trouble and constant care in the conflict with want, and with death in prospect. Everything in life shows that earthly happiness is destined to be frustrated or recognized as an illusion. The grounds of this lie deep in the nature of things. Accordingly the life of most men is troubled and short. Those who are comparatively happy are so, for the most part, only apparently, or else, like men of long life, they are rare exceptions, a possibility of which there had to be,—as decoy-birds. Life presents itself as a continual

From *The World as Will and Idea*, translated by R. B. Haldane and J. Kemp, 1883.

deception in small things as in great. If it has promised, it does not keep its word, unless to show how little worth desiring were the things desired: thus we are deluded now by hope, now by what was hoped for. If it has given, it did so in order to take. The enchantment of distance shows us paradises which vanish like optical illusions when we have allowed ourselves to be mocked by them. Happiness accordingly always lies in the future, or else in the past, and the present may be compared to a small dark cloud which the wind drives over the sunny plain: before and behind it all is bright, only it itself always casts a shadow. The present is therefore always insufficient; but the future is uncertain, and the past irrevocable. Life with its hourly, daily, weekly, yearly, little, greater, and great misfortunes, with its deluded hopes and its accidents destroying all our calculations, bears so distinctly the impression of something with which we must become disgusted, that it is hard to conceive how one has been able to mistake this and allow oneself to be persuaded that life is there in order to be thankfully enjoyed, and that man exists in order to be happy. Rather that continual illusion and disillusion, and also the nature of life throughout, presents itself to us as intended and calculated to awaken the conviction that nothing at all is worth our striving, our efforts and struggles, that all good things are vanity, the world in all its ends bankrupt, and life a business which does not cover its expenses;—so that our will may turn away from it.

The way in which this vanity of all objects of the will makes itself known and comprehensible to the intellect which is rooted in the individual, is primarily *time*. It is the form by means of which that vanity of things appears as their perishableness; for on account of this all our pleasures and joys disappear in our hands, and we afterwards ask astonished where they have remained. That nothingness itself is therefore the only *objective* element in time, i.e., that which corresponds to it in the inner nature of things, thus that of which it is the expression. Just on this account time is the *a priori* necessary form of all our perceptions; in it everything must present itself, even we ourselves. Accordingly, first of all, our life is like a payment which one receives in nothing but copper pence, and yet must then give a discharge for: the copper pence are the days; the discharge is death. For at last time makes known the judgment of nature concerning the work of all the beings which appear in it, in that it destroys them:—

> And rightly so, for all that arises
> Is worthy only of being destroyed.
> Hence were it better that nothing arose.

Thus old age and death, to which every life necessarily hurries on, are the sentence of condemnation on the will to live, coming from the hands of nature itself, and which declares that this will is an effort which frustrates itself. "What thou hast wished," it says, "ends thus: desire something better." Hence the instruction which his life affords to every one consists, as a whole, in this, that the objects of his desires continually delude, waver, and fall, and accordingly bring more misery than joy, till at last the whole foundation upon which they all stand gives way, in that his life itself is destroyed and so he receives the last proof that all his striving and wishing was a perversity, a false path:—

Then old age and experience, hand in hand,
Lead him to death, and make him understand,
After a search so painful and so long,
That all his life he has been in the wrong.

We shall, however, enter into the details of the matter, for it is in these views that I have met with most contradiction. First of all, I have to confirm by the following remarks the proof given in the text of the negative nature of all satisfaction, thus of all pleasure and all happiness, in opposition to the positive nature of pain.

We feel pain, but not painlessness; we feel care, but not the absence of care; fear, but not security. We feel the wish as we feel hunger and thirst; but as soon as it has been fulfiled, it is like the mouthful that has been taken, which ceases to exist for our feeling the moment it is swallowed. Pleasures and joys we miss painfully whenever they are wanting; but pains, even when they cease after having long been present, are not directly missed, but at the most are intentionally thought of by means of reflection. For only pain and want can be felt positively, and therefore announce themselves; well-being, on the other hand, is merely negative. Therefore we do not become conscious of the three greatest blessings of life, health, youth, and freedom, so long as we possess them, but only after we have lost them; for they also are negations. We only observe that days of our life were happy after they have given place to unhappy ones. In proportion as pleasures increase, the susceptibility for them decreases: what is customary is no longer felt as a pleasure. Just in this way, however, is the susceptibility for suffering increased, for the loss of what we are accustomed to is painfully felt. Thus the measure of what is necessary increases through possession, and thereby the capacity for feeling pain. The hours pass the quicker the more agreeably they are spent, and the slower the more painfully they are spent; because pain, not pleasure, is the positive, the presence of which makes itself felt. In the same way we become conscious of time when we are bored, not when we are diverted. Both these cases prove that our existence is most happy when we perceive it least, from which it follows that it would be better not to have it. Great and lively joy can only be conceived as the consequence of great misery, which has preceded it; for nothing can be added to a state of permanent satisfaction but some amusement, or the satisfaction of vanity. Hence all poets are obliged to bring their heroes into anxious and painful situations, so that they may be able to free them from them. Dramas and Epics accordingly always describe only fighting, suffering, tormented men; and every romance is a rareeshow in which we observe the spasms and convulsions of the agonised human heart. . . .

Before so confidently affirming that life is a blessing worth desiring or giving thanks for, let one compare calmly the sum of the possible pleasures which a man can enjoy in his life with the sum of the possible sorrows which may come to him in his life. I believe the balance will not be hard to strike. At bottom, however, it is quite superfluous to dispute whether there is more good or evil in the world: for the mere existence of evil decides the matter. For the evil can never be annulled, and consequently can never be balanced by the good which may exist along with it or after it.

Mille piacer' non vagliono un tormento.—Petrarch
(A thousand pleasures are not worth one torment.)

For that a thousand had lived in happiness and pleasure would never do away with the anguish and death-agony of a single one; and just as little does my present well-being undo my past suffering. If, therefore, the evils in the world were a hundred times less than is the case, yet their mere existence would be sufficient to establish a truth which may be expressed in different ways, though always somewhat indirectly, the truth that we have not to rejoice but rather to mourn at the existence of the world;—that its non-existence would be preferable to its existence;—that it is something which at bottom ought not to be. . . .

But since now our state is rather something which had better not be, everything about us bears the trace of this,—just as in hell everything smells of sulphur—for everything is always imperfect and illusory, everything agreeable is displaced by something disagreeable, every enjoyment is only a half one, every pleasure introduces its own disturbance, every relief new difficulties, every aid of our daily and hourly need leaves us each moment in the lurch and denies its service, the step upon which we place our foot so often gives way under us, nay, misfortunes great and small are the element of our life; and, in a word, we are like Phineus, whose food was all tainted and made uneatable by the harpies. Two remedies for this are tried: first, prudence, foresight, cunning; it does not fully instruct us, is insufficient, and leads to defeat. Secondly, the stoical equanimity which seeks to arm us against all misfortunes by preparedness for everything and contempt of all: practically it becomes cynical renunciation, which prefers once for all to reject all means of relief and all alleviations—it reduces us to the position of dogs, like Diogenes in his tub. The truth is, we ought to be wretched, and we are so. The chief source of the serious evils which affect men is man himself. . . . Whoever keeps this last fact clearly in view beholds the world as a hell, which surpasses that of Dante in this respect, that one man must be the devil of another. For this, one is certainly more fitted than another; an arch-fiend, indeed, more fitted than all others, appearing in the form of a conqueror, who places several hundred thousand men opposite each other, and says to them: "To suffer and die is your destiny; now shoot each other with guns and cannons," and they do so.

In general, however, the conduct of men towards each other is characterised as a rule by injustice, extreme unfairness, hardness, nay, cruelty: an opposite course of conduct appears only as an exception. Upon this depends the necessity of the State and legislation, and upon none of your false pretences. But in all cases which do not lie within the reach of the law, that regardlessness of his like, peculiar to man, shows itself at once; a regardlessness which springs from his boundless egoism, and sometimes also from wickedness. How man deals with man is shown, for example, by black slavery, the final end of which is sugar and coffee. But we do not need to go so far: at the age of five years to enter a cotton-spinning or other factory, and from that time forth to sit there daily, first ten, then twelve, and ultimately fourteen hours, performing the same mechanical labour, is to purchase dearly the satisfaction of drawing breath. But this is the fate of millions, and that of millions more is analogous to it.

We others, however, can be made perfectly miserable by trifling misfortunes; perfectly happy, not by the world. Whatever one may say, the happiest moment of the happy man is the moment of his falling asleep, and the unhappiest moment of the unhappy that of his awaking. An indirect but certain proof of the fact that men feel themselves unhappy, and consequently are so, is also abundantly afforded by the fearful envy which dwells in us all, and which in all relations of life, on the occasion of any superiority, of whatever kind it may be, is excited, and cannot contain its poison. Because they feel themselves unhappy, men cannot endure the sight of one whom they imagine happy; he who for the moment feels himself happy would like to make all around him happy also. . . .

If life were in itself a blessing to be prized, and decidedly to be preferred to non-existence, the exit from it would not need to be guarded by such fearful sentinels as death and its terrors. But who would continue in life as it is if death were less terrible? And again, who could even endure the thought of death if life were a pleasure! But thus the former has still always this good, that it is the end of life, and we console ourselves with regard to the suffering of life with death, and with regard to death with the suffering of life. The truth is, that the two inseparably belong to each other, for together they constitute a deviation from the right path, to return to which is as difficult as it is desirable.

If the world were not something which, expressed *practically*, ought not to be, it would also not be *theoretically* a problem; but its existence would either require no explanation, inasmuch as it would be so entirely self-evident that wonder concerning it or a question about it could arise in no mind, or its end would present itself unmistakably. Instead of this, however, it is indeed an insoluble problem; for even the most perfect philosophy will yet always contain an unexplained element, like an insoluble deposit or the remainder which the irrational relation of two quantities always leaves over. Therefore if one ventures to raise the question why there is not rather nothing than this world, the world cannot be justified from itself, no ground, no final cause of its existence can be found in itself, it cannot be shown that it exists for its own sake, i.e., for its own advantage. In accordance with my teaching, this can certainly be explained from the fact that the principle of its existence is expressly one which is without ground, a blind will to live, which as thing in itself cannot be made subject to the principle of sufficient reason, which is merely the form of the phenomenon, and through which alone every why is justified. But this also agrees with the nature of the world, for only a blind will, no seeing will, could place itself in the position in which we behold ourselves. A seeing will would rather have soon made the calculation that the business did not cover the cost, for such a mighty effort and struggle with the straining of all the powers, under constant care, anxiety, and want, and with the inevitable destruction of every individual life, finds no compensation in the ephemeral existence itself, which is so obtained, and which passes into nothing in our hands. Hence, then, the explanation of the world from . . . a will accompanied by *knowledge*, necessarily demands optimism to excuse it, which accordingly is set up and maintained in spite of the loudly crying evidence of a whole world full of misery. Life is there given out to be a gift, while it is evident that every one would have declined such a gift if he could have seen it and tested it beforehand; just as Lessing admired the understanding of his son, who, because he had absolutely declined to enter life, had to be forcibly brought into it with the forceps, but was scarcely there when he hurried away from it again. On the other hand, it is then well said that life should be, from one end to the other, only a lesson; to which, however, any one might reply: "For this very reason I wish I had been left in the peace of the all-sufficient nothing, where I would have had no need of lessons or of anything else." If indeed it should now be added that he must one day give an account of every hour of his life, he would be more justified in himself demanding an account of why he had been transferred from that rest into such a questionable, dark, anxious, and painful situation. To this, then, we are led by false views. For human existence, far from bearing the character of a *gift*, has entirely the character of a *debt* that has been contracted. The calling in of this debt appears in the form of the pressing wants, tormenting desires, and endless misery established through this existence. As a rule, the whole life-time is devoted to the paying off of this debt; but this only meets the interest. The payment of the capital takes place through death. And when was this debt contracted? At the begetting. . . .

An outcry has been made about the melancholy and disconsolate nature of my philosophy; yet it lies merely in the fact that instead of inventing a future hell as the equivalent of sin, I show that where guilt lies in the world there is also already something akin to hell; but whoever is inclined to deny this can easily experience it.

And to this world, to this scene of tormented and agonised beings, who only continue to exist by devouring each other, in which, therefore, every raven-ous beast is the living grave of thousands of others, and its self-maintenance is a chain of painful deaths; and in which the capacity for feeling pain increases with knowledge, and therefore reaches its highest degree in man, a degree which is the higher the more intelligent the man is; to this world it has been sought to apply the system of optimism, and demonstrate to us that it is the best of all possible worlds. . . .

But indeed to the palpably sophistical proofs . . . that this is the best of all possible worlds, we may seriously and honestly oppose the proof that it is the worst of all possible worlds. For possible means, not what one may construct in imagination, but what can actually exist and continue. Now this world is so arranged as to be able to maintain itself with great difficulty; but if it were a little worse, it could no longer maintain itself. Consequently a worse world, since it could not continue to exist, is absolutely impossible: thus this world itself is the worst of all possible worlds. For not only if the planets were to run their heads together, but even if any one of the actually appearing perturba-tions of their course, instead of being gradually balanced by others, continued to increase, the world would soon reach its end. Astronomers know upon what accidental circumstances—principally the irrational relation to each other of the periods of revolution—this depends, and have carefully calculated that it will always go on well; consequently the world also can continue and go on. We will hope that . . . they have not miscalculated, and consequently that the mechanical perpetual motion realised in such a planetary system will not also, like the rest, ultimately come to a standstill. Again, under the firm crust of the planet dwell the powerful forces of nature which, as soon as some accident affords them free play, must necessarily destroy that crust, with everything living upon it, as has already taken place at least three times upon our planet, and will probably take place oftener still. The earthquake of Lisbon, the earthquake of Haiti, the destruction of Pompeii, are only small, playful hints of what is possible. A small alteration of the atmosphere, which cannot even be chemically proved, causes cholera, yellow fever, black death, &c., which carry off millions of men; a somewhat greater alteration would extinguish all life. A very moderate increase of heat would dry up all the rivers and springs. The brutes have received just barely so much in the way of organs and powers as enables them to procure with the greatest exertion sustenance for their own lives and food for their offspring; therefore if a brute loses a limb, or even the full use of one, it must generally perish. Even of the human race, powerful as are the weapons it possesses in understanding and reason, nine-tenths live in constant conflict with want, always balancing themselves with difficulty and effort upon the brink of destruction. Thus throughout, as for the continuance of the whole, so also for that of each individual being the conditions are barely and scantily given, but nothing over. The individual life is a ceaseless battle for existence itself; while at every step destruction threatens it. Just because this threat is so often fulfiled provision had to be made, by means of the enormous excess of the germs, that the destruction of the individuals should not involve that of the species, for which alone nature really cares. The world is therefore as bad as it possibly can be if it is to continue to be at all. Q. E. D. The fossils of the entirely different kinds of animal species which formerly inhabited the planet afford us, as a proof of our calculation, the records of worlds the continuance of which was no longer possible, and which consequently were somewhat worse than the worst of possible worlds.

Optimism is at bottom the unmerited self-praise of the real originator of the world, the will to live, which views itself complacently in its works; and accordingly it is not only a false, but also a pernicious doctrine. For it presents life to us as a desirable condition, and the happiness of man as the end of it. Starting from this, every one then believes that he has the most just claim to happiness and pleasure; and if, as is wont to happen, these do not fall to his lot, then he believes that he is wronged, nay, that he loses the end of his existence; while it is far more correct to regard work, privation, misery, and suffering, crowned by death, as the end of our life. . . .

If now, in conclusion, to confirm my view, I were to give what has been said by great men of all ages in this anti-optimistic spirit, there would be no end to the quotations, for almost every one of them has expressed in strong language his knowledge of the misery of this world. Thus, not to confirm, but merely to embellish this chapter, a few quotations of this kind may be given at the end of it.

First of all, let me mention here that the Greeks . . . were . . . deeply affected by the wretchedness of existence. This is shown even by the invention of tragedy, which belongs to them. Another proof of it is afforded us by the custom of the Thracians, which is first mentioned by Herodotus, though often referred to afterwards—the custom of welcoming the new-born child with lamentations, and recounting all the evils which now lie before it; and, on the other hand, burying the dead with mirth and jesting, because they are no longer exposed to so many and great sufferings. . . .

Shakspeare puts the words in the mouth of the old king Henry IV.:—

O heaven! that one might read the book of fate,
And see the revolution of the times,
   .   .   .   .   .   how chances mock,
And changes fill the cup of alteration
With divers liquors! O, if this were seen,
The happiest youth,—viewing his progress through,
What perils past, what crosses to ensue,—
Would shut the book, and sit him down and die.

Finally, Byron:—

Count o'er the joys thine hours have seen,
  Count o'er thy days from anguish free,
And know, whatever thou hast been,
  'Tis something better not to be.

UTILITARIANISM

John Stuart Mill

John Stuart Mill (1806–1873), the leading British philosopher of the nineteenth century, defended utilitarianism against critics. He stressed that pleasures differ qualitatively and that the higher pleasures, such as those of intellect, imagination, and moral sentiment, are the source of genuine happiness, while the lower pleasures offer mere contentment. As he put it, "It is better to be a human being dissatisfied than a fool satisfied; better to be Socrates dissatisfied than a fool satisfied."

CHAPTER II

What Utilitarianism Is

The creed which accepts as the foundation of morals "utility" or the "greatest happiness principle" holds that actions are right in proportion as they tend to promote happiness; wrong as they tend to produce the reverse of happiness. By happiness is intended pleasure and the absence of pain; by unhappiness, pain and the privation of pleasure. To give a clear view of the moral standard set up by the theory, much more requires to be said; in particular, what things

From *Utilitarianism* (1863).

it includes in the ideas of pain and pleasure, and to what extent this is left an open question. But these supplementary explanations do not affect the theory of life on which this theory of morality is grounded—namely, that pleasure and freedom from pain are the only things desirable as ends; and that all desirable things (which are as numerous in the utilitarian as in any other scheme) are desirable either for pleasure inherent in themselves or as means to the promotion of pleasure and the prevention of pain.

Now such a theory of life excites in many minds, and among them in some of the most estimable in feeling and purpose, inveterate dislike. To suppose that life has (as they express it) no higher end than pleasure—no better and nobler object of desire and pursuit—they designate as utterly mean and groveling, as a doctrine worthy only of swine, to whom the followers of Epicurus were, at a very early period, contemptuously likened; and modern holders of the doctrine are occasionally made the subject of equally polite comparisons by its German, French, and English assailants.

When thus attacked, the Epicureans have always answered that it is not they, but their accusers, who represent human nature in a degrading light, since the accusation supposes human beings to be capable of no pleasures except those of which swine are capable. If this supposition were true, the charge could not be gainsaid, but would then be no longer an imputation; for if the sources of pleasure were precisely the same to human beings and to swine, the rule of life which is good enough for the one would be good enough for the other. The comparison of the Epicurean life to that of beasts is felt as degrading, precisely because a beast's pleasures do not satisfy a human being's conceptions of happiness. Human beings have faculties more elevated than the animal appetites and, when once made conscious of them, do not regard anything as happiness which does not include their gratification. I do not indeed, consider the Epicureans to have been by any means faultless in drawing out their scheme of consequences from the utilitarian principle. To do this in any sufficient manner, many Stoic, as well as Christian, elements require to be included. But there is no known Epicurean theory of life which does not assign to the pleasures of the intellect, of the feelings and imagination, and of the moral sentiments a much higher value as pleasures than to those of mere sensation. It must be admitted, however, that utilitarian writers in general have placed the superiority of mental over bodily pleasures chiefly in the greater permanency, safety, uncostliness, etc., of the former—that is, in their circumstantial advantages rather than in their intrinsic nature. And on all these points utilitarians have fully proved their case; but they might have taken the other and, as it may be called, higher ground with entire consistency. It is quite compatible with the principle of utility to recognize the fact that some kinds of pleasures are more desirable and more valuable than others. It would be absurd that, while in estimating all other things quality is considered as well as quantity, the estimation of pleasure should be supposed to depend on quantity alone.

If I am asked what I mean by difference of quality in pleasures, or what makes one pleasure more valuable than another, merely as a pleasure, except its being greater in amount, there is but one possible answer. Of two pleasures, if there be one to which all or almost all who have experience of both give a decided preference, irrespective of any feeling of moral obligation to prefer it, that is the more desirable pleasure. If one of the two is, by those who are competently acquainted with both, placed so far above the other that they prefer it, even though knowing it to be attended with a greater amount of discontent, and would not resign it for any quantity of the other pleasure which their nature is capable of, we are justified in ascribing to the preferred enjoyment a superiority in quality so far outweighing quantity as to render it, in comparison, of small account.

Now it is an unquestionable fact that those who are equally acquainted with and equally capable of appreciating and enjoying both do give a most marked preference to the manner of existence which employs their higher faculties. Few human creatures would consent to be changed into any of the lower animals for a promise of the fullest allowance of a beast's pleasures; no intelligent human being would consent to be a fool, no instructed person would be an ignoramus, no person of feeling and conscience would be selfish and base, even though they should be persuaded that the fool, the dunce, or the rascal is better satisfied with his lot than they are with theirs. They would not resign what they possess more than he for the most complete satisfaction of all the desires which they have in common with him. If they ever fancy they would, it is only in cases of unhappiness so extreme that to escape from it they would exchange their lot for almost any other, however undesirable in their own eyes. A being of higher faculties requires more to make him happy, is capable probably of more acute suffering, and certainly accessible to it at more points, than one of an inferior type; but in spite of these liabilities, he can never really wish to sink into what he feels to be a lower grade of existence. We may give what explanation we please of this unwillingness; we may attribute it to pride, a name which is given indiscriminately to some of the most and to some of the least estimable feelings of which mankind are capable; we may refer it to the love of liberty and personal independence, an appeal to which was with the Stoics one of the most effective means for the inculcation of it; to the love of power or to the love of excitement, both of which do really enter into and contribute to it; but its most appropriate appellation is a sense of dignity, which all human beings possess in one form or other, and in some, though by no means in exact, proportion to their higher faculties, and which is so essential a part of the happiness of those in whom it is strong that nothing which conflicts with it could be otherwise than momentarily an object of desire to them. Whoever supposes that this preference takes place at a sacrifice of happiness—that the superior being, in anything like equal circumstances, is not happier than the inferior—confounds the two very different ideas of happiness and content. It is indisputable that the being whose capacities of enjoyment are low has the greatest chance of having them fully satisfied; and a highly endowed being will always feel that any happiness which he can look for, as the world is constituted, is imperfect. But he can learn to bear its imperfections, if they are at all bearable; and they will not make him envy the being who is indeed unconscious of the imperfections, but only because he feels not at all the good which those imperfections qualify. It is better to be a human being dissatisfied than a pig satisfied; better to be Socrates dissatisfied than a fool satisfied. And if the fool, or the pig, are of a different opinion, it is because they only know their own side of the question. The other party to the comparison knows both sides.

It may be objected that many who are capable of the higher pleasures occasionally, under the influence of temptation, postpone them to the lower. But this is quite compatible with a full appreciation of the intrinsic superiority of the higher. Men often, from infirmity of character, make their election for the nearer good, though they know it to be the less valuable; and this no less when the choice is between two bodily pleasures than when it is between bodily and mental. They pursue sensual indulgences to the injury of health, though perfectly aware that health is the greater good. It may be further objected that many who begin with youthful enthusiasm for everything noble, as they advance in years, sink into indolence and selfishness. But I do not believe that those who undergo this very common change voluntarily choose the lower description of pleasures in preference to the higher. I believe that, before they devote themselves exclusively to the one, they have already become incapable of the other. Capacity for the nobler feelings is in most natures a very tender plant, easily killed, not only by hostile influences, but by mere want of sustenance; and in the majority of young persons it speedily dies away if the occupations to which their position in life has devoted them, and the society into which it has thrown them, are not favorable to keeping that higher capacity in exercise. Men lose their high aspirations as they lose their intellectual tastes, because they have not time or opportunity for indulging them; and they addict themselves to inferior pleasures, not because they deliberately prefer them, but because they are either the only ones to which they have access or the only ones which they are any longer capable of enjoying. It may be questioned whether anyone who has remained equally susceptible to both classes of pleasures ever knowingly and calmly preferred the lower, though many, in all ages, have broken down in an ineffectual attempt to combine both.

From this verdict of the only competent judges, I apprehend there can be no appeal. On a question which is the best worth having of two pleasures, or which of two modes of existence is the most grateful to the feelings, apart from its moral attributes and from its consequences, the judgment of those who are qualified by knowledge of both, or, if they differ, that of the majority among them, must be admitted as final. And there needs be the less hesitation to accept this judgment respecting the quality of pleasures, since there is no other tribunal to be referred to even on the question of quantity. What means are there of determining which is the acutest of two pains, or the intensest of two pleasurable sensations, except the general suffrage of those who are familiar with both? Neither pains nor pleasures are homogeneous, and pain is always heterogeneous with pleasure. What is there to decide whether a particular pleasure is worth purchasing at the cost of a particular pain, except the feelings and judgment of the experienced? When, therefore, those feelings and judgment declare the pleasures derived from the higher faculties to be preferable *in kind*, apart from the question of intensity, to those of which the animal nature, disjoined from the higher faculties, is susceptible, they are entitled on this subject to the same regard.

I have dwelt on this point as being a necessary part of a perfectly just conception of utility or happiness considered as the directive rule of human conduct. But it is by no means an indispensable condition to the acceptance of the utilitarian standard; for that standard is not the agent's own greatest happiness, but the greatest amount of happiness altogether; and if it may possibly be doubted whether a noble character is always the happier for its nobleness, there can be no doubt that it makes other people happier, and that the world in general is immensely a gainer by it. Utilitarianism, therefore, could only attain its end by the general cultivation of nobleness of character, even if each individual were only benefited by the nobleness of others, and his own, so far as happiness is concerned, were a sheer deduction from the benefit. But the bare enunciation of such an absurdity as this last renders refutation superfluous.

According to the greatest happiness principle, as above explained, the ultimate end, with reference to and for the sake of which all other things are desirable—whether we are considering our own good or that of other people—is an existence exempt as far as possible from pain, and as rich as possible in enjoyments, both in point of quantity and quality; the test of quality and the rule for measuring it against quantity being the preference felt by those who, in their opportunities of experience, to which must be added their habits of self-consciousness and self-observation, are best furnished with the means of comparison. This, being according to the utilitarian opinion the end of human action, is necessarily also the standard of morality, which may accordingly be defined "the rules and precepts for human conduct," by the observance of which an existence such as has been described might be, to the greatest extent possible, secured to all mankind; and not to them only, but, so far as the nature of things admits to, to the whole sentient creation.

Against this doctrine, however, arises another class of objectors who say that happiness, in any form, cannot be the rational purpose of human life and action; because, in the first place, it is unattainable; and they contemptuously ask, What right hast thou to be happy?—a question which Mr. Carlyle clinches by the addition, What right, a short time ago, hadst thou even *to be?* Next they say that men can do *without* happiness; that all noble human beings have felt this, and could not have become noble but by learning the lesson of *Entsagen,* or renunciation; which lesson, thoroughly learned and submitted to, they affirm to be the beginning and necessary condition of all virtue.

The first of these objections would go to the root of the matter were it well founded; for if no happiness is to be had at all by human beings, the attainment of it cannot be the end of morality or of any rational conduct. Though, even in that case, something might still be said for the utilitarian theory, since utility includes not solely the pursuit of happiness, but the prevention or mitigation of unhappiness; and if the former aim be chimerical, there will be all the greater scope and more imperative need for the latter, so long at least as mankind think fit to live and do not take refuge in the simultaneous act of suicide recommended under certain conditions by Novalis. When, however, it is thus positively asserted to be impossible that human life should be happy, the assertion, if not something like a verbal quibble, is at least an exaggeration. If by happiness be meant a continuity of highly pleasurable excitement, it is evident enough that this is impossible. A state of exalted pleasure lasts only moments or in some cases, and with some intermissions, hours or days, and is the occasional brilliant flash of enjoyment, not its permanent and steady flame. Of this the philosophers who have taught that happiness is the end of life were as fully aware as those who taunt them. The happiness which they meant was not a life of rapture, but moments of such, in an existence made up of few and transitory pains, many and various pleasures, with a decided predominance of the active over the passive, and having as the foundation of the whole not to expect more from life than it is capable of bestowing. A life thus composed, to those who have been fortunate enough to obtain it, has always appeared worthy of the name of happiness. And such an existence is even now the lot of many during some considerable portion of their lives. The present wretched education and wretched social arrangements are the only real hindrance to its being attainable by almost all.

The objectors perhaps may doubt whether human beings, if taught to consider happiness as the end of life, would be satisfied with such a moderate share of it. But great numbers of mankind have been satisfied with much less. The main constituents of a satisfied life appear to be two, either of which by itself is often found sufficient for the purpose: tranquility and excitement. With much tranquility, many find that they can be content with very little pleasure; with much excitement, many can reconcile themselves to a considerable quantity of pain. There is assuredly no inherent impossibility of enabling even the mass of mankind to unite both, since the two are so far from being incompatible that they are in natural alliance, the prolongation of either being a preparation for, and exciting a wish for, the other. It is only those in whom indolence amounts to a vice that do not desire excitement after an interval of respose; it is only those in whom the need of excitement is a disease that feel the tranquility which follows excitement dull and insipid, instead of pleasurable in direct proportion to the excitement which preceded it. When people who are tolerably fortunate in their outward lot do not find in life sufficient enjoyment to make it valuable to them, the cause generally is caring for nobody but themselves. To those who have neither public nor private affections, the excitements of life are much curtailed, and in any case dwindle in value as the time approaches when all selfish interests must be terminated by death; while those who leave after them objects of personal affection, and especially those who have also cultivated a fellow-feeling with the collective interests of mankind, retain as lively an interest in life on the eve of death as in the vigor of youth and health. Next to selfishness, the principal cause which makes life unsatisfactory is want of mental cultivation. A cultivated mind—I do not mean that of a philosopher, but any mind to which the fountains of knowledge have been opened, and which has been taught, in any tolerable degree, to exercise its faculties—finds sources of inexhaustible interest in all that surrounds it: in the objects of nature, the achievements of art, the imaginations of poetry, the incidents of history, the ways of mankind, past and present, and their prospects in the future. It is possible, indeed, to become indifferent to all this, and that too without having exhausted a thousandth part of it, but only when one has had from the beginning no moral or human interest in these things and has sought in them only the gratification of curiosity.

Now there is absolutely no reason in the nature of things why an amount of mental culture sufficient to give an intelligent interest in these objects of contemplation should not be the inheritance of everyone born in a civilized country. As little is there an inherent necessity that any human being should be a selfish egotist, devoid of every feeling or care but those which center in his own miserable individuality. Something far superior to this is sufficiently common even now, to give ample earnest of what the human species may be made. Genuine private affections and a sincere interest in the public good are possible, though in unequal degrees, to every rightly brought up human being. In a world in which there is so much to interest, so much to enjoy, and so much also to correct and improve, everyone who has this moderate amount of moral and intellectual requisites is capable of an existence which may be called enviable; and unless such a person, through bad laws or subjection to the will of others, is denied the liberty to use the sources of happiness within his reach, he will not fail to find this enviable existence, if he escapes the positive evils of life, the great sources of physical and mental suffering—such as indigence, disease, and the unkindness, worthlessness, or premature loss of objects of affection. The main stress of the problem lies, therefore, in the contest with these calamities from which it is a rare good fortune entirely to escape; which, as things now are, cannot be obviated, and often cannot be in any material degree mitigated. Yet no one whose opinion deserves a moment's consideration can doubt that most of the great positive evils of the world are in themselves removable, and will, if human affairs continue to improve, be in the end reduced within narrow limits. Poverty, in any sense implying suffering, may be completely extinguished by the wisdom of society combined with the good sense and providence of individuals. Even that most intractable of enemies, disease, may be indefinitely reduced in dimensions by good physical and moral education and proper control of noxious influences, while the progress of science holds out a promise for the future of still more direct conquests over this detestable foe. And every advance in that direction relieves us from some, not only of the chances which cut short our own lives, but, what concerns us still more, which deprive us of those in whom our happiness is wrapt up. As for vicissitudes of fortune and other disappointments connected with wordly circumstances, these are principally the effect either of gross imprudence, of ill-regulated desires, or of bad or imperfect social institutions. All the grand sources, in short, of human suffering are in a great degree, many of them almost entirely, conquerable by human care and effort; and though their removal is grievously slow—though a long succession of generations will perish in the breach before the conquest is completed, and this world becomes all that, if will and knowledge were not wanting, it might easily be made—yet every mind sufficiently intelligent and generous to bear a part, however small and inconspicuous, in the endeavour will draw a noble enjoyment from the contest itself, which he would not for any bribe in the form of selfish indulgence consent to be without.

And this leads to the true estimation of what is said by the objectors concerning the possibility and the obligation of learning to do without happiness. Unquestionably it is possible to do without happiness; it is done involuntarily by nineteen-twentieths of mankind, even in those parts of our present world which are least deep in barbarism; and it often has to be done voluntarily by the hero or the martyr, for the sake of something which he prizes more than his individual happiness. But this something, what is it, unless the happiness of others or some of the requisites of happiness? It is noble to be capable of resigning entirely one's own portion of happiness, or chances of it; but, after all, this self-sacrifice must be for some end, it is not its own end; and if we are told that its end is not happiness but virtue, which is better than happiness, I ask, would the sacrifice be made if the hero or martyr did not believe that it would earn for others immunity from similar sacrifices? Would it be made if he thought that his renunciation of happiness for himself would produce no fruit for any of his fellow creatures, but to make their lot like his and place them also in the condition of persons who have renounced happiness? All honor to those who can abnegate for themselves the personal enjoyment of life when by such renunciation they contribute worthily to increase the amount of happiness in the world; but he who does it or professes to do it for any other purpose is no more deserving of admiration than the ascetic mounted on his pillar. He may be an inspiriting proof of what men *can* do, but assuredly not an example of what they *should*.

Though it is only in a very imperfect state of the world's arrangements that anyone can best serve the happiness of others by the absolute sacrifice of his own, yet, so long as the world is in that imperfect state, I fully acknowledge that the readiness to make such a sacrifice is the highest virtue which can be found in man. I will add that in this condition of the world, paradoxical as the assertion may be, the conscious ability to do without happiness gives the best prospect of realizing such happiness as is attainable. For nothing except that consciousness can raise a person above the chances of life by making him feel that, let fate and fortune do their worst, they have not power to subdue him; which, once felt, frees him from excess of anxiety concerning the evils of life and enables him, like many a Stoic in the worst times of the Roman Empire, to cultivate in tranquility the sources of satisfaction accessible to him, without concerning himself about the uncertainty of their duration any more than about their inevitable end.

Meanwhile, let utilitarians never cease to claim the morality of self-devotion as a possession which belongs by as good a right to them as either to the Stoic or to the Transcendentalist. The utilitarian morality does recognize in human beings the power of sacrificing their own greatest good for the good of others. It only refuses to admit that the sacrifice is itself a good. A sacrifice which does not increase or tend to increase the sum total of happiness, it considers as wasted. The only self-renunciation which it applauds is devotion to the happiness, or to some of the means of happiness, of others, either of mankind collectively or of individuals within the limits imposed by the collective interests of mankind.

I must again repeat what the assailants of utilitarianism seldom have the justice to acknowledge, that the happiness which forms the utilitarian standard of what is right in conduct is not the agent's own happiness but that of all concerned. As between his own happiness and that of others, utilitarianism requires him to be as strictly impartial as a disinterested and benevolent spectator. In the golden rule of Jesus of Nazareth, we read the complete spirit of the ethics of utility. "To do as you would be done by," and "to love your neighbor as yourself," constitute the ideal perfection of utilitarian morality. As the means of making the nearest approach to this ideal, utility would enjoin, first, that laws and social arrangements should place the happiness or (as, speaking practically, it may be called) the interest of every individual as nearly as possible in harmony with the interest of the whole; and, secondly, that education and opinion, which have so vast a power over human character, should so use that power as to establish in the mind of every individual an indissoluble association between his own happiness and the good of the whole, especially between his own happiness and the practice of such modes of conduct, negative and positive, as regard for the universal happiness prescribes; so that not only he may be unable to conceive the possibility of happiness to himself, consistently with conduct opposed to the general good, but also that a direct impulse to promote the general good may be in every individual one of the habitual motives of action, and the sentiments connected therewith may fill a large and prominent place in every human being's sentient existence. If the impugners of the utilitarian morality represented it to their own minds in this its true character, I know not what recommendation possessed by any other morality they could possibly affirm to be wanting to it; what more beautiful or more exalted developments of human nature any other ethical system can be supposed to foster, or what springs of action, not accessible to the utilitarian, such systems rely on for giving effect to their mandates.

The objectors to utilitarianism cannot always be charged with representing it in a discreditable light. On the contrary, those among them who entertain anything like a just idea of its disinterested character sometimes find fault with its standard as being too high for humanity. They say it is exacting too much to require that people shall always act from the inducement of promoting the general interests of society. But this is to mistake the very meaning of a standard of morals and confound the rule of action with the motive of it. It is the business of ethics to tell us what are our duties, or by what test we may know them; but no system of ethics requires that the sole motive of all we do shall be a feeling of duty; on the contrary, ninety-nine hundredths of all our actions are done from other motives, and rightly so done if the rule of duty does not condemn them. It is the more unjust to utilitarianism that this particular misapprehension should be made a ground of objection to it, inasmuch as utilitarian moralists have gone beyond almost all others in affirming that the motive has nothing to do with the morality of the action, though much with the worth of the agent. He who saves a fellow creature from drowning does what is morally right, whether his motive be duty or the hope of being paid for his trouble; he who betrays the friend that trusts him is guilty of a crime, even if his object be to serve another friend to whom he is under greater obligations. But to speak only of actions done from the motive of duty, and in direct obedience to principle: it is a misapprehension of the utilitarian mode of thought to conceive it as implying that people should fix their minds upon so wide a generality as the world, or society at large. The great majority of good actions are intended not for the benefit of the world, but for that of individuals, of which the good of the world is made up; and the thoughts of the most virtuous man need not on these occasions travel beyond the particular persons concerned, except so far as is necessary to assure himself that in benefiting them he is not violating the rights, that is, the legitimate and authorized expectations, of anyone else. The multiplication of happiness is, according to the utilitarian ethics, the object of virtue: the occasions on which any person (except one in a thousand) has it in his power to do this on an extended scale—in other words, to be a public benefactor—are but exceptional; and on these occasions alone is he called on to consider public utility; in every other case, private utility, the interest or happiness of some few persons, is all he has to attend to. Those alone the influence of whose actions extends to society in general need concern themselves habitually about so large an object. In the case of abstinences indeed—of things which people forbear to do from moral considerations, though the consequences in the particular case might be beneficial—it would be unworthy of an intelligent agent not to be consciously aware that the action is of a class which, if practiced generally, would be generally injurious, and that this is the ground of the obligation to abstain from it. The amount of regard for the public interest implied in this recognition is no greater than is demanded by every system of morals, for they all enjoin to abstain from whatever is manifestly pernicious to society.

The same considerations dispose of another reproach against the doctrine of utility, founded on a still grosser misconception of the purpose of a standard of morality and of the very meaning of the words "right and "wrong." It is often affirmed that utilitarianism renders men cold and unsympathizing; that it chills their moral feelings toward individuals; that it makes them regard only the dry and hard consideration of the consequences of actions, not taking into their moral estimate the qualities from which those actions emanate. If the assertion means that they do not allow their judgment respecting the rightness or wrongness of an action to be influenced by their opinion of the qualities of the person who does it, this is a complaint not against utilitarianism, but against any standard or morality at all; for certainly no known ethical standard decides an action to be good or bad because it is done by a good or bad man, still less because done by an amiable, a brave, or a benevolent man, or the contrary. These considerations are relevant, not to the estimation of actions, but of persons; and there is nothing in the utilitarian theory inconsistent with the fact that there are other things which interest us in persons besides the rightness and wrongness of their actions. The Stoics, indeed, with the paradoxical misuse of language which was part of their system, and by which they strove to raise themselves above all concern about anything but virtue, were fond of saying that he who has that has everything; that he, and only he, is rich, is beautiful, is a king. But no claim of this description is made for the virtuous man by the utilitarian doctrine. Utilitarians are quite aware that there are other desirable possessions and qualities besides virtue, and are perfectly willing to allow to all of them their full worth. They are also aware that a right action does not necessarily indicate a virtuous character, and that actions which are blamable often proceed from qualities entitled to praise. When this is apparent in any particular case, it modifies their estimation, not certainly of the act, but of the agent. I grant that they are, notwithstanding, of opinion that in the long run the best proof of a good character is good actions; and resolutely refuse to consider any mental disposition as good of which the predominant tendency is to produce bad conduct. This makes them unpopular with many people, but it is an unpopularity which they must share with everyone who regards the distinction between right and wrong in a serious light; and the reproach is not one which a conscientious utilitarian need be anxious to repel.

If no more be meant by the objection than that many utilitarians look on the morality of actions, as measured by the utilitarian standards, with too exclusive a regard, and do not lay sufficient stress upon the other beauties of character which go toward making a human being lovable or admirable, this may be admitted. Utilitarians who have cultivated their moral feelings, but not their sympathies, nor their artistic perceptions, do fall into this mistake; and so do all other moralists under the same conditions. What can be said in excuse for other moralists is equally available for them, namely, that, if there is to be any error, it is better that it should be on that side. As a matter of fact, we may affirm that among utilitarians, as among adherents of other systems, there is every imaginable degree of rigidity and of laxity in the application of their standard; some are even puritanically rigorous, while others are as indulgent as can possibly be desired by sinner or by sentimentalist. But on the whole, a doctrine which brings prominently forward the interest that mankind have in the repression and prevention of conduct which violates the moral law is likely to be inferior to no other in turning the sanctions of opinion against such violations. It is true, the question "What does violate the moral law?" is one on which those who recognize different standards of morality are likely now and then to differ. But difference of opinion on moral questions was not first introduced into the world by utilitarianism, while the doctrine does supply, if not always an easy, at all events a tangible and intelligible, mode of deciding such differences.

It may not be superfluous to notice a few more of the common misapprehensions of utilitarian ethics, even those which are so obvious and gross that it might appear impossible for any person of candor and intelligence to fall into them; since persons, even of considerable mental endowment, often give themselves so little trouble to understand the bearings of any opinion against which they entertain a prejudice, and men are in general so little conscious of this voluntary ignorance as a defect that the vulgarest misunderstandings of ethical doctrines are continually met with in the deliberate writings of persons of the greatest pretensions both to high principle and to philosophy. We not uncommonly hear the doctrine of utility inveighed against as a *godless* doctrine. If it be necessary to say anything at all against so mere an assumption, we may say that the question depends upon what idea we have formed of the moral character of the Deity. If it be a true belief that God desires, above all things, the happiness of his creatures, and that this was his purpose in their creation, utility is not only a godless doctrine, but more profoundly religious than any other. If it be meant that utilitarianism does not recognize the revealed will of God as the supreme law of morals, I answer that a utilitarian who believes in the perfect goodness and wisdom of *God* necessarily believes that whatever God has thought fit to reveal on the subject of morals must fulfill the requirements of utility in a supreme degree. But others besides utilitarians have been of opinion that the Christian revelation was intended, and is fitted, to inform the hearts and minds of mankind with a spirit which should enable them to find for themselves what is right, and incline them to do it when found, rather than to tell them, except in a very general way, what it is; and that we need a doctrine of ethics, carefully followed out, to *interpret* to us the will of God. Whether this opinion is correct or not, it is superfluous here to discuss; since whatever aid religion, either natural or revealed, can afford to ethical investigation is as open to the utilitarian moralist as to any other. He can use it as the testimony of God to the usefulness or hurtfulness of any given course of action by as good a right as others can use it for the indication of a transcendental law having no connection with usefulness or with happiness.

Again, utility is often summarily stigmatized as an immoral doctrine by giving it the name of "expediency," and taking advantage of the popular use of that term to contrast it with principle. But the expedient, in the sense in which it is opposed to the right, generally means that which is expedient for the particular interest of the agent himself; as when a minister sacrifices the interests of his country to keep himself in place. When it means anything better than this, it means that which is expedient for some immediate object, some temporary purpose, but which violates a rule whose observance is expedient in a much higher degree. The expedient, in this sense, instead of being the same thing with the useful, is a branch of the hurtful. Thus it would often be expedient, for the purpose of getting over some momentary embarrassment, or attaining some object immediately useful to ourselves or others, to tell a lie. But inasmuch as the cultivation in ourselves of a sensitive feeling on the subject of veracity is one of the most useful, and the enfeeblement of that feeling one of the most hurtful, things to which our conduct can be instrumental; and inasmuch as any, even unintentional, deviation from truth does that much toward weakening the trustworthiness of human assertion, which is not only the principal support of all present social well-being, but the insufficiency of which does more than any one thing that can be named to keep back civilization, virtue, everything on which human happiness on the largest scale depends—we feel that the violation, for a present advantage, of a rule of such transcendent expediency is not expedient, and that he who, for the sake of convenience to himself or to some other individual, does what depends on him to deprive mankind of the good, and inflict upon them the evil, involved in the greater or less reliance which they can place in each other's word, acts the part of one of their worst enemies. Yet that even this rule, sacred as it is, admits of possible exceptions is acknowledged by all moralists; the chief of which is when the withholding of some fact (as of information from a malefactor, or of bad news from a person dangerously ill) would save an individual (especially an individual other than oneself) from great and unmerited evil, and when the withholding can only be effected by denial. But in order that the exception may not extend itself beyond the need, and may have the least possible effect in weakening reliance on veracity, it ought to be recognized and, if possible, its limits defined; and, if the principle of utility is good for anything, it must be good for weighing these conflicting utilities against one another and marking out the region within which one or the other preponderates.

Again, defenders of utility often find themselves called upon to reply to such objections as this—that there is not time, previous to action, for calculating and weighing the effects of any line of conduct on the general happiness. This is exactly as if anyone were to say that it is impossible to guide our conduct by Christianity because there is not time, on every occasion on which anything has to be done, to read through the Old and New Testaments. The answer to the objection is that there has been ample time, namely, the whole past duration of the human species. During all that time mankind have been learning by experience the tendencies of actions; on which experience all the prudence as well as all the morality of life are dependent. People talk as if the commencement of this course of experience had hitherto been put off, and as if, at the moment when some man feels tempted to meddle with the property or life of another, he had to begin considering for the first time whether murder and theft are injurious to human happiness. Even then I do not think that he would find the question very puzzling; but, at all events, the matter is now done to his hand. It is truly a whimsical supposition that, if mankind were agreed in considering utility to be the test of morality, they would remain without any agreement as to what *is* useful, and would take no measures for having their notions on the subject taught to the young and enforced by law and opinion. There is no difficulty in proving any ethical standard whatever to work ill if we suppose universal idiocy to be conjoined with it; but on any hypothesis short of that, mankind must by this time have acquired positive beliefs as to the effects of some actions on their happiness; and the beliefs which have thus come down are the rules of morality for the multitude, and for the philosopher until he has succeeded in finding better. That philosophers might easily do this, even now, on many subjects; that the received code of ethics is by no means of divine right; and that mankind have still much to learn as to the effects of actions on the general happiness, I admit or rather earnestly maintain. The corollaries from the principle of utility, like the precepts of every practical art, admit of indefinite improvement, and, in a progressive state of the human mind, their improvement is perpetually going on. But to consider the rules of morality as improvable is one thing; to pass over the intermediate generalization entirely and endeavor to test each individual action directly by the first principle is another. It is a strange notion that the acknowledgment of a first principle is inconsistent with the admission of secondary ones. To inform a traveler respecting the place of his ultimate destination is not to forbid the use of landmarks and direction-posts on the way. The proposition that happiness is the end and aim of morality does not mean that no road ought to be laid down to that goal, or that persons going thither should not be advised to take one direction rather than another. Men really ought to leave off talking a kind of nonsense on this subject, which they would neither talk nor listen to on other matters of practical concernment. Nobody argues that the art of navigation is not founded on astronomy because sailors cannot wait to calculate the Nautical Almanac. Being rational creatures, they go to sea with it ready calculated; and all rational creatures go out upon the sea of life with their minds made up on the common questions of right and wrong, as well as on many of the far more difficult questions of wise and foolish. And this, as long as foresight is a human quality, it is to be presumed they will continue to do. Whatever we adopt as the fundamental principle of morality, we require subordinate principles to apply it by; the impossibility of doing without them, being common to all systems, can afford no argument against any one in particular; but gravely to argue as if no such secondary principles could be had, and as if mankind had remained till now, and always must remain, without drawing any general conclusions from the experience of human life is as high a pitch, I think, as absurdity has ever reached in philosophical controversy. . . .

CHAPTER III

Of the Ultimate Sanction of the Principle of Utility

The question is often asked, and properly so, in regard to any supposed moral standard—What is its sanction? what are the motives to obey? or, more specifically, what is the source of its obligation? whence does it derive its binding force? It is a necessary part of moral philosophy to provide the answer to this question, which, though frequently assuming the shape of an objection to the utilitarian morality, as if it had some special applicability to that above others, really arises in regard to all standards. It arises, in fact, whenever a person is called on to *adopt* a standard, or refer morality to any basis on which he has not been accustomed to rest it. For the customary morality, that which education and opinion have consecrated, is the only one which presents itself to the mind with the feeling of being *in itself* obligatory; and when a person is asked to believe that this morality *derives* its obligation from some general principle round which custom has not thrown the same halo, the assertion is to him a paradox; the supposed corollaries seem to have a more binding force than the original theorem; the superstructure seems to stand better without than with what is represented as its foundation. He says to himself, I feel that I am bound not to rob or murder, betray or deceive; but why am I bound to promote the general happiness? If my own happiness lies in something else, why may I not give that the preference?

If the view adopted by the utilitarian philosophy of the nature of the moral sense be correct, this difficulty will always present itself until the influences which form moral character have taken the same hold of the principle which they have taken of some of the consequences—until, by the improvement of education, the feeling of unity with our fellow creatures shall be (what it cannot be denied that Christ intended it to be) as deeply rooted in our character, and to our own consciousness as completely a part of our nature, as the horror of crime is in an ordinarily well-brought up young person. In the meantime, however, the difficulty has no peculiar application to the doctrine of utility, but is inherent in every attempt to analyze morality and reduce it to principles; which, unless the principle is already in men's minds invested with as much sacredness as any of its applications, always seems to divest them of a part of their sanctity.

The principle of utility either has, or there is no reason why it might not have, all the sanctions which belong to any other system of morals. Those sanctions are either external or internal. Of the external sanctions it is not necessary to speak at any length. They are the hope of favor and the fear of displeasure from our fellow creatures or from the Ruler of the universe, along with whatever we may have of sympathy or affection for them, or of love and awe of Him, inclining us to do His will independently of selfish consequences. There is evidently no reason why all these motives for observance should not attach themselves to the utilitarian morality as completely and as powerfully as to any other. Indeed, those of them which refer to our fellow creatures are sure to do so, in proportion to the amount of general intelligence; for whether there be any other ground of moral obligation than the general happiness or not, men do desire happiness; and however imperfect may be their own practice, they desire and commend all conduct in others toward themselves by which they think their happiness is promoted. With regard to the religious motive, if men believe, as most profess to do, in the goodness of God, those who think that conduciveness to the general happiness is the essence or even only the criterion of good must necessarily believe that it is also that which God approves. The whole force therefore of external reward and punishment, whether physical or moral, and whether proceeding from God or from our fellow men, together with all that the capacities of human nature admit of disinterested devotion to either, become available to enforce the utilitarian morality, in proportion as that morality is recognized; and the more power-fully, the more the appliances of education and general cultivation are bent to the purpose.

So far as to external sanctions. The internal sanction of duty, whatever our standard of duty may be, is one and the same—a feeling in our own mind; a pain, more or less intense, attendant on violation of duty, which in properly cultivated moral natures rises, in the more serious cases, into shrinking from it as an impossibility. This feeling, when disinterested and connecting itself with the pure idea of duty, and not with some particular form of it, or with any of the merely accessory circumstances, is the essence of conscience; though in that complex phenomenon as it actually exists, the simple fact is in general all encrusted over with collateral associations derived from sympathy, from love, and still more from fear; from all the forms of religious feeling; from the recollections of childhood and of all our past life; from self-esteem, desire of the esteem of others, and occasionally even self-abasement. This extreme com-plication is, I apprehend, the origin of the sort of mystical character which, by a tendency of the human mind of which there are many other examples, is apt to be attributed to the idea of moral obligation, and which leads people to believe that the idea cannot possibly attach itself to any other objects than those which, by a supposed mysterious law, are found in our present experience to excite it. Its binding force, however, consists in the existence of a mass of feel-ing which must be broken through in order to do what violates our standard of right, and which, if we do nevertheless violate that standard, will probably have to be encountered afterwards in the form of remorse. Whatever theory we have of the nature or origin of conscience, this is what essentially consti-tutes it.

The ultimate sanction, therefore, of all morality (external motives apart) being a subjective feeling in our own minds, I see nothing embarrassing to those whose standard is utility in the question, What is the sanction of that particular standard? We may answer, the same as of all other moral standards —the conscientious feelings of mankind. Undoubtedly this sanction has no binding efficacy on those who do not possess the feelings it appeals to; but neither will these persons be more obedient to any other moral principle than to the utilitarian one. On them morality of any kind has no hold but through the external sanctions. Meanwhile the feelings exist, a fact in human nature, the reality of which, and the great power with which they are capable of acting on those in whom they have been duly cultivated, are proved by experience. No reason has ever been shown why they may not be cultivated to as great inten-sity in connection with the utilitarian as with any other rule of morals.

There is, I am aware, a disposition to believe that a person who sees in moral obligation a transcendental fact, an objective reality belonging to the province of "things in themselves," is likely to be more obedient to it than one who believes it to be entirely subjective, having its seat in human consciousness only. But whatever a person's opinion may be on this point of ontology, the force he is really urged by is his own subjective feeling, and is exactly measured by its strength. No one's belief that duty is an objective reality is stronger than the belief that God is so; yet the belief in God, apart from the expectation of actual reward and punishment, only operates on conduct through, and in proportion to, the subjective religious feeling. The sanction, so far as it is disinterested, is always in the mind itself; and the motion, therefore, of the transcendental moralists must be that this sanction will not exist *in* the mind unless it is believed to have its root out of the mind; and that if a person is able to say to himself, "That which is restraining me and which is called my conscience is only a feeling in my own mind," he may possibly draw the conclusion that when the feeling ceases the obligation ceases, and that if he find the feeling inconvenient, he may disregard it and endeavor to get rid of it. But is this danger confined to the utilitarian morality? Does the belief that moral obligation has its seat outside the mind make the feeling of it too strong to get rid of? The fact is so far otherwise that all moralists admit and lament the ease with which, in the generality of minds, conscience can be silenced or stifled. The question, "Need I obey my conscience?" is quite as often put to themselves by persons who never heard of the principle of utility as by its adherents. Those whose conscientious feelings are so weak as to allow of their asking this question, if they answer it affirmatively, will not do so because they believe in the transcendental theory, but because of the external sanctions.

It is not necessary, for the present purpose, to decide whether the feeling of duty is innate or implanted. Assuming it to be innate, it is an open question to what objects it naturally attaches itself; for the philosophic supporters of that theory are now agreed that the intuitive perception is of principles of morality and not of the details. If there be anything innate in the matter, I see no reason why the feeling which is innate should not be that of regard to the pleasures and pains of others. If there is any principle of morals which is intuitively obligatory, I should say it must be that. If so, the intuitive ethics would coincide with the utilitarian, and there would be no further quarrel between them. Even as it is, the intuitive moralists, though they believe that there are other intuitive moral obligations, do already believe this to be one; for they unanimously hold that a large *portion* of morality turns upon the consideration due to the interests of our fellow creatures. Therefore, if the belief in the transcendental origin of moral obligation gives any additional efficacy to the internal sanction, it appears to me that the utilitarian principle has already the benefit of it.

On the other hand, if, as is my own belief, the moral feelings are not innate but acquired, they are not for that reason the less natural. It is natural to man to speak, to reason, to build cities, to cultivate the ground, though these are acquired faculties. The moral feelings are not indeed a part of our nature in the sense of being in any perceptible degree present in all of us; but this, unhappily, is a fact admitted by those who believe the most strenuously in their transcendental origin. Like the other acquired capacities above referred to, the moral faculty, if not a part of our nature, is a natural outgrowth from it;

capable, like them, in a certain small degree, of springing up spontaneously; and susceptible of being brought by cultivation to a high degree of development. Unhappily it is also susceptible, by a sufficient use of the external sanctions and of the force of early impressions, of being cultivated in almost any direction, so that there is hardly anything so absurd or so mischievous that it may not, by means of these influences, be made to act on the human mind with all the authority of conscience. To doubt that the same potency might be given by the same means to the principle of utility, even if it had no foundation in human nature, would be flying in the face of all experience.

But moral associations which are wholly of artificial creation, when the intellectual culture goes on, yield by degrees to the dissolving force of analysis; and if the feeling of duty, when associated with utility, would appear equally arbitrary; if there were no leading department of our nature, no powerful class of sentiments, with which that association would harmonize, which would make us feel congenial and incline us not only to foster it in ourselves—if there were not, in short, a natural basis of sentiments for utilitarian morality, it might well happen that this association also, even after it had been implanted by education, might be analyzed away.

But there *is* this basis of powerful natural sentiment; and that it is which, when once the general happiness is recognized as the ethical standard, will constitute the strength of the utilitarian morality. This firm foundation is that of the social feelings of mankind—the desire to be in unity with our fellow creatures, which is already a powerful principle in human nature, and happily one of those which tend to become stronger, even without express inculcation, from the influences of advancing civilization. The social state is at once so natural, so necessary, and so habitual to man, that, except in some unusual circumstances or by an effort of voluntary abstraction, he never conceives himself otherwise than as a member of a body; and this association is riveted more and more, as mankind are further removed from the state of savage independence. Any condition, therefore, which is essential to a state of society becomes more and more an inseparable part of every person's conception of the state of things which he is born into, and which is the destiny of a human being. Now society between human beings, except in the relation of master and slave, is manifestly impossible on any other footing than that of the interests of all are to be consulted. Society between equals can only exist on the understanding that the interests of all are to be regarded equally. And since in all states of civilization, every person, except an absolute monarch, has equals, everyone is obliged to live on these terms with somebody; and in every age some advance is made toward a state in which it will be impossible to live permanently on other terms with anybody. In this way people grow up unable to conceive as possible to them a state of total disregard of other people's interests. They are under a necessity of conceiving themselves as at least abstaining from all the grosser injuries, and (if only for their own protection) living in a state of constant protest against them. They are also familiar with the fact of co-operating with others and proposing to themselves a collective, not an individual, interest as the aim (at least for the time being) of their actions. So long as they are co-operating, their ends are identified with those of others; there is at least a temporary feeling that the interests of others are their own interests. Not only does all strengthening of social ties, and all healthy growth of society, give to each individual a stronger personal interest in practically consulting the welfare of others, it also leads him to identify his *feelings* more and more with their good, or at least with an even greater degree of practical consideration for it. He comes, as though instinctively, to be conscious of himself as a being who *of course* pays regard to others. The good of others becomes to him a thing naturally and necessarily to be attended to, like any of the physical conditions of our existence. Now, whatever amount of this feeling a person has, he is urged by the strongest motives both of interest and of sympathy to demonstrate it, and to the utmost of his power encourage it in others; and even if he has none of it himself, he is as greatly interested as anyone else that others should have it. Consequently, the smaller germs of the feeling are laid hold of and nourished by the contagion of sympathy and the influences of education; and a complete web of corroborative association is woven round it by the powerful agency of the external sanctions. This mode of conceiving ourselves and human life, as civilization goes on, is felt to be more and more natural. Every step in political improvement renders it more so, by removing the sources of opposition of interest and leveling those inequalities of legal privilege between individuals or classes, owing to which there are large portions of mankind whose happiness it is still practicable to disregard. In an improving state of the human mind, the influences are constantly on the increase which tend to generate in each individual a feeling of unity with all the rest; which, if perfect, would make him never think of, or desire, any beneficial condition for himself in the benefits of which they are not included. If we now suppose this feeling of unity to be taught as a religion, and the whole force of education, of institutions, and of opinion directed, as it once was in the case of religion, to make every person grow up from infancy surrounded on all sides both by the profession and the practice of it, I think that no one who can realize this conception will feel any misgiving about the sufficiency of the ultimate sanction for the happiness morality. To any ethical student who finds the realization difficult, I recommend, as a means of facilitating it, the second of M. Comte's two principal works, the *Traité de politique positive.* I entertain the strongest objections to the system of politics and morals set forth in that treatise, but I think it has superabundantly shown the possibility of giving to the service of humanity, even without the aid of belief in a Providence, both the psychological power and the social efficacy of a religion, making it take hold of human life, and color all thought, feeling, and action in a manner of which the greatest ascendancy ever exercised by any religion may be but a type and foretaste; and of which the danger is, not that it should be insufficient, but that it should be so excessive as to interfere unduly with human freedom and individuality.

Neither is it necessary to the feeling which constitutes the binding force of the utilitarian morality on those who recognize it to wait for those social influences which would make its obligation felt by mankind at large. In the comparatively early state of human advancement in which we now live, a person cannot, indeed, feel that entireness of sympathy with all others which would make any real discordance in the general direction of their conduct in life impossible, but already a person in whom the social feeling is at all developed cannot bring himself to think of the rest of his fellow creatures as struggling rivals with him for the means of happiness, whom he must desire to see defeated in their object in order that he may succeed in his. The deeply rooted conception which every individual even now has of himself as a social being tends to make him feel it one of his natural wants that there should be harmony between his feelings and aims and those of his fellow creatures. If differences of opinion and of mental culture make it impossible for him to share many of their actual feelings—perhaps make him denounce and defy those feelings—he still needs to be conscious that his real aim and theirs do not conflict; that he is not opposing himself to what they really wish for, namely, their own good, but is, on the contrary, promoting it. This feeling in most individuals is much inferior in strength to their selfish feelings, and is often wanting altogether. But to those who have it, it possesses all the characters of a natural feeling. It does not present itself to their minds as a superstition of education or a law despotically imposed by the power of society, but as an attribute which it would not be well for them to be without. This conviction is the ultimate sanction of the greatest happiness morality. This it is which makes any mind of well-developed feelings work with, and not against, the outward motives to care for others, afforded by what I have called the external sanctions; and, when those sanctions are wanting or act in an opposite direction, constitutes in itself a powerful internal binding force, in proportion to the sensitiveness and thoughtfulness of the character, since few but those whose mind is a moral blank could bear to lay out their course of life on the plan of paying no regard to others except so far as their own private interest compels.

CHAPTER IV

Of What Sort of Proof the Principle of Utility Is Susceptible

. . . [Q]uestions of ultimate ends do not admit of proof, in the ordinary acceptation of the term. To be incapable of proof by reasoning is common to all first principles, to the first premises of our knowledge, as well as to those of our conduct. But the former, being matters of fact, may be the subject of a direct appeal to the faculties which judge of fact—namely, our senses and our internal consciousness. Can an appeal be made to the same faculties on questions of practical ends? Or by what other faculty is cognizance taken of them?

Questions about ends are, in other words, questions what things are desirable. The utilitarian doctrine is that happiness is desirable, and the only thing desirable, as an end; all other things being only desirable as means to that end. What ought to be required of this doctrine, what conditions is it requisite that the doctrine should fulfill—to make good its claim to be believed?

The only proof capable of being given that an object is visible is that people actually see it. The only proof that a sound is audible is that people hear it; and so of the other sources of our experience. In like manner, I apprehend, the sole evidence it is possible to produce that anything is desirable is that people do actually desire it. If the end which the utilitarian doctrine proposes to itself were not, in theory and in practice, acknowledged to be an end, nothing could ever convince any person that it was so. No reason can be given why the general happiness is desirable, except that each person, so far as he believes it to be attainable, desires his own happiness. This, however, being a fact, we have not only all the proof which the case admits of, but all which it is possible to require, that happiness is a good, that each person's happiness is a good to that person, and the general happiness, therefore, a good to the aggregate of all persons. Happiness has made out its title as *one* of the ends of conduct and, consequently, one of the criteria of morality.

But it has not, by this alone, proved itself to be the sole criterion. To do that, it would seem, by the same rule, necessary to show, not only that people desire happiness, but that they never desire anything else. Now it is palpable that they do desire things which, in common language, are decidedly distinguished from happiness. They desire, for example, virtue and the absence of vice no less really than pleasure and the absence of pain. The desire of virtue is not as universal, but it is as authentic a fact as the desire of happiness. And hence the opponents of the utilitarian standard deem that they have a right to infer that there are other ends of human action besides happiness, and that happiness is not the standard of approbation and disapprobation.

But does the utilitarian doctrine deny that people desire virtue, or maintain that virtue is not a thing to be desired? The very reverse. It maintains not only that virtue is to be desired, but that it is to be desired disinterestedly, for itself. Whatever may be the opinion of utilitarian moralists as to the original conditions by which virtue is made virtue, however they may believe (as they do) that actions and dispositions are only virtuous because they promote another end than virtue, yet this being granted, and it having been decided, from considerations of this description, what *is* virtuous, they not only place virtue at the very head of the things which are good as means to the ultimate end, but they also recognize as a psychological fact the possibility of its being, to the individual, a good in itself, without looking to any end beyond it; and hold that the mind is not in a right state, not in a state conformable to utility, not in the state most conducive to the general happiness, unless it does love virtue in this manner—as a thing desirable in itself, even although, in the individual instance, it should not produce those other desirable consequences which it tends to produce, and on account of which it is held to be virtue. This opinion is not, in the smallest degree, a departure from the happiness principle. The ingredients of happiness are very various, and each of them is desirable in itself, and not merely when considered as swelling an aggregate. The principle of utility does not mean that any given pleasure, as music, for instance, or any given exemption from pain, as for example health, is to be looked upon as means to a collective something termed happiness, and to be desired on that account. They are desired and desirable in and for themselves; besides being means, they are a part of the end. Virtue, according to the utilitarian doctrine, is not naturally and originally part of the end, but it is capable of becoming so; and in those who live it disinterestedly it has become so, and is desired and cherished, not as a means to happiness, but as a part of their happiness.

To illustrate this further, we may remember that virtue is not the only thing originally a means, and which if it were not a means to anything else would be and remain indifferent, but which by association with what it is a means to comes to be desired for itself, and that too with the utmost intensity. What, for example, shall we say of the love of money? There is nothing originally more desirable about money than about any heap of glittering pebbles. Its worth is solely that of the things which it will buy; the desires for other things than itself, which it is a means of gratifying. Yet the love of money is not only one of the strongest moving forces of human life, but money is, in many cases, desired in and for itself; the desire to possess it is often stronger than the desire to use it, and goes on increasing when all the desires which point to ends beyond it, to be compassed by it, are falling off. It may, then, be said truly that money is desired not for the sake of an end, but as part of the end. From being a means to happiness, it has come to be itself a principal ingredient of the individual's conception of happiness. The same may be said of the majority of the great objects of human life: power, for example, or fame, except that to each of these there is a certain amount of immediate pleasure annexed, which has at least the semblance of being naturally inherent in them—a thing which cannot be said of money. Still, however, the strongest natural attraction, both of power and of fame, is the immense aid they give to the attainment of our other wishes; and it is the strong association thus generated between them and all our objects of desire which gives to the direct desire of them the intensity it often assumes, so as in some characters to surpass in strength all other desires. In these cases the means have become a part of the end, and a more important part of it than any of the things which they are means to. What was once desired as an instrument for the attainment of happiness has come to be desired for its own sake. In being desired for its own sake it is, however, desired as *part* of happiness. The person is made, or thinks he would be made, happy by its mere possession; and is made unhappy by failure to obtain it. The desire of it is not a different thing from the desire of happiness any more than the love of music or the desire of health. They are included in happiness. They are some of the elements of which the desire of happiness is made up. Happiness is not an abstract idea but a concrete whole; and these are some of its parts. And the utilitarian standard sanctions and approves their being so. Life would be a poor thing, very ill provided with sources of happiness, if there were not this provision of nature by which things originally indifferent, but conducive to, or otherwise associated with, the satisfaction of our primitive desires, become in themselves sources of pleasure more valuable than the primitive pleasures, both in permanency, in the space of human existence that they are capable of covering, and even in intensity.

Virtue, according to the utilitarian conception, is a good of this description. There was no original desire of it, or motive to it, save its conduciveness to pleasure, and especially to protection from pain. But through the association thus formed it may be felt a good in itself, and desired as such with as great intensity as any other good; and with this difference between it and the love of money, of power, or of fame—that all of these may, and often do, render the individual noxious to the other members of the society to which he belongs, whereas there is nothing which makes him so much a blessing to them as the cultivation of the disinterested love of virtue. And consequently, the utilitarian standard, while it tolerates and approves those other acquired desires, up to the point beyond which they would be more injurious to the general happiness than promotive of it, enjoins and requires the cultivation of the love of virtue up to the greatest strength possible, as being above all things important to the general happiness.

It results from the preceding considerations that there is in reality nothing desired except happiness. Whatever is desired otherwise than as a means to some end beyond itself, and ultimately to happiness, is desired as itself a part of happiness, and is not desired for itself until it has become so. Those who desire virtue for its own sake desire it either because the consciousness of it is a pleasure, or because the consciousness of being without it is a pain, or for both reasons united; as in truth the pleasure and pain seldom exist separately, but almost always together—the same person feeling pleasure in the degree of virtue attained, and pain in not having attained more. If one of these gave him no pleasure, and the other no pain, he would not love or desire virtue, or would desire it only for the other benefits which it might produce to himself or to persons whom he cared for.

We have now, then, an answer to the question, of what sort of proof the principle of utility is susceptible. If the opinion which I have now stated is psychologically true—if human nature is so constituted as to desire nothing which is not either a part of happiness or a means of happiness—we can have no other proof, and we require no other, that these are the only things desirable. If so, happiness is the sole end of human action, and the promotion of it the test by which to judge of all human conduct; from whence it necessarily follows that it must be the criterion of morality, since a part is included in the whole.

And now to decide whether this is really so, whether mankind do desire nothing for itself but that which is a pleasure to them, or of which the absence is a pain, we have evidently arrived at a question of fact and experience, dependent, like all similar questions, upon evidence. It can only be determined by practiced self-consciousness and self-observation, assisted by observation of others. I believe that these sources of evidence, impartially consulted, will declare that desiring a thing and finding it pleasant, aversion to it and thinking of it as painful, are phenomena entirely inseparable or, rather, two parts of the same phenomenon—in strictness of language, two different modes of naming the same psychological fact; that to think of an object as desirable (unless for the sake of its consequences) and to think of it as pleasant are one and the same thing; and that to desire anything except in proportion as the idea of it is pleasant is a physical and metaphysical impossibility.

So obvious does this appear to me that I expect it will hardly be disputed; and the objection made will be, not that desire can possibly be directed to anything ultimately except pleasure and exemption from pain, but that the will is a different thing from desire; that a person of confirmed virtue or any other person whose purposes are fixed carries out his purposes without any thought of the pleasure he has in contemplating them or expects to derive from their fulfillment, and persists in acting on them, even though these pleasures are much diminished by changes in his character or decay of his passive sensibilities, or are outweighed by the pains which the pursuit of the purposes may bring upon him. All this I fully admit and have stated it elsewhere as positively and emphatically as anyone. Will, the active phenomenon, is a different thing from desire, the state of passive sensibility, and, though originally an offshoot from it, may in time take root and detach itself from the parent stock, so much so that in the case of a habitual purpose, instead of willing the thing because we desire it, we often desire it only because we will it. This, however, is but an instance of that familiar fact, the power of habit, and is nowise confined to the case of virtuous actions. Many indifferent things which men originally did from a motive of some sort they continue to do from habit. Sometimes this is done unconsciously, the consciousness coming only after the action; at other times with conscious volition, but volition which has become habitual and is put in operation by the force of habit, in opposition perhaps to the deliberate preference, as often happens with those who have contracted habits of vicious or hurtful indulgence. Third and last comes the case in which the habitual act of will in the individual instance is not in contradiction to the general intention prevailing at other times, but in fulfillment of it, as in the case of the person of confirmed virtue and of all who pursue deliberately and consistently any determinate end. The distinction between will and desire thus understood is an authentic and highly important psychological fact; but the fact consists solely in this—that will, like all other parts of our constitution, is amenable to habit, and that we may will from habit what we no longer desire for itself, or desire only because we will it. It is not the less true that will, in the beginning, is entirely produced by desire, including in that term the repelling influence of pain as well as the attractive one of pleasure. Let us take into consideration no longer the person who has a confirmed will to do right, but him in whom that virtuous will is still feeble, conquerable by temptation, and not to be fully relied on; by what means can it be strengthened? How can the will to be virtuous, where it does not exist in sufficient force, be implanted or awakened? Only by making the person *desire* virtue—by making him think of it in a pleasurable light, or of its absence in a painful one. It is by associating the doing right with pleasure, or the wrong with pain, or by eliciting and impressing and bringing home to the person's experience the pleasure naturally involved in the one or the pain in the other, that it is possible to call forth that will to be virtuous which, when confirmed, acts without any thought of either pleasure or pain. Will is the child of desire, and passes out of the dominion of its parent only to come under that of habit. That which is the result of habit affords no presumption of being intrinsically good; and there would be no reason for wishing that the purpose of virtue should become independent of pleasure and pain were it not that the influence of the pleasurable and painful associations which prompt to virtue is not sufficiently to be depended on for unerring constancy of action until it has acquired the support of habit. Both in feeling and in conduct, habit is the only thing which imparts certainty; and it is because of the importance to others of being able to rely absolutely on one's feelings and conduct, and to oneself of being able to rely on one's own, that the will to do right ought to be cultivated into this habitual independence. In other words, this state of the will is a means to good, not intrinsically a good; and does not contradict the doctrine that nothing is a good to human beings but in so far as it is either itself pleasurable or a means of attaining pleasure or averting pain.

But if this doctrine be true, the principle of utility is proved. Whether it is so or not must now be left to the consideration of the thoughtful reader.

HAPPINESS AND DUTY

Henry Sidgwick

The Englishman Henry Sidgwick (1838–1900) was for many years
professor of moral philosophy at Cambridge University. In his highly
regarded work *The Methods of Ethics*, he examined systematically the various procedures that have been tried to determine what ought to be
done. A problem that he found enormously difficult was how to reconcile the requirements of a person's moral duty with that individual's
desire for happiness.

§ 1. The belief in the connexion of Happiness with Duty is one to which we
find a general tendency among civilised men, at least after a certain stage in
civilisation has been reached. But it is doubtful whether it would be affirmed,
among ourselves, as a generalisation from experience, and not rather as a
matter of direct Divine Revelation, or an inevitable inference from the belief
that the world is governed by a perfectly Good and Omnipotent Being. To
examine thoroughly the validity of the latter belief is one of the most important
tasks that human reason can attempt: but involving as it does an exhaustive
inquiry into the evidences of Natural and Revealed Religion, it could hardly be
included within the scope of the present treatise. Here, then, I shall only consider the coincidence of Duty and Happiness in so far as it is maintained by
arguments drawn from experience and supposed to be realised in our present
earthly life. Perhaps, as so restricted, the coincidence can hardly be said to be
"currently believed": indeed it may be suggested that the opposite belief is
implied in the general admission of the necessity of rewards and punishments
in a future state, in order to exhibit and realise completely the moral government of the world. But reflection will show that this implication is not necessary; for it is possible to hold that even here virtue is always rewarded and
vice punished, so far as to make the virtuous course of action always the most
prudent; while yet the rewards and punishments are not sufficient to satisfy
our sense of justice. Admitting that the virtuous man is often placed on earth
in circumstances so adverse that his life is not as happy as that of many less
virtuous; it is still possible to maintain that by virtue he will gain the maximum
of happiness that can be gained under these circumstances, all appearances
to the contrary notwithstanding. And this view has certainly been held by
moralists of reputation on grounds drawn from actual experience of human
life; and seems often to be confidently put forward on similar grounds by
popular preachers and moralisers. It appears therefore desirable to subject
this opinion to a careful and impartial examination. In conducting this examination, at the present stage of our inquiry, we shall have to use the received
notions of Duty without further definition or analysis: but it is commonly

From *The Methods of Ethics*, Seventh Edition (1906).

assumed by those whose view we are to examine that these conceptions—as they are found in the moral consciousness of ordinary well-meaning persons—are at least approximately valid and trustworthy. . . .

§ 2. Accepting, then, the common division of duties into self-regarding and social, it may be conceded that as far as the first are concerned the view that we are examining is not likely to provoke any controversy: for by "duties towards oneself" are commonly meant acts that tend directly or indirectly to promote one's happiness. We may therefore confine our attention to the social department of Duty, and consider whether by observing the moral rules that prescribe certain modes of behaviour towards others we shall always tend to secure the greatest balance of happiness to ourselves.

Here it will be convenient to adopt with some modification the terminology of Bentham; and to regard the pleasures consequent on conformity to moral rules, and the pains consequent on their violation, as the "sanctions" of these rules. These "sanctions" we may classify as External and Internal. The former class will include both "Legal Sanctions," or penalties inflicted by the authority, direct or indirect, of the sovereign; and "Social Sanctions," which are either the pleasures that may be expected from the approval and goodwill of our fellow-men generally, and the services that they will be prompted to render both by this goodwill and by their appreciation of the usefulness of good conduct, or the annoyance and losses that are to be feared from their distrust and dislike. The internal sanctions of duty—so far as it diverges from the conduct which self-interest apart from morality would dictate—will lie in the pleasurable emotion attending virtuous action, or in the absence of remorse, or will result more indirectly from some effect on the mental constitution of the agent produced by the maintenance of virtuous dispositions and habits. This classification is important for our present purpose, chiefly because the systems of rules to which these different sanctions are respectively attached may be mutually conflicting. The Positive Morality of any community undergoes development, and is thus subject to changes which affect the consciences of the few before they are accepted by the many; so that the rules at any time sustained by the strongest social sanctions may not only fall short of, but even clash with, the intuitions of those members of the community who have most moral insight. For similar reasons Law and Positive Morality may be at variance, in details. For though a law could not long exist, which it was universally thought wrong to obey; there may easily be laws commanding conduct that is considered immoral by some more or less enlightened fraction of the community, especially by some sect or party that has a public opinion of its own: and any individual may be so much more closely connected with this fraction than with the rest of the community, that the social sanction may in his case practically operate against the legal.

This conflict of sanctions is of great importance in considering whether these sanctions, as at present capable of being foreseen, are sufficient in all cases to determine a rational egoist to the performance of social duty: for the more stress we lay on either the legal or the social sanctions of moral conduct, the greater difficulty we shall have in proving the coincidence of duty and self-interest in the exceptional cases in which we find these sanctions arrayed against what we conceive to be duty.

But even if we put these cases out of sight, it still seems clear that the external sanctions of morality alone are not always sufficient to render immoral conduct also imprudent. We must indeed admit that in an even tolerably well-ordered society—i.e., in an ordinary civilised community in its normal condition—all serious open violation of law is contrary to prudence, unless it is an incident in a successful process of violent revolution: and further, that violent revolutions would very rarely—perhaps never—be made by a combination of persons, all perfectly under the control of enlightened self-love; on account of the general and widespread destruction of security and of other means of happiness which such disturbances inevitably involve. Still, so long as actual human beings are not all rational egoists, such times of disorder will be liable to occur: and we cannot say that *under existing circumstances* it is a clear universal precept of Rational Self-love that a man should "seek peace and ensue it"; since the disturbance of political order may offer to a cool and skilful person, who has the art of fishing in troubled waters, opportunities of gaining wealth, fame, and power, far beyond what he could hope for in peaceful times. In short, though we may admit that a society composed entirely of rational egoists would, when once organised, tend to remain in a stable and orderly condition, it does not follow that any individual rational egoist will always be on the side of order in any existing community.

But at any rate, in the most orderly societies with which we are acquainted, the administration of law and justice is never in so perfect a state as to render *secret* crimes always acts of folly, on the score of the legal penalties attached to them. For however much these may outweigh the advantages of crime, cases must inevitably occur in which the risk of discovery is so small, that on a sober calculation the almost certain gain will more than compensate for the slight chance of the penalty. And finally, in no community is the law actually in so perfect a state that there are not certain kinds of flagrantly anti-social conduct which slip through its meshes and escape legal penalties altogether, or incur only such legal penalties as are outweighed by the profit of law-breaking.

§ 3. Let us proceed, then, to consider how far the social sanction in such cases supplies the defects of the legal. No doubt the hope of praise and liking and services from one's fellow-men, and the fear of forfeiting these and incurring instead aversion, refusal of aid, and social exclusion, are considerations often important enough to determine the rational egoist to law-observance, even in default of adequate legal penalties. Still these sanctions are liable to fail just where the legal penalties are defective; social no less than legal penalties are evaded by secret crimes; and in cases of criminal revolutionary violence, the efficacy of the social sanction is apt to be seriously impaired by the party spirit enlisted on the side of the criminal. For it has to be observed that the force of the social sanction diminishes very rapidly, in proportion to the number of dissidents from the common opinion that awards it. Disapprobation that is at once intense and quite universal would be so severe a penalty as perhaps to outweigh any imaginable advantages; since it seems impossible for a human being to live happily, whatever other goods he may enjoy, without the kindly regards of some of his fellows: and so, in contemplating the conventional portrait of the tyrant, who is represented as necessarily suspicious of those nearest him, even of the members of his own family, we feel prepared to admit that such a life must involve the extreme of unhappiness. But when we turn to contemplate the actual tyrannical usurpers, wicked statesmen, successful leaders of unwarranted rebellion, and, speaking generally, the great criminals whose position raises them out of the reach of legal penalties, it does not appear that the moral odium under which they lie must necessarily count for much in an egoistic calculation of the gain and loss resulting from their conduct. For this disesteem is only expressed by a portion of the community: and its utterance is often drowned in the loud-voiced applause of the multitude whose admiration is largely independent of moral considerations. Nor are there wanting philosophers and historians whose judgment manifests a similar independence.

It seems, then, impossible to affirm that the external sanctions of men's legal duties will always be sufficient to identify duty with interest. And a corresponding assertion would be still more unwarranted in respect of moral duties not included within the sphere of Law. In saying this, I am fully sensible of the force of what may be called the Principle of Reciprocity, by which certain utilitarians have endeavoured to prove the coincidence of any individual's interest with his social duties. Virtues (they say) are qualities either useful or directly agreeable to others: thus they either increase the market value of the virtuous man's services, and cause others to purchase them at a higher rate and to allot to him more dignified and interesting functions; or they dispose men to please him, both out of gratitude and in order to enjoy the pleasures of his society in return: and again—since man is an imitative animal—the exhibition of these qualities is naturally rewarded by a reciprocal manifestation of them on the part of others, through the mere influence of example. I do not doubt that the prospect of these advantages is an adequate motive for cultivating many virtues and avoiding much vice. Thus on such grounds a rational egoist will generally be strict and punctual in the fulfilment of all his engagements, and truthful in his assertions, in order to win the confidence of other men; and he will be zealous and industrious in his work, in order to obtain gradually more important and therefore more honourable and lucrative employment; and he will control such of his passions and appetites as are likely to interfere with his efficiency; and will not exhibit violent anger or use unnecessary harshness even towards servants and subordinates; and towards his equals and superiors in rank he will be generally polite and complaisant and good-humoured, and prompt to show them all such kindness as costs but little in proportion to the pleasure it gives. Still, reflection seems to show that the conduct recommended by this line of reasoning does not really coincide with moral duty. For, first, what one requires for social success is that one should *appear*, rather than *be*, useful to others: and hence this motive will not restrain one from doing secret harm to others, or even from acting openly in a way that is really harmful, though not perceived to be so. And again, a man is not useful to others by his virtue only, but sometimes rather by his vice; or more often by a certain admixture of unscrupulousness with his good and useful qualities. And further, morality prescribes the performance of duties equally towards all, and that we should abstain as far as possible from harming any but on the Principle of Reciprocity we should exhibit our useful qualities chiefly towards the rich and powerful, and abstain from injuring those who can retaliate; while we may reasonably omit our duties to the poor and feeble, if we find a material advantage in so doing, unless they are able to excite the sympathy of persons who can harm us. Moreover, some vices (as for example, many kinds of sensuality and extravagant luxury) do not inflict any immediate or obvious injury on any individual, though they tend in the long-run to impair the general happiness: hence few persons find themselves strongly moved to check or punish this kind of mischief.

Doubtless in the last-mentioned cases the mere disrepute inevitably attaching to open immorality is an important consideration. But I do not think that this will be seriously maintained to be sufficient always to turn the scales of prudence against vice—at least by any one who has duly analysed the turbid and fluctuating streams of social opinion upon which the good or ill repute of individuals mainly depends, and considered the conflicting and divergent elements that they contain. Many moralists have noticed the discrepancy in modern Europe between the Law of Honour (or the more important rules maintained by the social sanction of polite persons) and the morality professed in society at large. This is, however, by no means the only instance of a special code, divergent in certain points from the moral rules generally accepted in the community where it exists. Most religious sects and parties, and probably the majority of trades and professions, exhibit this phenomenon in some degree. I do not mean merely that special rules of behaviour are imposed upon members of each profession, corresponding to their special social functions and relations: I mean that a peculiar moral opinion is apt to grow up, conflicting to a certain extent with the opinion of the general public. The most striking part of this divergence consists generally in the approval or excusal of practices disapproved by the current morality: as (e.g.) licence among soldiers, bribery among politicians in certain ages and countries, unveracity of various degrees among priests and advocates, fraud in different forms among tradesmen. In such cases there are generally strong natural inducements to disobey the stricter rule (in fact it would seem to be to the continual pressure of these inducements that the relaxation of the rule has been due): while at the same time the social sanction is weakened to such an extent that it is sometimes hard to say whether it outweighs a similar force on the other side. For a man who, under these circumstances, conforms to the stricter rule, if he does not actually meet with contempt and aversion from those of his calling, is at least liable to be called eccentric and fantastic: and this is still more the case if by such conformity he foregoes advantages not only to himself but to his relatives or friends or party. Very often this professional or sectarian excusal of immorality of which we are speaking is not so clear and explicit as to amount to the establishment of a rule, conflicting with the generally received rule: but is still sufficient to weaken indefinitely the social sanction in favour of the latter. And, apart from these special divergences, we may say generally that in most civilised societies there are two different degrees of positive morality, both maintained in some sort by common consent; a stricter code being publicly taught and avowed, while a laxer set of rules is privately admitted as the only code which can be supported by social sanctions of any great force. By refusing to conform to the stricter code a man is often not liable to incur exclusion from social intercourse, or any material hindrance to professional advancement, or even serious dislike on the part of any of the persons whose society he will most naturally seek; and under such circumstances the mere loss of a certain amount of reputation is not likely to be felt as a very grave evil, except by persons peculiarly sensitive to the pleasures and pains of reputation. And there would seem to be many men whose happiness does not depend on the approbation or disapprobation of the moralist—and of mankind in general in so far as they support the moralist—to such an extent as to make it prudent for them to purchase this praise by any great sacrifice of other goods.

§ 4. We must conclude, then, that if the conduct prescribed to the individual by the avowedly accepted morality of the community of which he is a member, can be shown to coincide with that to which Rational Self-love would prompt, it must be, in many cases, solely or chiefly on the score of the internal sanctions. In considering the force of these sanctions, I shall eliminate those pleasures and pains which lie in the anticipation of rewards and punishments in a future life: for as we are now supposing the calculations of Rational Egoism to be performed without taking into account any feelings that are beyond the range of experience, it will be more consistent to exclude also the pleasurable or painful anticipations of such feelings.

Let us, then, contemplate by itself the satisfaction that attends the performance of duty as such (without taking into consideration any ulterior consequences), and the pain that follows on its violation. . . . I shall not of course attempt to weigh exactly these pleasures and pains against others; but I see no empirical grounds for believing that such feelings are always sufficiently intense to turn the balance of prospective happiness in favour of morality. This will hardly be denied if the question is raised in respect of isolated acts of duty. Let us take an extreme case, which is yet quite within the limits of experience. The call of duty has often impelled a soldier or other public servant, or the adherent of a persecuted religion, to face certain and painful death, under circumstances where it might be avoided with little or no loss even of reputation. To prove such conduct always reasonable from an egoistic point of view, we have to assume that, in all cases where such a duty could exist and be recognised, the mere pain that would follow on evasion of duty would be so great as to render the whole remainder of life hedonistically worthless. Surely such an assumption would be paradoxical and extravagant. Nothing that we know of the majority of persons in any society would lead us to conclude that their moral feelings taken alone form so preponderant an element of their happiness. And a similar conclusion seems irresistible even in more ordinary cases, where a man is called on to give up, for virtue's sake, not life, but a considerable share of the ordinary sources of human happiness. Can we say that all, or even most, men are so constituted that the satisfactions of a good conscience are certain to repay them for such sacrifices, or that the pain and loss involved in them would certainly be outweighed by the remorse that would follow the refusal to make them?

Perhaps, however, so much as this has scarcely ever been expressly maintained. What Plato in his *Republic* and other writers on the same side have rather tried to prove, is not that at any particular moment duty will be, to every one on whom it may devolve, productive of more happiness than any other course of conduct; but rather that it is every one's interest on the whole to choose the life of the virtuous man. But even this it is very difficult even to render probable: as will appear, I think, if we examine the lines of reasoning by which it is commonly supported.

To begin with Plato's argument. He represents the soul of the virtuous man as a well-ordered polity of impulses, in which every passion and appetite is duly obedient to the rightful sovereignty of reason, and operates only within the limits laid down by the latter. He then contrasts the tranquil peace of such a mind with the disorder of one where a succession of baser impulses, or some ruling passion, lords it over reason: and asks which is the happiest, even apart from external rewards and punishments. But we may grant all that Plato claims, and yet be no further advanced towards the solution of the question before us. For here the issue does not lie between Reason and Passion, but rather—in Butler's language—between Rational Self-love and Conscience. We are supposing the Egoist to have all his impulses under control, and are only asking how this control is to be exercised. Now we have seen that the regulation and organisation of life best calculated to attain the end of self-interest appears prima facie divergent at certain points from that to which men in general are prompted by a sense of duty. In order to maintain Plato's position it has to be shown that this appearance is false; and that a system of self-government, which under certain circumstances leads us to pain, loss, and death, is still that which self-interest requires. It can scarcely be said that our nature is such that only this anti-egoistic kind of regulation is possible; that the choice lies between this and none at all. It is easy to imagine a rational egoist, strictly controlling each of his passions and impulses—including his social sentiments—within such limits that its indulgence should not involve the sacrifice of some greater gratification: and experience seems to show us many examples of persons who at least approximate as closely to this type as any one else does to the ideal of the orthodox moralist. Hence if the regulation of Conscience be demonstrably the best means to the individual's happiness, it must be because the order kept by Self-love involves a sacrifice of pleasure on the whole, as compared with the order kept by Conscience. And if this is the case, it would seem that it can only be on account of the special emotional pleasure attending the satisfaction of the moral sentiments, or special pain or loss of happiness consequent on their repression and violation.

Before, however, we proceed further, a fundamental difficulty must be removed which has probably some time since suggested itself to the reader. If a man thinks it reasonable to seek his own interest, it is clear that he cannot himself disapprove of any conduct that comes under this principle or approve of the opposite. And hence it may appear that the pleasures and pains of conscience cannot enter into the calculation whether a certain course of conduct is or is not in accordance with Rational Egoism, because they cannot attach themselves in the egoist's mind to any modes of action which have not been already decided, on other grounds, to be reasonable or the reverse. And this is to a certain extent true; but we must here recur to the distinction . . . between the general impulse to do what we believe to be reasonable, and special sentiments of liking or aversion for special kinds of conduct, independent of their reasonableness. In the moral sentiments as they exist in ordinary men, these two kinds of feeling are indistinguishably blended; because it is commonly believed that the rules of conduct to which the common moral sentiments are attached are in some way or other reasonable. We can, however, conceive the two separated: and in fact, as was before said, we have experience of such separation whenever a man is led by a process of thought to adopt a different view of morality from that in which he has been trained; for in such a case there will always remain in his mind some quasi-moral likings and aversions, no longer sustained by his deliberate judgment of right and wrong. And thus there is every reason to believe that most men, however firmly they might adopt the principles of Egoistic Hedonism, would still feel sentiments prompting to the performance of social duty, as commonly recognised in their society, independently of any conclusion that the actions prompted by such sentiments were reasonable and right. For such sentiments would always be powerfully supported by the sympathy of others, and their expressions of praise and blame, liking and aversion: and since it is agreed that the conduct commonly recognised as virtuous is *generally* coincident with that which enlightened self-love would dictate, a rational egoist's habits of conduct will be such as naturally to foster these (for him) "quasi-moral" feelings. The question therefore arises—not whether the egoist should cherish and indulge these sentiments up to a certain point, which all would admit—but whether he can consistently encourage them to grow to such a pitch that they will always prevail over the strongest opposing considerations; or, to put it otherwise, whether prudence requires him to give them the rein and let them carry him whither they will. We have already seen ground for believing that Rational Self-love will best attain its end by limiting its conscious operation and allowing free play to disinterested impulses: can we accept the further paradox that it is reasonable for it to abdicate altogether its supremacy over some of these impulses?

On a careful consideration of the matter, it will appear, I think, that this abdication of self-love is not really a possible occurrence in the mind of a sane person, who still regards his own interest as the reasonable ultimate end of his actions. Such a man may, no doubt, resolve that he will devote himself unreservedly to the practice of virtue, without any particular consideration of what appears to him to be his interest: he may perform a series of acts in accordance with this resolution, and these may gradually form in him strong habitual tendencies to acts of a similar kind. But it does not seem that these habits of virtue can ever become so strong as to gain irresistible control over a sane and reasonable will. When the occasion comes on which virtue demands from such a man an extreme sacrifice—the imprudence of which must force itself upon his notice, however little he may be in the habit of weighing his own pleasures and pains—he must always be able to deliberate afresh, and to act (as far as the control of his will extends) without reference to his past actions. It may, however, be said that, though an egoist retaining his belief in rational egoism cannot thus abandon his will to the sway of moral enthusiasm, still, supposing it possible for him to change his conviction and prefer duty to interest,—or supposing we compare him with another man who makes this choice,—we shall find that a gain in happiness on the whole results from this preference. It may be held that the pleasurable emotions attendant upon such virtuous or quasi-virtuous habits as are compatible with adhesion to egoistic principles are so inferior to the raptures that attend the unreserved and passionate surrender of the soul to virtue, that it is really a man's interest—even with a view to the present life only—to obtain, if he can, the convictions that render this surrender possible; although under certain circumstances it must necessarily lead him to act in a manner which, considered by itself, would be undoubtedly imprudent. This is certainly a tenable proposition, and I am quite disposed to think it true of persons with specially refined moral sensibilities. But—though from the imperfections of the hedonistic calculus the proposition cannot in any case be conclusively disproved—it seems, as I have said, to be opposed to the broad results of experience, so far as the great majority of mankind are concerned. Observation would lead me to suppose that most men are so constituted as to feel far more keenly pleasures (and pains) arising from some other source than the conscience; either from the gratifications of sense, or from the possession of power and fame, or from strong human affections, or from the pursuit of science, art, etc.; so that in many cases perhaps not even early training could have succeeded in giving to the moral feelings the requisite predominance: and certainly where this training has been wanting, it seems highly improbable that a mere change of ethical conviction could develop their moral susceptibilities so far as to make it clearly their earthly interest to resolve on facing all sacrifices for the fulfilment of duty.

To sum up: although the performance of duties towards others and the exercise of social virtue seem to be *generally* the best means to the attainment of the individual's happiness, and it is easy to exhibit this coincidence between Virtue and Happiness rhetorically and popularly; still, when we carefully analyse and estimate the consequences of Virtue to the virtuous agent, it appears improbable that this coincidence is complete and universal. We may conceive the coincidence becoming perfect in a Utopia where men were as much in accord on moral as they are now on mathematical questions, where Law was in perfect harmony with Moral Opinion, and all offences were discovered and duly punished: or we may conceive the same result attained by intensifying the moral sentiments of all members of the community, without any external changes (which indeed would then be unnecessary). But just in proportion as existing societies and existing men fall short of this ideal, rules of conduct based on the principles of Egoistic Hedonism seem liable to diverge from those which most men are accustomed to recognise as prescribed by Duty and Virtue.

ON THE USES AND DISADVANTAGES OF HISTORY FOR LIFE

Friedrich Nietzsche

Friedrich Nietzsche (1844–1900) was a German philosopher and classical scholar whose unconventional views and aphoristic style of writing led to his being regarded as one of the most controversial figures in the history of modern philosophy. In this early essay he maintained that happiness requires not being chained by memories of the past but learning to live in the moment.

From *Untimely Meditations*, translated by R. J. Hollingdale, Cambridge University Press, 1997. Used by permission of the publisher.

Consider the cattle, grazing as they pass you by: they do not know what is meant by yesterday or today, they leap about, eat, rest, digest, leap about again, and so from morn till night and from day to day, fettered to the moment and its pleasure or displeasure, and thus neither melancholy nor bored. This is a hard sight for man to see; for, though he thinks himself better than the animals because he is human, he cannot help envying them their happiness —what they have, a life neither bored nor painful, is precisely what he wants, yet he cannot have it because he refuses to be like an animal. A human being may well ask an animal: "Why do you not speak to me of your happiness but only stand and gaze at me?" The animal would like to answer, and say: "The reason is I always forget what I was going to say"—but then he forgot this answer too, and stayed silent: so that the human being was left wondering.

But he also wonders at himself, that he cannot learn to forget but clings relentlessly to the past: however far and fast he may run, this chain runs with him. And it is a matter for wonder: a moment, now here and then gone, nothing before it came, again nothing after it has gone, nonetheless returns as a ghost and disturbs the peace of a later moment. A leaf flutters from the scroll of time, floats away—and suddenly floats back again and falls into the man's lap. Then the man says "I remember" and envies the animal, who at once forgets and for whom every moment really dies, sinks back into night and fog and is extinguished for ever. Thus the animal lives *unhistorically*: for it is contained in the present, like a number without any awkward fraction left over; it does not know how to dissimulate, it conceals nothing and at every instant appears wholly as what it is; it can therefore never be anything but honest. Man, on the other hand, braces himself against the great and ever greater pressure of what is past: it pushes him down or bends him sideways, it encumbers his steps as a dark, invisible burden which he can sometimes appear to disown and which in traffic with his fellow men he is only too glad to disown, so as to excite their envy. That is why it affects him like a vision of a lost paradise to see the herds grazing or, in closer proximity to him, a child which, having as yet nothing of the past to shake off, plays in blissful blindness between the hedges of past and future. Yet its play must be disturbed; all too soon it will be called out of its state of forgetfulness. Then it will learn to understand the phrase "it was": that password which gives conflict, suffering and satiety access to man so as to remind him what his existence fundamentally is—an imperfect tense that can never become a perfect one. If death at last brings the desired forgetting, by that act it at the same time extinguishes the present and all existence and therewith sets the seal on the knowledge that existence is only an uninterrupted has-been, a thing that lives by negating, consuming and contradicting itself.

If happiness, if reaching out for new happiness, is in any sense what fetters living creatures to life and makes them go on living, then perhaps no philosopher is more justified than the Cynic: for the happiness of the animal, as the perfect Cynic, is the living proof of the rightness of Cynicism. The smallest happiness, if only it is present uninterruptedly and makes happy, is incomparably more happiness than the greatest happiness that comes only as an episode, as it were a piece of waywardness or folly, in a continuum of joylessness, desire and privation. In the case of the smallest or of the greatest happiness, however, it is always the same thing that makes happiness happiness:

the ability to forget or, expressed in more scholarly fashion, the capacity to feel *unhistorically* during its duration. He who cannot sink down on the threshold of the moment and forget all the past, who cannot stand balanced like a goddess of victory without growing dizzy and afraid, will never know what happiness is—worse, he will never do anything to make others happy. Imagine the extremest possible example of a man who did not possess the power of forgetting at all and who was thus condemned to see everywhere a state of becoming: such a man would no longer believe in his own being, would no longer believe in himself, would see everything flowing asunder in moving points and would lose himself in this stream of becoming: like a true pupil of Heraclitus, he would in the end hardly dare to raise his finger. Forgetting is essential to action of any kind, just as not only light but darkness too is essential for the life of everything organic. A man who wanted to feel historically through and through would be like one forcibly deprived of sleep, or an animal that had to live only by rumination and ever repeated rumination. Thus: it is possible to live almost without memory, and to live happily moreover, as the animal demonstrates; but it is altogether impossible to *live* at all without forgetting. Or, to express my theme even more simply: *there is a degree of sleeplessness, of rumination, of the historical sense, which is harmful and ultimately fatal to the living thing, whether this living thing be a man or a people or a culture.*

To determine this degree, and therewith the boundary at which the past has to be forgotten if it is not to become the gravedigger of the present, one would have to know exactly how great the *plastic power* of a man, a people, a culture is: I mean by plastic power the capacity to develop out of oneself in one's own way, to transform and incorporate into oneself what is past and foreign, to heal wounds, to replace what has been lost, to recreate broken moulds. There are people who possess so little of this power that they can perish from a single experience, from a single painful event, often and especially from a single subtle piece of injustice, like a man bleeding to death from a scratch; on the other hand, there are those who are so little affected by the worst and most dreadful disasters, and even by their own wicked acts, that they are able to feel tolerably well and be in possession of a kind of clear conscience even in the midst of them or at any rate very soon afterwards. The stronger the innermost roots of a man's nature, the more readily will he be able to assimilate and appropriate the things of the past; and the most powerful and tremendous nature would be characterized by the fact that it would know no boundary at all at which the historical sense began to overwhelm it; it would draw to itself and incorporate into itself all the past, its own and that most foreign to it, and as it were transform it into blood. That which such a nature cannot subdue it knows how to forget; it no longer exists, the horizon is rounded and closed, and there is nothing left to suggest there are people, passions, teachings, goals lying beyond it. And this is a universal law: a living thing can be healthy, strong and fruitful only when bounded by a horizon; if it is incapable of drawing a horizon around itself, and at the same time too self-centred to enclose its own view within that of another, it will pine away slowly or hasten to its timely end. Cheerfulness, the good conscience, the joyful deed, confidence in the future—all of them depend, in the case of the individual as of a nation, on the existence of a line dividing the bright and discernible from the unilluminable and dark; on one's being just as able to forget at the right time as to remember at the right time; on the possession of a powerful instinct for sensing when it is necessary to feel historically and when unhistorically. This, precisely, is the proposition the reader is invited to meditate upon: *the unhistorical and the historical are necessary in equal measure for the health of an individual, of a people and of a culture.*

First of all, there is an observation that everyone must have made: a man's historical sense and knowledge can be very limited, his horizon as narrow as that of a dweller in the Alps, all his judgments may involve injustice and he may falsely suppose that all his experiences are original to him—yet in spite of this injustice and error he will nonetheless stand there in superlative health and vigour, a joy to all who see him; while close beside him a man far more just and instructed than he sickens and collapses because the lines of his horizon are always restlessly changing, because he can no longer extricate himself from the delicate net of his judiciousness and truth for a simple act of will and desire. On the other hand we have observed the animal, which is quite unhistorical, and dwells within a horizon reduced almost to a point, and yet lives in a certain degree of happiness, or at least without boredom and dissimulation; we shall thus have to account the capacity to feel to a certain degree unhistorically as being more vital and more fundamental, inasmuch as it constitutes the foundation upon which alone anything sound, healthy and great, anything truly human, can grow. The unhistorical is like an atmosphere within which alone life can germinate and with the destruction of which it must vanish. It is true that only by imposing limits on this unhistorical element by thinking, reflecting, comparing, distinguishing, drawing conclusions, only through the appearance within that encompassing cloud of a vivid flash of light—thus only through the power of employing the past for the purposes of life and of again introducing into history that which has been done and is gone—did man become man: but with an excess of history man again ceases to exist, and without that envelope of the unhistorical he would never have begun or dared to begin. What deed would man be capable of if he had not first entered into that vaporous region of the unhistorical? Or, to desert this imagery and illustrate by example: imagine a man seized by a vehement passion, for a woman or for a great idea: how different the world has become to him! Looking behind him he seems to himself as though blind, listening around him he hears only a dull, meaningless noise; whatever he does perceive, however, he perceives as he has never perceived before—all is so palpable, close, highly coloured, resounding, as though he apprehended it with all his senses at once. All his valuations are altered and disvalued; there are so many things he is no longer capable of evaluating at all because he can hardly feel them any more: he asks himself why he was for so long the fool of the phrases and opinions of others; he is amazed that his memory revolves unwearyingly in a circle and yet is too weak and weary to take even a single leap out of this circle. It is the condition in which one is the least capable of being just; narrow-minded, ungrateful to the past, blind to dangers, deaf to warnings, one is a little vortex of life in a dead sea of darkness and oblivion: and yet this condition—unhistorical, antihistorical through and through—is the womb not only of the unjust but of every just deed too; and no painter will paint his picture, no general achieve his victory, no people attain its freedom without having first desired and striven for it in an unhistorical condition such as that described. As he who acts is, in Goethe's words, always without a conscience, so is he also always without knowledge; he forgets most things so as to do one thing, he is unjust towards what lies behind him, and he recognizes the rights only of that which is now to come into being and no other rights whatever. Thus he who acts loves his deed infinitely more than it deserves to be loved: and the finest deeds take place in such a superabundance of love that, even if their worth were incalculable in other respects, they must still be unworthy of this love.

If, in a sufficient number of cases, one could scent out and retrospectively breathe this unhistorical atmosphere within which every great historical event has taken place, he might, as a percipient being, raise himself to a *suprahistorical* vantage point such as Niebuhr once described as the possible outcome of historical reflection. "History, grasped clearly and in detail", he says, "is useful in one way at least: it enables us to recognize how unaware even the greatest and highest spirits of our human race have been of the chance nature of the form assumed by the eyes through which they see and through which they compel everyone to see—compel, that is, because the intensity of their consciousness is exceptionally great. He who has not grasped this quite definitely and in many instances will be subjugated by the appearance of a powerful spirit who brings to a given form the most impassioned commitment." We may use the word "suprahistorical" because the viewer from this vantage point could no longer feel any temptation to go on living or to take part in history; he would have recognized the essential condition of all happenings—this blindness and injustice in the soul of him who acts; he would, indeed, be cured for ever of taking history too seriously, for he would have learned from all men and all experiences, whether among Greeks or Turks, from a single hour of the first or of the nineteenth century, to answer his own question as to how or to what end life is lived. If you ask your acquaintances if they would like to relive the past ten or twenty years, you will easily discover which of them is prepared for this suprahistorical standpoint: they will all answer No, to be sure, but they will have different reasons for answering No. Some may perhaps be consoling themselves: "but the next twenty will be better"; they are those of whom David Hume says mockingly:

> And from the dregs of life hope to receive
> What the first sprightly running could not give.

Let us call them historical men; looking to the past impels them towards the future and fires their courage to go on living and their hope that what they want will still happen, that happiness lies behind the hill they are advancing towards. These historical men believe that the meaning of existence will come more and more to light in the course of its *process*, and they glance behind them only so that, from the process so far, they can learn to understand the present and to desire the future more vehemently; they have no idea that, despite their preoccupation with history, they in fact think and act unhistorically, or that their occupation with history stands in the service, not of pure knowledge, but of life.

But our question can also be answered differently. Again with a No—but with a No for a different reason: with the No of the suprahistorical man, who sees no salvation in the process and for whom, rather, the world is complete and reaches its finality at each and every moment. What could ten more years teach that the past ten were unable to teach!

Whether the sense of this teaching is happiness or resignation or virtue or atonement, suprahistorical men have never been able to agree; but, in opposition to all historical modes of regarding the past, they are unanimous in the proposition: the past and the present are one, that is to say, with all their diversity identical in all that is typical and, as the omnipresence of imperishable types, a motionless structure of a value that cannot alter and a significance that is always the same. Just as the hundreds of different languages correspond to the same typically unchanging needs of man, so that he who understood these needs would be unable to learn anything new from any of these languages, so the suprahistorical thinker beholds the history of nations and of individuals from within, clairvoyantly divining the original meaning of the various hieroglyphics and gradually even coming wearily to avoid the endless stream of new signs: for how should the unending superfluity of events not reduce him to satiety, over-satiety and finally to nausea! So that perhaps the boldest of them is at last ready to say to his heart, with Giacomo Leopardi:

Nothing lives that is worthy
Thy agitation, and the earth deserves not a sigh.
Our being is pain and boredom and the world is dirt—nothing more.
Be calm.

FORLORNNESS

JEAN-PAUL SARTRE

Jean-Paul Sartre (1905–1980) was a French philosopher, novelist, and dramatist who defended existentialism, according to which human agents, through their own thoughts and activities, freely shape themselves but, having no prior concepts on which to rely, are condemned to forlornness.

Let us consider some object that is manufactured, for example, a book or a paper-cutter: here is an object which has been made by an artisan whose inspiration came from a concept. He referred to the concept of what a paper-cutter

From *Existentialism and Human Emotions*, translated by Bernard Frechtman, A Philosophical Library Book, Citadel, 2001. Reprinted by permission of Kensington Publishing Corp.

is and likewise to a known method of production, which is part of the concept, something which is, by and large, a routine. Thus, the paper-cutter is at once an object produced in a certain way and, on the other hand, one having a specific use; and one can not postulate a man who produces a paper-cutter but does not know what it is used for. Therefore, let us say that, for the paper-cutter, essence—that is, the ensemble of both the production routines and the properties which enable it to be both produced and defined—precedes existence. . . .

When we conceive God as the Creator, He is generally thought of as a superior sort of artisan. . . . He knows exactly what He is creating. Thus, the concept of man in the mind of God is comparable to the concept of paper-cutter in the mind of the manufacturer, and, following certain techniques and a conception, God produces man, just as the artisan, following a definition and a technique, makes a paper-cutter. Thus, the individual man is the realization of a certain concept in the divine intelligence. . . .

Atheistic existentialism, which I represent, . . . states that if God does not exist, there is at least one being in whom existence precedes essence, a being who exists before he can be defined by any concept, and that this being is man. . . . What is meant here by saying that existence precedes essence? It means that, first of all, man exists, turns up, appears on the scene, and only after-wards, defines himself. If man, as the existentialist conceives him, is indefin-able, it is because at first he is nothing. Only afterward will he be something, and he himself will have made what he will be. Thus, there is no human nature, since there is no God to conceive it. Not only is man what he conceives himself to be, but he is also only what he wills himself to be after this thrust toward existence.

Man is nothing else but what he makes of himself. Such is the first prin-ciple of existentialism. . . .

The existentialist . . . thinks it very distressing that God does not exist, because all possibility of finding values in a heaven of ideas disappears along with Him; there can no longer be an a priori Good, since there is no infinite and perfect consciousness to think it. Nowhere is it written that the Good exists, that we must be honest, that we must not lie, because the fact is we are on a plane where there are only men. Dostoevsky said, "If God didn't exist, every-thing would be possible." That is the very starting point of existentialism. Indeed, everything is permissible if God does not exist, and as a result man is forlorn, because neither within him nor without does he find anything to cling to. He can't start making excuses for himself.

If existence really does precede essence, there is no explaining things away by reference to a fixed and given human nature. In other words, there is no determinism, man is free, man is freedom. On the other hand, if God does not exist, we find no values or commands to turn to which legitimize our conduct. So, in the bright realm of values, we have no excuse behind us, nor justification before us. We are alone, with no excuses.

That is the idea I shall try to convey when I say that man is condemned to be free. Condemned, because he did not create himself, yet, in other respects is free; because, once thrown into the world, he is responsible for everything he does. . . . But then we are forlorn.

To give you an example which will enable you to understand forlornness better, I shall cite the case of one of my students who came to see me under the following circumstances: his father was on bad terms with his mother, and, moreover, was inclined to be a collaborationist; his older brother had been killed in the German offensive of 1940, and the young man, with somewhat immature but generous feelings, wanted to avenge him. His mother lived alone with him, very much upset by the half-treason of her husband and the death of her older son; the boy was her only consolation.

The boy was faced with the choice of leaving for England and joining the Free French Forces—that is, leaving his mother behind—or remaining with his mother and helping her to carry on. He was fully aware that the woman lived only for him and that his going-off—and perhaps his death—would plunge her into despair. He was also aware that every act that he did for his mother's sake was a sure thing, in the sense that it was helping her to carry on, whereas every effort he made toward going off and fighting was an uncertain move which might run aground and prove completely useless; for example, on his way to England he might, while passing through Spain, be detained indefinitely in a Spanish camp; he might reach England or Algiers and be stuck in an office at a desk job. As a result, he was faced with two very different kinds of action: one, concrete, immediate, but concerning only one individual; the other concerned an incomparably vaster group, a national collectivity, but for that very reason was dubious, and might be interrupted en route. And, at the same time, he was wavering between two kinds of ethics. On the one hand, an ethics of sympathy, of personal devotion; on the other hand, a broader ethics, but one whose efficacy was more dubious. He had to choose between the two.

Who could help him choose? Christian doctrine? No. Christian doctrine says, "Be charitable, love your neighbor, take the more rugged path, etc., etc." But which is the more rugged path? Whom should he love as a brother? The fighting man or his mother? Which does the greater good, the vague act of fighting in a group, or the concrete one of helping a particular human being to go on living? Who can decide a priori? Nobody. No book of ethics can tell him. The Kantian ethics says, "Never treat any person as a means, but as an end." Very well, if I stay with my mother, I'll treat her as an end and not as a means; but by virtue of this very fact, I'm running the risk of treating the people around me who are fighting, as means; and, conversely, if I go to join those who are fighting, I'll be treating them as an end, and, by doing that, I run the risk of treating my mother as a means.

If values are vague, and if they are always too broad for the concrete and specific case that we are considering, the only thing left for us is to trust our instincts. That's what this young man tried to do; and when I saw him, he said, "In the end, feeling is what counts. I ought to choose whichever pushes me in one direction. If I feel that I love my mother enough to sacrifice everything else for her—my desire for vengeance, for action, for adventure—then I'll stay with her. If, on the contrary, I feel that my love for my mother isn't enough, I'll leave."

But how is the value of a feeling determined? What gives his feeling for his mother value? Precisely the fact that he remained with her. I may say that I like so-and-so well enough to sacrifice a certain amount of money for him, but I may say so only if I've done it. I may say "I love my mother well enough to remain with her" if I have remained with her. The only way to determine the value of this affection is, precisely, to perform an act which confirms and defines it. But, since I require this affection to justify my act, I find myself caught in a vicious circle.

On the other hand, Gide has well said that a mock feeling and a true feeling are almost indistinguishable; to decide that I love my mother and will remain with her, or to remain with her by putting on an act, amount somewhat to the same thing. In other words, the feeling is formed by the acts one performs; so, I cannot refer to it in order to act upon it. Which means that I can neither seek within myself the true condition which will impel me to act, nor apply to a system of ethics for concepts which will permit me to act. You will say, "At least, he did go to a teacher for advice." But if you seek advice from a priest, for example, you have chosen this priest; you already knew, more or less, just about what advice he was going to give you. In other words, choosing your adviser is involving yourself. The proof of this is that if you are a Christian, you will say, "Consult a priest." But some priests are collaborating, some are just marking time, some are resisting. Which to choose? If the young man chooses a priest who is resisting or collaborating, he has already decided on the kind of advice he's going to get. Therefore, in coming to see me he knew the answer I was going to give him, and I had only one answer to give: "You're free, choose, that is, invent." No general ethics can show you what is to be done; there are no omens in the world. The Catholics will reply, "But there are." Granted—but, in any case, I myself choose the meaning they have.

When I was a prisoner, I knew a rather remarkable young man who was a Jesuit. He had entered the Jesuit order in the following way: he had had a number of very bad breaks; in childhood, his father died, leaving him in poverty, and he was a scholarship student at a religious institution where he was constantly made to feel that he was being kept out of charity; then, he failed to get any of the honors and distinctions that children like; later on, at about eighteen, he bungled a love affair; finally at twenty-two, he failed in military training, a childish enough matter, but it was the last straw.

This young fellow might well have felt that he had botched everything. It was a sign of something, but of what? He might have taken refuge in bitterness or despair. But he very wisely looked upon all this as a sign that he was not made for secular triumphs, and that only the triumphs of religion, holiness, and faith were open to him. He saw the hand of God in all this, and so he entered the order. Who can help seeing that he alone decided what the sign meant?

Some other interpretation might have been drawn from this series of set-backs; for example, that he might have done better to turn carpenter or revolutionist. Therefore, he is fully responsible for the interpretation. Forlornness implies that we ourselves choose our being.

Part Two

CONTEMPORARY THEORIES

A. Happiness as Pleasure

PLEASURE AND HAPPINESS

Wayne Davis

Wayne Davis is professor of philosophy at Georgetown University. He defends the view that pleasure and happiness are identical.

I believe two vocabularies are used to denote one set of mental phenomena. One centers around the term "happiness," the other around "pleasure." Both are complex, and they are not isomorphic. My goal is to delineate the structure of the two vocabularies, and map one onto the other. The paper is therefore a partial analysis of the concepts of pleasure and happiness, and a defense of the thesis that pleasure and happiness are the same thing.

I begin by distinguishing between *the occurrent and dispositional senses of happiness*. In the occurrent sense, "*A* is happy" means that *A* feels happy or is *experiencing* happiness; he is in high or good spirits, is in a good mood, and feels good. In the dispositional sense, "*A* is happy" means that *A* is *predominantly* happy in the occurrent sense. The dispositionally happy man may occasionally be unhappy (for example, when a friend dies), and he may at the moment be asleep or unconscious. That someone is smiling, has sparkling eyes, looks healthy and rested, and is bubbling effusively about a favorite hobby is good evidence of occurrent happiness. That someone is moderately wealthy, loves his wife, enjoys his work, and has robust health is good evidence of dispositional happiness. "Happy" is ambiguous in the same way "warm" is. "It is warm in Florida" may describe the current weather there (as in the daily paper) or the normal weather (as in a geography book). In both senses, a man may be happy now, unhappy later. Even dispositional happiness may end, as when an accident paralyzes a man and kills his wife. Elsewhere,[1] I define occurrent happiness in terms of belief, desire, and occurrent thought.

The previous paragraph concerns happiness as a *nonrelational* state. There are in addition various types of *relational* happiness. The adjective "happy" can either stand alone, or it can take various complements such as "that" and "with." *Happy that* expresses a propositional attitude. *A is happy that p only if A*

From *Philosophical Studies*, vol. 39 (1981). With kind permission from Springer Science and Business Media.

believes and desires that p. It is presupposed in addition that the person *knows* that *p*. Someone is unhappy that *p* only if he believes that *p* but desires that not-*p*. How happy *A* is that *p* is determined by how much he desires that *p*. It follows from my analysis of occurrent happiness that, other things equal, the happier a person is that *p*, the happier he is, provided the thought that *p* is occurring to him.[2] *Happy to* can always be transformed into "happy that." Thus "John is happy to be alive" means John is happy that he is alive, and "John is happy to get his income tax refund" means John is happy that he has just gotten it. "Happy" in these contexts is synonymous with *glad*, "unhappy" with *sorry*.

A person can *be* happy that *p* even though it does not *make* him happy that *p*. I am happy that I went to Redford High School, but it no longer makes me happy that I did so. I am happy that my alma mater has a good football team even though, due to lack of sufficient personal interest, it does not make me happy that they do. One goal of the present paper is to explain what it is for something to make a person happy. A person is *happy with X* only if he is happy with *X as it is*, as opposed to how it was or will be. You are happy with your wife only if you are happy with her as she is. This suggests that a person is happy with X only if he is happy *that X is the way it is*, and only if he has in mind a specific idea of the way *X* is (which he may or may not be able to articulate). This is insufficient, however. I am happy that my alma mater's football team is good, but I am not happy with my alma mater's team. The reason for this, I believe, is that it does not make me happy that the team is good. So, *A is happy with X if, and only if, it makes A happy that X is the way it is*. Finally, *A* is happy *about X* if X, or some fact about X, makes *A* happy. John is happy about his promotion if his promotion makes him happy. Mary is happy about the fact that she is married provided it makes her happy that she is married. And I am happy about my car because it makes me happy that it runs so well. Note that while I am happy that I went to Redford High, I am no longer happy about the fact that I went there.

We see that the general phenomenon of happiness can be divided into three basic categories: nonrelational happiness (being happy), propositional happiness (being happy that *p*), and "happification" (making happy). The third remains to be defined. We will see later that there are two basic types of happification, epistemic and nonepistemic. They will be defined separately.

I believe that *pleasure* can be identified with occurrent, nonrelational happiness. *A person experiences pleasure if, and only if, he experiences happiness.* And the happier he is, the more pleasure he is experiencing. McDougall objected to the identification of pleasure and happiness on the grounds that an unhappy man can experience pleasure:

> Consider the case of a man whose lifelong ambition and hopes have recently been dashed to the ground. If he were fond of music, he might, when the first shock of disappointment had passed away, attend a concert and derive pleasure from the music . . . and yet be continuously unhappy (1923, p. 160).

Such cases only show, however, that pleasure cannot be identified with *dispositional* happiness. If the man had not been occurrently happy during the concert, he could not be said to have enjoyed it. It is often objected that happiness is more lasting and durable than pleasure, which is transitory. This objection also collapses once occurrent happiness is distinguished from dispositional. True, we may suppose that a cup of coffee provides a derelict with a moment of pleasure without supposing that it makes him a happy man; nevertheless, at that moment he did experience happiness. Occurrent happiness can be as fleeting as pleasure. Another ineffective objection is that many sources of pleasure are not sources of "true" happiness, that a man can enjoy life without being *really* happy. I am identifying pleasure with happiness, not with true happiness.[3] The identification of pleasure with happiness does not entail that long term happiness can be achieved by indulging in any old momentary pleasure, nor in every whim or passing fancy. Long term happiness (or pleasure) often requires pain (or unhappiness) and sacrifice today, as every student should realize. And some pleasures, such as drinking before driving, endanger future happiness. We could not identify present pleasure with long term happiness any more than we could identify present happiness with long term happiness.

"Pleasure" is ambiguous too. In another sense, to experience pleasure is to have *pleasure-sensations*. A variety of stimuli commonly cause pleasure-sensations, such as stimulating the erogenous zones, massaging a tense muscle, scratching an itch, and stepping into a warm shower on a cold day. Pleasure-sensations have bodily location in the same way aches and pains do, but in contrast almost never last as long. Happiness is a feeling, but it is not composed of bodily sensations. It is not located in any part of the body, nor all over the body. Feeling happy does not even depend on somatic sensations in the way feeling sick or fatigued does. Pleasure-sensations do contribute to happiness, because we are happy that they occur. There are also two types of pain. "Physical" pain denotes the having of an all too familiar type of sensation. "Psychological" pain denotes suffering, misery, grief, heartache, and similar mental states. Psychological pain is unhappiness. Physical pain contributes to unhappiness.[4]

I do not deny that "pleasure" and "happiness" have different *connotations*. They certainly do. "Pleasure" suggests wordly, trivial, animal, and short-range pursuits, while "happiness" suggests spiritual, profound, noble, and long-range pursuits. These connotations have crystallized in idioms like "pleasure-seeker," "the life of pleasure," and "giving oneself over to pleasure" on the one hand, and "the happy life," "overcome by happiness," and "transports of happiness" on the other. I am not even asserting that "pleasure" and "happiness" are *synonymous*. I maintain only that in one sense the terms *refer to the same mental state*. If we want to cheer up a glum friend, to make him happy, then wine, women and song may be just the prescription. And the conditions of happiness, be they health, wealth, and self-fulfillment, are equally conditions of a pleasureful life. Intense pleasure can be derived from scientific discovery, artistic creation, and any of the noblest achievements. It is particularly evident, finally, that extreme happiness—joy—is pleasure, and that extreme unhappiness—suffering, grief, etc.—is pain.

So in one sense pleasure is a nonrelational state. There are several associated relations. Things can *please* us. Pleasing can be identified with happifying.

If X pleases A, then either A is pleased *by* X or A is pleased *with* X. I am pleased by (not with) the sound of a piano, and pleased with (not by) the condition of my piano. To be pleased by something is to *get pleasure from* it. Each type of relational pleasure is equivalent to a type of relational happiness. *A is pleased with X iff A is happy with X.* I am pleased with the condition of my piano because it makes me happy that it is in good condition. *A is pleased by X iff A is made happy by X.* I am pleased by the sound of a piano when it makes me happy. It follows that A is pleased with X iff A is pleased by the fact that X is the way it is. I am pleased by the fact that the condition of my piano is what it is. To be pleased *about* something is to be happy about it. We would expect that to be pleased *that* something is the case is to be happy that it is. Not so.[5] I am happy that the Second World War is over, but the war ended so long ago I can no longer say I am pleased that it is over. I am glad that the Russian dancer defected, but I do not care enough to be pleased that he did. Instead, we have the following equivalence: *A is pleased that p iff it makes A happy that p.* It no longer makes me happy that the war is over, and it does not make me happy that the dancer defected. It follows that to be pleased *that p* is to be pleased *by the fact that p.* I am pleased (by the fact) that I have a good job. Finally, *pleased to* can always be transformed into "pleased that." I should note that "I am pleased" is an incomplete or elliptical sentence, unlike "I am happy" or "I am experiencing pleasure." "Pleased" demands a complement.

"Please" has different contraries in different contexts. We are *pained by* the death of a loved one, *displeased with* a lousy car. Something pains us if it makes us unhappy, and displeases us if we are unhappy with it. "Pleased by" is synonymous with *gratified by.* "Gratified with" is improper, though. "Pleased with" has two near synonyms: *satisfied with* and *content with.* Pleasure is stronger than satisfaction, though. The representatives of a defeated nation may well be satisfied with the terms of the surrender, though we could hardly expect them to be pleased with the terms.[6] We may be satisfied, but not pleased, with a mediocre performance.[7] Pleasure, we might say, is positive, while satisfaction is merely non-negative. This suggests the following equation: *S is satisfied or content with X iff S is not unhappy with X*, provided S has some belief about the way X is. The fact that our performance was mediocre may not make us unhappy, but it will hardly make us happy. It follows, of course, that being pleased with something entails being satisified with it.[8] *Dissatisfaction* and satisfaction are not merely contrary, but contradictory. We must be either satisfied or dissatisfied with our performance (provided we have any beliefs about it). We can, in contrast, be neither pleased nor displeased with it. Consequently, S is dissatisfied or discontent with X iff S is unhappy with X. So dissatisfaction and displeasure are the same thing even though satisfaction and pleasure are not.

In one sense, you *like* something iff it pleases you. There are therefore as many ways of liking something as there are ways of being pleased. I like the sound of a piano, and the condition of my piano; John may like seducing young girls, and he may like the fact that he seduces them. Bedford (1959, p. 73) and Taylor (1963, p. 13) pointed out, though, that it would be impolite for a guest, while in order for the hostess, to say that she is pleased with the dessert. The guest would be guilty of no impropriety if she said only that she liked the dessert: that would be a compliment. This suggests that "X pleases A" and "A likes X" do not after all have the same truth conditions. The suggestion is misleading. It would not be at all inappropriate, let alone false, for the guest to answer "Yes" if the hostess asked, "Are you pleased with your dessert?" The conditions under which it is proper to make a statement are not always its truth conditions.

To be pleased or made happy by something is to get pleasure from it. There are, however, two different ways of getting pleasure from something.[9] John may get pleasure from seducing sixteen year old girls, or he may get pleasure from the fact that he seduces sixteen year old girls. The ways are independent. John may get pleasure from seducing young girls even though he does not get pleasure from the fact that he does; indeed, it may distress him severely that he seduces young girls, which may send him to a psychiatrist. On the other hand, John may get pleasure from the fact that he seduces young girls (he takes it as sign of youthfulness and sex appeal), even though he does not get pleasure from the act of seducing young girls (due to some physical disorder); indeed, it may hurt him to seduce young girls, and that may send him to a doctor. We can begin to see how the two ways in which something can make us happy differ by noting the following. John could not get pleasure from the fact that he seduces sixteen year old girls without knowing that he does so; but he could still get pleasure from seducing them (he might not know the age of the girls he seduces, or he might think they seduce him). A father could get pleasure from the fact that his daughter plays the piano beautifully without ever having heard her play, but he could not then get pleasure from her beautiful piano playing.

In both cases, getting pleasure from something entails being *aware* of it. But the types of awareness involved are different. We must distinguish *non-epistemic* from *epistemic* awareness.[10] This is the distinction between being aware of Heifetz playing the violin, and being aware (of the fact) *that* Heifetz is playing the violin. The latter entails knowing and believing that Heifetz is playing the violin; the former entails direct perceptual contact with Heifetz's violin playing. A person can be aware of Heifetz playing the violin even if he does not know who Heifetz is, or how to tell the difference between a violin and a viola. A person can be aware that Heifetz is playing the violin while in a sound-proof windowless monitoring booth surrounded by dials and meters. Facts or true propositions are the objects of epistemic awareness. Concrete objects, events, or states of affairs are the objects of non-epistemic awareness. John can get pleasure from seducing young girls only if he is aware of seducing them, so I call this *nonepistemic happifying or gratifying*. John can get pleasure from the fact that he seduces young girls only if he is aware that he seduces them, so this is *epistemic happifying or gratifying*.[11]

Nonepistemic gratifying is *enjoyment*. To enjoy seducing young girls is to get pleasure from seducing them, not to get pleasure from the fact that one seduces them. What is it to derive pleasure from, or be made happy by something in this way? I believe the basic idea is that the object of enjoyment *causes* one to experience happiness or pleasure. More precisely, *A is enjoying X iff A is experiencing happiness or pleasure at least in part because he is nonepistemically aware of X*. If I am enjoying the music, I must be occurrently happy, i.e., experiencing pleasure; furthermore, I must be aware of the music; and finally, I must be happy at least partly because of the music. I say at least partly, because my happiness may be a result of other things as well, such as the drink I am having and the woman I am with. To enjoy something, it is not necessary to experience any pleasure-sensations, nor is it necessary to be dispositionally happy. How much we are enjoying something can be identified with how happy we are when we are enjoying it. The happier I am when I enjoy the music, the more I enjoy the music.[12]

The above equivalence holds only if X is something other than A himself. A is enjoying *himself* iff he is enjoying *what he is doing*. Suppose John is practicing the piano. Then he is enjoying himself provided he is enjoying practicing. It follows that if someone is enjoying himself, then he is experiencing happiness and pleasure. But a person may experience happiness or pleasure without enjoying himself. John might be happy despite the fact that he is performing some unpleasant chore, such as cleaning up after his dog.

"Pleasure," used above as an abstract singular term, also occurs as a general term, as in "His pleasures are few," "It is a pleasure to meet you," and "the pleasures of dancing." A pleasure (general term) is a *source* of pleasure (singular term). A pleasure is something that makes us happy, not the state of happiness itself. More specifically, a pleasure is an object of enjoyment, something we get pleasure from nonepistemically. Playing the piano is one of my pleasures, not the fact that I play the piano. Ryle's claim (1949, p. 108) that "His digging was his pleasure, and not a vehicle of his pleasure" is therefore a false dichotomy. The common objection to ethical hedonism (pleasure is the only intrinsic good) that some pleasures are bad (such as excessive drinking, adultery, etc.), is similarly misguided. "The pleasures of dancing" refers to those aspects of dancing people enjoy. In contrast, "The pleasure of dancing" refers to the enjoyment of dancing, as in "I dance for the pleasure of dancing." Hence Kenny's complaint that on a theory of pleasure like mine, "It would be quite a contingent matter that the pleasure of drinking did not occur while eating . . ." (1963, p. 133), is mistaken. The enjoyment of drinking cannot occur, i.e., we cannot enjoy drinking, except while drinking; this follows from the definition of enjoyment given. Similarly, from the fact that the pleasure of drinking is different from the pleasure of eating, it does not follow that there is no psychological state present both when we are enjoying drinking and enjoying eating. In both cases, we experience pleasure. The pleasure of eating is different from the pleasure of drinking simply because eating is different from drinking.[13] We can agree that "a pleasure" never means "a pleasure-sensation." In contrast, "a pain" almost always means "a pain sensation," seldom "a source of pain." "Happiness" is never a general term. There is instead the idiom "Happiness is X (a cold glass of beer, being in love, freedom from want, etc.)," which means that X is a source or condition of happiness. "Happiness consists in X" means the same.

An evaluative distinction is often made between higher and lower pleasures (not to be confused with the distinction between psychological and physical pleasure, drawn above[14]). Unfortunately, the distinction is vague. It is clear that eating, drinking, and sex are to be counted lower, while the activities of the poet, artist, and mathematician are higher. There seem to be three criteria. Lower pleasures are: (a) shared with the lower animals; (b) sources of pleasure in part because they produce pleasant bodily sensations; and (c) valued less than higher pleasures by mature, cultured, and sophisticated people. These criteria conflict. Wine-tasting is higher by (a) and (c), lower by (b). Listening to country music is higher by (a) and (b), lower by (c). Pornography is lower by (b) and (c), higher by (a). I wish to emphasize that this distinction is a distinction among pleasures, sources of pleasure. The singular term "pleasure" has no parallel ambiguity. Furthermore, the term "pleasure" is strongly associated with lower pleasures, which is unfortunate, since the association is a psychological obstacle to the identification of pleasure with happiness. There is absolutely no factual basis for this association, however: there are countless sources of pleasure in addition to eating, drinking, and sex.

Two cognates of the noun "pleasure" are the adjectives *pleasant* and *pleasing*. These adjectives are equivalent, though *"pleasant* usually imputes a quality to the object to which it is applied, while *pleasing* suggests merely the effect of the object upon one" (*Webster's New Dictionary of Synonyms*). While "pleasant" has the contrary "unpleasant," "pleasing" as an adjective has no contrary. *Something is pleasant or pleasing iff it is disposed to give pleasure nonepistemically.* In other words, people are disposed to enjoy what is pleasant. We cannot say that something is pleasant only if it *actually* or *normally* gives pleasure. The view from a certain spot may be pleasant even though no one has ever enjoyed it. This may be because no one has ever been there to view it, or because the heat, humidity, and mosquitos are unendurable.[15] The view is still *disposed* to give pleasure, though in the latter case the manifestation of this disposition is inhibited by external factors. To say that something *normally* does something is much stronger than saying it is disposed to do it. Here, I believe, lies the difference between "pleasant" and *pleasurable*: the latter denotes what normally gives pleasure nonepistemically. People do enjoy what is pleasurable. I should emphasize that what is pleasurable or pleasant must be something we are pleased *by*. We may be pleased with the price of something, but that does not make the price pleasant. Furthermore, what is pleasurable or pleasant must give pleasure *nonepistemically*. Playing tennis is pleasurable, and the thought that I will play tennis today is pleasant; but the fact that I will play tennis today is neither, even though I am pleased by the fact that I will.

Pleasantness can be relativized. Something is pleasant *to A* provided it is disposed to please *A*. Something is pleasant *absolutely* provided it is disposed to please a *normal* person. Thus pain-sensations are unpleasant, even if they are pleasant to a masochist. Masochists are abnormal. The unpleasantness of pain-sensations can apparently be reduced or eliminated by a prefrontal lobotomy, a rare operation. We often describe our sensations and bodily feelings as pleasant. Pleasure-sensations are an obvious case. It must be emphasized, however, that sensations and mental entities in general are not the only pleasant things. *Any* object of nonepistemic awareness (the weather, a waitress, music) can be pleasant or unpleasant.[16] It should also be noted that pleasure-sensations are not the only pleasant sensations: the senses of taste, sight, and sound furnish countless examples. Similarly, not all unpleasant sensations are pains, e.g., an itch. Finally, note that while pleasantness is definable in terms of pleasure, they are quite different things. Pleasure is a mental state, pleasantness is not.

Pleasantness is a disposition some mental and physical objects have to pro-mote that mental state.[17]

Pleasantness and unpleasantness are contraries: nothing can be both pleas-ant and unpleasant to the same person at the same time. It is possible, however, to have two experiences, one pleasant, the other unpleasant. This would occur if I took a sip of Coke while suffering from a sore foot. A person cannot, of course, experience pleasure (happiness) and pain (unhappiness) simultane-ously. One stimulus can be *more* pleasant or unpleasant than another. A deep cut is more unpleasant than a pinprick. A is more pleasant than B provided people are disposed to enjoy A more than B. A precise degree of pleasantness cannot be assigned to an object, however. For people in different circumstances enjoy the same thing to different extents. It follows that the pleasantness of two stimuli presented together cannot be expressed as the sum of the degrees of pleasantness of the separate stimuli.[18]

So much for nonepistemic happifying. What about epistemic? It is time we specified the conditions under which it makes A happy that p. One necessary condition is that A is happy that p, from which it follows that A knows that p. It makes me happy that I won the tournament only if I am happy that I won. However, as noted above, this condition is not sufficient. Many people are glad that Kennedy defeated Nixon in the 1960 election. But if anyone were to say now (over twenty years later) that it makes him happy that Kennedy won the election, we would—as Perry[19] put it—wonder where he'd been. Most of us would be glad that the crop in Ethiopia was good last year, but unless we had some personal interest in the matter it would not make us happy that the crop was good. My suggestion is that due to lapse of time or lack of inter-est, we are not happy *enough* that these things are the case. How happy do we have to be? Happy enough to influence our happiness. This obviously needs clarification.

First observe, though, that it can make John happy that he seduces young girls even though at the moment he is not seducing anyone. He need not even be thinking about seducing young girls. However, when he does think about seducing young girls, he must have some tendency to be happy. The thought that he seduces young girls must tend to cause him to be happy. Now recall my remark that, other things equal, the happier a person is that p, the happier he is, provided the thought that p is occurring to him. I therefore suggest the following definition of epistemic happification: *It makes A happy that p iff A is happy enough that p so that he tends to be happy when thinking that p.* A need not be happy every time the thought that p occurs to him. For other unhappy thoughts might outweigh it. It may make John happy that he won the tourna-ment. But if his family was killed in an auto accident the next day, we would not expect him to be happy even if he is reminiscing about the tournament. Indeed, it may make John happy that he won even though, for one reason or another, he is generally unhappy. He must, however, have some *tendency* to be happy when he is thinking about the fact that he won. Furthermore, he must have this tendency at least in part *because* he is so happy that he won. It would not suffice for John always to be happy and also happy that he won (in which case he would tend to be happy when thinking about the win). I agree that "A is happy enough that p so that he tends to be happy when thinking that p" is vague. But so is "It makes A happy that p," in about the same way.

We can similarly say that it makes A *unhappy* that p iff A is unhappy enough that p so that he tends to be unhappy when he is thinking that p. It follows that we are satisfied with our mediocre performance provided we are not unhappy enough that it was mediocre so that we are unhappy when we think about it. This might of course be due to the fact that we are happy that it was that way. Finally, it makes A *very* happy that p iff A is happy enough that p so that he tends to be very happy when thinking about it.

NOTES

1. See "A theory of happiness," *American Philosophical Quarterly* 18 (1981): 111–20.

2. See "A theory of happiness."

3. See "A theory of happiness"; also Goldstein (1973) and Thomas (1968, p. 105).

4. Much of the philosophical literature on pleasure has been concerned with the question of whether or not pleasure is a sensation or feeling. See Ryle (1949, ch. 4; 1954a, ch. 4; 1954b), Gallie (1954), Penelhum (1957), Manser (1960–1), Zink (1962, ch. III), Von Wright (1963, ch. 4), Taylor (1963), Kenny (1963, ch. VI), Pitcher (1965), Alston (1967), Perry (1967, ch. IV), Cowan (1968, ch. 2), Gosling (1969, ch. 2), Puccetti (1969), McCloskey (1971), Momeyer (1975), and Edwards (1975).

5. See Bedford (1959, p. 85) and Perry (1967, p. 145ff).

6. This example is due to Perry (1967, p. 56).

7. Something we are pleased with is *satisfying*; something we are merely satisfied with is *satisfactory*; see Benditt (1974, p. 8).

8. If I am *quite* satisfied, or *very* content with something, then I am pleased with it.

9. This was noticed by Anscombe (1967, p. 609); a similar distinction was noticed by Gordon (1969, p. 410ff). Cf. Also Penelhum (1964, p. 82) and Perry (1967, p. 129).

10. This distinction is carefully drawn for visual awareness by Dretske (1969, ch. III).

11. There are some linguistic differences. When "X gives A pleasure" expresses epistemic pleasure-getting, it can be transformed into a sentence of the form "It gives A pleasure *that p*." And "X is giving A pleasure" can only express nonepistemic pleasure-getting.

12. The analysis of enjoyment sketched in this paragraph is developed more fully in "A Causal Theory of Enjoyment."

13. Contrast Quinn (1968, p. 582ff).

14. See Perry (1967, p. 66); contrast Edwards (1975).

15. Cf. Cowan, "The view may be a very pleasant one indeed but rendered completely unenjoyable by the swarms of mosquitos" (1968, p. 20). Contrast Hall, "The noun *pleasure* is used of that feature of human experience common to all occasions on which pleasant objects are experienced" (1966–7, p. 36). Also contrast Brandt (1979, pp. 35–42), who identifies what is pleasant with what is being enjoyed by someone.

16. Cf. Beebe-Center (1932, ch. XI).

17. An incredible amount of confusion has resulted from failure to distinguish pleasure from pleasantness, and from trying to construe pleasantness as a mental state or process. See, for example, Titchener (1909, pp. 225–264).

18. Tatarkiewicz (1976, p. 38).

19. I am indebted to Bedford (1959, p. 85) and Perry (1967, p. 45ff).

BIBLIOGRAPHY

Alston, W. P.: 1967, "Pleasure," *The Encyclopedia of Philosophy* 6, pp. 341–7.

Anscombe, G. E. M.: 1967, "On the Grammar of 'Enjoy,' " *Journal of Philosophy* 64, pp. 607–14.

Bedford, E.: 1959, "Pleasure and belief," *Proceedings of the Aristotelian Society* Supplementary vol. 33, pp. 73–92.

Beebe-Center, J. G.: 1932, *The Psychology of Pleasantness and Unpleasantness* (Van Nostrand).

Benditt, T.: 1974, "Happiness," *Philosophical Studies* 25, pp. 1–20.

Brandt, R. B.: 1969, *A Theory of the Good and the Right* (Clarendon).

Cowan, J. L.: 1968, *Pleasure and Pain* (St. Martin's Press).

Davis, W. A.: 1981, "A theory of happiness," *American Philosophical Quarterly* 18, pp. 111–20.

Davis, W. A.: "A Causal Theory of Enjoyment," unpublished.

Dretske, F. I.: 1969, *Seeing and Knowing* (U. of Chicago Press).

Edwards, R. B.: 1975, "Do pleasures and pains differ qualitatively?" *Journal of Value Inquiry* 9, pp. 270–281.

Gallie, W. B.: 1954, "Pleasure," *Proceedings of the Aristotelian Society* Supplementary vol. 28, pp. 147–164.

Goldstein, I.: 1973, "Happiness: The role of non-hedonistic criteria in its evaluation," *International Philosophical Quarterly* 13, pp. 523–34.

Gordon, R. M.: 1969, "Emotions and knowledge," *Journal of Philosophy* 66, pp. 408–13.

Gosling, J. C. B.: 1969, *Pleasure and Desire* (Clarendon).

Hall, J. C.: 1966–7, "Quantity of pleasure," *Proceedings of the Aristotelian Society* 67, pp. 35–52.

Kenny, A.: 1963, *Action, Emotion, and Will* (Humanities Press).

Manser: 1960–1, "Pleasure," *Proceedings of the Aristotelian Society* 61, pp. 223–38.

McCloskey, M. A.: 1971, "Pleasure," *Mind* 80, pp. 542–551.

McDougall, W.: 1923, *Social Psychology* (Luce).

Momeyer, R. W.: 1975, "Is pleasure a sensation?" *Philosophy and Phenomenological Research* 36, pp. 113–121.

Penelhum, T.: 1957, "The Logic of Pleasure," *Philosophy and Phenomenological Research* 17, pp. 488–503.

Penelhum, T.: 1964, "Pleasure and falsity," *American Philosophical Quarterly* 1, pp. 81–91.

Perry, D. L.: 1967, *The Concept of Pleasure* (Mouton).

Pitcher, G.: 1965, "Emotion," *Mind* 74, pp. 326–346.

Puccetti, R.: 1969, "The sensations of pleasure," *British Journal of Philosophy of Science* 20, pp. 239–245.

Quinn, W. S.: 1968, "Pleasure—disposition or episode?" *Philosophy and Phenomenological Research* 28, pp. 578–586.

Ryle, G.: 1949, *The Concept of Mind* (Barnes and Noble).

Ryle, G.: 1954a, *Dilemmas* (Cambridge).

Ryle, G.: 1954b, "Pleasure," *Proceedings of the Aristotelian Society* Supplementary vol. 28, pp. 135–46.

Tatarkiewicz, W.: 1976, *Analysis of Happiness* (Martinus Nijhoff).

Taylor, C. C. W.: 1963, "Pleasure," *Analysis* 23 Supplement, pp. 2–19.

Thomas, D. A. L.: 1968, "Happiness," *Philosophical Quarterly* 18, pp. 97–113.

Titchener, E. B.: 1909, *Textbook of Psychology* (Macmillan).

Von Wright, G. H.: 1963, *The Varieties of Goodness* (Routledge and Kegan Paul).

Zink, S.: 1962, *Concepts of Ethics* (St. Martins).

WHY HEDONISM IS FALSE

Daniel Haybron

Daniel Haybron is assistant professor of philosophy at Saint Louis University. He argues against hedonistic theories that identify happiness with pleasure.

1. INTRODUCTION

Some unlucky soul might, over a period of time, be depressed, despondent, beset with anxiety, "stressed out," seething with rage, overwhelmed by fear, worried sick, heartbroken, grief-stricken, lonely, in low spirits, burdened with shame, overcome with boredom, deeply dissatisfied with life, haunted by a sense of dread or by feelings of emptiness, or simply be melancholy. A more fortunate counterpart might be in high spirits, joyful, exhilarated, elated, jubilant, carefree, deeply contented, at peace, delighted with her life, or blessed with a profound sense of fulfillment or well-being. Persons of the former sort we naturally deem *unhappy*. Those of the latter we call *happy*. Indeed, these would seem to be prototypical cases of unhappiness and happiness, at least in one important sense of these expressions. Concerned parents probably have circumstances like these in mind when they inquire as to whether their children are happy. Likewise for young job seekers who worry that they may not be happy if they choose the wrong vocation.

Let "hedonism" denote the venerable doctrine that happiness, so construed, reduces completely to a subject's balance of pleasure over displeasure: happiness is merely the condition of having a favorable balance of pleasure over displeasure. I wish to argue that this theory is false. Indeed, it never had a chance of being true, for it fundamentally misconstrues the nature of the mental states that could constitute anything plausibly called happiness. . . .

2. PRELIMINARIES

We can mean any number of things by "happiness."[1] In such cases as the foregoing—henceforth the "paradigm cases"—we typically intend to denote nothing more profound than a state of mind. In our more lyrical moments, we might refer to it as a condition of the soul or spirit. Though such talk bears unfortunate connotations of cheap New Age sentimentality, these terms are here used in a common secular and naturalistic sense, and are meant to suggest something psychologically deep, intimate and important to us. To distinguish our subject from other things commonly called happiness, we may call this

From Daniel Haybron, "Happiness and Pleasure," *Philosophy and Phenomenological Research*, vol. 62 (2001). Used by permission of the journal.

state of mind *psychological happiness*. So construed, happiness is a purely psychological, nonevaluative kind.[2]

Philosophers often use "happiness" with other meanings, most frequently to denote a particularly enviable condition in life: a type of well-being or flourishing. Thus we commonly see the patently evaluative Greek expression *"eudaimonia"* translated as "happiness." This evaluative kind I refer to as *prudential happiness*. Whereas a correct theory of prudential happiness is determined by asking what sorts of lives make us better off, the task of providing a theory of psychological happiness—our task—is to determine the nature of a certain type of psychological state.[3] We can distinguish other senses of "happiness," but the foregoing remarks should suffice for our purposes.[4]

Of more immediate concern is the possibility that there may be no single psychological kind answering to the psychological sense of "happiness." Or maybe the vernacular notion is so ill-defined that it admits of no satisfactory analysis. Maybe there *is* no well-defined folk notion to analyze. No doubt such worries have led many philosophers to conclude that happiness is not a worthwhile object of study. Let us suppose, for the sake of argument, that these concerns are well-founded. It hardly follows that there is no subject matter worth studying. There are clearly aspects of our psychology that we denote, however imprecisely or confusedly, under the guise of happiness. These aspects are almost universally taken to be immensely valuable—indeed, to comprise a central element of human well-being. We have no reason to doubt this belief. We therefore ought to *learn* something about these phenomena. Even if they simply reduce to familiar psychological categories, we shall have discovered something important; and then we can determine just how valuable happiness is. Maybe, when all is said and done, we will find that happiness is not so valuable after all. And if the resulting kind or kinds do not correspond neatly to our vernacular notion of happiness, we may need to revise our concept somewhat. If more than one kind answers to the name, then we may wish to distinguish further senses of "happiness," restrict its proper use to just one of the kinds, or dispense with the term altogether. But the idea that such weighty matters do not deserve serious philosophical scrutiny at all is simply *obtuse*. . . .

3. WHY HEDONISM IS FALSE

The most obvious problem with existing hedonistic theories is that they are too inclusive: all sorts of shallow, fleeting pleasures are made to count towards happiness. Yet such pleasures manifestly play no constitutive role in determining how happy a person is. One's enjoyment of eating crackers, hearing a good song, sexual intercourse, scratching an itch, solving a puzzle, playing football, and so forth need not have the slightest impact on one's level of happiness (though, of course, they may). I enjoy, get pleasure from, a cheeseburger, yet I am patently not happier *thereby*.[5] Conversely for superficial displeasures. The problem does not concern the intensity of such pleasures: an orgasm may well be intensely pleasurable, yet still fail to *move* one, to make one any happier (consider anonymous sex or masturbation). Might the brief duration of the event be misleading our intuitions here? Not likely: it is not just that any particular superficial pleasure seems irrelevant. Even the whole *pattern* of such pleasures over time appears to be. We would certainly expect that someone who underwent an unrelenting succession of minor irritations would not be very happy at the end of it all. But this expectation is based not on the aggregation of particular pleasures but rather on the likely effect of these pleasures on some deeper aspect of one's psychology: one's mood, perhaps inter alia. Intuitively, the trouble seems to be that such pleasures don't reach "deeply" enough, so to speak. They just don't *get* to us; they flit through consciousness and that's the end of it.

This consideration alone appears to undermine any hedonistic account of which I am aware. It also demonstrates the error of equating talk of hedonic states with talk of happiness, as many commentators are wont to do. The pleasures of happiness are not the only pleasures to be had, though perhaps they are the most desirable. Perhaps some restricted form of hedonism could suffice: happiness is a matter of pleasure, but only a certain kind of pleasure— "deep" pleasure, maybe, or the Epicurean pleasures of tranquillity. This sort of proposal also has serious problems. To show why, I shall discuss a couple of alternative theories and explain what distinguishes them from hedonism. Doing so will clarify the errors that beset all forms of hedonism. . . .

Recall the paradigm cases cited at the beginning of this paper—e.g., profound depression and anxiety on the one hand, and a deep sense of well-being and joy on the other. What is it that makes them examples of happiness and unhappiness? Right away, it seems more than a bit odd to say that these people are happy or unhappy simply by virtue of experiencing a great deal of pleasure or displeasure. They certainly are experiencing those. But that is not what constitutes their being happy. If it were, then we might as well add to our list of prototypically unhappy people someone who is experiencing serious chronic pain. No doubt, we should expect such a person to be unhappy. But his pain is not his unhappiness, if he is indeed unhappy (perhaps he is a highly disciplined Buddhist monk). It is, rather, the *source* of his unhappiness.

Instead, we would suppose that—him most likely not being a Buddhist monk—his pain *gets him down*. It makes him depressed and irritable, not to mention highly dissatisfied with his lot in life. And it is far more plausible to suppose that he is unhappy in virtue of *these* underlying states, caused by the physical pain. One who is depressed, irritable, and dissatisfied with his life, then, is thereby unhappy. In light of such considerations, one natural proposal is that happiness consists in a person's emotional state: insofar as one's emotional state is basically positive, one is happy. Thus such positive emotional conditions as a predominance of joyfulness, high-spiritedness, peace of mind, etc. would exemplify happiness, while a predominance of their negative counterparts—depression, anxiety, fear, anger, feelings of discontent, etc.— would typify unhappiness. . . .

At the root of the problem is the fact that hedonistic happiness consists of nothing but a series of conscious events: to know that someone is happy on this view is only to know that his recent experience has been mostly positive. So construed, ascriptions of happiness are little more than capsule summaries or histories of subjects' conscious episodes. . . . Hedonistic happiness is an essentially *episodic* and backward-looking phenomenon. But happiness is obviously not just the having of a certain kind of experience, or even lots of them. It is rather a deeper psychological condition incorporating the more or less stable underlying mental states that *determine*, in part and among other things, the kinds of experiences that will occur. It is a substantially dispositional phenomenon. It tells us not just about subjects' histories, but also about their current condition and propensities for the near future. It is forward-looking. Being in a certain sort of mood state or thymic state is such a condition. So, it would seem, is having a certain attitude towards one's life. Experiencing pleasure is not. Hedonism is thus fundamentally wrong about the kind of mental state that happiness is. It appears to commit something of a category mistake.

An important aspect of hedonism's error is that pleasure lacks what we may call *causal depth*. All appearances are that happiness has deep, far-reaching, and typically lasting consequences for a person's state of mind and behavior. Theories ought to respect this appearance, or explain why they need not if they do not. Causal depth has three aspects. First, causally deep states or conditions are *productive*. That is, they are prolific in their causal effects. Second, they are *wide-ranging* in their effects; their effects are not limited to a narrow class of states. Third and most importantly, they are in some sense psychologically *deep*: they affect one's psychological condition at a very profound and basic level, in typically lasting ways, and not simply in superficial and transient ways. This is partly a matter of disposing one to have certain mental states rather than others. Pleasure does not have causal depth to anything like the extent that, say, thymic states do. Hedonism does little more than skim the phenomenal surface off of our emotional states and call it happiness. But happiness runs much deeper than that. . . .

The hedonist might object that *any* credible conception of happiness is bound to be backward-looking. For ascriptions of happiness typically do not simply report on subjects' current states, but mostly characterize the general tenor of their states in the recent past. A subject's present condition, one might argue, will comprise only a small part of what's described, making happiness only marginally forward-looking at best. Hedonists who raise this concern will be sorry they asked, since it not only fails, its manner of failure reveals another of hedonism's shortcomings. To understand why the objection misfires we should consider the time frame relative to which happiness is defined in ordinary ascriptive practice. Is it a week, a month, a lifetime? In fact the appropriate period of time depends on the context, and is often somewhat indeterminate; a person may be happy with respect to the present year, yet unhappy today. Is there a minimum? For all intents and purposes, no: asked if I am happy, I might sensibly reply that, while I'm generally very happy these days, I'm nonetheless pretty unhappy at the moment. (For I am momentarily upset over a flat tire.) Also, one's level of happiness may change dramatically in a very short time frame: informed of a child's sudden death, for example, a parent will immediately undergo profound and thoroughgoing changes in her state of mind—will pass, that is, from a state in which she may be quite happy to a state of extreme unhappiness. But this state may not continue for long if she quickly learns that she was misinformed, and that her child is just fine. (Doubtless it will take her a while to recover from the shock, but this probably needn't be more than a few hours.) So there appears to be enormous flexibility in the temporal reach of happiness ascriptions.

That said, happiness is normally ascribed over the long term. When the context fails to supply specific temporal cues, we tend to fall back on certain defaults, and these are invariably lengthy ones. So if I simply report that I am happy, that will generally be taken to apply to some extended period of time—probably whatever I see as the current period of my life, which itself is likely to be fairly indefinite and context-sensitive. Despite their predominantly long-term character, happiness ascriptions possess an interesting and important connection to the present: unqualified true attributions of happiness strongly suggest, and appear to entail, that the subject is happy *now*. They do not merely summarize the subject's recent psychological history, but tell us something about the subject's present condition. Thus if a person's state of mind has been consistently favorable for the last month, but plummeted in just the last hour on hearing terrible news concerning her child we would not want to describe her simply as happy. We would instead rate her as very unhappy, though we may well wish to point out that she had until recently been quite the opposite. Contrast this with the . . . example involving a flat-tire-induced bad mood. There also we refer specifically to the subject's present state. But notice that the emphasis is reversed, and rests on the subject's broader condition. Thus we say that I am happy "generally," but not at the moment.

Is this a problem for my claim about (what we may call) the present-anchored focus of happiness ascriptions? No, but it is a problem for hedonism. For what anchors our ascriptions is not the quality of our immediate experience, which may be anomalous. The anchoring is performed, rather, by some deeper aspect of our psychology that better reflects our general disposition. . . . Hedonism . . . would seem to treat the flat tire and aggrieved parent cases more or less identically: in each case the subject's experience has been pleasant until now. There is in these examples a difference in intensity, but it would not be hard to construct parallel cases in which the intensity ordering is different. *That's* not the problem. The problem is that something psychologically deep and (typically) lasting has happened in one case but not the other. Hedonism fails to distinguish deeper and shallower aspects of happiness and therefore lacks the power to handle such cases. . . .

In short, happiness is not backward-looking in the extreme manner that hedonism takes it to be, for ascriptions are anchored firmly in the present. It is doubtful whether hedonism can respect this property of happiness ascriptions at all. If it does—thus handling cases like the aggrieved parent—it appears to do so only at the cost of getting cases like the flat tire wrong. (We would not want to say simply that this individual is unhappy, for his bad mood is anomalous and highly misleading about his general frame of mind, which is typically what interests us with respect to happiness. Yet the hedonist who takes this course essentially reduces happiness ascriptions to claims about the pleasantness of one's immediate experience.) Even if hedonism can anchor happiness in the present, its characterization of subjects' present conditions is so superficial as to license little in the way of prediction. That my experience is now pleasant says next to nothing about my propensities for the future— maybe I just like the ice cream I am eating—whereas the fact that my mood or attitude towards my life . . . is positive would certainly seem to say rather more. This is yet another problem.

NOTES

1. To simplify matters I shall generally refer only to happiness, assuming that whatever is said of happiness also applies, *mutatis mutandis*, to unhappiness.

2. Philosophers who appear to accept hedonism about psychological happiness include, among many others, such historical thinkers as Bentham, Locke, and Sidgwick; and more recently, Brandt (1959; 1979; 1989; 1992); Campbell (1973); Carson (1978a; 1978b; 1979; 1981); Davis (1981b; 1981a); Ebenstein (1991); Griffin (1979; 1986); Mayerfeld (1996; 1999); Sen (1987); Sprigge (1987; 1991); and Wilson (1968). Casual references to happiness in the philosophical literature frequently assume it to be hedonistic. Hedonism has adherents in psychology as well, such as Allen Parducci (1995) and Daniel Kahneman (1999).

3. I use terms like "kind" and "category" very loosely here, with no particular metaphysical commitments in mind. For instance, the relevant psychological kinds may have no place in scientific, versus folk, psychology. I talk of psychological kinds only to distinguish the present concept from evaluative notions such as that of prudential happiness.

To illustrate: one might wish to argue that psychological happiness is the proper measure of well-being—and many have done so (mistakenly, in my view). But this is different from making an a priori stipulation that happiness—whatever it is—must characterize what it is to have an especially enviable life. The theorists who do so are not involved in the same business that engages us here. Thus even if well-being consists solely in the psychological state of pleasure, well-being is still an evaluative, and not psychological, kind.

4. For more on the uses of "happiness" and cognates, see my (2000; unpublished ms-c), as well as Davis (1981b), Goldstein (1973), and Thomas (1968).

5. Though perhaps soul food is so-called for a putative capacity to produce just such an impact!

BIBLIOGRAPHY

Brandt, R. B. (1959). *Ethical Theory*. Englewood Cliffs, New Jersey, Prentice-Hall.
Brandt, R. B. (1979). *A Theory of the Good and the Right*. New York, Oxford University Press.
Brandt, R. B. (1989). "Fairness to Happiness." *Social Theory & Practice* 15: 33–58.
Brandt, R. B. (1992). *Morality, Utilitarianism, and Rights*. New York, Cambridge University Press.
Campbell, R. (1973). "The Pursuit of Happiness." *Personalist*: 325–37.
Cowan, J. L. (1968). *Pleasure and Pain: A Study in Philosophical Psychology*. New York, Macmillan.
Davis, W. (1981a). "Pleasure and Happiness." *Philosophical Studies* 39: 305–18.
Davis, W. (1981b). "A Theory of Happiness." *American Philosophical Quarterly* 18: 111–20.
Ebenstein, A. O. (1991). *The Greatest Happiness Principle: An Examination of Utilitarianism*. New York, Garland.
Goldstein, I. (1973). "Happiness: The Role of Non-Hedonic Criteria in Its Evaluation." *International Philosophical Quarterly* 13: 523–34.
Goldstein, I. (1980). "Why People Prefer Pleasure to Pain." *Philosophy* 55: 349–62.
Goldstein, I. (1989). "Pleasure and Pain: Unconditional, Intrinsic Values." *Philosophy and Phenomenological Research* 50(2): 255–76.
Griffin, J. (1979). "Is Unhappiness Morally More Important Than Happiness?" *Philosophical Quarterly*: 47–55.
Griffin, J. (1986). *Well-Being: Its Meaning, Measurement, and Moral Importance*. Oxford, Clarendon Press.

Haybron, D. M. (unpublished ms-a). Happiness and the Importance of Life Satisfaction. Department of Philosophy, Rutgers University.

Kahneman, D. (1999). Objective Happiness. *Well-Being: The Foundations of Hedonic Psychology.* D. Kahneman, E. Diener and N. Schwarz. New York, Russell Sage Foundation: 3–25.

Mayerfeld, J. (1996). "The Moral Asymmetry of Happiness and Suffering." *Southern Journal of Philosophy* 34: 317–38.

Mayerfeld, J. (1999). *Suffering and Moral Responsibility.* New York, Oxford University Press.

Parducci, A. (1995). *Happiness, Pleasure, and Judgement: The Contextual Theory and Its Applications.* Mahwah, New Jersey, L. Erlbaum Associates.

Sen, A. (1987). *Commodities and Capabilities.* New York, Oxford University Press.

Sprigge, T. L. S. (1987). *The Rational Foundations of Ethics.* New York, Routledge and Kegan Paul.

Thomas, D. A. L. (1968). "Happiness." *Philosophical Quarterly* 18: 97–113.

Wilson, J. (1968). "Happiness." *Analysis* 29: 13–21.

B. Happiness as Satisfaction

ATTITUDINAL AND EPISODIC HAPPINESS

John Kekes

John Kekes is Emeritus Professor of Philosophy at the University at Albany, State University of New York. He argues that happiness has two aspects: an attitude and a collection of episodes that contribute to forming the attitude.

I

In this paper I propose a way of understanding happiness. My main interest is in the kind of lasting happiness that a man's whole life can possess. My strategy is to begin with the commonsensical view of this kind of happiness and then go on to refine it by noticing the complexities implicit in this simple view and by criticizing some inadequate philosophical approaches to it.

According to common sense, then, a happy man is satisfied with his life. He would like it to continue the same way. If asked, he would say that things are going well for him. His most important desires are being satisfied. He

From John Kekes, "Happiness," *Mind,* vol. 91 (1982). Used by permission of the journal.

is doing and having most of what he wants. He frequently experiences joy, contentment, and pleasure. Such a man is not divided about his life, for, on the whole, it is as he wants it to be. He is not often beset by fundamental inner conflicts. He is not given to depression, anxiety, or frustration. He does not contemplate fundamental changes in the way he lives; has no serious regrets about important decisions he has taken; nor is he lastingly resentful, envious, guilty, ashamed, or jealous.

Happiness has two aspects: one is an attitude, the other is a collection of episodes contributing to forming the attitude. The episodes are satisfactions derived from what one does and has. The attitude is satisfaction with one's life as a whole. A man's life is largely composed of what he does and has. Of course, possessions need not be material goods. They may be talents, personal relationships, the respect of others, worldly success, or a private sense of well-being. Nor should activities be thought of merely as publicly observable behaviour. Reflectiveness, aesthetic appreciation, feelingfulness, quiet amusement are private activities, yet they are conducive to happiness.

The attitudinal aspect of happiness is more than a succession of satisfying episodes. For the attitude requires that the significance of the episodes be appraised in terms of one's whole life. This appraisal need not involve conscious reflection, although it frequently does. It may simply be an unspoken feeling of approval of one's life and a sense that particular episodes fit into it. The episodes may be goals achieved, obstacles overcome, experiences enjoyed, or just a seamless continuation of the approved pattern of one's life.

Without many such episodes, the attitude cannot be maintained. But the connection between satisfying episodes and an attitude of satisfaction with one's life is not simple. Polus in *Gorgias* is a typical spokesman for the simple view that if a man does and has what he wants, he is happy.[1] It is clearly true that if someone cannot have or do anything he wants, he cannot be happy. Happiness is incompatible with complete frustration. However, Polus is mistaken in thinking that the satisfaction of one's wants assures happiness.

Consider a man who has all he wants. To begin with, some wants are important and lasting, while others are trivial and transitory. Wanting the waiter to hurry up with my lunch is not in a class with Hume's ruling passion. All of us can tolerate unsatisfied minor wants, and these only exceptionally stand in the way of happiness. So we must concentrate on a man who has all he seriously wants. But suppose that he wants only one thing; he pursues it single-mindedly, to the exclusion of everything else, and while he gets it, his soul shrivels. Rich misers, successful avengers, triumphant climbers of greasy poles notoriously find themselves empty, once their obsessions are satisfied. Or a man may want only what he does not have, and when he gets it, like Don Juan, he no longer wants it. Yet others are mistaken in thinking that what they want will satisfy them. The glittering sophistication of an inner circle may pale once the outsider finds himself accepted. Having what one wants, therefore, is no guarantee of happiness.

Nor should it be supposed that doing all that one really wants leads to happiness. Of course, not being able to do anything one wants makes happiness impossible. But doing what one wants is not sufficient for it, because a man may want to do something with the full realization that it will not make him happy. He may want to commit suicide, do his duty at great cost to himself, choose the happiness of his child, parent, or lover over his own, or continue with a deadly routine out of fear, resignation, or lack of imagination. Nor can we say that doing all that one wants is necessary for happiness. For a happy man can tolerate frustrated wants. A woman may be happy in her life even though she realizes that her career is incompatible with having the children she wants. The cost of happiness is frequently to leave some wants unsatisfied. Life forces one to choose. Happiness is not unconnected with the capacity to prevent frustration from spoiling what one has.

So we must reject with Socrates the simple view of Polus. In its place, I offer the suggestion that if a man is satisfied with many of the important things he does and has, then one condition of his happiness is met. Doing and having what one wants figure as formal notions in this suggestion. The advantage of this is that we can say what happiness consists in without having to specify the particular possessions and activities that may be conducive to it. Happiness essentially involves satisfactions. But, having learned from Polus's mistake, we can say that there is no particular satisfaction indispensable to happiness, nor a dissatisfaction inevitably prohibiting it.

The satisfaction of important wants involves the episodic aspect of happiness. Happiness, however, also has an attitudinal aspect. We have already observed that this aspect is also connected with satisfaction. But the object of satisfaction here is one's life as a whole. The connection between these two aspects can be approached through the notion of importance. Happiness requires the satisfaction of many important wants. Important wants depend on what someone wants to make of his life.

We should thus distinguish between first and second-order wants and also between first and second-order satisfactions.[2] A first-order want is wanting to do or have something. A second-order want is wanting to have a life in which important first-order wants are generally satisfied. A first-order satisfaction is derived from the fulfilment of first-order wants, while second-order satisfaction consists in having satisfied the second-order want. Thus a man has many first-order wants and satisfaction, but only one second-order want and satisfaction.

First-order wants and satisfactions belong in the context of the episodic aspect of happiness. Their objects are specific activities and possessions. The second-order want and satisfaction occur in the context of the attitudinal aspect of happiness. Their object is the total life of a man. Second-order satisfactions logically depend on first-order satisfactions and the second-order want logically involves first-order wants. The precise nature of this logical connection, however, cannot be given. For it is impossible to specify what particular wants, how many of them, with what frequency, and to what extent must be satisfied so that a man could reasonably judge that he is satisfied with his life as a whole. What is possible to specify is one necessary condition of a happy life, namely, a man has it only if his second-order want is satisfied.

This has important implications. First, a man is extremely unlikely to have a happy life without having a more or less clearly formed view about what his life should be. If a seeker of haphazard satisfactions can truly claim to have enjoyed a great many of them, he still cannot be said to have a happy life. For his satisfactions may be of unimportant wants or of only a few of his important wants. It is just a fact that one must choose between satisfactions. The more direction one has given to his life, the more intelligent choice is likely to contribute to his overall happiness, and the less direction there is, the smaller is the chance of achieving a happy life. Therefore, happiness involves the balanced pursuit of first-order satisfactions. If we did not live in a condition of scarcity, if we did not have a conflict between short and long-range satisfactions, if the stages in life's way did not affect our wants and satisfactions, then this balance would not be required. I am not denying that imbalance is compatible with many episodic satisfactions; I am denying that these episodes add up to a happy life.

We might mark this point by distinguishing between feeling happy and being lastingly happy. The feeling is a temporary result of a first-order satisfaction. A demanding task well done, sexual gratification, the experience of a work of art may produce it. Being lastingly happy comes from the second-order satisfaction involving one's whole life. It does not depend on any particular first-order satisfaction. A man cannot be lastingly happy unless he frequently feels happy. But one can feel happy and yet not be lastingly happy, for the transitory satisfaction may not amount to overall satisfaction with one's life.

The second implication has to do with pleasure and pain. A man can put up with a great deal of pain and still have a happy life. In the first place, physical and psychological suffering may be episodic and such episodes may be outweighed by others in the long run. God presumably did not fail to look after Job in this manner. Furthermore, even if a man is frequently in pain, he may enjoy overall happiness, provided very many of his other important wants are satisfied. It is not impossible for a marathon runner to be happy.

The connection between happiness and pleasure, of course, informs the history of this subject. It is an elementary point that if pleasure is taken to mean all forms of satisfaction, then happiness is necessarily connected with pleasure. But this is just a misleading way of noting the obvious. On the other hand, if pleasure is regarded as a specific physical sensation, then it is clearly false that happiness is necessarily connected with it. For there are many forms of satisfaction—aesthetic appreciation, parental love, being given one's due —which have nothing to do with this physical sensation. A life without any pleasure, in this second sense, probably cannot be happy. But it is wrong to suppose that pleasure is part of every episode of satisfaction.

Happiness comes in degrees. The extent to which a man is happy depends, first of all, on the satisfaction of his important first-order wants. These satisfactions are quantitative, having to do with number and frequency. And they are also qualitative, depending on the intensity of particular satisfaction. But the degree to which a man is happy depends also on the kind of first-order want he regards as important. Men differ about this and so it is not to be expected that when different men are correctly described as being, as opposed to feeling, happy, then it is reasonable to make quantitative or qualitative comparisons between them. The cluster of satisfactions Falstaff, Saint Theresa, Disraeli, Picasso, and Montaigne regarded as important were different, to put it mildly. Each was happy to a degree, and even if we could succeed in ascertaining that they were happy to the same degree—whatever same could mean here—it would be fatuous to suppose that they were in similar states. I labour this point, because cruder forms of utilitarianism rest on the supposition that a hedonic calculus could be constructed for measuring the extent to which different men approximate the same state of happiness.

A reasonable man wants to be as happy as possible, for this comes to wanting to satisfy his important first-order wants. But wanting to be happy does not mean that all reasonable men want the same thing, nor does it mean that they want it unconditionally. Happiness differs from man to man, because different men have different clusters of important first-order wants. And the pursuit of happiness is not unconditional, because a man may come to believe that his important first-order wants are incompatible, harmful, injurious to those he loves, or that the requirements of his family, country, or profession take precedence over the satisfaction of his own wants. So we can say that a reasonable man wants to be happy, and, unless there are reasons not to do so, he should aim to increase his happiness. But I do not mean that the pursuit of happiness is the only or the most important aim a reasonable man can have.

II

How should a man decide which of his wants are important? Aristotle has an answer: "Everyone who has the power to live according to his own choice should . . . set up for himself some object for the good life to aim at . . . by reference to which he will do all that he does, since not to have one's life organized in view of some end is a sign of great folly."[3] Thus one should plan his life for the attainment of an end. An important want depends on this end. Aristotle also tells us what this end is: it is "the activity of soul in accordance with virtue, and if there are more than one virtue, in accordance with the best and most complete."[4] This turns out to be "For man . . . the life according to reason is best and pleasantest, since reason more than anything else is man. This life therefore is also the happiest" (NE, 1178n5–9). Aristotle makes clear that the reason is theoretical (NE, X, 7–8).

Hardie[5] argues that Aristotle's answer is open to two interpretations: one defensible, the other not. The interpretations hinge on the distinction between dominant and inclusive ends. "A man, reflecting on his various desires and interests, notes that some mean more to him than others, that some are more, some less, difficult and costly to achieve, that the attainment of one may, in different degrees, promote or hinder the attainment of others. By such reflection he is moved to plan to achieve at least his most important objectives as fully as possible. The following of such a plan is roughly what is meant by the pursuit of happiness" (pp. 299–300). Happiness, understood in this way, is an inclusive end. But Aristotle frequently thinks of happiness as a dominant end, that is, as the exercise of one particular virtue: theoretical reason. On the interpretation of happiness as an inclusive end, reason is required for the construction of a life-plan that makes the pursuit of happiness possible. But if happiness is taken to be a dominant end, it consists in the exercise of theoretical reason.

The interpretation of happiness as a dominant end makes Aristotle's position indefensible. For the single-minded pursuit of one end dooms a man to a life of frustration, since his other wants will remain unsatisfied. The exclusive pursuit of a single end is a vice. Thinking of rationality and happiness in this way gives both a bad name, as Oakeshott has convincingly argued.[6] I shall interpret happiness as an inclusive end. This end, then, is a rational life-plan for the satisfaction of first-order wants. What want is important depends on one's life-plan.

The satisfaction of important first-order wants has a dual significance. One aspect of it is obtaining its object and thereby finding first-order satisfaction. The other is the influence of the satisfied first-order want on the life of the agent. For each satisfied first-order want is an episode contributing to the formation of the man's attitude to his life as a whole. So a reasonable man seeking happiness will ask himself two questions about satisfying any of his important first-order wants: how should I go about satisfying it? and should I want to have the kind of life in which this kind of want, rather than another, is regarded as important? The pursuit of happiness, therefore, is not just the pursuit of first-order satisfactions, but also the construction of one's life. These carefree grazers in the field of satisfaction for whom Polus speaks miss the importance of the second question. As a result, they can perhaps feel happy if luck is with them, but they cannot be happy. This, I think, is the substance of the Socratic dictum that the unexamined life is not worth living.

The second question, about the kind of life one wants, is answered in terms of a life-plan. A life-plan is the hierarchical ordering of first-order wants. When a man has decided about the place of a want in his life, he has, I shall say, made a commitment. Commitments function as standards by which wants are judged.

Three kinds of commitments need to be distinguished: unconditional, defeasible, and loose,[7] depending on their importance to the man being or becoming what he wants to be. Robert Bolt's portrayal of Thomas More[8] provides a good example for discussing them.

As Bolt tells it, More was prepared to, and eventually did, go to his death, because he would not take an oath falsely. The details are irrelevant, but I mention in passing that they concern the question of whether Henry VIII was legally and morally entitled to marry Anne Boleyn. What matters is that More had an unconditional commitment to a certain kind of morality; that is, he wanted, more than anything else, to be a certain kind of man. He was unwilling to violate this unconditional commitment, not even to save his own life.

An unconditional commitment can be dishonoured, but only at the cost of inflicting great psychological damage upon oneself. More was a hero and a saint, and he died for his unconditional commitment. Most of us are made of softer stuff. But the violation of these commitments is no less damaging to weaker men. There is a crisis, we do something, and we realize that we cannot come to terms with what we did. The man we have considered ourselves being would not have done that. We did it, so we are not what we took ourselves to be. The result is that an abyss opens up at the centre of our being. We disintegrate, go mad, or carry on in a desultory way looking in vain for a chance to undo the dreadful thing we had done.

There are many examples of what happens when unconditional commitments are violated. One is Lord Jim who spent a lifetime expiating for his one cowardly act. Another is the tragedy of many survivors of concentration camps who suspect that they survived, at the expense of others who did not, because they accommodated themselves to unspeakable evils which the dead, their betters, rejected. A further case in point is the man who finds himself guilty of what he regards as sacrilege, as Oedipus was of incest and parricide. Or Othello and King Lear who, in the throes of their respective passions, injured those who loved them most.

Unconditional commitments are not universal, for they vary from man to man. Nor are they categorical, for a man may decide to violate them. They are unconditional, because they are fundamental conditions of a man being what he wants to be. This is the point at which happiness and morality connect. For both essentially involve a clear sense of basic commitments and the extreme seriousness of their violation. (I shall return to this.)

Many men have no unconditional commitments. This means that they have no clear sense of themselves. The moral consequence is that they may be nice, but not good.[9] Such men are afloat in conventional morality, but they have not made its requirements their own. This is one source of moral relativism. If morality is seen as conventional, then, they erroneously conclude, ultimately nothing matters. As Ivan Karamazov says: if there is no God, everything is permitted. But this is a simple, though ubiquitous, mistake. It rests on the mistaken assumption that a commitment can be unconditional only if it is universal. I see no reason why personal commitments could not be unconditional. Indeed, it is just such commitments that give a man integrity, a sense of identity, and make his happiness possible by providing a standard for ordering first-order wants. It is quite irrelevant to the unconditionality of these standards how many others share them.

The second kind of commitments are defeasible. They are normally honoured, but they can be overriden by countervailing reasons. The difference between unconditional and defeasible commitments is that, normally, in the case of the former, but not of the latter, no reason will be accepted by the agent, in a cool moment, that could override them. For the most weighty reasons are just those that appeal to unconditional commitments. Of course, these commitments and reasons can change. But the change, as we have seen, results in a drastic alteration of a man's life and view of himself.

As Bolt describes him, More was deeply in love with his wife and he loved his children no less. His commitment to them, however was defeasible, because he decided, upon due reflection, that his commitment to God was deeper. So he went to his death and left his family to fend for themselves. When it came to the point, someone in More's position could have decided to take the oath falsely, because his obligation to his family came first. But that decision could only have been made by another man—a man More could change into. More, however, was what he was, because he placed his commitment to God above his commitment to his family.

Defeasible commitments guide our everyday practices. They overlap with conventional morality; they include the commitments incurred by one's station and duties and also the ways in which a man goes about satisfying his first-order wants. A man can be happy, successful, and upright just by living up to his defeasible commitments. The appeal to unconditional commitments is made only in crises, when the guidance of defeasible commitments is unclear.

This may occur when defeasible commitments systematically conflict. Typical conflicts of this sort are between charity and justice, love and self-interest, short and long-range satisfaction.

Loose commitments are on the outer fringes of our lives. They usually concern the particular forms taken by the fulfilment of unconditional and defeasible commitments. These forms are the products of a man's culture, education, and society. More was a patriotic man, his commitment to England was defeasible. The form it took was fealty to his King. But this, for More, was a loose commitment, for the author of *Utopia* understood better than most that the demands of patriotism are historically and socially conditioned. Loose commitments are comparable to the style of an artist. He must have some style or another, but whatever it is, it should be a proper vehicle for the expression of substance. Similarly for man: conditional and defeasible commitments must be expressed, but the particular ways in which this is done is of secondary importance.

The claim I have been supporting up to now is that the satisfaction of one's second-order want is necessary to being happy. The achievement of this second-order satisfaction, in turn, depends both on the satisfaction of many of one's important first-order wants and on the possession of a life-plan. A life-plan is a three-tiered structure of commitments. These commitments determine the kind of man one wants to be, and, thus, guide the distinction between more and less important first-order wants. Without the satisfaction of many important first-order wants a man cannot be happy, for his most important aspirations would then be frustrated. Equally, unless first-order wants are balanced in terms of his life-plan, a man will not achieve happiness, for he does not then know how to resolve inevitable conflicts between first-order wants, and thus how to go about satisfying his own wants.

III

Is the satisfaction of one's second-order want sufficient, and not merely necessarily, for being happy? That is, can we say that happiness consists in having a life-plan and in satisfying one's first-order wants in accordance with it? This question can be approached from the first-person internal point of view and also from the external third-person one. The former has a man ask whether he himself is happy if these conditions are met; the latter is formulated about a man and it is asked by witnesses to his life. I shall call the first the subjective view of happiness, and the second the objective view.[10]

According to the objective view, if a man judges that he is happy, on the grounds that his first-order wants are satisfied in accordance with his life-plan, then one necessary condition of his happiness is met. But this is not sufficient for happiness, because he may be mistaken. The subjective view is that if a man judges himself to be happy on these grounds, then he is happy; the judgement is both necessary and sufficient for happiness.

It is important to recognize that this disagreement does not turn on the distinction between feeling and being happy. The subjective view is not that if a man feels happy, then he is happy. Both the subjective and the objective views allow for the distinction between first and second-order wants. Thus both can say that the satisfaction of first-order wants and the consequent feeling of happiness are not sufficient for being happy. For a man can be satisfied in many ways and yet be dissatisfied with his life.

Both the subjective and objective views interpret happiness in the inclusive sense: it involves the satisfaction of one's second-order want. At issue between them is the possibility of a man making a mistake about being happy. How could one reasonably say of someone else: he really thinks that he is happy with his life, but he is not? What could a mistake be here? How could a man be corrected in this allegedly mistaken judgement?

This is one of the great divides in moral philosophy. Plato, Aristotle, and Christian moralists think that there are certain kinds of life proper to man and it is a mistake to suppose oneself happy unless he lives one of these. Emotivists, existentialists, and egoists, on the other hand, think that a man's life is what he makes of it and if he sincerely judges it happy, then it is. John Stuart Mill is an instructive case of someone agonizing over the issue. He thinks that it is better to be Socrates dissatisfied than a pig satisfied, yet he repudiates the kind of paternalistic interference with people for their own good that objectivism encourages.

My own view is that the objectivist is right, but not for the reasons traditionally given. A man's judgement about his own happiness can be mistaken and the mistake can be pointed out to him by others. What makes this possible is not the existence of objective standards of happiness, but the rational appraisal of subjective standards.

The key to the resolution of this ancient dispute is the distinction between two senses in which standards of happiness can be objective and subjective. This requires the replacement of the traditional twofold distinction by a fourfold one. It should be recognized that both subjective and objective standards can be interpreted ontologically and epistemologically.[11] What I have in mind is the following scheme for standards:

	Subjective	Objective
Ontological	Made by personal decision	Exists independently of personal decision
Epistemological	Acceptance or rejection depends only on personal decision	Acceptance or rejection can be rationally appraised independently of personal decision

Plato, Aristotle, and Christian moralists think that standards of happiness are objective both ontologically and epistemologically. This means that a man's commitments to structuring his first-order wants can be rationally evaluated with reference to standards that exist independently of what he thinks or does. Emotivists, existentialists, and egoists think that a man's commitments are subjective in both senses. That is, his commitments are made by him and cannot be justified with reference to anything outside of him. I think that standards of happiness are ontologically subjective and epistemologically objective. In other words, a man's commitments are made by him, but nevertheless they can be justified and criticized independently of what he thinks or does.

The making of commitments is open to a misunderstanding I want to guard against. A commitment involves two components. One is an act: the summoning up of a resolve. The other is the content: whatever is the object of the resolve. The act is the component of commitments that is always made. For unless a man voluntarily and deliberately summons up the resolve, he cannot be said to have a commitment. Without the resolve, he may be obedient, habit-ridden, conventional, or indoctrinated, but not committed. On the other hand, the content of the commitment may or may not be, and, in fact, rarely is made. For the contents are ideals of satisfactions that men usually take over from their culture. So making a commitment is making a resolve to abide by an ideal, but it is only exceptionally the making of an ideal.

If a man has made a commitment in this sense, then his commitment is ontologically subjective—it exists only because he made it. But it is epistemo-logically objective, because the commitment can be justified or criticized inde-pendently of what the man who made it thinks or does. That is, a man's sincere judgement that his first-order wants are satisfied in accordance with his life-plan, and that he is happy, is open to rational evaluation. And the evaluation may be adverse. This is the reason why a man's sincere judgement that he is happy is only necessary and not sufficient for his happiness. If, however, his judgement is supported by independent rational evaluation, then, I claim, both necessary and sufficient conditions of his happiness are met. I must now argue for this claim.

IV

The fundamental reason for thinking that a man's sincere judgement that he is happy can be overruled by others is that he can be shown to be mistaken in his own terms. How can this be? The temporal perspective is crucial here. A man can view his life retrospectively, just as his biographer might. Or, some-one planning for his future may construct scenarios about how he hopes it will go; this is the adolescent's view. But I want to consider a man judging his own life in midstream. He is clear about the hierarchy of his commitments, he is engaged in satisfying his important first-order wants, he sincerely claims that he is satisfied with the way his life is going, and yet he is mistaken in thinking that his life is happy. His mistake can take two forms. One derives from inter-nal defects of his life-plan. He can be shown that even though things are presently going well for him, he is doomed to fail. The other has its source in the man having chosen the wrong way of going about the realization of his life-plan. He will inevitably encounter daunting obstacles, even if he has not yet done so.

Let us begin by describing some ways in which the first sort of mistake may occur. One thing that can be wrong with a life-plan is that it contains incompatible elements. It may be that a man has unconditional commitments to two mutually exclusive wants: to social activism and scholarship, for instance. So far he has managed to combine them, because he is young and energetic. But, even though he has done well at both, he has not done as well as he might, because the demands of one already interfere with the demands of the other. The danger signals are there, although he may not have noticed them. As time goes on, he must slow down. He will not be able to live up to both of these commitments, and since they are unconditional, he is doomed to disappointment. He himself will come to see that as time goes on. If he is reasonable, he can be shown now that this is so.

Another thing that can go wrong with a life-plan is that it is humanly impossible. A man can be engaged in shaping himself in the direction he is resolved to develop, he may justly claim to have made progress, and yet he cannot achieve the life he regards as satisfying, because it is beyond human reach. I think that Simone Weil lived such a life. But if that case is contentious, the point can be made generally in terms of the Christian ideal of *imitatio Christi*. The man who would be God, cannot be happy. A man can come to understand this, even about himself.

Yet a third fault with a life-plan may be that it does not suit the man who has it. Someone may have first-order wants whose satisfaction requires character-traits, talents, intelligence, or feelings that he does not have or has only to a small extent. Imagine, for instance, a principled man of considerable strength of character, who is morally fastidious, stubborn, unwilling to compromise what he thinks is right, and he is led by his convictions to become a politician. He is unconditionally committed to political work for the common good. Politics being what it is, he cannot be happy with such a life-plan. Woodrow Wilson is a case in point. He may have thought, before Versailles, that he was a happy man. But he would have been wrong. The satisfying episodes of his life do not add up to happiness, as the public calamity of Versailles and the private tragedy of his own disintegration show. His life as a politician was doomed to failure, so his life-plan was faulty. I doubt that he would have believed someone explaining this to him before Versailles, but that does not make it unreasonable to claim that that man should not have had that life-plan, if he wanted a happy life.

The last internal defect of life-plans I shall mention is perhaps the most common of all. Many men have unconditional commitments to wants capable only of transitory satisfactions. The trouble with the lives of gourmands and sexual conquistadores is that early peaks are followed by doldrums, and, the flesh being what it is, by middle-aged incapacity. It does not require great sagacity to see that a life-plan designed to pursue this sort of satisfaction will not make a man happy, even though it may yield some intensely satisfying experiences.

In all these cases, the life-plan was faulty. A reasonable man can be shown this, and the life thus criticized may be his own. If this happens, he may be able to change his life, or he may resign himself to lack of happiness. I want to emphasize that one can do the latter. I am not suggesting that happiness is the only aim in life. The thesis I am defending is not that a life-plan is faulty if it does not lead to happiness. My claim is that if a man aims at happiness, his life-plan can be shown to be faulty if it frustrates this aim. And this can be shown even if the man judges otherwise.

But there is also a second form mistakes about one's happiness can take. A life-plan may be free of internal defects and yet be unrealizable due to its context. One way this can happen is to have a life-plan radically out of step with one's times. The classic example is Don Quixote. The attempt to find happiness in courtly love, single combat, the fealty of servants, and knightly honour cannot succeed at a time when one's lovers, enemies, subordinates and peers are guided by entirely different considerations.

Another kind of conflict between a life-plan and its context is due to the failure to observe the legal and moral constraints imposed upon one's pursuit of happiness by the society in which he lives. A man whose life-plan involves frequent violation of the legal and moral standards of his society cannot be happy; this is so even if he rejects these standards. Systematic life-long dissimulation and lying are required for living at odds with one's society. Trust, relaxation, and intimate personal relationships are impossible, for one's true sentiments must always be hidden. As Philippa Foot observes: "Philosophers often speak as if a man could thus hide himself from those around him, but the supposition is doubtful, and in any case the price in vigilance would be colossal. If he lets even a few people see his true attitude he must guard himself against them; if he lets no one into the secret he must always be careful in case the least spontaneity betray him."[12]

The kind of internal exile that opposition to one's society requires may have the highest moral credentials. If a society is evil, resisting its vicious legal and moral requirements is good. My point is not to condemn such behavior, but to call attention to its incompatability with happiness. If a man wants to have a happy life, his life-plan should not be at radical odds with his society. Of course, in some societies one ought not to strive to be happy at the exclusion of other things. In any case, if a man aims at happiness, then one way of showing him that he cannot succeed is to point at the unavoidable implications of there being a radical conflict between his life-plan and the prevailing legal and moral code.

Yet another way of showing someone that he is mistaken has to do with features a life-plan must have, but his actually lacks. Imagine, for instance, a performing artist, say a violinist, who is so concerned with maintaining faultless technique as to render his approach to music largely analytical, leaving little room for feeling. He may see himself succeeding, and yet be paving the way to ultimate failure. Or consider a mother so intent upon avoiding laying upon her children the kind of authoritarian demands from which she suffered as a child as to overlook the children's need for discipline. If successful motherhood is what would make her happy, she is failing at it, even if she sees herself as succeeding. And this, of course, can be called to her attention.

V

Let us now sum up the argument. In Section I, I argued that one necessary condition of a happy life is the satisfaction of one's second-order want. This involves the satisfaction of many important first-order wants. What wants are important is decided by a man's life-plan. In Section II, I described the three-tiered structure of commitments that compose a life-plan. These commitments function as standards of happiness, for it is through them that a man decides what satisfactions he should seek. In Section III, I distinguished between the subjective and objective views of happiness. According to the subjective view, a man's sincere judgement that he is happy is both necessary and sufficient for happiness. The objective view agrees about its necessity, but denies its sufficiency. In order to explain the objective view, I distinguished between ontological and epistemological objectivity, and argued that standards of happiness are only epistemologically objective. This implies that a man's sincere judgement that he is happy can be mistaken. In Section IV, I discussed several cases to show some of the ways in which a man's sincere judgement about his happiness can be overruled. Each of these cases serves as a counterexample to the subjective view of happiness.

What must be done now is to show how standards of happiness can be epistemologically objective; that is, how personal commitments can be rationally justified. This involves two stages, one simple and one complicated. The simple one is to find out whether the judgement that a man is satisfied with his life is true. It makes no difference from the point of view of justification who does the finding out: it may be the man himself, or it may be others. A man is satisfied with his life if he wants it to go on without radical changes; if he is not seriously frustrated; and if he has frequent experiences of joy, pleasure, or contentment. These are factual questions to which straight factual answers can be given. An affirmative answer establishes that one necessary condition of justifying his commitments is met, for they do lead to the satisfaction of his first-order wants in accordance with his life-plan.

The second and complicated stage is to supply the other necessary condition for the justification of personal commitments. The complication enters because the true judgement that a man is satisfied with his life involves a temporal dimension. The judgement is made as a man is living his life, and the question is whether the judgement will remain true as his life unfolds. What is at stake is whether his life-plan will continue to yield satisfactions conducive to his happiness. A man can think so and be wrong, just as observers of his life may be wrong. What meeting this necessary condition for justifying his commitments demands is the elimination of error.

But how could this be done? How could anyone be sure that a life-plan contains no serious, but hitherto hidden faults? How could anyone know that the agent's character, talents, weaknesses, and strengths will continue to be served by his life-plan? The answer is that we cannot know, not with certainty. Lack of certainty, however, does not mean that the grounds for reasonable belief are also lacking. It is possible and common to make judgements about how men's lives are likely to go. Such judgements are predictions based on present imperfect knowledge. Some men are good at making such judgements, while others are poor. Good judgements require what Aristotle called practical wisdom and what we tend to call knowledge of human nature. Judges, novelists, personnel officers are supposed to excel at it. So reasonable judgements can be made. My claim is that the second necessary condition of the justification of personal commitments is reasonable judgement of this sort in favour of them and the absence of reasonable judgement against them.

My conclusion is that happiness requires the fulfilment of two conditions: individually necessary and jointly sufficient. The first is that the judgment that a man's life is happy should be true; the second is that it should be reasonable to believe and unreasonable to doubt that this judgement will continue to hold in the future. The substance of my argument has been to show what is involved in meeting these conditions.

VI

In closing, it is necessary to say something about the large question of the connection between happiness and morality. There are two widely accepted contemporary answers: the Utilitarian and the Kantian. The Utilitarian answer is that the purpose of morality is to increase general happiness. The central difficulty with this is that there are immoral ways to accomplishing this. Therefore, morality must be richer than Utilitarians think. The Kantian answer is that morality is indifferent to happiness, for its purpose is to command men to do their duty. The problem here is that there is no acceptable answer to the question of why a reasonable man would want to be moral. These difficulties have been endlessly debated, but it does not seem to me that they have been removed. If this is so, there is a reason for looking further to understand the connection between happiness and morality.

A more promising answer can be derived from the classical view of morality, that of Plato's and Aristotle's. According to it, the purpose of morality is to teach men how to live good lives. And since happiness is one form a good life can take, happiness and morality are connected; as Utilitarians correctly insist. One objection frequently raised against this view is that the pursuit of happiness is self-regarding and morality is other-regarding, so they cannot be connected. But this is a mistaken objection. For what makes a man happy may well include other-regarding considerations, such as unconditional commitment to the well-being of those he loves.

Yet the connection between happiness and morality is not necessary, for a morally good man may be unhappy and a happy man may be immoral. The connection between them rests on unconditional commitments. That happiness involves such commitments, we have seen. That morality also involves them is the large element of truth in Kantian morality. For morality requires that moral agents obey categorical imperatives. But the unconditional commitments involved in both morality and happiness need not be the same. As unconditional commitments may or may not lead to happiness, so they may or may not be morally commendable. The outstanding question about happiness and morality is whether there are some unconditional commitments required by both. I think there are, but I cannot support this belief here.

NOTES

1. There is an excellent discussion of this in I. Dilman's *Morality and the Inner Life* (London: Macmillan, 1979), Chapter Four.

2. This distinction has been suggested to me by H. G. Frankfurt's "Freedom of the Will and the Concept of a Person," *Journal of Philosophy*, **68** (1971), pp. 5–20.

3. *Eudemian Ethics*, 1241b 6–14.

4. *Nicomachean Ethics*, 1098a 16–18.

5. W. F. R. Hardie, "The Final Good in Aristotle's Ethics," *Aristotle*, ed. J. M. E. Moravcsik (New York: Doubleday, 1967), pp. 297–322.

6. M. Oakeshott, "Rationalism in Politics," *Rationalism and Politics* (London: Methuen, 1962), pp. 1–36.

7. I am relying on S. Hampshire's "three-tiered conception of morality" developed in "Morality and Pessimism," *Public and Private Morality* (Cambridge: University Press, 1978), pp. 1–22.

8. R. Bolt, *A Man for All Seasons* (New York: Random House, 1963).

9. I. Murdoch's *The Nice and the Good* (London: Chatto and Windus, 1968), is an illustration of this.

10. In this discussion I both follow and disagree with R. Kraut's "Two Conceptions of Happiness," *Philosophical Review*, **88** (1979), pp. 167–197. I follow Kraut's excellent statement of the issues, but we part company because he attacks and I defend the objective view of happiness.

11. I have been helped to see this point by B. Ellis's "Truth as a Mode of Evaluation, " *Pacific Philosophical Quarterly*, **61** (1980), pp. 85–99. He makes this distinction with respect to theories of truth.

12. Foot, "Moral Beliefs," *Aristotelian Society Proceedings*, **59** (1958–9), p. 102.

HAPPINESS AND TIME

Wladyslaw Tatarkiewicz

Wladyslaw Tatarkiewicz (1886–1980) was a philosopher who taught at several universities in his native Poland. He examined the relationship between happiness and the past, present, and future.

Happiness is an ambiguous word. In this paper it is used in the sense of satisfaction with one's life as a whole. Such use of the term is a natural one, accepted in common parlance and at the same time corresponding with the definitions of philosophers. . . .

When understood in this way, happiness is certainly not something that could be exactly ascertained and measured; many people cannot decide whether or not they are happy in this sense. Sometimes they feel happy, sometimes not, sometimes neither happy nor unhappy. But at least some people, at some moments of their lives, are happy, i.e., satisfied with their lives as a whole, and some are unhappy, i.e., unsatisfied with their lives. This forms a sufficient basis for an examination of the matter. The purpose of this essay is to examine it in relation to time.

From Wladyslaw Tatarkiewicz, "Happiness and Time," *Philosophy and Phenomenological Research*, vol. 27 (1966). Used by permission of the journal.

* * *

Satisfaction with life as a whole must be a satisfaction not only with that which is, but also with that which was and that which will be: not only with the present, but also with the past, and the future. Therefore the feeling of happiness includes not only an agreeable present state, but also a favorable assessment of the past, and good prospects for the future. This plurality of satisfaction is essential to happiness. The present moment, however pleasant, cannot ensure the happiness of a being endowed with reason—a being who remembers the past and is concerned with the future. Not only things which exist in present time and directly affect the individual, but also those which are no longer, or not yet in existence, have a bearing upon his happiness. Happiness is, by the nature of things, both retrospective and prospective in character.

The three chronological components of happiness: the past, the present, and the future, are never isolated in their influence upon the feeling of happiness: they are interrelated and simultaneous in action, combining to bring about that feeling. An agreeable present is not only delightful in itself; it sheds its light on the still uncertain future and even on the past; when seen through the prism of a joyful moment, past sufferings are minimized, and past pleasures magnified. But once the present has deteriorated, both past and future can appear in a less favorable light. Similarly, good or bad past experiences are not only pleasant or unpleasant in themselves, they also form the basis for a favorable or unfavorable evaluation of the past and present: they cast a rosy glow or a black shadow not only on the unknown future but also the known present. Even the future, which has not yet arrived, can color the past and the present—at least for people of a certain psychological type: in some cases they view the past and present in the light of their dreams of the future, in others, anxiety about the future precludes all enjoyment of the present. All this is natural enough, as every reality can indeed be perceived as better or worse, and purely psychological factors can lessen or increase, suffering, even physical pain.

In spite of the interaction of these three elements, each has its own distinct role in human happiness. These roles are not coequal. It is generally held that the present is of paramount importance, because it exists in reality. To quote the French verse: "ce qui n'est plus ne fut jamais"; whatever has passed by, no longer exists, neither does that which has yet to take place. Certainly—and yet the supposition is false that happiness hinges mainly on the present. Of course, only the present actually exists and we experience only present feelings—nothing could be more certain—but present emotions are not aroused by present events alone. For beings endowed with memory and imagination, experiences which they recall or anticipate arouse emotions in time present, and thus things which are no longer, or not yet in existence contribute to human happiness and unhappiness. The satisfaction we feel is an actual and real one, but actual and real satisfaction need not necessarily be derived from things existing in present reality.

I. In fact, present events play a comparatively minor role in human happiness. They exist in the present and are therefore experienced directly—an experience all the more vivid for being direct. But these experiences are incomparably fewer than those derived from nonexistent things which one remembers or anticipates. The present is real, but fleeting. In his "*De brevitate vitae*" Seneca says that the present is so brief that some feel that it does not exist at all. "It has passed, even before it has arrived."[1]

Naturally, considerable differences exist between various people on that score: for some, the present moment carries a good deal more weight in the balance of happiness, than it does for others.[2] A child has few memories as yet, therefore it lives within the present; present pleasure and present pain determine its general state, its satisfaction or dissatisfaction with life. With adults it is a different matter: only very intense actual delights and sufferings can absorb their entire consciousness.

1. Our consciousness is seldom taken up entirely by the present, we are equally, or even more absorbed by our imagination and memory, by anticipation and recollection. When these occupy our consciousness to a greater extent, the pleasure and distress they bring play a greater part in our general satisfaction and dissatisfaction, in our happiness and unhappiness.

2. If the present comes into conflict with the past or future, it does not necessarily gain the upper hand. Acute pain can blot out the most delightful memories, and overshadow the most pleasant expectations; but also it is difficult for someone who has met with a great misfortune, or is desperately anxious about the future, to find some amusement, some present pleasure to change his trend of thought, and free him from memories and anxieties; he feels no interest in the most brilliant stage performance, no delight in the most exquisite dish.

3. Pleasures and annoyances which we consider to be those of the present do not always originate in the present. They are leavened with the relaxation or fatigue of yesterday, and with yesterday's successes or disappointments. These events of yesterday often make themselves felt in today's pleasure or distress. Even when the object of one's emotions belongs to the present, the source of those emotions may lie in the past. A voice or a fragrance which delights us today often does so because it conjures up an experience of long ago.

4. Sometimes present pleasures alone seem to suffice in inducing a state of contentment—but this can be so only when one is troubled by neither past nor future. Present delights in the full sense of the term—like satiety, good food, and drink—do in fact generate a feeling of well-being. But that is only possible when one's digestion is in good order, and one's mind clear of worries and anxieties.

It is often stated that work, particularly intellectual activity, brings happiness. If this is so, then it is due only to a minor extent to immediate pleasure, in which the work is often entirely lacking—being more frequently linked with effort, fatigue, struggle, and even suffering. Only when accompanied by the thought of the final results—whether achieved or anticipated—can it become a source of happiness.

5. Of course it is impossible to maintain that the present is irrelevant to happiness. The entire store of man's experience, the basis for his joy and sadness, his happiness and unhappiness, is the product of the fleeting, ephemeral

moments which make up the present. One should differentiate, however, between the present as the source of present satisfaction and as the material for future satisfaction. Some people are unable to derive direct enjoyment from the present, and for them the present can be, at most, a springboard for the future.

Present moments are by no means immaterial to happiness. But their importance is less than is commonly supposed: it cannot be denied that it is quite considerable for some, for others, on the contrary, it is very little. And nothing, perhaps, is more conducive to happiness than an awareness that the present is unimportant, that life is yet to be lived and all that is good and valuable lies ahead. Such an attitude makes the unavoidable imperfections of the present lose their significance and cease to be an obstacle to happiness.

II. The influence of the past on man's happiness or unhappiness is indubitable. Firstly, the memory of what has been accompanies him and permeates his consciousness. Secondly, his present conjectures and judgments were formed in the past; the past has caused his outlook to become serene or gloomy, his attitude trusting or mistrusting. And thirdly, the conjectures and judgements formed in the past comprise the "basis of apperception" according to which he understands and evaluates the present. Practically every aspect of present reality can be viewed in a more or less favorable light, and thus it can be experienced with joy as well as with distress. Two men get a headache, let us say; one knows from experience that it will hurt for a while and then stop, so he does not take the pain seriously and feels it less acutely; the other knows that this is the first symptom of many a dangerous and protracted illness, he cannot wrench his apprehensive thoughts away from the pain and the illness looming over him, and thus his suffering is intensified.

Therefore it follows that: 1. The contribution of the past to happiness and unhappiness lies not only in the fact that it is the object of satisfaction or dissatisfaction, but also partly in the fact that it is the cause of satisfaction or dissatisfaction with the present. In the first instance we are consciously delighted with the past, in the second we need not realize that we owe our delight to the past. Thus the influence of the past on happiness can be dual: conscious or unconscious.

2. Satisfaction with the past, however, is not indispensable to happiness: people can be happy although dissatisfied with their past. Their satisfaction can be due to a past which was far from satisfactory, because the awareness of having freed oneself from a disagreeable past intensifies the enjoyment of an agreeable present. In this case dissatisfaction with the past intensifies one's satisfaction with the present, and with life as a whole.

3. If our imagination is capable of distorting the present, it is even more capable of distorting the past. The past, after all, is nothing more than an image, and of course imagination can more easily change images than perceptions. Like a stage upon which various floodlights are played, the image of the past can take on a rosy glow or a grey and dismal hue in accordance with the mood of the moment. When we evaluate the past emotionally, we evaluate it not as it really was, but as it has been transformed by our imagination. And so our happiness or unhappiness can be determined not only by the past as it really was, but also by an imaginary past which had never been. On the

whole, this distortion is often the ally of happiness. How many people idealize the "good old days" and live in a cloud of past happiness which had never existed. Quite often, on the other hand, people derive no joy from that imaginary happiness; on the contrary, they are dejected at its supposed passing; by using an imagined happy past as a yardstick for the present, they perceive the present as worse than it really is—consequently their suffering caused by a supposedly disagreeable present exceeds their enjoyment of the supposedly agreeable past.

4. The contribution of the past to happiness is impermanent. "Sometimes an agreeable memory is more delightful than the agreeable present" wrote de Musset.[3] But according to Dante, no suffering is more galling than the recollection of past happiness. This also holds for unhappiness: some things leave a wound which never heals and rankles with every memory. Sometimes, however, the reverse is true: "The more one suffers, the sweeter one's memories" in the words of the Polish 17th century poet, Waclaw Potocki. The manner in which a good or bad past affects happiness depends not only on that past, but also on whether the present is good and whether good prospects exist for the future.

5. Our evaluation of the past is often at variance with what it was when that past was still the present. This is indicated in the conversation about happiness between Croesus and Solon,[4] which was famous in antiquity. Croesus had considered his existence to be a happy one, as long as it was the present, but on his deathbed, when his life, seen in retrospect, was relegated to the past, he could perceive no happiness in it. More often, however, the opposite is true: people appreciate happiness only when it has fled.

6. It seems to be a peculiarity of the past that—no matter whether it was agreeable or disagreeable—it contributes more frequently, and to a greater extent, to happiness than to unhappiness. This peculiarity is linked with what is described as the "optimistic tendency of memory." It has a dual aspect. Firstly, one's memory usually shuns unpleasant experiences and dwells on those which are pleasant—it seems to act by design, selecting recollections which have a favorable effect on the psyche. This is doubtless because, by dint of being recalled more frequently, pleasant memories become more firmly rooted in the mind. Secondly, memory transmutes emotional states from the negative to the positive: quite often something which meant distress and tears in one's childhood is enjoyed as a pleasant memory in later years.

And finally: 7. In time present, we are subject to thousands of stimuli, some pleasant, some unpleasant; their plurality and diversity sometimes make it difficult for us to state with conviction whether the present is on the whole happy or otherwise. For the most part, it shimmers with a profusion of highlights, and is more seldom bathed in a steady light. But when our present seems to be happy to us, we are often afraid of admitting the fact to others, and even to ourselves; we are afraid of calling ourselves happy too soon.

While the present is undefined, the future is uncertain, and therefore to be feared. With the past, it is another matter: it has passed by, so we need not fear it and we can state whether it was happy or not. In it alone can we see happiness without uncertainty, and also without anxiety. It is in this sense that one can interpret Guyau's strange dictum which relegates happiness and unhappiness alike to the past: "Happiness and unhappiness are already the past, that is, something which can no longer be."[5]

III. The future—though it is not yet here—affects the feeling of happiness and the assessment of life, to no less degree than the past does. It happens not infrequently that the future, and practically the future alone, determines that feeling. The past? An old adage goes: "What was and is no longer, does not enter into account." Only the present and the future remain. *"Aut praesentibus torquemur aut futuris"* wrote Seneca, deleting the past from the calculation of happiness. The present? It is, after all, only a moment—and I can endure even the most dreadful moment, provided I know that things will be better soon. Many people feel this way. Consciously or otherwise, they link their happiness exclusively with the future, they measure it up to something which has not yet come, and perhaps will never come. But they experience that future in advance, they see it and feel it as good or evil. This is no doubt largely a matter of personality: some people live in the present moment, or in the past, while others live in the future. The happiness of the latter is dependent upon faith in the future, even if it is illusory, while their unhappiness is due to misgivings about the future, even if they are unfounded. On the other hand, faith or misgivings are often based on past or present experience. Though not always: there exist incurable optimists and incurable pessimists, whose vision of the future runs counter to what the past and the present have taught them.

Fear of pain is often more oppressive than the pain itself; the prospect of amusement can be more delightful than the amusement itself. For imagination corrects reality, it enhances colors, and the habitual greyness of life, composed of both light and sombre tones, is intensified by imagination to the pitch of black and white.

We do not fear the past, since we have left it behind, and we often commend it even though it was unfavorable. Neither do we fear the present, because we know that it will soon pass, that its very existence is nothing more than a sinking into the past. But the future weighs heavily upon our consciousness. And therefore the expectation of good or evil has greater significance for happiness or unhappiness than their recollection or even experience. The past and the present have less significance in this respect than prospects for the future. Possession signifies less than hope.

The past, the present, and the future exert an influence on the way we experience the successive moments of our lives; each participates in the satisfaction and dissatisfaction we derive from each moment, and which we accumulate to form our ultimate satisfaction and dissatisfaction with life as a whole. Each plays a different part, but the parts are interwoven. Retained in memory, the past affects the way one experiences the present and future. The present moment is not only something we experience directly, it is also the prism through which we see the past and future. Similarly the future, before it comes, has a bearing upon our experience of the past and present. The anticipation of a good future enables one to forget a bad past and to accept a bad present, while the fear of a bad future can erase all the good one has hitherto experienced.

The real past, the real present, and the real future, even when combined, do not yet determine happiness and unhappiness. Acting simultaneously with them there is the past which never existed (but which we see in the vista of time) as well as the present which does not exist, and the future which will never exist. For in happiness and unhappiness alike, it is not a matter of what was, is, and will be in reality, but also of that which we imagine and feel.

These chronological reflections on happiness suggest two conclusions. Firstly, the fact that in connection with the interrelation of the past, present, and future, there arise distortions of reality, which have a bearing upon the feeling of happiness. These distortions—of an entirely different nature than those caused by pathological euphoria or depression—do not create a complete illusion, but they alter the perspective of the image of reality. These are mainly illusions as to location—or, to be more exact, as to the location in time—of the sources of satisfaction and dissatisfaction. Because we praise or disparage the present for that which springs from the past, and vice versa.

Secondly, it follows from these reflections that the direct experience of good and evil makes up only a fragment, and by no means the most important fragment, of happiness and unhappiness. Recollection, and even more so, anticipation, mean as such, or more. Imagination often means as much as, or more than experience, anticipation means as much as, or more than the present with all its reality. And thus happiness is also determined by things which never were and never will be. It is determined not only by real things and events experienced at first hand, but also by the unreal. If both the past and future are reflected in momentary pleasure or distress, they are reflected to an even greater extent in happiness which is a satisfaction with the whole of life.

This is connected with the preponderance of psychological over physical factors in happiness. Pain can be effectively blunted by a mental attitude. It did not take Coué to realize that willpower and purely psychical activity can be used to overcome pain and awaken joy of living. Marcus Aurelius advised: "In every circumstance which saddens you, remember the rule: it is not unhappiness." The reverse can also be true: purely physical experiences often determine one's mental attitude; they persist in memory, in our ideas about things, and in the hopes we entertain for the future. The strength of psychological factors lies in that they embrace the past and future, while physical elements extend no further than the present. We derive our sensations only from what is, while imagination also draws upon what was and what will be. Epicurus, a greater connoisseur of worldly delights than most, considered mental pleasures to be superior, all his materialism and sensualism notwithstanding.

The very limited participation of the present in happiness or unhappiness may appear to be the most extraordinary thing about this problem. This conclusion, which is at variance with current ideas on the matter, can be easily explained: one should simply bear in mind the ambiguity which exists in the concept of the present.

According to one notion, the present is made up of what one is experiencing at the given moment. According to another, it is made up of everything which is in existence at that moment. But one does not immediately experience everything at the moment in which it exists. A good deal has been experienced earlier, and even more will be experienced later. A considerable amount of time may sometimes elapse before that which exists and is happening now reaches one's consciousness—and it may have ceased to exist in the meantime.

Present events pass by at the moment in which they have taken place, but they persist for a longer span of time in one's consciousness. As a rule, we experience them not in a single moment, but over a certain period of time, which can be of longer or shorter duration. A lottery prize is drawn in a single moment, but the winner's enjoyment continues for a much longer time—until the money runs out, in fact. And conversely, present experiences often last but a single moment, while the things which caused them continue to exist. In other words, that which lasts but a moment in reality, extends over a period of time in our experience, while that which we experienced for but a moment often continues in reality over a long period of time.

As a rule the same combination of circumstances which exists within the present moment already existed in the time immediately preceding, and will exist in the time immediately following that moment. This allows us to link moments immediately following and immediately preceding, with the present moment and to include them in it. And that is precisely what we do. Then the present ceases to be a single *moment*, and becomes a *period of time*. It is the period of time which comprises the same combination of circumstances as the present moment. *A period which surrounds the moment actually being experienced.*

This period keeps pace with our life, moving forwards simultaneously with it. By moving forwards, it shifts and changes. It does not embrace a constant number of days, months, or years; it is sometimes narrowed down to just a few days, or it extends far into the past and future; sometimes it leans more towards the past, or towards the future. On the day when we embark on a new period in life, yesterday already belongs to the past, and on the contrary when we are confronted by changed unfamiliar circumstances, the present ends today, and tomorrow already belongs to the future.

This concept of the present as something which extends over a period of time is the one in common currency. And if the present is so understood, then time is no longer composed of *two* periods—the past and the future—separated as if by a line, by the present moment; it is divided into three equivalent periods. One can say with Seneca: "Life is divided into three periods: that which is, that which was, and that which will be."[6]

The participation in human happiness or unhappiness of a present which is conceived of in this way—as a period—is of course different than that of the present moment alone. The part played by the present moment is exiguous; it is the material for, rather than the object of satisfaction. On the other hand, the part played by the present period is considerable. This present cannot be described as one which has passed before we have become aware of it. It is no longer only every last moment of the past, or every first moment of the future. It is no longer only the material for happiness, it is its object. If one is satisfied with it, one already possesses a major portion of what one needs to be satisfied with life as a whole. The vast majority of people are indifferent to the remote past; but the recent past, yesterday's sufferings and joys, cause as much pain and delight as those of today. Most people are unconcerned about the distant future, but the importance of tomorrow is equal, if not greater for them, than that of the present day.

NOTES

1. Seneca, *De brevitate vitae*, "Ante desinit esse quam venit."

2. J. W. Goethe, "Die Gegenwart allein ist unser Glück."

3. A. de Musset, "Un souvenir heureux est peut-être sur terre plus vrai que le bonheur."

4. *Herodotus*, I, 30.

5. J. M. Guyau, *Esquisse d'une morale sans obligation ni sanction*, 1885.

6. Seneca, *Epistolae ad Lucilium*, XII: "In tria tempora vita dividitur: quod est, quod fuit, et quod futurum est."

C. Happiness as More Than Satisfaction

TWO CONCEPTIONS OF HAPPINESS

Richard Kraut

Richard Kraut is professor of philosophy at Northwestern University. He compares Aristotle's way of judging happiness to our own.

I

In this paper, I want to contrast two ways of judging whether people are leading happy lives: Aristotle's and our own. I will argue that there are some striking similarities between these two conceptions of happiness. To live happily, for both Aristotle and for us, is to have certain attitudes towards one's life, and to measure up to certain standards. Where we and Aristotle sharply disagree is over the standards to be used in evaluating lives. Roughly, he insists on an objective and stringent standard, whereas our test is more subjective and flexible. I will also argue that we have good reason to reject his conception of happiness, for his standards can be employed only by those who know things we do not. If we ever acquired such knowledge, we might make judgments about happiness that are like the ones Aristotle makes in the *Nicomachean Ethics*. We would, in other words, drop our present conception of happiness and adopt something like his.

From *The Philosophical Review*, vol. 88 (1979). Used by permission of the journal.

The approach I am taking to this subject differs from the usual one. Scholars and philosophers who study the *Ethics* often claim that Aristotle has no conception of happiness at all, in our sense of the word. They notice that when his term *eudaimonia* receives the traditional translation, "happiness," a number of his points sound dubious and even silly. For example, he is made to say that everything should be sought for the sake of happiness, and that children and evil adults are never happy because they have not developed such traits as justice, courage, and self-control. Furthermore, *eudaimonia* does not name a feeling or emotion, whereas we think that happiness is, or at least involves, a certain state of mind. And so we are warned, for example, by Henry Sidgwick, that the word "happiness" that we find in translations of Aristotle does not have its contemporary meaning in English.[1] Occasionally a different translation is proposed: W. D. Ross suggests "well-being"[2] (despite the fact that he sticks to "happiness" in the Oxford edition of the *Ethics*); John Cooper proposes "flourishing."[3] The idea is that we should assign a meaning to *eudaimonia* that makes Aristotle disagree with us as little as possible. Since we believe that some children definitely are happy, and that some evil people might very well be, Aristotle's *eudaimonia* cannot mean "happiness" in its usual sense.

I think this approach rests on an oversimplified view both of happiness and of *eudaimonia*. Sidgwick makes the dubious claim that our term is "commonly used in Bentham's way as convertible with Pleasure."[4] Ross tells us that " 'happiness' means a state of feeling, differing from 'pleasure' only by its suggestion of permanence, depth and serenity."[5] And Cooper says that it "tends to be taken as referring exclusively to a subjective psychological state."[6] The common error here is the belief that the only thing we mean when we judge a person happy is that he is in a certain state of mind. As I will argue, we often mean something more than this: we are saying that the individual is happy because his life meets a certain standard (a subjective one). Furthermore, when Aristotle calls someone *eudaimon*, he means not only that the individual meets a certain standard (an objective one), but that he is in a certain state of mind— the very same state we say people are in when we call them happy. To think that happiness just involves a psychological condition and that *eudaimonia* does not is to get both concepts wrong.

It is an illusion, at any rate, to think that we foster a better understanding of Aristotle if we use "well-being" or "flourishing" as translations of *eudaimonia*, rather than "happiness." If we use these words, Aristotle will be made to say that children and evil men do not attain well-being, or do not flourish. Are these claims any more plausible than the ones they are supposed to replace? If a young tree can flourish in the right conditions, why not a young person?[7] Why say that well-being is beyond the reach of children and evil people? Certainly we do things for their well-being—don't we ever succeed?

We could of course leave *eudaimonia* untranslated and let its meaning be gathered from the statements Aristotle makes about it. But that would leave unanswered a question I think we should ask: When we say that a person is leading a happy life, and Aristotle says that the same person is not *eudaimon*, do we have anything to argue about? I think we do. As I will try to show, the conception of *eudaimonia* in the *Nicomachean Ethics* is best interpreted as a challenge to the way we go about judging people to be happy. If we were convinced that what Aristotle says about *eudaimonia* is true, we would no longer believe that children or evil people can be happy. And if we began to make judgments of happiness in the way he makes judgments of *eudaimonia*, we would not be changing the meaning of "happiness."

II

Aristotle thinks that the most *eudaimon* individual is someone who has fully developed and regularly exercises the various virtues of the soul, both intellectual and moral. Such a person engages in philosophical activity (since this is the full flowering of his capacity to reason theoretically) and also in moral activities, which display his justice, generosity, temperance, etc. Though he may experience minor mishaps, he cannot have recently suffered any severe misfortunes, such as the death of close friends or dearly loved children. Aristotle thinks that a virtuous person will make the best of any situation, but that in extreme circumstances *eudaimonia* is lost. It may be regained, but only after a long period of time during which many fine things have been achieved.[8]

Consider such a person—a philosopher and a good man—at a time of life that is not marred by misfortunes. Aristotle thinks he would in these conditions be as *eudaimon* as any human being can be. I want to ask: is he a happy person? Is he in the same psychological state as any individual who is leading a happy life? When we say that someone is living happily, we imply that he has certain attitudes towards his life: he is very glad to be alive; he judges that on balance his deepest desires are being satisfied and that the circumstances of his life are turning out well. Does Aristotle's paradigm of *eudaimonia* have these same attitudes? I think so. For such a person loves the activities he regularly and successfully engages in. He thinks that exercising one's intellectual and moral capacities is the greatest good available to human beings, and he knows he possesses this good.[9] Furthermore, he has all the other major goods he wants. His desire for such external goals as honor, wealth, and physical pleasure is moderate, and should be easy enough to satisfy in a normal life.[10] If, however, some great misfortune does occur—if, for example, he is totally deprived of honor—then Aristotle insists that he is no longer *eudaimon*.[11] So, the individual who is most *eudaimon* on Aristotle's theory passes our tests for happiness with flying colors. All his major goals are being achieved, to a degree that satisfies him. Knowing this, he greatly enjoys his life and has nothing serious to complain of.

Furthermore, there is a passage in which Aristotle explicitly tells us how a *eudaimon* individual will look upon his life. It occurs in the midst of an involved proof that whoever is *eudaimon* needs friends: "All men desire (life), and particularly those who are good and supremely happy (*makarious*), for to such men life is most desirable, and their existence is the most supremely happy (*makariōtatē*)" (1170a26–29). To put it somewhat differently: one who is good and highly *eudaimon* has an especially strong desire for life, and this psychological condition is based on the perception of how very desirable his life is. Now, when Aristotle says that one who is virtuous and *eudaimon* particularly desires life, he cannot mean that he will struggle to stay alive at any cost. Rather, he must mean that such individuals are more glad to be alive than others; the kind of existence they enjoy gives them a heightened love of life. As Aristotle says elsewhere (1117b9–13), these are the people who have the most reason to live, and therefore the thought of death—even death in battle— is especially painful to them. In their attitude towards themselves and their lives, they are the very opposite of the sort of individual who is so miserable and filled with self-hatred that he contemplates suicide (1166b11–28). It is undeniable, then, that the *eudaimon* individual, as Aristotle depicts him, is fully satisfied with his life. He is, in other words, a happy person.

There is another way of arriving at this same conclusion. Let us for the moment ignore Aristotle's belief that *eudaimonia* consists in virtuous activity. He has many other convictions about the *eudaimon* life besides this one, and from these alone we can infer that whoever is *eudaimon* must be happy with his life. Consider the following points, all of which Aristotle affirms or pre-supposes: We human beings are different from plants, in that we would never be able to attain our good with any regularity, unless we had effective desires for what we think is worthwhile. Since we are creatures with strong desires for the good, as we variously conceive it, it is natural and inevitable for us to develop a deep interest in whether or not such desires are being satisfied. An animal with first-order desires, but no strong second-order interest in whether those first-order desires are being fulfilled, would not be fully human. Put otherwise: no person would choose a life in which he remains continually unaware of whether or not he possesses the good; that would be a life befitting plants, not human beings.[12] Now, any deep desire which develops naturally and universally is a desire which must be satisfied, if we are to attain our good. Satisfying that desire is in fact part of our good.[13] So a major human good is the second-order good which consists in the perception that our major first-order desires are being satisfied. And this second-order good is one we must have in order to be *eudaimon*, since a *eudaimon* life can have no serious deficiency (1097b14–15). Even if someone correctly understood his good and attained it, he still would not be *eudaimon*, if he mistakenly thought that he lacked a major part of that good. For example, suppose someone whose family is living abroad is told that they have recently been killed. Let us assume that he is deeply affected, and views his loss as a great tragedy. Even if he should discover, after a year's time, that he was misinformed, that his family has all this time been alive and well, it remains true that he lacked *eudaimonia* during that year.[14] His life may in fact have possessed every first-order good that a well-lived life requires; still, it undeniably contained a serious second-order evil. To think, over a long period of time, that dear friends or family members have recently died, is by itself a major misfortune. For it involves the perception—or, in the case imagined, the misperception—that one lacks a great good, and this in itself is a great evil. *Eudaimonia* involves the recognition that one's desire for the good is being fulfilled, and therefore one who attains *eudaimonia* is neces-sarily happy with his life. His deepest desires are being satisfied, and realizing this, he has an especially affirmative attitude towards himself and his life.[15]

Notice that in reaching this conclusion, no appeal was made to Aristotle's theory that the best life is devoted to virtuous activity. So, if the argument

I have just reconstructed is correct, then all of the various and conflicting theories of the good life ought to recognize that a *eudaimon* individual, whatever else may be true of him, has a certain attitude toward his life. Even if one disagrees with Aristotle about the importance of virtue, that is no reason for denying the connection between *eudaimonia* and the perceived satisfaction of major desires. For that connection depends solely on some highly general features of human nature, and the point that a *eudaimon* life is without major defects. Therefore, any adequate theory of the best human life—whether it identifies the good with honor or pleasure or virtue—ought to characterize a *eudaimon* individual as someone who knowingly satisfies his deepest desires. Furthermore, if *eudaimonia* and desire-satisfaction are connected in the way described, then there is a fair empirical test by which competing theories of *eudaimonia* can be partially evaluated. If the individuals who are pronounced *eudaimones* by a certain theory of *eudaimonia* believe there is little reason to be alive, and are given to thoughts of suicide, then that theory cannot be right. Contrariwise, if those who are pronounced *eudaimones* have a highly positive attitude towards their lives, and those who are alleged to be quite distant from *eudaimonia* are deeply dissatisfied with themselves, then that is some confirmation for the theory which reaches this result. A theory of *eudaimonia*, in other words, ought to harmonize, at least partly,[16] with the way people feel about their lives: that is the upshot of our argument linking *eudaimonia* and the perception that one's major desires are being fulfilled. And Aristotle can claim that his own particular theory, which connects *eudaimonia* with virtuous activity, satisfies this requirement. For, as we have seen, he thinks that the virtuous and *eudaimon* individual is especially glad to be alive, whereas the individual who most sorely lacks *eudaimonia*—the evil man, hated for his misdeeds—is given to thoughts of suicide.

Let me emphasize two points about my interpretation. First, I have not said that the word *eudaimon*, by virtue of its everyday meaning, could only have been applied to satisfied individuals. Perhaps, as K. J. Dover claims, a Greek could have applied that term, without irony or contradiction, to a person who was deeply dissatisfied with his life.[17] What I want to emphasize is that Dover's thesis about ordinary Greek usage does not conflict with my own thesis about Aristotle. The *Nicomachean Ethics* does not merely record linguistic conventions about the term *eudaimon*, and in many ways Aristotle's treatment of this subject is controversial. His idea that *eudaimonia* consists in contemplation, for example, is no part of the meaning of the word *eudaimonia*, but is instead a product of philosophical argument. Similarly, the psychological condition presupposed by Aristotle—that *eudaimonia* requires full and conscious satisfaction of desire—is a product of his own reflections, and need not have been a linguistic convention or a matter of universal agreement. So if we ever find among Greek authors genuine cases in which a deeply dissatisfied individual is called *eudaimon*, we merely will have discovered an application of that term against which Aristotle would protest, just as he protests against those who call only the wealthy *eudaimones*.[18]

Second, I am not saying that, according to Aristotle, whoever perceives that his major desires are being satisfied is *eudaimon*. Complete fulfillment of desire is a necessary condition of *eudaimonia*, but not a sufficient one. For on

Aristotle's theory, those desires must be directed at worthwhile goals, and they must be proportionate in strength to the value of those goals; otherwise, one is not *eudaimon*, however satisfied one feels. Now, it might be claimed that this is a striking difference between *eudaimonia* and happiness. If a person's desires are fully satisfied—so the claim goes—then he is happy; but, as I have just said, this condition is not sufficient, in Aristotle's eyes, for *eudaimonia*. And it might be said that this difference is enough to show that "happiness" is not a good translation of Aristotle's *eudaimonia*. In the remaining sections of this paper, I will be presenting my reply to this line of argument. For now, I would like to stress the point that, however one wants to translate Aristotle's term *eudaimonia*, one ought to have a clear understanding of the similarities and differences between that notion and our notion of a happy life. And one remarkable similarity, which scholars have not recognized,[19] is this: A *eudaimon* individual, as Aristotle conceives him, is in the very same psychological state as a person who is living happily. Such individuals have a highly affirmative attitude towards their lives, since they perceive that their major desires are being fulfilled. In spite of the fact that "happiness" is the traditional translation of *eudaimonia*, one of the most important connections between the two concepts has curiously been ignored.[20]

III

Let us take a closer look now at how we judge whether someone is happy. The following example will help focus our ideas: Suppose a man is asked what his idea of happiness is, and he replies, "Being loved, admired, or at least respected by my friends. But I would hate to have friends who only pretend to have these attitudes towards me. If they didn't like me, I would want to know about it. Better to have no friends at all, and realize it, than to have false friends one cannot see through." Suppose that what this man hates actually comes to pass. His so-called friends orchestrate an elaborate deception, giving him every reason to believe that they love and admire him, though in fact they don't. And he is taken in by the illusion.

Is this a happy life? Is he a happy man? Some people will say yes, without a moment's thought. On their view (which I will call "extreme subjectivism"), happiness is a psychological state and nothing more; it involves, among other things, the belief that one is getting the important things one wants, as well as certain pleasant affects that normally go along with this belief.[21] So the deceived man is living just as happily as he would be if he were not deceived. Just as unfounded fear is still fear, so unfounded happiness is still happiness. For consider what we would say if the deceived man became suspicious of his friends, and came upon an opportunity to discover what they really think of him. Would we say that he is finding out whether he is really happy? Wouldn't it be more natural to say that he is finding out whether his happiness has been based on an illusion?

I think extreme subjectivism is a half-truth. Our reaction to the case of the deceived man is really more complicated than this doctrine admits. We do have some tendency to say that the deceived man is happy, but at the same time we have a definite reluctance to say this. The basis for our reluctance seems to be this: When a person is asked what his idea of happiness is, he quite naturally answers by describing the kind of life he would like to lead. It would therefore be misleading for the man in the above example to reply that he will be happy whether his friends deceive him or not. That would imply that he attaches some significant value to the situation in which he is deceived. Evidently, when we ask someone, "What will make you happy? What is your idea of happiness?", we are not requesting that he specify the conditions under which he will be in a certain psychological state. It is not like asking, "What will make you angry?" Rather, it is inquiring about the standards he imposes on himself, and the goals he is seeking. And this makes us hesitant to say that the deceived man is happy or has a happy life. Judged by his own standards of happiness, he has not attained it, though he is in the same psychological condition he would be in if he had attained it. Merely being in that psychological state is not something to which he attaches any value, and so it is odd to say that he has attained a happy life merely by being in that psychological state.[22]

I think we can improve on the way extreme subjectivism describes our use of "happiness." We are not at all reluctant to say that the deceived man *feels happy* about his life. But we are quite reluctant to say that *the life he is leading is a happy life*. And we are at sea when we have to decide whether he is *happy*; the word "happiness" seems to lean in two directions, sometimes referring to the *feeling* of happiness, sometimes to the kind of *life* that is happy. For a person to be living happily, or to have a happy life, he must attain all the important things he values, or he must come reasonably close to this standard. But one can feel happy with one's life even if one comes nowhere near this goal; one need only believe that one is meeting one's standard. The deceived man, then, has a feeling of happiness, but when he is asked what he thinks happiness is, he is not being asked for the conditions under which he will have this feeling. Rather, he is being asked for his view about what a happy life is. If he discovers that his friends were deceiving him, he should say that although his feeling of happiness was based on an illusion, it really did exist. At no time, however, was he really leading a happy life.

In what follows, I will, for the sake of convenience, use the terms "happiness" and "a happy life" interchangeably. I am not denying that it is sometimes correct to call a person happy merely because he feels that way about his life. Aristotle never uses *eudaimonia* in this way, and in this respect his term differs markedly from our own. But once this point is made, an important question remains: What is the difference between being *eudaimon* and leading a happy life?

IV

On our view, a person is living happily only if he realizes that he is attaining the important things he values, or if he comes reasonably close to this high standard. Of course, this is not the only condition one must meet. One must also find that the things one values are genuinely rewarding, and not merely the best of a bad range of alternatives.[23] And perhaps further conditions are necessary as well. What I want to focus on is a certain subjectivism in our conception of happiness. On our view, a person is happy only if he meets the standards *he* imposes on his life. Even if many others consider his standards too low, and would never switch places with him, he can still have a happy life. Consider, for example, a person who is severely retarded and thus quite limited in his aims and abilities. Though we would never wish for such a fate, we still think that under favorable conditions such a person can lead a happy life. For he can achieve the things he values, given the right circumstances. It is irrelevant that more fortunate individuals have more ambitious goals and would not be satisfied if their achievements were so very limited.

Contrast this with a more objective way of determining whether people are leading happy lives. We can define "objectivism" as the view that people should not be considered happy unless they are coming reasonably close to living the best life they are capable of. According to the objectivist, each person has certain capacities and talents which can be fully developed under ideal conditions. And if someone is very distant from his full development, he is not and should not be considered happy, even if he meets the standards he imposes on his life. For he could have been leading a much better life, as determined by some ideal standard. The objectivist thinks that it is not up to you to determine where your happiness lies; it is fixed by your nature, and your job is to discover it.

The objective conception of happiness is in some important ways modeled on Aristotle's conception of *eudaimonia*. He thinks that to be *eudaimon* one must completely fulfill the function of a human being, or come reasonably close to doing so. And in his opinion, most people don't know what their function is; they may not even believe that they have one. Therefore they never attain *eudaimonia*, whether they realize it or not. Now, even though the objective view of happiness is patterned after Aristotle's approach to *eudaimonia*, a modern-day objectivist need not be as narrow. The *Nicomachean Ethics* argues that there is just one life that is best for everyone—the philosophical life—but objectivists can disagree. They might believe that for each of us there is a large class of ideal lives, and that to be happy we have to come reasonably close to one of those lives. And an objectivist can also say that different types of individuals have different capacities, so that what is ideal for one person may not be ideal for another. We can think of the objectivist as a reformed Aristotelian: he wants us to make judgments of happiness in somewhat the way the *Ethics* makes judgments of *eudaimonia*, but he is free to modify Aristotle's doctrine here and there, so that his own proposal will be more reasonable.

It is important not to overestimate the differences between the subjective and objective ways of judging a person to be living happily.[24] The objectivist, like us, recognizes that a happy person must have certain attitudes towards himself; he must be satisfied with the way his life is going, and he must find his projects fulfilling. Furthermore, we are like the objectivist in that we believe that living happily does not merely consist in having a highly positive attitude towards one's life. We agree that to lead a happy life a person must actually meet a certain standard; seeming to meet it is not enough. Finally, we resemble the objectivist in this further respect: in our assessment of how happy a person is, we take into account the extent to which he has realized his capacities. We think that if someone falls far short of developing himself, then although he may be happy, he is not as happy as he might have been. For example, even if a retarded person manages to achieve a happy life, he might have been happier had he realized to a greater degree the normal capacities of a human being. In better circumstances, he could have chosen his interests from a wider range of alternatives, and he would have found more rewarding activities for himself. Much the same can be said of normal individuals who grow up in environments that do not elicit their talents and abilities. They too might have led happier lives, though they can be successful in pursuing the things they value, and therefore be happy.[25]

But the objectivist says that a person is not happy if he is very distant from leading the best life he is capable of. We say instead that such a person is happy, though he might have been happier. What sort of disagreement is this, and how important is it?

V

Is the difference between subjectivism and objectivism merely verbal? Does the objectivist assign a different meaning to the word "happiness?" Should we say that he is only adopting a misleading way of talking, and that he would make his point more clearly and effectively if he used a different word instead of "happiness?" We might recommend, for example, that he express himself in this way: "A person can be happy if his life meets his own standards, but *to flourish* he must realize his capacities and come reasonably close to the best life he is capable of. So one can be happy but not flourish."

I think the objectivist has good reason to reject this proposal. He is someone who sees, in a number of cases, a huge gap between the lives people are leading and the lives that would be best for them. He may want to shock them into the realization that they are doing a terrible job with their lives. In this way perhaps they will change for the better, and at any rate others will not be tempted to imitate them. Furthermore, the objectivist may succeed in changing people's minds about whether their lives have been happy. He may convince them that their lives have been sorely lacking in qualities whose importance they suddenly recognize. After reevaluating themselves in the light of newly acquired standards, they may thank the objectivist for making them see that they have unknowingly been leading unhappy lives.[26] Since such reevaluations do take place, it is hardly appropriate to tell the objectivist that he is misusing the word "happiness." Notice too that it is not very disturbing to be told that although one is happy one could be even happier. Quite naturally, people will reply that they are satisfied just to be happy: why should they keep striving for more and more? Why should we make radical changes in our lives, as the objectivist urges, merely to exchange a happy life for a happier one? Similarly, no one is going to be upset if he is told that he is not flourishing (most people will wonder what flourishing amounts to) or fully realizing his talents. Happiness is what people want for themselves, and the objectivist is right in his conviction that people are unlikely to change drastically for their own sake unless they believe that they are not presently leading happy lives.

So if we take the word "happiness" away from the objectivist, we take away a strategic tool, which he rightly insists on using.

Furthermore, the objectivist may challenge us in the following way: "As you saw earlier, a person is not leading a happy life if he falsely believes that he is achieving his most valued goals. But can't people suffer from an illusion that is equally bad for them, if not worse? They can have radically false beliefs about what goals they should pursue. If a person wants to lead the best life he is capable of, but is deeply mistaken about what this life consists in or how it is to be accomplished, then he is in as sorry a state as the man who is deceived into believing that he is loved by his friends. Both think they are leading a certain sort of life, but they are far from it, and so neither is living a happy life— though they may *feel* happy."

We can reply to this challenge by showing what the difficulties of objectivism are, and I will be doing that in a later section. But enough has been said to show that the objectivist is not simply adopting an arbitrary and misleading way of talking. He thinks that the way we talk about happiness deceives people into leading what is, from their own point of view, the wrong kind of life. So we would be missing his point if we were to look upon his way of judging people happy to be nothing but a misuse of the word.

Nor would it be correct to say that the objectivist is proposing a new meaning for the word "happiness." To see this, consider the following analogy: Suppose that a certain society takes tallness to be an invaluable property, though the greatest height attained is five feet. A group of scientists discovers that under optimal conditions human beings can reach a height of between five and seven feet, and they propose that steps be taken to achieve these conditions, so that young people and future generations will achieve their ideal height. To make people sense the urgent need for change, they stop calling anyone—even five-footers—tall, and they recommend that everyone else adopt this new standard. It would be a strategic mistake for them to introduce a new word to mean "attaining one's ideal height." Since "tallness" is already a familiar term for an esteemed property, they should simply deny what their society has affirmed: that a five-foot person is tall.

It would be wrong to say that these scientists are proposing a new meaning for the word "tall." To be tall is to meet or exceed a specified standard of height, and the scientists are not trying to change this definition. Rather, they are proposing a different standard. They think that tallness should no longer be a matter of exceeding the norm, but of coming close to an ideal, and there is no more a change of meaning here than in any other case in which standards for the application of a term are revised. What once passed for a good recording, for example, would no longer do so, but that hardly shows that the meaning of "good recording" has changed.[27]

The objective conception of happiness should be treated in the same way. It proposes that we drop our current subjective standard of happiness,[28] and judge each person instead by a more severe and objective test. And the objectivist can reasonably argue that when he talks about a happy life, "happy" means just what it does for the subjectivist: a happy person has a highly affirmative attitude towards his life, and comes reasonably close to attaining the important things he values; a happy life, furthermore, is one that is highly desirable from the standpoint of the person leading it. But how should we characterize that standpoint? The objectivist says that a life is desirable from your own standpoint only if it comes fairly close to your ideal life, whereas the subjectivist thinks your current goals fix the standpoint from which your life should be evaluated. This difference hardly amounts to a difference in the meaning of the term "happiness."[29]

I think this bears on the question of how to translate Aristotle. For the objectivist wants us to use the expression "living happily" in very much the way the *Ethics* uses *eudaimonia*. As we have seen, Aristotle thinks that if someone is *eudaimon*, then he has a highly affirmative attitude towards his life, and his deepest desires are being satisfied. Aristotle differs from us only in that he thinks a *eudaimon* life must come very close to the ideal, whereas our judgments of happiness rely on a subjective standard. And as I have just argued, this sort of difference is not plausibly viewed as a difference in meaning.

VI

We can get a clearer picture of the objectivist's proposal if we ask what it is to wish someone future happiness. More specifically, what are we wishing for when we say of a new-born baby, "I hope he has a happy life"? The subjectivist might be tempted to reply: "We are wishing the child success in attaining the things he will come to value, whatever these things are; and we are hoping he will find these goals, whatever they are, fulfilling." But I do not think this is the right account. For think of all the terrible things that would not be excluded by the wish for happiness, if this were all it amounted to. A newborn child might become retarded—yet still live happily; he might be enslaved, or blinded, or severely incapacitated in other ways—yet still live happily. Even though these are awful misfortunes, they do not so restrict us that a happy life becomes impossible, given the subjective account of happiness. Yet when we wish a happy life to a new-born baby, we are wishing for something better than such lives as these. The child's parents, upon hearing our wishes, do not respond: "But why are you being so ungenerous? Why don't you wish our baby all the best, rather than a merely happy life? You've said nothing so far to exclude the major misfortunes—things one should not wish even upon one's enemies!"

Why don't parents make this accusation of ungenerosity? To answer this question, it will be useful to remind ourselves that there is a close linguistic connection between happiness and good fortune. "Hap" means chance; a hapless person is luckless; a happy turn of events is always good news; the first dictionary definition of "happy" is: "characterized by luck or good fortune."[30] I suggest that when we wish a child a life of happiness, we are tacitly relying on this connection between hap and happiness. We hope that the child will achieve the things he values, and find these things rewarding; but we also hope that the child's range of choices will not be restricted by unfortunate—that is, unhappy—circumstances. This explains why we do not react in different ways to the wish that a baby have all the best and the wish that he lead a life of happiness.[31]

As children grow up and their lives take on a definite shape, their parents and others will employ our usual subjective test for determining whether they are happy. A parent might judge that his children are very distant from the best life that was available to them, but that they are nonetheless happy. We are objective in our early hopes and subjective in our later judgments. That is, when we wish someone a happy life, we hope he comes as close as possible to one of the best lives available to him; yet later our assessments of happiness abandon any reference to an ideal. The objectivist's proposal is that we bring our judgments of happiness into line with our early wishes. He says that we should only judge a person happy if he is leading the kind of life we should have wished for him when he was a new-born baby. Some explanation is needed of why we do not adopt this practice.

Notice, by the way, how silly it would be to say that "happiness" has two different meanings: one when we wish children a happy life, and another when we assess the happiness of adults. Quite clearly what is happening is not a change in meaning but a change in standards. We include more in a happy life, when we wish it to the new-born, than we require of such a life, when we judge that someone has achieved it. All the more reason, then, to think that objectivists and subjectivists mean the same by "happiness," and that Aristotle's *eudaimon* is properly rendered, "leading a happy life."

VII

The objectivist wants us to change our linguistic habits and use his test for determining whether people are happy. To convince us, he must give us a definite idea of how to use that test. That is, he must tell us how to determine what the ideal life (or set of ideals) is for each person. We must have a fairly complete picture of what must be included in such lives and of what can safely be left out. Further, the objectivist must convince us that the lives he calls ideal really deserve that name. When people engage in the activities he calls ideal, and refrain from the ones he thinks unimportant, they must find their lives more rewarding than they were before. Conversely, when people move away from lives the objectivist considers ideal, and try different alternatives, they must come to regret their decisions. And the objectivist ought to have some explanation of why people prefer the kind of life which he says is best for them. He must point to certain deep-seated facts of human nature and social organization which incline people to find a certain way of life best from their own point of view. Without such an explanation we may suspect that the objectivist merely has acquired a powerful hold over people who cannot consider themselves happy unless they do what he tells them. Furthermore, the objectivist must say something about what it is for a person to come *reasonably* close to leading his ideal life. Obviously, he cannot require that a happy life be absolutely perfect—there are no such lives. But unless we have some idea of what deviations from the ideal are compatible with happiness, it would be pointless to try to judge whether anyone is living happily. It would be like trying to decide whether London is reasonably close to Bristol.[32]

The trouble with objectivism is that no one has worked out a detailed and plausible theory that satisfies these demands. And so even if we are attracted by the objectivist's proposal, we have very little idea of how to put it into practice.[33] For example, suppose we read Aristotle's discussion of *eudaimonia* as a recommendation about how to determine whether people are living happily. (This is how he should be read, if *eudaimonia* means "leading a happy life.") The idea that the best life is philosophical seems much too narrow, so let us leave this aside and consider Aristotle's claim that the best life must make an excellent use of reason. Two questions arise: First, might someone make a poor use of his reasoning abilities, but make such excellent use of other capacities and talents that he comes reasonably close to leading one of the lives that could be ideal for him? Aristotle does not give any convincing reason for believing that this cannot happen. Second, there is the question of what constitutes an excellent use of reason. Here Aristotle has a lot to say. Using reason in an excellent way about practical matters requires exercising the virtues as he interprets them: one must be temperate in matters of physical pleasure, rather than a sensualist or an ascetic; one must be courageous, chiefly on the battlefield; and so on. Here too, Aristotle has worked out his theory too narrowly. There is no reason to believe that a person fully realizes his capacities only if he adopts Aristotle's attitudes towards physical pleasure and the use of force. Any objective theory of happiness which tries to do better than Aristotle's conception of *eudaimonia* will have to avoid his narrowness, without becoming so vague and general as to be useless.

I want to emphasize that I am making a limited point against objectivism. I do not claim that in principle such a theory cannot be found.[34] Great figures have claimed to see what the ideal life is for each individual, and the only rational response to these philosophies is to examine them case by case. Perhaps with more work we can provide objectivism with the philosophical foundations it requires. My point is that at present we have no defensible method for discovering each person's distance from his ideal lives. And so if we drop our subjective judgments of happiness, we have no workable and systematic alternative to put in their place.[35] Unless some incoherence can be found in our subjective conception of happiness—and so far none has—we have good reason to continue our present practice. Even so, our interest in the alternative provided by objectivism is bound to continue. For subjectivism says so little about how we should lead our lives: it tells us that if we want to be happy we should make up our minds about what we value most, and this is of little help to those who are uncertain about what kind of life to lead. Subjectivism requires less of a philosophical foundation than objectivism, but as a result it is, from a practical standpoint, the less informative theory.

VIII

One final complaint must be lodged against Aristotle's particular brand of objectivism: the standard by which he evaluates lives is too rigid. To see this, consider his doctrine of natural slavery.[36] He thinks there are individuals who are constitutionally incapable of rational deliberation (1260a12, 1280a32–34), and for whom the best life is one of docile subordination to a wise master (1254b16–20, 1278b34–35). These natural slaves are not wholly devoid of reason (1254b22–23). Like all human beings, and unlike other animals, they are capable of emotions and desires which are persuaded and therefore altered by rational argument. But since they cannot rationally plan their lives on their own, they need to attach themselves to a benevolent superior who will regularly do this for them. If natural slaves discipline themselves so that their emotions and desires conform with their masters' correct conception of the good, they will achieve a low-grade form of virtue (1260a34–36). But even so—and this is the point I want to emphasize—Aristotle says that they can never attain *eudaimonia*, no matter how well they do within their limits (1280a33–34). Evidently, his test for *eudaimonia* is not how well one is doing, given one's limitations, but how close one comes to a perfect human life. Since the best a slave can do still falls far short of the ideal available to some, he can never be *eudaimon*. An objective theory of happiness that follows Aristotle on this point will say that a mentally retarded person can never live happily, even in the best of circumstances. Is there something wrong with this uncompromising form of objectivism?

Aristotle's inflexibility might be defended in this way: even if a slave cannot achieve *eudaimonia*, he nonetheless has every reason to try to come as near as he possibly can to that ultimate end. Certain ways of life will move him closer to this ideal and others will move him farther away, so his conception of *eudaimonia* will influence him as much as it influences those who can actually achieve it. What harm is done, then, if Aristotle's rigid standard makes the slave incapable of *eudaimonia*?

The answer is that Aristotle's inflexibility makes it difficult, if not impossible, for seriously handicapped individuals to maintain their self-esteem and vitality. On his view, only a *eudaimon* life is well lived (1095a18–20), and so slaves cannot justifiably believe that they are doing a good job of living their lives. The most favorable point they can make about their existence is that among the bad lives theirs are not the worst: quite a negative judgment about the worth of being alive. Similarly, a slave is never justified in congratulating himself on the way he is living, nor can others justifiably congratulate him. For to congratulate someone on his life is to call him *eudaimon*[37]—and the slave is utterly distant from that end. Now, just as a dedicated singer would find it hard to live with the public recognition that he sings poorly, so a person who wants to see some good in his being alive will find it hard to do so if he and others judge that his life can never be well lived. The singer, at least, can try to change his role, but one cannot turn to some other activity besides living one's life. The slave is kept going by the biological urge for survival and can develop no justified confidence that his existence is preferable to death. Aristotle himself suggests that when we ask what *eudaimonia* is, we are asking what makes life worth living, that is, what reasons there are to choose to stay alive (*Eudemian Ethics* I 5). Since the slave has such a small sampling of those goods that make life worthwhile, he can never be *eudaimon*, and can find little reason to be glad that he is alive. Aristotle's conception of self-love (*NE* IX 4) yields the same dismal conclusion: the less virtuous one is, the less one can justifiably love oneself, and so, since the slave can at best achieve a reduced form of virtue, he is entitled to little self-regard.

I suggest that there is something inhumane about Aristotle's doctrine, and that an objective theory of happiness should depart from his lead in some way. Objectivism, as I have described it, takes happiness to be a highly valuable goal, and it urges us to be dissatisfied with our lives if they are not objectively happy. But if a person is permanently handicapped, there is no reason why we should persuade him to be unhappy with his life, distant though it may be from the ideal he might have achieved. Rather, objectivism will be a more humane doctrine if it evaluates each person's life by a standard which reflects his unalterable capacities and circumstances.[38] What an objectivist should say is this: Happy individuals can fall far short of the ideal they might have achieved, but they must do reasonably well with whatever restrictions currently surround their lives. A person is happy only if: (1) he meets the standards he has set for himself, and finds his life highly desirable; and (2) nothing he can now do would make his life significantly better.[39]

Notice that the objectivist who takes this line must give up a claim made earlier, in Section VI. He said that we ought to call someone happy only if he is leading the kind of life we should have wished for him when he was a new-born baby. But what happens when a normal baby later receives severe physical injuries which cause some retardation? Humane objectivists would not have wished such a life upon this unfortunate person, but they will nonetheless judge him happy if he is doing his best under the circumstances. So flexible objectivists, no less than subjectivists, allow for a discrepancy between early wishes and later judgments. When they wish a baby a happy life, they mean to exclude certain events which, if they occur at a later time, do not prevent them from calling that life happy.

By tailoring each person's ideal to fit his current limitations, and thus departing from Aristotle's conception of *eudaimonia*, objectivism can be a humane outlook. But its main difficulty still remains. It requires us to judge someone happy only if his life cannot be significantly better; but we do not know how to determine this, in so many cases. Of course, all of our lives, or nearly all, could be somewhat better—but could they be significantly better?[40] To answer this question, the objectivist will have to say what the best attainable life is for each of us, and he must provide some reasonable way of measuring our distance from this reachable ideal.

To summarize, let me turn back once more to Aristotle: his differences with us stem from the fact that he calls someone *eudaimon* only if that person comes fairly close to the ideal life for all human beings, whereas our standard of happiness is more subjective and flexible. We do not have a defensible theory about which lives are ideal, and even if we did, we would not want to judge people happy only if they come close to the best life a human being can lead. So, when Aristotle says that a slave cannot be *eudaimon*, and we say that in certain conditions he can be happy, we are not, strictly speaking, contradicting each other. He is measuring the slave's distance from the ideal for all human beings, while we are saying that the slave's life can meet his own reduced standards. But even though we are not contradicting Aristotle on this point, we still have something to argue about. He would accuse us, and we should accuse him, of measuring people's lives by an inappropriate standard.[41]

NOTES

1. *The Methods of Ethics*, 7th ed. (London, 1907), pp. 92–93.

2. *Aristotle: A Complete Exposition of His Works and Thought*, Meridian ed. (Cleveland, 1959), p. 186. Unless otherwise noted, quotations are from the Ross translation.

3. *Reason and Human Good in Aristotle*, (Cambridge, Massachusetts, 1975), pp. 89–90, n. 1. Cooper says that "happiness" is not a good translation since "much that Aristotle says about *eudaimonia* manifestly fails to hold true of happiness as ordinarily understood." (Ibid.) To support this point, he calls attention to Aristotle's claim at 1100*a*1–4 that a child can be called *eudaimon* only in the expectation that he will achieve *eudaimonia* as an adult.

4. Op. cit., p. 92.

5. Op. cit., p. 186.

6. Op. cit., p. 89, n. 1.

7. It would be desirable, in translating Aristotle's *eudaimonia*, to find an English expression that plays pretty much the same role in our language that *eudaimonia* played in his. On this score, "flourishing" is quite inadequate:

A. *Eudaimon* and its cognates were everyday words that occurred frequently not only in philosophical works, but also in Greek drama, oratory and poetry. Our term "flourishing" is less common. If a student in a philosophy course were asked, "What is human flourishing?" his first reaction would be that this is a philosopher's question that has no obvious connection with ordinary life. But when Aristotle asked in his classroom what *eudaimonia* is, his audience immediately recognized this as a common and urgent practical question. (In this respect, asking "what is happiness?" is very much like asking what *eudaimonia* is.)

B. When "flourishing" is used in common speech, it is most often attached to nonhuman subjects; ant colonies, flowers, towns, businesses, etc., are much more likely to be called flourishing than human beings. *Eudaimonia*, on the other hand, is attributed only to human and divine persons. (Notice how odd it would be to say that an animal or plant is leading a happy life. Though dogs and cats can be happy, they still do not lead happy lives; the latter expression has pretty much the same range of application as *eudaimonia*.)

C. When human beings are said to flourish, it is often meant that they flourish in a certain role or activity. For example: artists do not flourish in military dictatorships, pornographers flourish in democracies, and evil men flourish when moral standards are too lax or too strict. Roughly what is meant is that they succeed in these roles under the conditions specified. This common use of the term "flourish" is far from Aristotle's use of *eudaimonia*. When he says that an evil man cannot be *eudaimon* under any conditions, he is hardly denying that evil can flourish.

8. This paragraph summarizes views Aristotle puts forward in several parts of the *Ethics*: I 7 1097*b*22–1098*a*20 (the function of man is to act virtuously); I 8 1099*a*31–1099*b*7 and I 9 1100*a*5–9 (the misfortunes that can spoil *eudaimonia*); I 10 1100*b*22–1101*a*13 (only major misfortunes take *eudaimonia* away, and it can be recovered); X 7–8 (the best life is philosophical). See "Aristotle on the Ideal Life" (unpublished) for my defense of the view that for Aristotle the best life combines both philosophical and ethical activities.

9. As is well known, the virtuous individual does not merely act virtuously: he also chooses such acts for their own sake (II 4 1105*a*30–32), prefers them to everything else (I 10 1100*b*19–20), and realizes he is a good person (IX 9 1170*b*4–9).

10. For the view that ethical virtue requires moderate desires for external goods, see esp. III 4 1119*a*11–20 and VII 4 1148*a*22–1148*b*4. Aristotle's doctrine that every ethical virtue lies in

a mean between two extremes should be distinguished from his belief that desires for external objects should be moderate in strength, though he himself may run these two theses together. For some brief discussion, see J. Urmson, "Aristotle's Doctrine of the Mean," *American Philosophical Quarterly* 10 (July, 1973), esp. pp. 225–226.

11. "Those who say that the victim on the rack or the man who falls into great misfortunes is happy if he is good, are, whether they mean to or not, talking nonsense" (VII 13 1153*b*19–21). Aristotle presumably does not mean that a brief experience of great physical pain, whatever its cause, is incompatible with *eudaimonia*. Otherwise, pains endured in honorable battle would also deprive someone of *eudaimonia*. No doubt, he is thinking of the rack as an instrument of punishment and therefore disgrace; the victim not only suffers pain, but also a severe loss of honor. To put the point more generally: Some external goods, like honor, are so important that they must be present, to some moderate degree, in any *eudaimon* life, and this is why severe deprivation of such goods is incompatible with *eudaimonia*. Such goods will be desired moderately by whoever understands what *eudaimonia* is, and so those who achieve *eudaimonia* will fully satisfy their desires for these major external goals. If Aristotle had held (1) that a virtuous individual can have ravenous appetites for external goods, and (2) if he had continued to hold that a *eudaimon* life need only contain a moderate amount of such goods, then (3) he would have to accept the conclusion that a *eudaimon* individual can want much more than he has.

12. Aristotle says in a number of places that a life of continual slumber is one no human being would choose, since it is the life of a plant. See *Eudemian Ethics* I 5 1216*a*2–6; *NE* I 5 1095*b*32–35, X 6 1176*a*34–35. The distinction between plants and animals lies in the latter's ability to perceive (*De Anima* II 2413*b*1–2, *NE* IX 9 1070*a*16–17); in sleep, one becomes plant-like, since perception ceases. Therefore, one of the capacities we must take advantage of if we are to lead lives that are not plant-like, is perception. And what one presumably wants to perceive are the goods available to higher beings: the good things in one's own life, in the lives of friends and one's city, and in the fixed nature of the universe. Merely to perceive the sorts of things that other animals can detect is to escape the condition of a plant, but it is not to lead a distinctively human life (I 7 1098*a*1–3).

13. Thus Aristotle says that pleasure is a good since all human beings desire it (X 2 1172*b*35–1173*a*4). In fact, it is so pervasive a feature of human life that all men "weave pleasure into their ideal of happiness" (VII 13 1153*b*14–15). Aristotle's own theory of *eudaimonia* also finds an important place for this good (I 8 1099*a*7–29). In general, anything that is deeply and universally desired must be part of our good.

14. Aristotle, of course, never discusses such an example. My point is that he has beliefs which commit him to denying that the individual described is *eudaimon*. Anyone who doubts this should recall Aristotle's view that one must have practical wisdom to be *eudaimon*. Judging from his discussion of this virtue in Book VI, it is doubtful that he would ascribe it to those who have radically mistaken beliefs about their own well being. Notice especially the connection between practical wisdom and understanding (VI 10), and the importance of recognizing specific matters of fact (1141*b*15 ff., 1142*a*20 ff.).

15. The connection between *eudaimonia* and desire-satisfaction is tacitly assumed at the beginning of *Eudemian Ethics* I 5: "While there are many different things as to which it is not easy to make a right judgment, this is especially the case with one about which everybody thinks that it is easy to judge and anybody can decide—*the question which of the things contained in being alive is preferable and which when attained would fully satisfy a man's desire*" (1215*b*15–18, tr. by H. Rackham, emphasis added). Obviously, the deceptively simple question posed here is a stand-in for the one Aristotle has been raising in the first four chapters of the *Eudemian Ethics*: "Which sort of life is most *eudaimon*?" Since Aristotle regards them as equivalent questions, he is presupposing that a life cannot be *eudaimon* unless it fully satisfies the desires of one who leads it. I take him to be talking about major desires—that is, long-standing desires which have great weight in determining how one conducts one's life. Small mishaps cannot deprive one of *eudaimonia* (*NE* I 10 1100*b*22–25), and the failure to satisfy a minor desire is a small mishap, at most.

16. I say "at least partly" because Aristotle leaves open the possibility that some lack *eudaimonia* even though they perceive that their deepest desires are satisfied. Consider, for example,

a person who is not evil, but who values honor, wealth, and physical pleasure more than they are worth. Because of these defective desires, he is not a virtuous person, and he therefore lacks *eudaimonia*. Yet he might be fully satisfied with his life. Satisfaction of desire is not a sufficient condition of *eudaimonia*, but even so a theory of *eudaimonia* is dubious if it fails to correspond roughly with experience. The most important cases are at the extremes: individuals deemed *eudaimones* or *athlioi* (miserable) ought to have opposite attitudes towards their lives.

17. *Greek Popular Morality in the Time of Plato and Aristotle* (Oxford, 1974), p. 174, and n. 5.

18. I doubt that Dover has found a genuine case. The lines he quotes, ibid., n. 5, are *Medea* 598–9, but the context strongly suggests that Medea is being ironic: some *eudaimon* life that would be, filled with worry and distress! If that is how she is to be understood, then her lines tell us just the opposite of what Dover reads into them. Her mental anguish is precisely what makes it outrageous to call her *eudaimon*. I am grateful to Gregory Vlastos and Elizabeth Gebhard for discussion of this point. Dover admits that *eudaimonia* "occasionally requires the translation 'happiness'." Ibid. So even if this is a poor translation in many contexts and authors (and I am not convinced it is), it may still be the most suitable translation of Aristotle. Notice that closeness of meaning is not necessarily transitive. Our expression "leading a happy life" may be close in meaning to Aristotle's term *eudaimonia*, and his use of that term may be close to the way it is used by his contemporaries and predecessors; yet some of them may mean by *eudaimon* something that is not close to our expression "leading a happy life."

19. This parallel is not mentioned by any of those who specifically discuss the relationship between *eudaimonia* and happiness: J. Austin, "*Agathon* and *Eudaimonia* in the *Ethics* of Aristotle," in J. Moravcsik (ed.), *Aristotle: A Collection of Critical Essays* (Garden City, N.Y., 1967), pp. 261–296, esp. 270–283; H. Joachim, *The Nicomachean Ethics* (Oxford, 1951), p. 28; J. Ackrill, "Aristotle on *Eudaimonia*," *Proceedings of the British Academy* 1974, pp. 3–23, esp. 12–13; S. Clark, *Aristotle's Man* (Oxford, 1975), p. 157; R. Sullivan, *Morality and the Good Life* (Memphis, 1977), p. 178; to which add the works of Sidgwick, Ross and Cooper, cited above in notes 1, 2, and 3.

20. For an exception, see G. Watson, "Happiness and *Eudaimonia*," read at the 1977 Princeton Colloquium on Aristotle's Ethics; his argument differs from my own. Hobbes too seems to connect *eudaimonia* with happiness. He says, "That whereby (men) signify the opinion they have of a man's felicity is by the Greeks called *makarismos*, for which we have no name in our tongue." *Leviathan*, I 6, penultimate sentence. A *makarismos* is a claim that someone is *makarios* or (equivalently) *eudaimon*. So Hobbes is saying that when *A* calls *B eudaimon*: (1) *A* thinks *B's* life is felicitous (i.e., happy), and (2) *A* is giving his opinion of (is praising or admiring) *B's* happy life.

21. I do not intend extreme subjectivism to be naive in its view about what kind of psychological state happiness consists in. It would be naive if it held that a happy person is simply one who is, at the time, in a euphoric mood. That is far too simple and episodic an account: a happy person may be so occupied with challenging activities that he rarely experiences the sort of mood we call "feeling happy." The important thing about extreme subjectivism is that it endorses these views: when a person's conception of reality is utterly mistaken, that fact can never be the basis for denying that he is happy; even when someone deeply desires his conception of the world to be correct, his happiness does not require that desire to be satisfied; a person must be wrong if he says that his happiness depends on reality being a certain way.

22. To vary the example somewhat: Suppose that, as a cruel trick, someone is voted the most popular student in his high school. In actuality, his fellow students can't stand him, but he is benighted enough to take the vote at face value. After a day of euphoria, he discovers that he has been tricked. Years later, he is asked what the happiest day of his life has been. If that day in high school was the one on which he felt most intensely happy, must he say that in fact it was the happiest day in his life? I think not. I can understand his saying that it was actually the unhappiest day of his life, however happy he felt. If the extreme subjectivist also wants to make this distinction between a happy day and a day on which someone feels happy, then he must explain why he does not distinguish a happy life from feeling happy with one's life. For further discussion, see n. 31.

23. "Attaining the important things one values" should not be construed narrowly, e.g., to mean that a happy person necessarily strives for future accomplishments, prizes, or successes. Happiness does not require "amounting to something," as that phrase is often used. One might attain the important things one values simply by being a certain sort of person, enjoying certain activities or relationships, and functioning in a certain way. Furthermore, to find an activity or goal "rewarding" is not merely to make an aseptic intellectual judgment that it is worthwhile. It is to be emotionally engaged in that activity, and to feel pleasure in its performance.

24. I will be assuming in this paper that both objectivists and subjectivists view happiness as a great good. This vague judgment, though arguable, is common in philosophy, and accurately reflects the role happiness plays in ordinary practical thought. Happiness has an important place, for example, in the ethics of philosophers as divergent as Kant and Mill. Of course, they disagree about how great a good it is; according to Mill it includes all other goods, whereas Kant assigns it a smaller but still significant place in our thinking. The precise value of happiness is a difficult issue which I want to avoid. It is separate from the problem of whether objective or subjective standards are more appropriate, and so in order to focus attention on this latter issue, I have objectivists and subjectivists agree roughly that happiness is a great good. Taking this as common ground, they can more easily isolate the issues that divide them. For further comments on the worth of a happy life, see n. 38. On those who deny happiness a central role in practical thought, see B. Williams, *Morality: An Introduction to Ethics* (New York, 1972), pp. 81–88. According to Aristotle, any adequate theory of *eudaimonia* must treat that end as one that cannot rationally be renounced. The *eudaimon* life, whatever it turns out to be, must be so good that no reasonable person would choose to have something else instead. (I 7 1097b14–20). Many suppose that happiness, for all its importance, does not have quite the value Aristotle attributes to *eudaimonia*. But we should not infer—as J. Ackrill does—that because of this disparity "happiness" is an unsuitable translation of Aristotle's term *eudaimonia*. See p. 13 of his paper, cited in n. 19. Mill, as I have said, thinks it is a conceptual truth that happiness includes all other desirable goals. Yet those who deny this point can still mean the same thing he does by "happiness." Similarly, the fact that *eudaimonia*, as Aristotle conceives it, cannot be rationally renounced hardly shows that "happiness" is a poor translation of his term.

25. How are we to take the claim that although someone is leading a happy life, he could be leading a happier one? Do such statements refer to a certain psychological state which the person is currently in, and which could be more intense in different circumstances? For example, do we mean that although the individual now has a highly positive attitude towards his life, it would have been more affirmative and enthusiastic had he chosen a different life? Sometimes this is meant, but not always. I am inclined to say that our conception of happiness, though largely subjective, nonetheless contains an objective component: Certain events—the ones that severely handicap us—are misfortunes, whatever a person's standards, attitudes or feelings. And a life afflicted by bad happenstance is, to that extent, less happy than it might otherwise have been. If a blind and a sighted person have the same positive attitude towards their existence, the latter's life is nonetheless happier, since it is not marred by serious misfortune. For futher discussion, see n. 31. So subjectivism borrows from objectivism, without accepting its central idea that to live happily one must come close to one's full development.

26. Suppose someone thinks back on an earlier period of his life, and decides that although he was achieving his goals and considered himself happy, those goals were actually worthless. Since he now deeply regrets having lived in that way, he may single out the days on which he became attracted to those empty ideals as the unhappiest days of his life. (See n. 22.) If this is a coherent way of describing those days, then it also makes sense for him to go further and to say that his life, during that whole period, was not happy. And if he does say this, his judgment cannot rely on a subjective conception of happiness. For he admits that (*A*) his life at that earlier time met the standards he then set, and that (*B*) he did have an affirmative attitude towards his existence. By subjective standards, he was then leading a happy life; the claim that he was then unhappy presupposes an objective conception of happiness. So when I say throughout this paper that our conception of happiness is subjective, I am oversimplifying. Subjectivism (with its objective component—see n. 25) is normally our view, but on occasion

(e.g., in the example just presented), some of us make statements that presuppose an objective test of happiness. For another example, see n. 40.

27. It might be suggested, contrary to what I claim in this paragraph, that a tall person is one who significantly exceeds the average height of individuals *currently alive*. If that is the correct definition, then the scientists in our imaginary society would be proposing a new meaning. But I doubt that this proposal captures the meaning of "tall person." Suppose we discover that ten billion human beings escaped from the earth in prehistoric times and have been living in a different galaxy. Their height varies from eight to ten feet. Are only some of them tall—the ones who exceed our newly computed average? Obviously, we would call *all* of them tall. And we would not be forced by the meaning of "tall" and "short" to consider all earthlings short.

28. This is a crucial feature of objectivism, as I conceive it. It is not the mild view that on occasion we are justified in using an objective standard, and that for the most part a subjective test of happiness is legitimate. Rather, the objectivist holds that our subjective test for happiness should never be employed.

29. It may help, at this point, to think about such expressions as: "that is a happy turn of phrase," "your plants are happy in that window," "my dog is happier when he's on the farm." These uses of the term "happy" are closely related to each other, and to the way "happy" is used when applied to human beings. A happy turn of phrase is one that is just right for the context in which it occurs: if a plant is happy in a sunny window, or a dog happy on a farm, that is because their needs and their environment are appropriately matched; and a person cannot be happy if his nature is totally unsuited for the situation in which he finds himself. In general, we speak of happiness only when there is a fit between a thing and its context. This fact is surely connected with our commonsense view that if a human being is happy then he is satisfying his major desires. Happiness requires a fit between a thing's nature and its surroundings, and since our desires form an important part of our nature, we cannot be happy unless they are fulfilled. The objectivist goes one step further and claims that a life can be unsuitable for someone's nature even if he satisfies his deepest desires. There is no absurdity or linguistic impropriety here.

30. See, e.g., *The American Heritage Dictionary* (Boston, 1969) and *Webster's New International Dictionary* (Springfield, Mass., 1966), *s.v.*

31. I think this connection between hap and happiness sheds light on some earlier points: (*A*) I claimed that the deceived man is not leading a happy life (Section III); in a parallel case, I said (n. 22) that when someone looks back at a day on which he was deceived into euphoria, he could sensibly call it the unhappiest day of his life. In both cases, we take note of the individual's values (friendship, popularity) and judge him unfortunate in the light of those values. And then we justifiably slide from talk of an unfortunate person or an unfortunate day to talk of an unhappy person and an unhappy day. (*B*) I also said (Section IV) that if individuals live in impoverished conditions, they can be happy, though not as happy as they might otherwise have been. The connection between hap and happiness helps explain why we think this way: impoverished conditions are a misfortune, and a life lived in happier circumstances is a happier life. To say that someone might have been happier in different conditions is not always to say that a certain psychological state might have been more intense. Notice that I have left unanswered the question of what makes something a misfortune. Why, for example, is blindness an objective misfortune, as I claim in n. 25, whereas the lack of perfect pitch is not? Is it because sight is so much more valuable as a means to further practical ends? I suspect that this is not the whole story. A blind person is cut off from a significant part of the real world, and so is worse off even if his practical aims do not require vision. A philosopher who denies the reality of the physical world has less reason to consider blindness a misfortune.

32. It might be thought that the subjective conception of happiness must tackle this same difficult problem. After all, it says that a happy person attains the important things he values, or *comes reasonably close* to this standard. But what is it to come reasonably close? The subjectivist, fortunately, can get himself off the hook in most cases by leaving it up to the individual to make the decision. There is no reason to establish a uniform way of measuring each person's distance from his ideal. Of course, a subjectivist cannot say that people are living happily so

long as they believe they are coming reasonably close to attaining what they value. That would mean that even the deceived man is leading a happy life. But what the subjectivist can say is this: when a person has a good idea of how close he is to meeting his goals, then it is up to him to determine whether his distance from these goals is so large as to make him unhappy. What one person considers reasonably close another may not, and the subjectivist need not be bothered by this. Nor need he be disturbed by the fact that many individuals are unsure whether to call themselves happy. Though they may know how close or far they are from attaining the things they value, they may not know whether their distance from their ideals is such as to deprive them of happiness. In these cases, the individual simply has to decide whether or not he should be happy with his life. That is not something the subjectivist can decide for him. The objectivist, however, is in a more difficult position, since *he* is the one to decide *in all* cases whether a person is leading a happy life.

33. I said earlier that when we wish a child a happy life, we are expressing the hope that he will come as close as possible to one of the best lives available to him. (See Section VI.) But now I say that we have no defensible method of determining what the class of best lives is. If this is an obstacle to making objective *judgments* of happiness, shouldn't it equally be an obstacle to making objective *wishes* for happiness? Should the subjectivist stop wishing someone all the best (i.e., wishing someone a happy life), since he doesn't know what that involves? To both of these questions, the answer is no. The fact that you can't tell whether someone will have achieved a certain goal does not argue against wishing for it. But if it is important to know whether someone has achieved that goal—and I assume we have a deep interest in knowing whether we are happy (see n. 24)—then we need a workable method for deciding when it has been attained. Our ignorance is no bar to wishing for an objectively happy life, but it does discredit our judgment that someone's life is objectively happy or unhappy.

34. Here I am in disagreement with G. von Wright, as I understand him. He says, "Whether a person is happy or not depends on *his own* attitude to his circumstances of life. The supreme judge of the case *must be* the subject himself. To think that it could be otherwise is false objectivism." *The Varieties of Goodness* (New York, 1963), pp. 100–101, his emphasis. I take this to mean that our way of judging people happy cannot change so that the supreme judge of happiness becomes a wise observer, rather than the subject himself. I have been arguing that this is false, when "happy person" is equated with "person leading a happy life." If our question is, "Does this person feel happy with his life?", then von Wright is correct in saying that the supreme judge is the subject who is not deceiving himself.

35. The objectivist might reply that we should abandon our subjective conception of happiness, and withhold judgments about the happiness of people's lives until we have developed a workable objective theory. But this proposal is quite weak. If we have an adequate theory, we justifiably continue to use it until a better one comes along. We don't drop it merely because a superior view might be developed.

36. All references in this paragraph are to the *Politics*. My interpretation follows that of W. Fortenbaugh, *Aristotle on Emotion* (London, 1975), pp. 53–55.

37. This is a point made by Austin, op. cit. at n. 19, p. 280. Cf. H. Liddell and R. Scott, *A Greek-English Lexicon*, 9th edn. (Oxford, 1940), *s.v. eudaimonisma*.

38. An objectivist could choose to depart from Aristotle in a different way: he might claim that the permanent absence of happiness is a minor disadvantage, since there are many other goods. On this view, there is nothing objectionable about inflexible standards of happiness, since the unavailability of happiness should mean little to us. I think, however, that this way of modifying Aristotle results in a less defensible theory. Normally we think that if a person gives up his chances to lead a happy life, he is making a great sacrifice. But if there are many other goods available to the unhappy person, has he really given up that much? The objectivist cannot easily combine these ideas: (*A*) a life that is not happy can still contain many good things; (*B*) if one's life contains many good things, then one should be happy with it; (*C*) if one's life is not happy, then it is inappropriate to be happy with it. Objectivism must affirm (*C*), and since (*B*) is more plausible than (*A*), the latter should be rejected. I see no reason why the objectivist should adopt (*A*) rather than the position I urge on him in the text.

39. Objectivism, thus modified, claims that a person is not living happily if his conception of the good is both alterable and radically defective. For such an individual fails to satisfy condition (2). Objectivists who think that defective conceptions of the good are unchangeable—and perhaps Aristotle is one of these—might find this amended version of their theory unattractive. But I am inclined to think that we can and often do revise our notions of what is worth pursuing.

40. There may be a few isolated cases in which we can already answer yes, without doing further philosophical work. For example, suppose sight could be restored to a certain blind person, who nonetheless willingly chooses to remain blind. Then even a subjectivist should admit that this individual's life could be significantly better, i.e., that he is far from an attainable life that is much happier. See n. 25. (I am assuming in this example that the restoration of sight would not bring with it countervailing misfortunes.) Even so, we may be reluctant to say that this person, in his blindness, is necessarily leading an unhappy life. For in so many other cases, we justifiably use a subjective standard of happiness, and this blind man may in fact meet that standard. Wouldn't we be picking on him, if we switched to an objective test and denied him the happiness we attribute to others on subjective grounds? Looking at the matter in this way, it may seem that objectivism has to work in a great many cases, or it won't work at all. But the point is debatable. We could also say that this blind man ought to be made dissatisfied with his present life, since a much better one is available. Why should we encourage him in his error by agreeing that his life is happy? Objectivism is supposed to help people view their lives correctly, and surely we are allowed to help a few even though we can't help everyone. On this view, there is nothing wrong with piecemeal objectivism. I am unable to decide between these two alternatives. But notice that even piecemeal objectivism, since it accepts subjective standards in many cases, is a far cry from the objective conception of happiness discussed throughout this paper. See n. 28.

41. I am grateful to D. Blumenfeld, C. Chastain, G. Dworkin, R. Meerbote, G. Watson, and two anonymous referees, for their comments on earlier drafts. I also profited from reading this paper to the Philosophy Departments at Northwestern University and the University of Wisconsin at Milwaukee.

VIRTUE ETHICS

Richard Taylor

Richard Taylor (1919–2003) was professor of philosophy at the University of Rochester. He argued that happiness consists in achieving fulfillment through the exercise of creative intelligence.

Underlying all the moral philosophy of the ancients were two questions: What is happiness? And how is it attained? Those are the questions to which we now, finally, turn.

Happiness has to be the basic concern of all ethics, for if human beings had no capacity for it and for its opposite, there would be no point in reflecting

From Richard Taylor, *Virtue Ethics* (Amherst, NY: Prometheus Books, 2002). Copyright © 2002 by Richard Taylor. Reprinted with permission of the publisher.

about ethics at all. This was so obvious to the ancients that it seemed to them to need no defense. All these classical moralists justified their systems, finally, by claiming that the ideals they portrayed were the ingredients of a happy life. Even Plato felt the need to justify the austere lives of the guardians of his republic by claiming that they were, notwithstanding appearances, happy; and he recognized the suggestion that they were not as a possibly fatal criticism. The Stoics, too, in spite of their unbending rectitude and the severity of their principles, maintained that their ideal life of reason and self-denial was the only genuinely happy one.

The idea of happiness is no less essential to modern moral philosophy than to the ancient systems, even though it is now more apt to be taken for granted than treated as a difficult and profoundly important idea in its own right. The role of happiness in determining questions of moral right and wrong is generally acknowledged, but then attention is forthwith focused not on the nature of happiness, but upon the distinction of right and wrong. Still, no philosopher could consider his theories tenable if he were compelled to admit that the application of them to human affairs would inevitably promote misery. Even those who reject hedonism, and the various forms of utilitarianism, would find it hard to render their views plausible if they had to assume that human beings have no more capacity for happiness than unfeeling stones. However one approaches ethics—whether from the ancient standpoint of virtue, or the modern one of duty, or from any other—what one finally asserts has to be something that makes a difference and this, in the last analysis, must be a difference with respect to human happiness. Otherwise, whatever is said will be simply pointless.

THE NATURE OF HAPPINESS

However much the ancient schools differed in their various conceptions of happiness, they were agreed about its importance. Their word for it, *eudaimonia*, is not even adequately translatable into English. It usually comes out, in translation, as "happiness," but not without loss. Something like "fulfillment" would in some ways be better, but we shall stay with happiness, keeping in mind its shortcomings.

Eudaimonia means, literally, to be possessed of a good demon, and this conveys the idea of extreme good fortune on the part of its possessor. One possessed of *eudaimonia* was thought of by the ancients as blessed beyond measure, as having won something of supreme worth and, at the same time, something very elusive and hence rare. Just what it *is* was seldom clear, even in the minds of the greatest moralists, but there was no doubt at all of its importance and value. To discover the nature of this *eudaimonia* and the path to its attainment seemed to many great moralists of that age to be the main task of philosophy.

Most people seem to think they know what happiness is, which is unfortunate, for this prevents them from learning. One has no incentive to inquire into what one thinks one already knows. In fact, however, there seem to be few things more infected with error and false notions than people's ideas of happiness. It is very common for people, in their ill-considered quest for personal happiness, to spend their lives pursuing some specious ideal—such as the accumulation of wealth—and then, having succeeded, to miss the happiness erroneously identified with it. Of course people are reluctant to come to terms with their own illusions, and few who have wasted their lives are very willing to admit it even to themselves; but their failure is often quite obvious to others. We tend to be tolerant of error here, for its only victims are the possessors of it. Another person's dashed expectations seldom threaten our own. And we are therefore content to suppose that if someone seems to himself or herself to be happy, perhaps he or she really is happy after all. But one can see how shallow this is by asking whether one would really wish to *be* that other person. It is hard to see why not, if that other person is believed to be truly happy. But we know, in fact, that such persons are not; they only seem so to themselves, largely because they are unwilling to admit their own folly.

It was from reflections such as these that ancient moralists were fond of quoting Solon, to the effect that no man should be deemed happy until he is dead (for example, Aristotle, *N. Ethics*, Bk. I, Ch. 10). This paradoxical remark seems to suggest that the dead are more happy than the living, but that is not what is meant at all. The point is, rather, that the search for happiness is the task of a lifetime and that it can elude one, even at the last moment. And indeed, it does elude most persons, even those who thought they were on the track of it.

It will be best to begin, then, by citing a few of the things that are most commonly confused with happiness and seeing where they fail. Having cleared the way of false conceptions, we can hope to see, however imperfectly, what happiness really is and how it might be won.

HAPPINESS AND PLEASURE

It is very common for modern philosophers, and others too, to confuse happiness with pleasure. John Stuart Mill even declared them to be one and the same. Others make the same mistake, sometimes speaking as if happiness were something which, like pleasures, can come and go or be artificially induced or evoked by stimulation. The ancients rarely did this. They were partly protected from this error by having a word, *eudaimonia*, far richer in its connotations than either of our words *happiness* or *pleasure*. The identification of happiness with pleasure would have sounded funny to them, whereas to us it may not.

The reason why modern philosophers are sometimes so eager to treat happiness and pleasure as the same is not hard to see. They want to think of happiness as something familiar, identifiable, and even measurable, rather than as something problematical or dubious. Pleasure, being an actual and common feeling, is certainly familiar and identifiable, and there seems to be no reason in principle why it should not be measurable. In short, the interest some moral philosophers have in the concept of pleasure is but a consequence of their predilection for empiricism. If, they think, ethics can be grounded in something plainly real and indisputable, then it ought to be possible to resolve the problems of ethics in a straightforward manner. This was certainly Mill's motive. He wanted to be able to define moral right and wrong (and hence duty) in terms of happiness and to identify happiness with pleasure, in order to remove questions of ethics from the realm of philosophical and religious polemic and to settle them beyond further controversy. And the motive of contemporary utilitarian philosophers is, at least in some cases, quite transparently similar. It has long been the hope of moral philosophers to be able to *prove* that certain things are right, certain things wrong, certain things dutiful, and it has seemed to some that basing the definitions of such normative terms on something non-normative, or factual and familiar to all, offers the best hope of being able to do that.

Familiar modes of discourse also suggest to some that pleasure and happiness might be equated. For example, being happy and being pleased seem, at one level, to be about the same. Someone who is happy with something— with his job, for instance—can also be described as pleased with it. And it is but a short step to equate being pleased with having feelings of pleasure.

Or again, it is perhaps quite impossible to imagine that someone might be happy while consistently and continuously exhibiting the symptoms of pain, or be thoroughly unhappy while continuously or repeatedly exhibiting the usual signs of pleasure. Thus do pleasure and happiness, or pain and unhappiness, seem clearly connected, not just causally, but logically. And it is not hard to suppose that the connection might be one of identity or, in other words, that happiness and pleasure might just be two words for one and the same thing.

In fact, however, happiness and pleasure have little in common other than that both are sought, and both are sometimes loosely referred to by the same vocabulary.

Pleasures, for example, can often be located in this or that part of the body. This is even more obvious in the case of pains. But one cannot speak of the happiness felt in his back when it is being massaged, or of the unhappiness in one's tooth or toe. Again, pleasures, like pains, come and go, and can be momentary; but one cannot momentarily be a happy person. One can momentarily exult or rejoice, to be sure, and while such states are typically ingredients of a happy existence, they are certainly not the same thing. Even persons who are quite plainly not happy can nevertheless feel occasional pleasures, just as those who are happy sometimes feel pain; and just as thoroughly unhappy people once in a while exult or rejoice, so do genuinely happy people sometimes feel dejection and frustration.

Again, pleasures sometimes arise from bad sources, just as pains sometimes arise from good ones; but one can hardly speak of genuine happiness as being rooted in evil or unhappiness growing from what is wholesome and good. There would, for example, be something incongruous in describing someone as achieving genuine and lasting happiness from the contemplation of suffering, though there are persons who apparently derive pleasure from such sources and from others as bad. And that reflection suggests another point of contrast, namely, that the term *happiness* is one of approbation, while pleasure is not, or at least not in the same way. Thus one can speak of happiness as an achievement, and admire those few people who manage to win it; but one hardly thinks of pleasures that way, not even those pleasures that are thought to be refined and even noble. It is at least moderately inspiring that someone, born to a wretched existence, should somehow die a happy person; but no comparable response is evoked by the thought of such a person dying with feelings of pleasure, even though this is, to be sure, preferable to its opposite. Happiness can even be thought of as the supreme good, as many philosophers have indeed described it; but it is hard to think of pleasures that way.

Furthermore, there are many different kinds of pleasures—the pleasures of eating, for instance, or of music, or of receiving praise. Pleasures are innumerable and varied. But there are not different kinds of happinesses, and indeed, even to use the word "happiness" in the plural is odd. No such oddness attaches to speaking of many pleasures. One is happy or he is not, or he is more or less so; but one cannot move from one happiness to another that is quite unlike it, as one sometimes moves from pleasure to pleasure.

And from that observation it can be noted that happiness and pleasure are really quite different kinds of things to begin with. Pleasures are, in the strictest sense, feelings, just as are pains; but happiness, and similarly unhappiness, are opposite states, not feelings. One can, to be sure, feel happy or unhappy—but not the way one feels a pleasure or pain. Feeling unhappy is feeling oneself to be in a certain general state. Pleasures and pains, on the other hand, are typically, and often quite literally, things felt—the pain of a toothache, for instance.

THE "HAPPINESS" OF LESSER BEINGS

Finally, it should be noted that children, idiots, barbarians, and even animals are perfectly capable of experiencing pleasure and pain, but none of these can become happy, in the sense in which the term is used here. One can, to be sure, speak correctly of a happy child, or a happy moron, but we need to attend carefully to what is being said in such cases. A happy child, for instance, is one who fares well *as a child*, or in other words, one for whom the benign conditions of well-being are met. These include affection, the sense of trust and security, loving discipline, and so on. Under such conditions a child can, indeed, be a *happy child*, in the sense of not being morose, disturbed, depressed, sullen, and so on, which is a perfectly clear sense of happiness. But the child is not happy in the sense that is important to philosophy, that is, in the sense of having achieved fulfillment or having been blessed with the highest personal good. This is the kind of happiness that can only be hoped for in time in the case of a child. The happiness of a happy child, though real and important, consists of little more than feeling good, a feeling that is rooted in certain salubrious conditions of life. It is a good, but it is not the great good that is the object of the moral life, the kind of good that normally takes the better part of a lifetime to attain.

The point is perhaps better made with the example of a happy moron. A person thus severely limited in those capacities that are so distinctively human can, like a child, feel happy. But that is about all his or her happiness is—a feeling. Such a person fares well, to be sure, but only as a moron, not as a person, in the full sense of the term. The point can be seen very readily if, contemplating a happy moron, one puts the matter to oneself this way: Happiness is the ultimate personal good, and this person is obviously happy. Would I not, then, be willing to be just like that moron, if I could thereby enjoy the same happiness? Of course the answer for any normal person is a resounding negative. This shows, not that happiness is not the ultimate personal good, but rather, that the happiness here illustrated is not the kind of happiness that a philosopher upholds as the highest good. Happiness, in this fuller sense, is much more than just a state of euphoria. It is the fulfillment of a person, as a person, and not as a child, or a moron, or whatever other limited person one might suggest.

PLEASURE AS AN INGREDIENT OF HAPPINESS

We can surely conclude, then, that happiness and pleasure are not the same, and that the concept of happiness, unlike that of pleasure, is a profound and difficult one.

Yet it would be rash to dismiss pleasure as having nothing to do with genuine happiness. It would be truer to say that pleasure, along with other things, is an ingredient of happiness, in the sense that no life that was utterly devoid of pleasures could ever be described as a fully happy one however estimable it might be otherwise.

Pleasure, then, should be included within that vast and heterogeneous assortment of things that the ancient moralists classed as *externals*. This apt term was applied to all those things of value to one's life, which result from accident or good fortune, or are bestowed by others. What others bestow, they can also withhold, and similarly, one can be cursed by chance as readily as one can be blessed. Externals, in short, do not depend upon oneself, are largely or entirely beyond one's own control, and are for that very reason called externals.

And it is clear that persons cannot, for the most part, bestow pleasures upon themselves. They need other things and other persons as the source of them. This does not render them bad, but it does make them largely a matter of luck. They belong in a happy life but cannot be made the whole point of it. Genuine happiness, on the other hand, while it can be utterly ruined by chance —by dreaded illness, for example, or other disaster—nevertheless depends on oneself, in case it is ever won. Wisdom, or the choice of the right path to happiness, cannot guarantee that one will win it; but on the other hand, one is certain to miss it without that wisdom.

It would thus be as narrow to identify happiness with pleasure as to identify it with any other external good, such as property, honor, youth, beauty, or whatever. External goods are goods, and while a happy life cannot be devoid of them all, neither can any sum of them, however great, add up to such a life.

HAPPINESS AND POSSESSIONS

It would be unnecessary even to consider the identification of happiness with the accumulation of wealth were it not that shallow people, who are very numerous, tend to make precisely that identification. The pursuit of happiness is simply assumed by many to be the quest for possessions, and the "good life" is thought by the same persons to be a life of affluence.

The explanation for this, too, is not hard to find. Possessions, up to a certain minimum, are essential even to life. They are needed, beyond that point, for leisure; and while life is possible without leisure, happiness is not. There is, accordingly, a natural and wise inclination in everyone to possess things. If we add to this that all persons tend to be covetous and envious, then we have most of the explanation for the widespread greed for possessions, and of the identification of happiness with the feeding of that greed. Indeed, accumulation, and the display of wealth, sometimes become important mainly as a means to inciting envy.

It should, however, be obvious to any thinking person that happiness cannot possibly be found in the sheer accumulation of possessions, even when they are used to purchase great power, or when they are philanthropically used for the public good, as sometimes happens. Such purchase of power and bestowals of wealth sometimes mitigate the ugliness of the greed lying behind them, but these cannot add up to happiness in anyone. And if happiness is the great goal in life, as it surely is, then there are obscure, unknown people, of modest possessions, far more to be envied for what they have than even the very richest.

The pursuit of possessions beyond a certain point, far from constituting or even contributing to happiness, is an obstacle to it; for one has no chance of finding the right path to anything if he is resolutely determined to follow the wrong one, convinced that he is already doing things exactly right. The feeling of power that great wealth sometimes nourishes, and the envy that is incited in others, are both exhilarating, but neither can be regarded as an important ingredient of personal happiness. At best they add zest and challenge to one's life, effectively banishing boredom, but this is a poor substitute for happiness. Indeed the lover of possessions, who indulges that love to the exclusion of things more important, can be compared to the glutton, who indulges his love for food. For food, too, is necessary for life; but gluttony, far from constituting or even contributing to a good life, is utterly incompatible with it. To set that as one's ideal of life would be grotesque, and the clearest possible example of a wasted life. The successful pursuit of great wealth is no less grotesque and as certainly the waste of one's life. Most persons who would be repelled by gluttony, however, seem strangely blind to this comparison.

And this is really sad. For each of us does, indeed, have but one life to live, and if possible that life should be lived successfully. The chance of this happening is greatly diminished when the term *success* is applied to a kind of life which, from the standpoint of philosophy, is incompatible with success. That term should be reserved for the achievement of genuine happiness, and not for some popularly accepted illusion of happiness. If, to pursue the comparison once more, there were a race of people who exalted food without limit, indulged in gluttony, and envied corpulence as the mark of success in this pursuit, then we would say with certainty that theirs was a false and in fact disgusting ideal; nor would we change our judgment of them even if they declared with one voice that this was their happiness. The illusion of happiness is not happiness, nor is the feeling of happiness always a mark of possessing it.

HONOR, FAME, AND GLORY

The same can be said of many of the other goals people set for themselves, although some of these, such as the love of honor, come closer to the ideal. A person is sometimes honored for what he actually is, and if this is something that is noble, then that honor is well placed and its recipient is, to some extent, justified in believing that he has achieved something worthwhile. Still, such things as honor, fame, and glory, though certainly not despicable, do depend upon others and must therefore be classed as externals. One can seek honor, for example, and even honor that is deserved; but whether one gets it will always depend upon the perceptions and values and, sometimes, the caprices of others. One cannot bestow honors upon oneself. People tend, moreover, to honor and applaud their own benefactors, or sometimes even people who merely make them feel very good, such as charismatic clergy and the like, rather than honoring virtue for its own sake. What they give then resembles the price of a purchase more than a gift. Thus a victorious general is honored, rather than a losing one, even though the latter might in fact have displayed more resourcefulness and courage than the former. Similarly, a person may become rich at the expense of others, then be honored for charitably returning part of it to the very public that was exploited.

Moreover, people sometimes honor and even glorify things that are neither honorable nor glorious such as sheer power, even when it is selfishly used. Also, the masses of people are often eager to raise to great fame persons whose uniqueness is some mere eccentricity; this is sometimes true of popular entertainers, or something of very little worth, as in the case of prizefighters. People can, in fact, be swept off their feet by trifles and are willing to heap great honor and wealth upon the producers of such trifles, as in the case of professional athletes, who represent no group and no ideal other than by the outright sale of their skills.

Perhaps the fairest thing to say concerning such things as we have been considering—wealth, honor, glory, and the like—is that, like pleasure, they often contribute to happiness but never add up to it. Personal excellence or even heroism are often parts of a lasting happiness, and the recognition of such qualities by others often adds to that happiness. But the real reward of personal excellence, of the kind that leads one to do, perhaps with almost superhuman effort and resourcefulness, what no one else has ever done, is simply the possession of that excellence itself. To be uniquely able to create an extraordinary piece of music of great merit, or a poem, or a story, or a philosophical treatise, or a painting, or a building, or to accomplish any feat of great significance requiring genius or exemplary courage—all such abilities are gifts in themselves that are not much embellished by the gifts added by others. What one finds satisfying are things belonging to oneself rather than things added. At the same time, it would be unrealistic to treat the recognition or acclaim of others as worth nothing. What we should say is that such honor and acclaim are sometimes a part of one's happiness, possibly even a necessary part; but they can never constitute the sum and substance of it.

EUPHORIA, JOY, AND EXUBERANCE

It is, as we have noted, common to treat happiness as if it were a mere feeling, and even to confuse it with the feelings of pleasure. But while such feelings, and particularly the feelings of joy and exuberance, are often the expressions of a real inner happiness, they are not the same. They are too fleeting and superficial, and sometimes nothing more than the expressions of mood or of momentary satisfaction. And they are rarely chosen. Happiness, on the other hand, is an essential part of one's very existence, in the case of those lucky enough to possess it. While it is not gained simply by choice, as if nothing more were required in order to have it, it is nevertheless something chosen as contrasted with something accidental or thrust upon one.

WHAT HAPPINESS IS

The idea of happiness, we have suggested, contains the idea of fulfillment. It is also something of great and perhaps even ultimate value, and except when destroyed by accident or disaster, it is enduring. It is not something that comes and goes from one hour to the next. We have also said that it is a state of being and not a mere feeling.

It can be compared with something like health, to derive a useful analogy. For while there is such a thing as the feeling of health, no one imagines that health itself is no more than a feeling. To be healthy is to be in a certain state, the description of which we will consider shortly. And like happiness, it is very precious. Again like happiness, health is something that is normally lasting; one is not momentarily healthy. Nor, like happiness, are there different kinds of health. One either possesses it or does not. And for this reason the word "health" like the word "happiness" can only be used in the singular. Health, when one has it, is usually lost only through accident or disaster not through choice; so again, the comparison with happiness is apt.

The one way in which the analogy of health to happiness breaks down significantly is with respect to choice. Health is normal and natural; one can almost say, that one is normally born with it. It is something chosen and worked for only under unusual circumstances and then only in a limited way, as in the case of someone who has lost it and strives to recover it. Happiness, on the other hand, is certainly not a gift of nature; it is quite rare and is always the fruit of choice and effort exercised over a long period of time. Effort is needed to keep or regain health but not to win it in the first place, and in this respect it is quite unlike happiness.

Still, the analogy is useful, for health, like happiness, is a kind of fulfillment. And here it is very easy to see, in a general way, just what that fulfillment consists of. One is healthy when his body and all its parts function as they should. A diseased or unhealthy body is one that functions poorly. Similarly, a diseased or unhealthy heart, or lung, or whatever, is one whose function has been partially or wholly lost, so that a diseased heart and a malfunctioning one, for example, are exactly the same thing.

HAPPINESS AND THE CONCEPT OF FUNCTION

The point of making those seemingly banal observations about health is to bring out the important point that it is understood and defined entirely in terms of *function*. And since the analogy between happiness and health appears so very close, we seem justified in supposing that happiness, too, may be understandable in terms of function.

But function of what? If health consists simply of a properly functioning body, then what is happiness? The idea of happiness is obviously larger than that of health because, although this has not been noted before, the former presupposes the latter: A person can be healthy and lack happiness but not the other way around. Someone lacking health, however courageous or otherwise estimable he or she may be, cannot be fully happy, unless one of those rare individuals who combines great inner strength with extraordinary creative power—as will be explained shortly.

And this suggests that happiness is understandable as consisting of the proper functioning of a person as a whole. With this reflection it will be seen that we have come around full circle and back to the viewpoint of the ancient moralists who defined virtue in much the same way. We see, abstractly, the plausibility of the claim they so often made, that virtue and happiness are inseparable.

Let us now look a little more closely at happiness as thus conceived and then see whether this conception of it is borne out by actual experience.

The ancients quite rightly singled out the intellectual side of human nature as constituting our uniqueness. The exercise of this was, they thought, our proper function, and excellence in this exercise our special virtue. They called this part of our nature "reason"; but this meant for them simply the exercise of intelligence in discovering truth as well as in governing conduct. Socrates and Plato construed reason more narrowly, sometimes identifying it with dialectic, that is, with philosophical argumentation. Modern philosophers have, for the most part, unfortunately gone along with this narrower conception.

Let us, then, think of reason or intelligence in a broader sense, to include not merely the activity of reasoning (as exhibited for example in philosophy) but also observation and reflection and, above all, creative activity. This is, certainly, what distinguishes us from everything else. Human beings are, by virtue of their intelligence, capable of *creating* things that are novel, unique, sometimes of great value, and even sometimes, though rarely, of overwhelming value. One thinks, for example, of scientific theories or great works of art or literature, or profound philosophical treatises like Spinoza's *Ethics*, or the great and lasting music that emerges from the creative genius of one person. It is here, certainly, that we see what distinguishes us from all other living things and entitles us to think of ourselves as akin to the gods. Other creatures have no history and are virtually incapable of even the most trivial innovation or novelty. What was done by the generations that preceded them is done also by them in an endless repetition. But it is not so with human beings. Their works rise and fall, to be replaced by others that no one could have foreseen. Human beings, in a word, think, reflect, and *create*. It is no wonder that we are referred to in Scripture as having been created "in the image of God," for this has traditionally been thought of as the primary attribute of God, namely, that God is the *creator*.

Aristotle thought of the pursuit of knowledge as the human virtue par excellence. But it is significant that he thought of this, not merely as something passive, a mere absorption of things seen to be true, but rather as an activity. And it is the nature of intellectual activity that it is creative. To the extent that the mind is active, it is also creative, and this is true even in the sciences, and in such things as mathematics, where there is thought to be the least scope for novelty and innovation.

If we think of happiness as fulfillment, then it must consist of the fulfillment of ourselves as human beings, which means the exercise of our creative powers. For we are, among the creatures of the earth, the only ones possessed of such power. The idea of fulfillment is without meaning apart from the idea of function, however, and thus, as our bodies are fulfilled in health, so are our bodies and minds together fulfilled in creative activity. There are no real substitutes. The appearance of health, and the feelings associated with it, are often marks of that underlying state, but such things are not identical with it. The former can be present when the latter is not. And similarly, the appearance of happiness and the feeling of happiness are often marks of that precious state itself, but by no means to be confused with it. A person can appear happy and not be, and what is less readily understood, can feel happy and not be. Children, idiots, and animals, as we have seen, sometimes feel good, indeed, characteristically do; but they cannot possibly be happy in the true sense of the term. There simply is nothing more to be said of them with respect to their happiness than that they feel good.

Of course one might be tempted at this point to protest that if someone feels happy, what more can be wanted? Is it not quite enough to feel perfectly happy, without making much of the sources of that feeling? And why withhold the term *happiness* from anyone if that person is totally content with his own condition?

What more is wanted is, of course, the genuine thing. And one sees this readily enough if one imagines someone in whom the feelings of happiness are present, but the proper fulfillment of function is not, as again in the case of someone severely retarded. Whatever may be that person's feelings of self-satisfaction and joy, no one capable of a genuinely intelligent and creative life could ever trade it for this other. Feelings of joy complement and add to the happiness that most persons are capable of, but they can never replace it.

WHAT IS CREATIVITY?

When we think of creativity, we are apt to construe it narrowly, as the creation of things, sometimes even limiting it to things belonging to the arts. But this is arbitrary. Creative intelligence is exhibited by a dancer, by athletes, by a chess player, and indeed in virtually any activity guided by intelligence. In some respects the very paradigm of creative activity is the establishment of a brilliant position in a game of chess, even though what is created is of limited worth.

Nor do such activities need to be the kind normally thought of as intellectual. For example, the exercise of skill in a profession, or in business, or even in such things as gardening and farming, or the rearing of a beautiful family, all such things are displays of creative intelligence. They can all be done badly or well and are always done *best* when done not by rule, rote, or imitation, but with successful originality. Nor is it hard to see that, in referring to such common-place activities as these, at the same time we touch upon some of the greatest and most lasting sources of human happiness.

Consider, for example, something both commonplace and yet fairly unusual as begetting and rearing a beautiful family. There is, to be sure, nothing in the least creative about the mere begetting of children. It is something anyone can do. But to raise them and convert them to successful, that is, well-functioning, happy adults, requires great skill, intelligence, and creativity. We see this at once when we compare those who succeed at it with the many who do not. And now let us consider someone who has succeeded at this and ask what that person's happiness consists of, and how it compares with some of the specious substitutes for happiness that we have alluded to.

With respect to the first question, that is, what such a person's happiness consists of, we can easily see that it is not mere feeling. To be sure, the feelings of happiness are there, but they are based upon a state of being that is far more precious and enduring, namely, upon the lasting realization of what has been wrought. Feelings of reward, or of praise, or of envy in others, may be worth something; but if, for example, they rested upon nothing real, or upon actual error or misperception, then they would be worth very little. There would then be no real happiness behind them, but only the feelings of happiness. And with respect to the comparison of this person with someone whose happiness is per-haps spectacular but nonetheless specious, it is again not hard to see who is more blessed. Consider a man whose wealth far exceeds his needs and which has simply flowed to him without any creative effort on his part, as in the case of wealth that is inherited. This person cannot possibly have the happiness of even the most ordinary person who has created something valuable and last-ing, even of a commonplace sort. To see this, you need only to get before your mind a clear image of both lives, and then ask not which one you envy, not which one is more honored by the masses of people, not which one shines with more glory, not which is filled with more feelings of exhilaration, but just simply: Which of these two persons is happier?

THE DEFEAT OF HAPPINESS

Happiness is often represented as something to be pursued, as something that might be conquered; and quite rightly, for this calls attention to the fact that it can also be lost, or that one might fail altogether to find it. It by no means flows automatically to those who wait for it, even when all the conditions for it are right. It must be chosen and sought.

Of course the clearest way in which it can be lost is by calamity, such as dreadful or life-destroying illness, and things of this nature, which either cannot be foreseen or cannot be warded off when they are foreseen. The Stoics maintained that even catastrophic setback or illness could not destroy one's happiness, but this was an extreme and unbelievable position. It is true that happiness cannot be conferred upon one, but it can certainly be taken away, and under some circumstances it is idle to speak of pursuing it.

The other ways in which one can fail to become happy are either: first, through ignorance of what happiness is, and hence an inability to distinguish genuine happiness from specious forms; or second, from lack of the creative intelligence necessary for its pursuit. We shall consider these in turn.

THE FAILURE FROM IGNORANCE

This has been dealt with incidentally. Thus, people who think happiness results from possession, for example, have no chance of becoming happy, for they go in the wrong direction. They may succeed in their pursuit of wealth, but having done that, they then find themselves using that wealth to pursue things equally specious, such as power over others or the envy of others, and other things totally unrelated to the kind of creative activity we have described; or else they find themselves going through the kinds of motions that have characterized their lives superfluously adding wealth to what they already have in great excess. The mere doing of things, perhaps on a large scale, achieves no more happiness than the mere defeat of boredom—for which, incidentally, most people appear quite willing to settle. Sheer boredom is indeed a baneful state. To escape it is, to some extent, a blessing though a negative one. Hence the incessant activity on the part of some—things done for no purpose beyond making more money; or travel undertaken for new sights and sounds passively absorbed; or projects pursued, sometimes on a grand scale, just to impress others; or things purchased for the same purpose. This is how many people live, escaping boredom, keeping busy, being preoccupied with something from one day to the next, giving little thought to life or to death. And this does achieve, for the moment, the banishment of boredom and loneliness; but that is as close to happiness as it gets. Meanwhile others who are wiser, having little of all this and almost never knowing boredom, go about life in their own way, creating from their own resources things original to themselves, quite unlike what others have done, things small, sometimes not small, sometimes even great and lasting, but every one of them something that is theirs and is the reflection of their own original power. Such people rejoice, perhaps unnoticed—and are happy.

THE WANT OF CREATIVE INTELLIGENCE

The second way to fail is through the sheer lack of what is needed to succeed. For if genuine happiness is found through the exercise of creative intelligence, then it is obvious that, without this, a person will have to be content with a specious kind of happiness, far less than the *eudaimonia* we have described. And many people, perhaps even most, are thus prevented.

Thus there are people whose every day is very much like the one just lived. They are essentially people without personal biographies except for the events which the mere passage of time thrusts upon them. In this they are like animals, each of whose lives is almost indistinguishable from others of its species, simply duplicating those of the generations before it. One sparrow does not differ from another. What it does, others have done and will do again, without creative improvement of any kind. Its life consists of what happens to it. And people who are like this have a similar uniformity. They do much as their neighbors do and as their parents have done, creating virtually no values of their own, but absorbing the values of those around them. Their lives are lived like clockwork, and thought, which should be the source of projects and ideals, is hardly more than a byproduct of what they are doing, an almost useless accompaniment like the ticking of a clock. You see these people everywhere, doing again today what they did yesterday, their ideas and feelings having about as little variation. And, it should be noted, such people are by the ordinary standards that prevail *quite happy*—that is, they are of good cheer, greet each sunrise with fresh anticipation, have friends, and spend much of their time exchanging empty remarks and pleasantries with others like them. They are, in a word, contented people who would declare with total sincerity, if asked, that they are perfectly happy, asking no more of the world than to escape those things, such as poverty or illness, which might threaten their contentment.

But we must not be misled by this. What such people have are certain feelings of happiness—feelings only. These are not bad, not even really illusory, but they do fall far short of the meaning of happiness the ancients tried to capture in the word *eudaimonia*. Such persons are not fulfilled but merely satisfied. They have a kind of contentment that is within the reach of anyone capable of suffering who luckily manages to escape suffering. What they have is not even distinctively personal or human. The measure of their happiness is nothing more than their lack of inclination to complain.

It is, to be sure, doubtful whether any normal person entirely fits this baneful description, but one can hardly fail to see that it expresses what is almost normal. Even the least creative among us are usually capable of something original, however innocuous it might be. But what is sad is that the kind of happiness that is within the reach only of human beings should be within the reach of so few of these. And what is sadder still is that those who have no clear idea of what happiness is, or worse, lack within themselves the resources to capture it, do not care. It is, in some ways, almost as if they had not even been born.

It is no wonder that the ancients thought of happiness as a blessing of almost divine worth, as something rare, and something that can be ascribed to someone only after he is dead.

THE EXPERIENCE MACHINE

Robert Nozick

Robert Nozick (1938–2002) was professor of philosophy at Harvard University. He argued that we desire a life in which we do certain things, not just have the experience of doing them.

Suppose there were an experience machine that would give you any experience you desired. Superduper neuropsychologists could stimulate your brain so that you would think and feel you were writing a great novel, or making a friend, or reading an interesting book. All the time you would be floating in a tank, with electrodes attached to your brain. Should you plug into this machine for life, preprogramming your life's experiences? If you are worried about missing out on desirable experiences, we can suppose that business enterprises have researched thoroughly the lives of many others. You can pick and choose from their large library or smorgasbord of such experiences, selecting your life's experiences for, say, the next two years. After two years have passed, you will have ten minutes or ten hours out of the tank, to select the experiences of your *next* two years. Of course, while in the tank you won't know that you're there; you'll think it's all actually happening. Others can also plug in to have the experiences they want, so there's no need to stay unplugged to serve them. (Ignore problems such as who will service the machines if everyone plugs in.) Would you plug in? *What else can matter to us, other than how our lives feel from the inside?* Nor should you refrain because of the few moments of distress between the moment you've decided and the moment you're plugged. What's a few moments of distress compared to a lifetime of bliss (if that's what you choose), and why feel any distress at all if your decision *is* the best one?

What does matter to us in addition to our experiences? First, we want to *do* certain things, and not just have the experience of doing them. In the case of certain experiences, it is only because first we want to do the actions that we want the experiences of doing them or thinking we've done them. (But *why* do we want to do the activities rather than merely to experience them?) A second reason for not plugging in is that we want to *be* a certain way, to be a certain sort of person. Someone floating in a tank is an indeterminate blob. There is no answer to the question of what a person is like who has long been in the tank. Is he courageous, kind, intelligent, witty, loving? It's not merely that it's difficult to tell; there's no way he is. Plugging into the machine is a kind of suicide. It will seem to some, trapped by a picture, that nothing about what we are like can matter except as it gets reflected in our experiences. But should it be surprising that what *we are* is important to us? Why should we be concerned only with how our time is filled, but not with what we are?

From Robert Nozick, *Anarchy, State, and Utopia* (New York: Basic Books, 1974). Used by permission of the publisher.

Thirdly, plugging into an experience machine limits us to a man-made reality, to a world no deeper or more important than that which people can construct. There is no *actual* contact with any deeper reality, though the experience of it can be simulated. Many persons desire to leave themselves open to such contact and to a plumbing of deeper significance.[1] This clarifies the intensity of the conflict over psychoactive drugs, which some view as mere local experience machines, and others view as avenues to a deeper reality; what some view as equivalent to surrender to the experience machine, others view as following one of the reasons *not* to surrender!

We learn that something matters to us in addition to experience by imagining an experience machine and then realizing that we would not use it. We can continue to imagine a sequence of machines each designed to fill lacks suggested for the earlier machines. For example, since the experience machine doesn't meet our desire to *be* a certain way, imagine a transformation machine which transforms us into whatever sort of person we'd like to be (compatible with our staying us). Surely one would not use the transformation machine to become as one would wish, and thereupon plug into the experience machine![2] So something matters in addition to one's experiences *and* what one is like. Nor is the reason merely that one's experiences are unconnected with what one is like. For the experience machine might be limited to provide only experiences possible to the sort of person plugged in. Is it that we want to make a difference in the world? Consider then the result machine, which produces in the world any result you would produce and injects your vector input into any joint activity. We shall not pursue here the fascinating details of these or other machines. What is most disturbing about them is their living of our lives for us. Is it misguided to search for *particular* additional functions beyond the competence of machines to do for us? Perhaps what we desire is to live (an active verb) ourselves, in contact with reality. (And this, machines cannot do *for* us.)

NOTES

1. Traditional religious views differ on the *point* of contact with a transcendent reality. Some say that contact yields eternal bliss or Nirvana, but they have not distinguished this sufficiently from merely a *very* long run on the experience machine. Others think it is intrinsically desirable to do the will of a higher being which created us all, though presumably no one would think this if we discovered we had been created as an object of amusement by some superpowerful child from another galaxy or dimension. Still others imagine an eventual merging with a higher reality, leaving unclear its desirability, or where that merging leaves *us*.

2. Some wouldn't use the transformation machine at all; it seems like *cheating*. But the one-time use of the transformation machine would not remove all challenges; there would still be obstacles for the new us to overcome, a new plateau from which to strive even higher. And is this plateau any the less earned or deserved than that provided by genetic endowment and early childhood environment? But if the transformation machine could be used indefinitely often, so that we could accomplish anything by pushing a button to transform ourselves into someone who could do it easily, there would remain no limits we *need* to strain against or try to transcend. Would there be anything left *to do*? Do some theological views place God outside of time because an omniscient omnipotent being couldn't fill up his days?

HAPPINESS AS ACHIEVEMENT

Julia Annas

Julia Annas is Regents Professor of Philosophy at the University of
Arizona. She argues that happiness is not only a positive state but also
an achievement in the way we live our lives.

Ten years ago, shortly after publishing a book called *The Morality of Happiness*
about the structure of ancient ethical theory, I received an email informing
me that I had been added to a bibliography of "happiness researchers" on a
website called the World Database of Happiness. I explored this site with
interest, only to find that this was not a research program that I felt myself to
be part of.

The website assumes, without discussion, that happiness is "subjective,"
that it is enjoyment or pleasure, and that it should be studied "empirically."
Philosophy is then derided for failing to "operationalize" happiness and to
produce "measures" of it. (Philosophy has a meager 88 entries in the bibliography, compared to 2,927 for the social sciences.) Empirical studies are lauded
for their measures of happiness, while the website claims that "preliminary
questions about conceptualization and measurement are now fairly well
solved."

The website, however, gives off a definite air of disappointment. No sound
body of knowledge on happiness, it admits, has yet been achieved. In the
present state of research, we can claim only that "there are obviously several
universal requirements for a happy life (such as food and possibly meaning)."

Philosophers (and some psychologists, too) will find it unsurprising that
if you rush to look for empirical measures of an unanalyzed "subjective" phenomenon, the result will be confusion and banality.[1] After all, what is it that
the social scientists on the World Database of Happiness are actually measuring? Here is the heart of the problem. Is happiness really something subjective? Is it simply a matter of pleasure, a positive feeling? We can at least hope
that it is not, and that we can come to conclusions better than the claim that
what anyone needs to be happy is food and possibly meaning.

For many years I have taught, discussed, and written on ancient ethical
theories, whose basic concepts are those of happiness and virtue. During this
time, philosophical interest in these theories has grown rapidly and has in
turn produced a crop of modern "virtue ethics" theories, a fair number of
which are eudaimonist—that is, theories which take happiness and virtue to
be basic concepts. Philosophers are now taking virtue and happiness more
seriously than they had for some time, and realizing the importance of clarify-
ing and deepening our understanding of these before rushing into empirical
studies. (Judging by recent publications, this concern is shared in some areas
of psychology.)

From *Daedalus* (Spring 2004). © 2004 by the American Academy of Arts and Sciences.

As a result, one of the best places to seek understanding of happiness is the study of ancient ethical theories and of those modern theories which share their eudaimonist concerns. For these recognize, and build on, some of our thoughts about happiness that have become overwhelmed by the kind of consideration that emerges in the claim that happiness is obviously subjective. Given the systematically disappointing results of the database approach, it is time to look seriously at our alternatives.

When it is asked what happiness is, a first answer may well be that it is some kind of feeling. Being happy is easily taken to be feeling happy—as when I wake up in the morning—a kind of smiley-face feeling. This line of thought takes us rapidly to the idea that I can be happy doing any old thing. Some people feel happy when helping old ladies across streets; others feel happy when torturing puppies: happiness comes down to whatever you happen to like.

But this line of thought cannot stay up for long. It is immediately obvious that when we talk about feelings we are talking about *episodes*; I wake up feeling happy but am depressed by the time I get to work, never mind lunchtime. Getting a smiley-face feeling from good deeds or bad deeds lasts only as long as the deeds do. And this kind of happiness does not matter to us all that much once we start to think in a serious way about our lives. As we bring up our children, what we aim for is not that they have episodes of smiley-face feeling, but that their lives go well as wholes: we come to think of happiness as the way a life as a whole goes well, and see that episodes of happiness are not what we build our lives around.

This point can produce a variety of responses. One is to say that when we are thinking of our lives as wholes, we should think in terms of flourishing or welfare or well-being rather than happiness. These terms may be useful in some circumstances to avoid misunderstanding, but we should not yield talk of happiness without further discussion to its most trivial contexts of use. In my experience, discussion rapidly reveals that we do talk about happiness over our lives as wholes, or at least over long stretches of them. We should not, then, restrict talk of happiness at the start to contexts of short-term feeling.

The point that these are the contexts which first occur to many people when they are asked about happiness indicates that our notion of happiness has indeed been affected by the notion of smiley faces, feeling good, and pleasant episodes. Doubtless this is the source of some of the empirical researcher's problems in trying to measure it. For if we try to measure the happiness of lives in terms of smiley-face feelings, the results will be grotesque. I have seen a survey that asks people to measure the happiness of their lives by assigning it a face from a spectrum with a very smiley face at one end and a very frowny face at the other. Suppose that you have just won the Nobel Prize; this surely merits the smiliest face. But suppose also that you have just lost your family in a car crash; this surely warrants the frowniest face. So, how happy are you? There is no coherent answer—unless you are supposed to combine these points by picking the indifferent face in the middle!

So, even if episodes first come to mind, we do think, centrally, of *living* happy lives. And this is because we think of our lives as wholes when we are thinking of how to live, what kind of people we are to aspire to be.

At this point, another characteristically modern, and more reasonable sounding, idea tends to come in. Surely having a happy life has something to do with getting what you want, rather than being frustrated and deprived of what you want? We all have desires; the happy person will be the person whose desires are fulfilled. The philosopher's term for this is the "desire-satisfaction" account, which appeals to more thoughtful ideas about happiness than our initial ones.

Why wouldn't a happy life be one of getting what you want? People, after all, can live happy lives in many different ways. We feel that there is something wrong in trying to build any particular content into our notion of happiness such that only people living certain kinds of life could be happy. The idea that happiness is desire-satisfaction seems suitably neutral on the content of happy lives, allowing happiness to the intellectual and the incurious alike as long as they are getting what they desire.

It is possible to think of happiness as desire-satisfaction if we are prepared to think of happiness—in the spirit of the suggestion that it is subjective—as something on which each of us is the authority. I am happy if I think I am, since I am getting what I want. For who could be a better authority than I am on the issue of whether I am getting what I want? Perhaps the idea that happiness is desire-satisfaction does justice to the initial thought that it is something subjective—without the obvious problems of the smiley-face-feeling interpretation.

Why might we be dissatisfied with this result? We would have to hold that anyone getting what he or she wants is happy, whatever the nature of the desire. Happiness would thus lose any purchase as an idea that could serve to rank or judge lives; Nelson Mandela, Bill Gates, and Madonna, if they are all getting what they want, are all happy, so any comparative judgments about their lives cannot involve the idea of happiness. We might accept this, thinking that there must be something else about lives which can be compared— perhaps well-being or some other kind of value on which the agent is not necessarily the best authority.

One thing the desire-satisfaction account disables us from doing is making judgments about the happiness of people whose desires are in obvious ways defective. Notoriously, some desires are based on radically faulty information or reasoning. Some desires are unresponsive to the agent's reasoning powers because of the force of addiction or obsession. At a deeper level, some desires are themselves deformed by social pressures. Girls who desire less for themselves than for their brothers, poor people who see desire for self-betterment as unimaginable—these are just two of many kinds of desires that are open to criticism, despite being honestly expressed and open to modification in the light of reason and information, because they spring from the internalization of ideas that deny the agents themselves proper respect.

Once again, the idea that happiness is desire-satisfaction can absorb these points and even deny their faults, at the cost of shrinking happiness to something where only I am authoritative. Suppose, however, that I am happy if I think I am, because I am happy if I am getting what I want, and I am the authority on whether I am getting what I want. If we take this point seriously, we can see that we have not really moved forward from the smiley-face-feeling conception of happiness. Happiness is still just a state I am in that I report on: getting what I want, rather than feeling good, but still a state, namely a state of having my desires fulfilled.

Both the smiley-face and desire-satisfaction accounts of happiness, despite their current popularity, especially among social scientists, turn out to conflict with two other surprisingly deep and far-reaching convictions about the meaning of happiness, convictions which emerge readily in simple discussion. These are the thought that happiness has an essential connection with my life as a whole and the thought that happiness is an *achievement* on my part.

Why should I even bother thinking about my life as a whole? It can seem, from a modern point of view, like an excessively cautious thing to do —prudential in the way that people are prudential who save and buy life insurance. But it is actually rather different, and it is something we all do all the time, since there are two perspectives which we take on our lives.

One is the linear perspective, from which we think of our lives as proceeding through time, one action being followed by another as we slowly get older. The other perspective opens up as soon as we ask of any action, *Why* I am doing it. Why am I getting up? A number of different kinds of answers suggest themselves, but we readily recognize one kind that is *purposive*: I get up *in order to* get to my classes. Why am I going to my classes? In order to major in Spanish. Why am I majoring in Spanish? In order to get a job as a translator. The answers collected by this question will not all be on the same level of generality. Taking a course is a particular goal that gets its salience from some more general goal, such as having a satisfying career. Our goals are in this way *nested*.

One feature of this way of thinking that soon becomes clear is its capacity to *unify*. I cannot have as concurrent aims the ambition to be a great ballet dancer *and* the ambition to be a lieutenant in the Marines; I have to find a way to sequence these aims coherently. As this way of thinking reveals to me what my aims are, I realize that they are constrained by considerations of consistency, available time, resources, and energy. These constraints come from the fact that *my* aims are the aims I have in the only life I have to live. Confused or self-undermining aims force me to get clearer about my priorities and to sort out competing claims on my time and energy.

So thinking about the way one action is done for the sake of another leads seamlessly into thinking about my life in a nonlinear way, one we can call *global*. I may not leap right away into thinking of my life as a whole; I might start by considering smaller units circumscribing various phases of my life, such as my twenties or my life at university. But when large aims, typically associated with careers or self-fulfillment, come in, I have to move to thinking of my life as a whole—a whole given in terms of my goals and the way they fit together overall—rather than as mere duration through time.

This way of thinking, we should notice, strikingly refutes the initial supposition of a timid, over-prudent way of thinking about my life. Such a perspective would come from assuming that I already know, at least in outline, what will happen in my life, and respond to this cautiously. What we are concerned with here, by contrast, is an exploratory way of thinking about my life in which my plans are *shaping* and actively *organizing* what is going to happen in it.

Suppose I recognize this perspective and realize that what faces me is not just a series of actions trailing into the future, but a task, namely the task of forming my life as a whole in and by the way I act. I then have, even if in a vague and muddled way, a conception of my life as a whole and of the overall way my endeavors are shaping it—my *telos* as the ancients put it.

Does this get us to happiness? Aristotle famously said that everybody agrees that our *telos* is happiness. We, however, do not so readily come to this conclusion. Some respond at this point by denying that happiness is our overarching aim in life. Others accept Aristotle's point verbally, but trivialize it by taking happiness just to be whatever you want, thereby expelling from discussions of happiness serious concern with the formation of our lives.

It is important, however, to note that Aristotle at once goes on to add that agreement that our final or overarching end is happiness does not settle anything, since people disagree as to what happiness is. Some think it is pleasure, others virtue; unreflective people think it is money or status.

We can now see that we have made progress after all; for once we recognize, even if at an indeterminate level, that we have a final end, questions and problems about happiness now occupy exactly the right place. Coming up with the proper specification of our overall goal in living will make us happy. But before this is helpful for us, we need to know what happiness is.

Is it pleasure? We now know that the right answer to this question must recognize that happiness specifies not a transient feeling, but our final end in a way that makes sense for us of the aims we pursue. Am I studying Spanish, ultimately, to get pleasure? We can see right away that if the answer is to be yes, then pleasure has to be explicated in a way that makes sense of its role as an aim I could have in studying Spanish as one way to shape my life. If this can be done, it will turn out to have little to do with smiley-face feeling; it will turn out to be a blander, Epicurean kind of pleasure.

We are on the right track, then, in looking for happiness in the search for the best way to live, the best way to understand our *telos*. Once we follow through this train of thought, we can see why the smiley-face-feeling and desire-satisfaction accounts were so hopeless. The issues that matter are issues about the living of our lives, not about feelings or desires. Once this is clear, we can avoid verbal disputes about whether happiness properly applies to feelings or to lives as a whole. We talk in terms of both; but the issues about happiness that concern us most are those that are formulated once we think about our lives in a global as well as a linear way.

Do we actually think about happiness in this way? Certainly a lot of our discourse implies it. When I wonder whether winning the lottery will make me really happy, this is the point in mind; I am not wondering whether it will produce smiley-face feeling or give me what I want.

Discussion and debate about others' lives also makes clear to us that we are disputing about what happiness really is, and that this is a point about our lives and the ways these have been shaped. Two people may dispute whether their colleague ruined her life or not when she lost her job as a result of acting in accordance with her values. (She blew the whistle on corrupt practices, say.) One onlooker may say that she has ruined her prospects for happiness; now she is unemployable, and all her training and ambition will go to waste. The other may say that she would never have been happy had she not acted as she did; had she failed to live up to her values, her life would have been infected by hypocrisy. This is a dispute about happiness that could not be settled by reports about her feelings or desire-satisfaction. It is a substantive dispute about what we are seeking overall in life, and resolving it requires substantive discussion of our values and priorities.

Why does this sort of discourse not spring more prominently to the minds of social scientists when they embark on happiness research? It seems to be at least as prominent in the way people think and talk about happiness as are thoughts about feelings. It does not, of course, fit into the framework that conceives of happiness as subjective—and perhaps this should lead us to doubt the assumption that we have a well-grounded idea of "subjective" happiness and that that assumption is the proper place to start our investigation of happiness. For, as we have seen, we do think of happiness as something to be achieved, or not, by living a life of one kind or another; and we do think of this issue as one to be discussed in terms of values and ideals. And this does not look "subjective" in any of the many ways in which that term is understood.

Is happiness really an achievement, though, in the way suggested? Suppose we agree that I aim at happiness by specifying my aims in life overall, and agree, further, that this is something for which competing accounts are available, so requiring choice and direction on my part. Still, is happiness itself aptly to be thought of as a matter of the direction I give my life?

We are used to theories that take happiness to be a *state*—a positive one, of course. On this view, shared by consequentialists of all kinds, aiming to be happy just is aiming to get myself into this positive state. In principle, somebody else could do the work for me, and if the work is laborious it is hard to see why I would insist on doing it myself.

But could happiness be a state of myself that I (or if I am lucky, others) bring about in myself? Here it is relevant to mention a discussion with students that I have had many times, but which I first borrowed from a former student, Kurt Meyers.

Kurt asked the students in his business ethics class, mostly business school students, what they thought a happy life consisted of. All mentioned material things like a large salary, a nice house, an SUV, and so on. Well, he said, suppose you find in the mail tomorrow that an unknown benefactor has left you lots of money, so that these material things are now yours for the having. Would this make you happy? Overwhelmingly they said no (and this is uniformly what I have found also).

What this little thought experiment shows is that it was not really the material things, the stuff, that they imagined would make their lives happy. Rather, they thought of a happy life as one in which they *earned* the money, *made* something of their lives so that these things were an appropriate reward for their effort, ambition, and achievement. Just having the stuff was not all they wanted.

This is a mundane enough example, yet it is surprisingly powerful when we take it seriously. How many people really think that stuff alone will make them happy, regardless of how they obtain it? That you could be made happy by money or an SUV, regardless of how you got them? The thought extends readily to other things that have been taken to be objective measures of happiness in numerous studies. Am I made happy by being strong, healthy, intelligent, beautiful? By having an income at or above the average in my society? By having a reasonably high status in my society? Once we bear in mind the importance to us not just of having these things but of having them in one kind of life rather than another, we can see that these questions cannot sensibly be thought of as having yes or no answers. They open the discussion rather than tell us what we need to know to close it.

So we are not so far as we might think from the ancient thought that happiness is an achievement, even given the fact that our thoughts have got confused by the association of happiness with feelings. We do have the thought that happiness comes from living in some ways and not others, that it is not something that others can give you, either by giving you stuff or by getting you into a particular state. Too often these reflections have been ignored by the social sciences, and this has been something to regret, and the source of much of the disappointing state of happiness studies in that area.

One final objection is worth mentioning: it is that the idea of happiness as achievement is unrealistically high-minded.

We see all around us, it is claimed, people who do think of happiness as some kind of positive state, and who seem not to care greatly whether it is their own efforts which produce this state for them, or those of others. If this is a common way of thinking, is it not too idealistic to think of happiness as achievement?

To this the right response is, I think, that low expectations should not automatically lead us to lower our ideals. People have low expectations for a number of reasons—prominently, social conditions that have discouraged them from having higher ones. If someone does not think of himself as having much control over the shape his life can take, it is natural that he should not readily think of happiness as something *he* can achieve, and he may rest content with the notion that happiness is a state that others can just as well bestow. But this example does not show that happiness as achievement is a hopelessly ideal notion. As I have indicated, it does not take a lot of reflection to find it.

To show that eudaimonism is the right form for ethical theory to take would require more argument than I can provide here, but I hope to have shown at least that the notion of happiness as achievement which forms the center of such theories is already a part of our reflective lives.

In the meantime, it is worth redirecting our attention to what we actually think about happiness. We are faced with the point that we do think of happiness as an achievement in the way we live our lives: one subject to dispute and disagreement that we will need theories to clarify, never mind settle. And even this much shows us that philosophy has more to contribute than social science has allowed, both in refocusing the study on the proper data and in giving it fruitful direction.

Smiley faces are fun as reward stickers in children's books, but they are no help in serious thought about happy lives. It is a pity that we need philosophers to point this out.

NOTE

1. For an amusing example, see <http://news.bbc.co.uk/2/hi/health/2630869.stm>, where "scientists" claim to have solved "one of the greatest mysteries plaguing mankind" by actually giving us a mathematical formula: $P + (5 \times E) + (3 \times H) = happiness$, where $P = $ personal characteristics, $E = $ existence, and $H = $ higher-order needs. You compute your formula by answering four questions.

D. Happiness and Virtue

VIRTUE AND EUDAIMONISM

Julia Annas

Julia Annas is Regents Professor of Philosophy at the University of Arizona. She explores the relationship between virtue and happiness.

I. INTRODUCTION

The two most important and central concepts in ancient ethical theory are those of virtue (*aretē*) and happiness (*eudaimonia*). This is well-known by now, as is the way that many scholars and philosophers have in recent years investigated the structure of ancient ethical theories, at least partly in the hope that this would help us in our modern ethical thinking by introducing us to developed theories which escape the problems that have led to so much frustration with deontological and consequentialist approaches.[1] And there has indeed been considerable interest in developing modern forms of ethics which draw inspiration, to a greater or lesser extent, from the ancient theories. However, there is an asymmetry here. Modern theories which take their inspiration from Aristotle and other ancient theorists are standardly called virtue ethics, not happiness ethics. We have rediscovered the appeal of *aretē*, but *eudaimonia* is still, it appears, problematic for us. This has an important consequence for us, for in ancient theories virtue is not discussed in isolation; it is seen as part of a larger structure in which the overarching concept is

From *Social Philosophy and Policy*, vol. 15 (1998). Used by permission of the journal.

happiness. If we focus on virtue alone and ignore its relation to happiness, we are missing a large part of the interest that study of the ancient theories can offer.

Of course, we may be interested in virtue from a purely modern perspective, and may feel it to be of no importance that ancient theories discuss it in relation to happiness. It is perfectly consistent to be interested in virtue but to consider ancient ethical theories to be too remote from ours to offer us any guidance. Without offering a full argument against this position, I think it worth pointing out two things. One is that few if any have thought that virtue can do all the work in a theory; the question arises at some point as to how we are to locate it in a wider structure. And ancient theories at least offer us examples of such structures, which ought to be of some use to us.[2] Secondly, one reason why much modern discussion of virtue ethics has remained at a relatively discursive and vague level has been reluctance to explore the ways in which virtue might be located in a systematic ethical theory. Focus on virtue has in some discussions been associated with a reluctance to move to ethical theory, as opposed to discussing particular aspects of the virtues; it has sometimes been assumed that virtue and character are untheoretical ideas, and that discussing them gets us away from the supposedly dehumanizing and self-alienating effects of abstract theorizing.[3] But this attitude often rests on an unrealistically rigid and monolithic view of what ethical theory is, and it is ironic if it is our reason for not investigating the structure of ancient ethical theories, since these offer models which lack those features of modern theories which have commonly been found alienating.[4]

II. VIRTUE, MODERN AND ANCIENT

I take it as uncontroversial that at the everyday level our conception of virtue is unorganized, indeed something of a mess. Virtue as a serious idea has been so long orphaned from any serious systematic context that our intuitions about it tend to be both vague and conflicting. In a recent issue of the magazine *George*,[5] a selection of famous people were asked to select a figure in public life best exemplifying their concept of virtue. The figures chosen, and the reasons given for choosing them, would be hard to bring under any single nontrivial characterization. Some of the interviewees identified virtue as a kind of vague do-gooding: virtue was seen as other-directed.[6] Some of the people interviewed, however, showed hostility to the idea of virtue, associating it with conservatism and self-righteousness; it was seen as self-directed, indeed egoistic, leading to a selfish indifference to others.[7] This sort of contradictory result would probably emerge from other informal attempts to poll people about virtue. Insofar as we have a more organized conception, it seems to be a timid and negative one. In a wonderful *Calvin and Hobbes* cartoon,[8] Calvin, about to throw a snowball at Susie, is restrained by Hobbes's observation that some philosophers think that *true* happiness is to be found in a life of virtue. Calvin tries out this idea: he tidies his room, shovels the snow, takes out the garbage, and so on. But of course he rebels and goes and throws a snowball at Susie anyway. As he and Hobbes flee from Susie's wrath, Hobbes declares that virtue needs some cheaper thrills. (Calvin's response is that he will write his own philosophy book when he grows up.) Not being in cultural studies, I will not give you a theoretical analysis of the content of this cartoon, but I take it to be right in holding that our pre-reflective view of virtue, even if free of contradictions, is of this repressed, rule-following kind. However, even Calvin can *try* to be happy by being virtuous; our intuitions about virtue may be messy and self-contradictory, but they are quite pliable. It is as though we realize that virtue is a powerful normative notion, and would like to make more use of it, but have somehow lost our grip on what it is.

Doubtless there are many reasons for this state of affairs, but one must surely be the way in which moral theories have demoted the status of the concept of virtue. For most of the twentieth century, moral theories have conceived themselves as mechanisms for producing answers to moral problems, or at least as being driven by the supposed need to provide answers to a range of exceptional or difficult moral dilemmas; they have focused on the extreme situation and the hard case. Virtues have typically been seen merely as dispositions to do the right thing, or to do the right thing reliably, and this has led to two predictable results. Virtues have been seen as trivial or uninteresting. Of course we would, *ceteris paribus*, prefer someone who does the right thing reliably to someone who is less reliable, but this seems merely a prima facie consideration; philosophers are good at thinking up counterexamples in which we would prefer the unreliable person who, in a nonstandard situation, does what is in fact the right thing. Seen in this light, stress on virtues can even seem dubious, displaying an ungrounded preference for the routine over the exceptional, for the rule-follower over the person who is always ready to apply the theory from scratch in every new situation. Moreover, if virtues are seen as dispositions to do the right thing, whatever that is, and if that is determined by the theory, then virtues can be reshaped to accommodate whatever is, according to the theory, the right thing, and their content just falls mechanically out of the theory. Thus, we get utilitarian virtues which are simply dispositions to do whatever is, from a utilitarian point of view, the right thing to do, and whose content must, obviously, be completely fluid. (Or else they are defined at a secondary place in the theory as dispositions to act in certain ways which have utilitarian value by being reliable, rather than by reliably producing certain results; but then we are back with the ungrounded preference for the routine.) It is easy to see why virtue, so conceived, is not very important or serious from a theoretical point of view. Perhaps this combination of secondary status and plasticity in theory has contributed to the general uncertainty at the everyday level as to what virtue is.

It is clear here that we are helped by turning to the ancient theories and their accounts of virtue, and it is also clear why: they are complex and structured. Whether we agree with them or not, the ancients are not in the kind of uncertainty about virtue that we tend to find ourselves in. Virtue is a disposition or state (something which, in turn, is the object of some attention in the metaphysical and logical parts of the ancient theories). It is something which goes deep in the person, and is a matter of their character, not a particular style of acting or living. The disposition involves two things, which develop together and are intertwined in practice. One is the ability to reason reflectively in the morally right way. (What this way will amount to, will differ among different theories. Aristotle puts, more weight on following role models, the Stoics more on formulating general rules.) The person who has developed this ability, the *sophos* or *phronimos*, will get things right, and make the correct decisions. The other thing involved in virtue is a developed habit of feeling and reacting in the right way, that is, the way that accords with the correct reasoning. Again, what this involves will differ from school to school; Stoics and Aristotelians disputed over the nature and role of the emotions. But there is no basic dispute as to virtue's being a settled and deeply rooted state of the person, involving a complex interaction of reasoning and feeling; the virtuous person picks out what are in fact the morally salient aspects of the relevant situation, and reacts to them in the appropriate way. Moreover, virtue is not the disposition to be "excellent" in some way; ancient virtues are the moral virtues—bravery, "temperance" or self-control, justice, and practical wisdom. Virtue is in ancient theories the locus of what we call morality. Forms of modern virtue ethics which miss this point, and erase the difference between moral virtue and nonmoral excellence lose contact with the ancient theories, and so do some modern translations of ancient texts which use "excellence" to translate *aretē*.[9] This account is, of course, very brief and crudely stated; I have defended these claims at length in part 1 of *The Morality of Happiness*.[10] Here I merely wish to make the point that the ancient conception of virtue is definite, coherent, and complex by comparison with the modern one, and thus that it is no surprise that some modern versions of "virtue ethics" have wished to appeal to it.

III. HAPPINESS, MODERN AND ANCIENT

But ancient theories, as I mentioned, do not just discuss virtue; for them it is part of a theory the overarching concept in which is happiness. Virtue is seen as a means to, or a part of, or as constituting the whole of, happiness (depending on the theory). And it is here that our real troubles begin, both as interpreters and as modern theorists hoping for insight from the ancients. For it is undeniable that any of these claims, even the weakest, sounds odd to us, and the thesis that virtue is actually sufficient for happiness tends to sound absurd. If, like Bentham, we think the whole idea self-evidently absurd, we will proceed no further,[11] but ironically the more prepared we are to take seriously the ancient notion of virtue, the more trouble we are apt to have with the notion of happiness which allows for these claims. Since the ancients do not see the need to argue against, or even seem to be aware of, any dismissive reactions like Bentham's to the idea that virtue might be sufficient for *eudaimonia*, it might well appear that *eudaimonia* cannot be happiness as that has been understood in the modern period.[12]

This is an important point both for historical interpretation and for modern moral thinking. The recent revival of interest in virtue ethics has often been associated with an isolated emphasis on virtue and a reluctance to locate virtue in a theoretical structure. And philosophers who have treated virtue systematically as part of a whole theory have taken their models from the modern rather than the ancient tradition.[13] If we are to take a systematic interest in ancient theories of virtue, it seems that we must pay attention to the way they locate virtue within an overall theory of happiness, and from the first this forces on us the question of how we are to understand the ancient conception of happiness. Can we regard it as a coherent version of a concept of which our own version is messier and more problematic? This certainly seems to be the case with virtue. Our intuitions about virtue are unsystematic and potentially in conflict, but we recognize that there is a powerful normative concept there, and we can recognize when another tradition has a more coherent version of it.

This might seem to be hopeless with respect to happiness, for a reason already brought out. Even if we think Bentham was willfully unsympathetic as an interpreter, we may well think it hopeless, either at the everyday level or at the level of moral philosophy, to defend the thesis that virtue is sufficient for happiness. Appreciating the more robust ancient conception of virtue does not seem to help; prima facie, it makes the matter worse.

What we should notice here, though, is that the thesis that virtue is sufficient for happiness was found a hard saying in the ancient world also. It was not thought to be nonsense, but many rejected it in favor of more intuitive views which gave a separate role in happiness to conventional goods like health and wealth. Thus, pointing out that some ancient theories claimed that virtue was sufficient for happiness, whereas if we tried to do this we should find it an unacceptable claim, closes too soon the issue of whether the ancient notion of happiness is quite different from ours. If we look at what are likely to be the stress points of a theory, we should not be surprised to find stress. If we find the sufficiency of virtue for happiness absurd, whereas the ancients found it difficult to accept but not absurd, then indeed our conception of happiness seems to come under more stress from the idea. But rather than try to measure degrees of stress here, it is more useful to look at areas of possible agreement between the ancient and the modern conceptions of happiness. For if we do this, it puts us in a better position to see just where the stress is coming from, for us, when we consider the thesis that virtue is sufficient for happiness.

The ancient conception of happiness appears, in Plato and Aristotle, as an obvious specification of our final end. We see this emerge, in a way that is presented as coming naturally on the everyday level, in Plato's *Euthydemus*.[14] Socrates impresses on a young man, Cleinias, the need to be serious about philosophy and not to treat it as a competitive game, as do the sophists in the dialogue. (The passage thus serves as a protreptic or exhortation to the philosophical life; Cleinias, the unformed boy who is to choose between the serious and the superficial ways of life, clearly makes the reader think about the way she would face such a choice in her own life.) Socrates begins from assumptions which are well-marked as being shared by all parties to the discussion. Everyone, he claims, wants to be happy; actually, it is a silly question to ask if everyone wants to be happy, since it would be absurd to deny it. Further, it would also be absurd to deny that being happy requires having many good things, and, moreover, good things which must benefit us.

The argument which follows is, though short, controversial; and I shall not go into the details of it here.[15] But one feature of it stands out. Cleinias has, as expected, very conventional views about happiness; the good things it requires are, he thinks, conventional goods like health, wealth, political power, and suchlike. Socrates argues that these things are not good at all; the only thing that is good is virtue (here identified with practical wisdom, the excellence of the virtuous person's practical reasoning), and the other things are only good as put to use by virtue. This is an astounding conclusion for such a short argument, but the argument was an influential one; we can see the Stoics developing a similar line of thought. What is most striking here is that Plato leaves standing the point about happiness—that it is what we seek in all we do—at the cost of throwing out the intuition that health, wealth, and other conventional goods are good things, which benefit us. Happiness must come from the possession and use of good things, and the argument is to persuade us that we can be very wrong about what those good things are—in fact, our values are completely mistaken. But we cannot, it seems, tinker with the idea that it would be absurd to deny that happiness is what everyone seeks. Plato does not even consider the idea that happiness is, in fact, what we intuitively think it to be—being benefited by goods like health and wealth—while virtue makes a different, and more insistent, claim, one which overrides that of happiness.

That the argument goes this way might be merely an idiosyncrasy—or perversity if you like—of Plato's, though it would be odd to insist so strongly on the intuitive nature of the premises and then make an obviously perverse move with respect to them. But we can see that Plato's reaction to this argument is not idiosyncratic if we turn to the famous passage in Aristotle's *Nicomachean Ethics* in which he says that everyone agrees that our final good is happiness, but everyone disagrees as to what it is.[16] The first disagreement he mentions is that between "the many" and "the wise": exactly the kind of division set up in the *Euthydemus*. Aristotle does not think that any argument is needed to show that all agree that our final good is happiness; clearly to him it seems as absurd to deny this as it does to Plato. Moreover, he immediately says that there is wide disagreement as to what happiness is, thus showing that disagreement about what is good, and so a way of achieving happiness, is normal; he never envisages an argument to replace happiness as our final end.

Is it similarly platitudinous for us that happiness is our final end, what we seek in everything we do? This turns out to be complex. On the one hand, there is a certain undeniable appeal to the idea. When the question is raised, it is generally easy to find people agreeing to the idea that everything we do is done for the sake of happiness. Philosophers teaching elementary ethics classes, for example, generally report that students find it obvious that happiness directs even altruistic behavior and self-sacrificing lives. (Philosophers' own intuitions on the subject, of course, are hopelessly infected by their discussion of theories.) This ready consensus may, of course, have a variety of sources, some of which may be dubious.[17] But there is undoubtedly some thought easily available to us which to some extent mirrors Aristotle's readiness to move from final end to happiness.

How well does this thought stand up to reflection about the nature of our final end? Here it is instructive to look at a passage in Plato's *Philebus*,[18] which is interesting for our purposes in that it appeals only to ordinary commonsense intuitions.[19] Formally the argument is about the good, but it is clearly said that what is being sought is what will make a human life happy.[20] Socrates and his interlocutor, Protarchus, agree that this good is what everything seeks, and that it must be perfect and sufficient. Since Protarchus is at this point a hedonist and Socrates is defending the claims of reason, their views about the content of the good life could hardly be more different, but they have no trouble agreeing on these points, which can fairly clearly be seen as formal points about our final good, analogous to the formal points that Aristotle makes.[21] If the good is complete, then nothing need be added to it for it to make the good life good. This formal point turns out to have considerable power; for when Protarchus holds that the life of pleasure is the good life, Socrates shows him that in that case pleasure would be complete, and could not be found to be lacking anything. However, a life of pleasure unaccompanied by any intellectual activity of any kind would be no life for a human to choose; it would be the life of a clam, whose pleasures come and go unaccompanied by any consciousness or memory. Similarly, a life purely of reason would be no life for a human to choose (though it would be fine for a god);[22] humans need a life made up in some way of both pleasure and reason. Here an important conclusion is reached simply by appealing to ordinary intuitions about completeness, and the result is decisive. It does not occur to Protarchus to question the assumption that a final aim must be complete. Hence, if pleasure is not complete—if it leaves out something important as an object of rational aim—then it cannot be the good that a human life aims at. And exactly the same goes for reason. There is no need for lengthy argument, since the crucial assumption about completeness is shared and regarded as not open to question.

Would modern intuitions about completeness be as robust? It would be rash to assert that an analogue of the *Philebus* argument would go through in such an uncomplicated way. It is much more likely that, if we had a plausible candidate for happiness, but it were pointed out that this candidate lacked something important to human life, the response would be that there is more to life than happiness. A modern analogue to Protarchus might claim that if pleasure lacks something important, this shows not that a life cannot be made happy by pleasure but rather that happiness is not the only reasonable aim in life.

It seems, then, that while we can easily come to agree that happiness is a thin specification of the end we seek in everything that we do, this is not as robust a thought for us as for the ancients, and we do not reject other thoughts on the basis of it as they do. We seem in fact to have divided intuitions about happiness, and they divide on the issue of completeness. We can agree that happiness is what we seek in everything that we do; but we also seem to have a more limited and demarcated notion of happiness, given which it could be reasonable to aim at other things in life as well. Obviously pleasure, enjoyment, and so on will be more plausible candidates for this limited notion of happiness than they can be for happiness if that is defined as complete.

IV. THE TRANSFORMATIVE ROLE OF VIRTUE

There is also a larger difference, which emerges when we look at the role of happiness in all the ancient theories, as the unreflective starting point of our thoughts, and also as the end point, when we have argued the matter through and adopted the right theory as to what happiness is. This point is not limited to theories which make virtue prominent in or sufficient for happiness, but it shows up most clearly in their case; and therefore I shall discuss it with reference to the theories of Socrates in the Socratic dialogues of Plato, and of the Stoics, who found inspiration in the figure of Socrates. Both Socrates and the Stoics claim that virtue is sufficient for happiness, and, before returning to the point that we tend to find this an unconvincing claim, it is worth looking more closely at how this claim is to be understood, and exactly where the disagreement lies.

Socrates[23] holds, as we have seen from the *Euthydemus* passage above, that happiness is our final end, and that we achieve this by having good things, which benefit us. What is striking in passages in other dialogues is the way in which Socrates stresses the idea that virtue is the only thing worth having, in a particularly strong and uncompromising way. Since Plato writes dialogues and not treatises, these claims are not explicitly brought into relation to the more theoretical discussion in the *Euthydemus*, and indeed when we look at some of the most familiar of these passages it requires some effort on our part to see them as part of a theory of happiness in the first place. In the *Gorgias*, Socrates puts forward, aware that it will be found deeply unconvincing, the claim that it is so important to do right and not to do wrong, that it is better to be wronged than to wrong others, and, if one does wrong others, better to be punished than to get away with it. And in two other dialogues whose uncompromising tone matches that of the *Gorgias*, he makes the point even clearer. "If it becomes clear," he says in the *Crito*, "that such conduct is unjust, I cannot help thinking that the question whether we are sure to die, or to suffer any other ill-effect for that matter, if we stand our ground . . . ought not to weigh with us at all in comparison with the risk of acting unjustly."[24] And in the *Apology*, Socrates says, "You are mistaken, my friend, if you think that a man who is worth anything ought to spend his time weighing up the prospects of life and death. He has only one thing to consider in performing any action: that is, whether he is acting justly or unjustly, like a good man or a bad one."[25]

This does not look to us like a position about happiness at all, let alone a plausible one. But we have reason to consider Socrates a eudaimonist, given the way that, in the *Euthydemus* passage, he readily accepted a radical redefinition of good such that virtue is the only thing that is good; rather than budge on the principle that happiness is what we seek in all we do. As is often the case, we can find the key to a good interpretation by looking at the later moral theory of the Stoics, who saw themselves as Socratics in this respect, but who have a more developed and technical theory which can serve as a template to bring out the overall shape of Socrates' ideas. The Stoics hold explicitly that virtue is not only necessary but also sufficient for happiness. If we grant the sufficiency of virtue for happiness (a big "if," of course; we shall shortly be looking at the thesis), we can see why Socrates can be a eudaimonist and yet be uncompromising about virtue. The virtuous person, just by being virtuous, has what matters for happiness, and thus can lose other things without losing what is sufficient for happiness. Hence it is a mistake even to let these things enter into one's deliberations and be weighed up against the prospect of wrongdoing; this is what Socrates rejects so violently in the above passages. For to think of the immoral action as an option for you is already to be thinking of things like life, health, and wealth as parts of happiness in their own right, and this is a fundamental mistake if indeed virtue is sufficient for happiness. Moreover, we can make sense of the counterintuitive position of the *Gorgias*: if virtue is indeed sufficient for happiness, then the wicked person is, in being wicked, harming himself; hence the conventional evil of punishment may actually improve his life, by giving him the chance to change and become virtuous, which is the only way to achieve happiness. Thus, conventional evils may be good for the bad person. And conventional good things can add nothing toward happiness: hence for the vicious person they are not good, since they do nothing to make him virtuous, which is all that matters for happiness, and may produce a misleading and dangerous illusion of happiness, or the means to develop as an even less virtuous person than he is. Nor do conventional goods form, for the virtuous person, a part of happiness in their own right, since the virtuous person already has what is sufficient for happiness.

In all this, something seems to be conspicuously missing. If virtue is sufficient for happiness in the way that Socrates is represented as trenchantly insisting, why should the virtuous person have any interest in anything other than virtue? Why should he have any reason to choose health over illness, wealth over poverty? Since these things make no contribution to happiness in their own right, why would he not be indifferent to them? There is a deafening silence in the Socratic dialogues on this point,[26] and we do not find the kind of answer that is needed until the Stoics introduce their idea of what they call "indifferents."

The Stoics hold that virtue, which is sufficient for happiness, has a value which is of a different sort from the value that other kinds of things have. Several important Stoic doctrines hang on this point.[27] Health, wealth, and other conventional goods are referred to as "indifferents" and have a different kind of value, called "selective" value, since we have reason to select among them, although what we do when we thus select is different in kind from what we do when we are motivated to pursue virtue, which is called "choosing" virtue to distinguish it from our attitude to the indifferents. Indifferents like health that we have reason to go for are said to be "preferred" because of the selective value they have; those that we have reason to avoid, like illness, correspondingly have selective disvalue, and so are dispreferred. The point of the special terminology is to make the point that the two kinds of value are different in kind. When the question arises, whether the virtuous person would have any reason to go for preferred indifferents, such as health and wealth, the answer takes up and extends the suggestion in the *Euthydemus* that things other than virtue are good only as put to use by virtue. For the Stoics take over the Socratic idea that virtue is a skill (*technē*): it is skill in living, and it works on the material of virtue, that is, the everyday things which have selective value and which we must select among to make our way through the day. Things that are indifferent and have merely selective value make a contribution to happiness only as part of the virtuous life, not in their own right. Health adds nothing to the vicious life, and does not make the vicious person happier, because it has not been taken up into the network of concerns that the virtuous person has; in the vicious person's life it is put to the wrong kind of use, and has the wrong kind of value.

We might try to express the idea by saying that things other than virtue which are conventionally good—health, wealth, and so on—have merely conditional value, whereas virtue has unconditional value. But this does not quite locate the important point, since the preferred indifferents do have a form of unconditional value, namely selective value. What matters here is their value as contributing to happiness; and *this* is conditional on their being given a place and function within a virtuous life—on their being "put to use" by the skill of virtue.

It is easy to feel, at this point, that the problems raised by an outrageous claim—that virtue is sufficient for happiness—have been resolved in an academic fashion, and that we still lack any real insight into the idea that virtue is sufficient for happiness. For what could it be, to recognize that you have reason to go for health rather than illness, and yet to think that health makes no contribution toward your happiness except as embedded in a life of virtue? On this view, the healthy vicious person is not happy, because he is vicious; his excellent health provides no compensation whatever, and makes him no happier than he would be being ill—indeed, it may perhaps be responsible for making him unhappier, since it provides means for him to sustain and increase his wickedness in a hale and hearty way.[28]

Something is playing a role here which is not picked out as such by any ancient concept, though the idea emerges from ancient discussions of virtue overall. Virtue is not just one disposition among many, though one which is mysteriously guaranteed to be of more significance for virtue than other aspects of your life. Virtue is of more importance than other things in your life because it controls the value that they have for you. Virtue, in a word, can transform a human life. It can do so because it can transform your view of what happiness is.[29] The virtuous person is not tempted to identify happiness with something like having a lot of money, for virtue enables you to correct ordinary valuations and arrive at a true estimate of value. Moreover, the virtuous person does not ascribe the wrong kind of value to money. She can perfectly well allow that normally, and ceteris paribus, we have reason to go for money rather than its absence; but she realizes that even though it has this selective value, this does not make it good in itself, regardless of context. Only the virtuous person properly knows how to put money to use and do the right things with it; and thus only in the virtuous person's life does money make a contribution to happiness.

We can see here a line of thought which is intuitively acceptable and attractive up to a point, taken further than we would normally be prepared to take it. We are familiar with the idea that money does not, just on its own, make a life happy. Many lives of the rich and famous are spectacularly unhappy because the person cares so much about money that he piles it up without taking thought as to the use to which to put it, and then finds himself at a loss. With money, doubtless some wish-fulfillment enters into our judgment that the rich and famous are not happy, but we frequently do make such judgments about people who have obvious shares of conventional goods such as beauty or political power. This idea, that conventional goods will benefit you, and thus make you happy, only if you have the right character to make good use of them, appears in Plato in a passage in the *Menexenus*, where it is part of a string of cliches uttered in an ultra-conventional speech, so we can be fairly sure that Plato took it to be part of common-sense intuition.[30]

Plato and the Stoics, however, take this idea far beyond what common sense makes of it. We are open to the idea that money just as such will not improve the life of the vicious person, and that getting rid of the relevant vices is the first step to take. It is a much stronger position to hold that a good person cannot be harmed, as Socrates says in the *Apology*, that there is no pain or loss which can have an important enough effect on the virtuous person for him to lose his happiness. For that to be the case, virtue must have transformed his life so much that he continues to regard himself as having what matters for happiness, despite the pain and loss (which he minds, of course; virtue does not transform your life to the point that you cease to notice them).

This idea of virtue as transformative of a life, and radically affecting the value of other things for the person, is obviously removed from modern, more limited ideas of virtue. But it is also a notable development of ancient ideas; people happy to accept the point made in the *Menexenus* would require effort to get them to accept, still less live by, the idea that virtue is actually sufficient for happiness. It is far from a given in ancient ethical thought that virtue has this transformative power; Aristotle, for example, sees its force as being much more limited than this, and allows that conventional goods do form a part of happiness in their own right (though only up to a point; virtue does determine the limit of what they can add).

It is clear from the progression of ideas that I have traced that we have located a very large difference between ancient and modern ideas about happiness. Even if we are willing to grant the starting point, that our final end is happiness, we find great difficulty in the idea that, by the time we allow that virtue can transform a life, we are still talking about happiness. This difficulty does not just arise from the idea that virtue can have this effect. Nor does it arise just from the idea that this is too demanding a theory. We are familiar with the objection to a moral theory, that it is too demanding. This may mean either that the theory is too lofty for human nature; it defines its goals so high that it takes itself out of the running as a moral theory. Or it may mean that, while recognizably a theory that we can attempt to pursue, it sets goals that so many will fail to reach so decisively that it is difficult to accept as a serious option. In the ancient world, the Socratic and Stoic theories were certainly seen as demanding, in contrast to less demanding theories such as Aristotle's. Indeed, this became a familiar topic of debate: Aristotelians attacked Stoic theories as unrealistic, while Stoics regarded Aristotelian theories as feeble in their concessions to weak human nature. But no school in the ancient world had the response that the demandingness of Stoic types of theory ruled them out as theories of happiness. On the question of demandingness itself, our reactions are not very different; we recognize that demanding theories can be seen as unrealistic, and less demanding theories as too concessive, while tending to assume that the onus is on the critic to show why morality must be shown to demand what human nature can readily come up with. However, many people now do tend to find the Stoic theory unacceptable as a theory of happiness, not just too demanding a theory, and this shows us that important modern assumptions about happiness are playing a role.

V. HAPPINESS TRANSFORMED

Happiness in ancient theories, from the *Euthydemus* on, is our final goal in life, even when our view of what it consists of is radically changed, so that we seek it in virtue rather than in conventional goods. Hence it is the goal we have at our starting point, when we begin to reflect about our lives, and also the goal we have at the end, when we are committed (say) to virtue's being the only good thing, and sufficient for happiness. Happiness is the continuing goal we have, but it can be transformed by virtue; we go on seeking happiness, but our conception of where to look for it and how we have to be to get it can be utterly reconfigured. Here, however, we run up against two aspects of the modern idea of happiness, to be discussed in what follows: firstly, the modern idea that happiness is *subjective*, and secondly, that it is *rigid*, not allowing significant modification of content.

One corollary of the ancient theories is that the person who has successfully transformed his idea of what happiness is, is now in a position to say that he was wrong before. He thought that happiness consisted in wealth and power, but he now sees that this was a mistake. Hence, he has to conclude that, when he was living the unenlightened life of wealth and power, he thought he was happy at the time, but was not. Here we collide with some strong modern intuitions. For it can be argued, as it has been by L. W. Sumner,[31] that our modern conception of happiness is subjective; if I think I am happy at a given time, then I am, and if I find out later that my happiness was based on mistakes of various kinds, then, while I can regret the mistakes, I cannot deny that I was happy. To do so involves an Orwellian rewriting of history.

Is our modern conception essentially subjective? I do not think that there is agreement on this; some have argued that, while we are drawn to the subjective way of thinking, we also feel the force of the idea that happiness is objective, in that happiness based on mistakes turns out not to be happiness at all; the mistaken person would in fact rewrite their past and say that they were not happy, though they thought they were.[32] It is possible that our reactions differ with the nature of the mistakes. Sumner describes a case of a woman who is happily married for ten years and then discovers that her husband had another partner all the time. She has much to regret, he says, but before being undeceived she was happy: she was not mistaken about *that*. Intuitions divide here, I suspect, and neither the position that she was happy nor the position that she was not commands a consensus. But I think that it is different with the person who has moved from seeking money and power to seeking virtue as a way of being happy. The ancient conception allows his transformed idea of happiness still to be happiness; but we have much more difficulty with the idea that a person whose values have changed for the better was not happy before that change in values.[33] Undoubtedly the modern conception of happiness has a subjective aspect—that is, even if we are not wholehearted about the subjectivity of happiness, some of our intuitions support it. Moreover, if others do not, we are less likely to claim that happiness is objective than we are to claim that our concept is internally inconsistent.

Even if we deny that our conception of happiness is subjective, there is another way in which it resists the ancient transformation by virtue. Our conception of happiness is rigid: it is not tolerant of much shifting of content, certainly not the wholesale redefining demanded by the thesis that virtue is sufficient for happiness. This rigidity is not a matter of being tied to one particular content; there have been many candidate accounts for happiness in modern philosophy—pleasure, welfare, desire-satisfaction, and so on. It is a rigidity of form rather than content: although there are competing accounts of the content, once we have settled on it we are reluctant to allow that there could be radical change while thinking that we are still talking about happiness.[34] We have problems with the idea that happiness might alter in content while retaining its role as our goal.

It seems undeniable that there are these differences at least between ancient and modern notions of happiness. It would be interesting to investigate further the sources of these differences, but I do not have the scope or the knowledge to do this here. It is tempting to trace the idea of happiness as subjective to the Utilitarians' insistence on defining it as pleasure and the absence of pain; but perhaps there are broader causes, and certainly neither Bentham nor Mill writes as though there were a serious objective conception of happiness familiar and available which needed replacement. Moreover, the rigidity of happiness, which also resists transformation by virtue, seems shared by the Utilitarians with Kant, who never doubts that happiness can always conflict with morality, and that happiness should be seen as opposed to morality rather than enlarged by it. Together, however, with the comparative weakness of our attachment to the idea of happiness as our final end, these factors compel us to see our idea of happiness as conflicted and uncertain by comparison with the ancient idea.

I suggested at the beginning that we can come to understand, and even accept, the ancient conception of virtue, despite the thinness, confusion, and uncertainty of our own conception of virtue. Is the same possible in the case of happiness? Can we see the ancient conception as a coherent and usable version of something that we have a strong attachment to as a normative notion, but find ourselves confused and uncertain about? Sumner has claimed that our modern notion is centrally a subjective one, and that this inhibits trying to line it up with ancient *eudaimonia*, which is so clearly not a subjective notion. He suggests that we identify *eudaimonia* instead with some more clearly objective modern notion, such as well-being. This is an interesting suggestion. It would not be true to the ancient idea of *eudaimonia* in that it would be an artificial and theory-dependent notion, whereas *eudaimonia* arises naturally out of everyday language, as happiness does (hence both are accompanied by adjectives and verbs which "well-being" lacks, making translation difficult).[35] Further, there is the intriguing fact that ancient moral philosophers seem to have had the chance to develop an ancient concept of well-being, and did not do so. Democritus, regarded as a competitor with Socrates for being the originator of moral philosophy, talked of both *eudaimonia* and *euestō*, the latter being Ionic Greek for "well-being."[36] But later philosophers note Democritus only for his ideas about *eudaimonia*; indeed, he is hailed as a pioneer for placing happiness in the soul.[37] *Euestō* never developed as a standard philosophical term.

We might also, however, consider the possibility that our modern conception of happiness, rather than being firmly subjective, might be formed from a variety of incompatible sources; if so, it might still offer the chance of being, as I have throughout assumed it to be, a suitable match for *eudaimonia*. By this I mean not that happiness might map exactly onto *eudaimonia*, but that it may stand to the ancient conception somewhat as our muddled and rather pathetic concept of virtue stands to that of the ancients. We have, of course, no prospects of ready acceptance of the consequences of the thesis that virtue is sufficient for happiness. But coming to understand our own moral ideas better in the light of the way they match and mismatch ancient ideas is always complex, and the hope would be that we can understand the ancient theories as theories about virtue and happiness, different though our own concepts of both of these may be.

What this shows is that we are faced by some important options, the choice of which makes a profound difference to our approach to moral philosophy. If we accept that our conception of happiness contains several different and incompatible elements, we may regard it as we do our conception of virtue, and try to understand the ancient ideas as more coherent and stronger versions of the conception which we recognize as important but have lost a consistent interpretation of. If, on the other hand, we think that we do have a conception of happiness which is fairly strongly centered on an idea, such as subjectivity, which is clearly alien to the ancient approaches, then we will, like Sumner, conclude that ancient theories are theories of well-being rather than of happiness.

Prominent in all this is the idea that virtue can transform a life by transforming the person's conception of what happiness is. It goes without saying that this presupposes a fairly strong version of moral realism, for the transformation in question is not like that which results in the changed worlds of the deluded or the psychopathic: it is a development which reveals to the person what true values are. Thus, it might be rejected by those who reject moral realism. But apart from this issue the idea that virtue can transform a life presses on our attention a question which I raised at the start. Modern versions of virtue ethics have tended to focus on virtue in isolation, and the question arises of how virtue fits into the larger structure of moral theory. If we cannot adjust our ideas of virtue and happiness to accommodate the transformative power of virtue on the person's happiness, then it seems that we have to forgo the prospect of a form of eudaimonism within which there is a certain conception of morality. This is a conception familiar to us since Kant, but it can also be seen in the uncompromising statement of Socrates quoted earlier in the essay: morality embodies a value different in kind from the values that nonmoral things have, and cannot be weighed up against these other values, but overrides them. It is commonly assumed that eudaimonism cannot accommodate this conception of morality, and indeed sometimes this is turned into an advantage by those who dislike this conception of morality, but find eudaimonism appealing. As I have argued in this essay, however, we see this conception in the Socratic and Stoic forms of eudaimonism. It has proved difficult for us to understand, and still harder to envisage as an option for ourselves. I have suggested that our ideas about virtue and happiness are both part causes of this difficulty, and that we must recognize the width of the gap we have to bridge if we are to understand, let alone adopt, a form of eudaimonism which allows its proper place to virtue.

NOTES

1. Both of these approaches have been increasingly criticized for unrealistic and abstract approaches to moral questions, and for their inability to give a convincing account of moral character and the role in individuals' moral thinking of a conception of their life as a whole.

2. Not the only such examples; the role of virtue in eighteenth-century writers such as Francis Hutcheson and Adam Smith is also receiving more attention, and it would be good to have informed comparisons of such theories with the ancient ones.

3. S. G. Clarke and E, Simpson, eds., *Anti-Theory in Ethics and Moral Conservatism* (Albany, NY: SUNY Press, 1989), contains many papers which put forward this viewpoint. A forthcoming book by Michele Svatos on the structure of virtue ethics builds on and contributes to more theoretically ambitious types of virtue ethics.

4. These features include a bias in favor of science or mathematics as proffering the right structure for an ethical theory, emphasis on formalization, and readiness to discard those aspects of ethical experience which do not lend themselves to economical and elegant structuring. In my *The Morality of Happiness* (Oxford: Oxford University Press, 1993), I argue against taking the antitheoretical urge to be central to a concern with virtue ethics.

5. *George*, April/May 1996.

6. The people asked tended to pick worthy figures from their own area of competence: an actor picked an actor, a singer a singer, a bureaucrat a bureaucrat, a black activist a black activist. Otherwise, the candidates were people who ran social programs, or had overcome handicaps, or provided good role models. Among those with a favorable attitude toward virtue, the minimal content of the idea seemed to be that virtue is something other-directed, involving some sacrifice on the agent's part, and worthy of praise.

7. This is how it was viewed in the associated essay by Joe Queenan: "[A]t heart, almost all of the virtue books emanate from the right. . . ." Queenan presents focus on virtue as a smug conservative attempt to justify ignoring the needs of others, thus linking it with social attitudes such as attacks an welfare. He never explains why virtue should be conceived as egoistic and self-satisfied.

8. Bill Watterson, *There's Treasure Everywhere: A Calvin and Hobbes Collection* (Kansas City: Andrews and McMeel, 1996), p. 96. In the Calvin and Hobbes cartoons, widely syndicated in the United States from the early eighties to 1996, Calvin is a small boy and Hobbes his tiger (a toy tiger to others, Hobbes shares an imaginative world with Calvin, in which one of the people they interact with is Susie, the girl next door).

9. *Aretē* does have a broad sense in which it covers the nonmoral excellence of various things, but ancient philosophical writers are clear that the relevant sense in ethics is what we would call moral virtue; see Annas, *The Morality of Happiness*, pp. 129–31.

10. Annas, *The Morality of Happiness* (*supra* note 4).

11. Bentham dismisses the idea of virtue's sufficiency for happiness as self-contradictory nonsense; see Jeremy Bentham, *Deontology, Together with A Table of the Springs of Action, and the Article on Utilitarianism*, ed. Amnon Goldworth (Oxford: Oxford University Press, 1933), p. 300. Bentham gives no reason for this other than the fact that he finds the idea absurd. It may be that he located the problem in the relevant notion of happiness, rather than in virtue, given that he devotes a chapter to dismissing the *summum bonum* as "consummate nonsense."

12. I am grateful to L. W. Sumner for presenting this issue in a forceful and well-argued way which has greatly clarified my own thinking on the matter.

13. See Michael Slote, *From Morality to Virtue* (Oxford: Oxford University Press, 1992).

14. Plato, *Euthydemus*, 278d–282e. The argument is couched in terms of "doing well" or *eu prattein*, but it is clear from 280b6 that this is regarded as synonymous with "being happy" or *eudaimonein*. (See also Aristotle, *Nicomachean Ethics*, 1095a18–20.)

15. See Gregory Vlastos, *Socrates, Ironist and Moral Philosopher* (Cambridge: Cambridge University Press, 1991), ch. 6; and my article "Virtue as the Use of Other Goods," in Terence Irwin and Martha C. Nussbaum, eds., *Virtue, Love, and Form: Essays in Memory of Gregory Vlastos* (Edmonton: Academic Printing and Publishing, 1993), pp. 53–66.

16. Aristotle, *Nicomachean Ethics*, 1095a17–22. Cf. the later passage at 1097b22–24, where Aristotle says that it is a platitude to say that the final good is happiness, and we seek further specification of it.

17. It may be that unreflective egoism plays a role in some people's ready assent to the idea that happiness is our final end, and that if egoism is rejected the assent is not nearly so ready. But what matters here is simply that at the intuitive level the assent is pretty ready.

18. Plato, *Philebus*, 20b–23b.

19. Unlike the surrounding material, which is methodologically among the most baffling in Plato.

20. Plato, *Philebus*, 11d4–6. Note the references to the lives of pleasure, etc., in the argument, as at 20e1–2, 21d8–9; and at 20d, it is said that everything strives for the good. These points are reminiscent of Aristotle's discussion of happiness. It remains odd that, although the *Philebus* is about the issues discussed in other dialogues in terms of virtue and happiness, these terms are mentioned very seldom in the dialogue, which focuses rather on pleasure and reason as factors in a human life.

21. At *Philebus*, 20d, the good is said to be complete or *teleon*, and sufficient or *hikanon*; at 22a9–b8, it is said that the lives of pleasure and reason on their own do not contain the good (that makes human lives happy), since if they did, they would have been sufficient, complete, and choiceworthy by all. Here even the terminology suggests Aristotle's establishment of the points that our final end must be complete and self-sufficient.

22. At *Philebus*, 33b, the life of reason without pleasure or pain is said to be most godlike; but this of course disqualifies it from being a good candidate for the human good.

23. I am ignoring all versions of the "Socratic problem" here, since they do not affect my point. I take it that there is a coherent position in Plato's Socratic dialogues which can be attributed to early Plato, using Socrates as the figure who holds (and embodies) this view.

24. Plato, *Crito*, 48d, in *The Last Days of Socrates*, trans. Hugh Tredennick and Harold Tarrant (London: Penguin, 1993).

25. Plato, *Apology*, 28b, in *The Last Days of Socrates*.

26. Indeed, Vlastos finds the silence so deafening that he takes the problem to be an indication that Socrates does not in fact hold that virtue is sufficient for happiness.

27. These doctrines include not just the sufficiency of virtue for happiness, but the theory of preferred indifferents and the account of right actions.

28. Moreover, this change in perspective affects our view of what the virtuous and vicious person can be said to accomplish. James Griffin has made the point that Wagner, not a good person, nonetheless could be said to have led a great life because of his many accomplishments. Ancient philosophers, however (at any rate those in the Socratic-Stoic tradition), would not regard Wagner's accomplishments as something neutrally assessable (perhaps to be weighed against his admitted defects). Rather, our view of what he accomplished would already be affected by our view of the place of these accomplishments in his life. In the *Gorgias*, Socrates is represented as uncompromisingly unimpressed by the Parthenon and the other Acropolis buildings that we admire so much; rather than letting their aesthetic qualities be weighed against the problematic way they were financed, he insists on discussing them in their context of imperialistic and demagogic policy.

29. Does this also require a revisionist view of virtue (a point raised by Fred Miller)? It certainly requires something very different from modern views of virtue. Yet a person in the ancient world might not be wrong about what virtue is (she might think of it as a disposition to do the right thing for the right reason, and this is correct in outline) but might nonetheless have a radically wrong view of the place and role of virtue in life. Aristotle, in *Rhetoric*, Book 1, ch. 5, retails ordinary views of happiness which give virtue rather low priority; they are defective in their grasp of the relation between virtue and other things, not in their view of what virtue is (just as they are wrong in their view of the importance of wealth, not in their view of what wealth is).

30. Plato, *Menexenus*, 246d–247a.

31. L. W. Sumner, "Happiness Now and Then," a Taft Lecture delivered as part of a conference on eudaimonia and well-being at the University of Cincinnati, May 1996.

32. See Richard Kraut, "Two Conceptions of Happiness," *Philosophical Review*, vol. 88, no. 2 (1979), pp. 167–97.

33. There is a range of cases here; I suspect that we might accept that someone was not really happy whose previous values were self-defeating or masochistic or in some obvious way defective; but it is harder to make the case for a change of values where the ones adopted depend on acceptance of a theory and are controverted by other theories. Would we be happy to say that the Emperor Charles V was never happy until he retired to a monastery?

34. This is a point I stress in *The Morality of Happiness*, ch. 22.

35. Despite the differences between *eudaimonia* and happiness which I have explored in this essay, and which are striking to philosophers reflecting on virtue and happiness, "happiness" is clearly the correct translation for *eudaimonia* in ancient literature of all kinds, and it would be a mistake to conclude that we should translate *eudaimonia* by some other term.

36. I owe this point to Dr. Emidio Spinelli.

37. Arius Didymus ap. Stobaeus, *Eclogae*, II, 52.13–14. The passage goes on to list *euestō* as one of the ways Democritus characterizes *eudaimonia*, along with more subjective ones such as *euthumia* (cheerfulness) and *ataraxia* (tranquillity). However, later accounts of Democritean moral theory stress happiness and its more subjective characterizations, particularly, cheerfulness, not *euestō*.

HAPPINESS AND IMMORALITY

Steven M. Cahn and Jeffrie G. Murphy

Steven M. Cahn, coeditor of this book, is professor of philosophy at the Graduate Center of The City University of New York. Jeffrie G. Murphy is Regents Professor of Law, Philosophy, and Religious Studies at Arizona State University. They take opposing sides on the issue of whether an immoral person can be happy.

Parts A and B are from "The Happy Immoralist," *Journal of Social Philosophy*, Vol. 35 (2004). Used by permission of Blackwell Publishing. Parts C and D are copyright © 2006 by Steven M. Cahn and used with his permission.

A. *The Happy Immoralist*

Steven M. Cahn

"Happiness," according to Philippa Foot, "is a most intractable concept." She commits herself, however, to the claim that "great happiness, unlike euphoria or even great pleasure, must come from something related to what is deep in human nature, and fundamental in human life, such as affection for children and friends, the desire to work, and love of freedom and truth."[1] I am not persuaded by this characterization of happiness and offer the following counterexample.

Consider Fred, a fictitious person, but an amalgamation of several people I have known. Fred's life has been devoted to achieving three aims: fame, wealth, and a reputation for probity. He has no interest whatever in friends or truth. Indeed, he is treacherous and thoroughly dishonest. Nevertheless, he has attained his three goals and is, in fact, a rich celebrity renowned for his supposed integrity. His acquiring a good name while acting unscrupulously is a tribute to his audacity, cunning, and luck. Now he rests self-satisfied, basking in renown, delighting in luxuries, and relishing praise for his reputed commitment to the highest moral standards.

That he enjoys great pleasure, even euphoria, is undeniable. But, according to Mrs. Foot, he is not happy. I would say, rather, that *we* are not happy with *him*. We do not wish to see shallowness and hypocrisy rewarded. Indeed, while numerous works of literature describe good persons who are doomed to failure, few works tell of evil persons who ultimately flourish. (An exception to the rule is Natasha in Chekhov's *The Three Sisters*, a play that causes most audiences anguish.)

We can define "happiness" so as to falsify the claim that Fred is happy. This philosophical sleight-of-hand, though, accomplishes little, for Fred is wholly contented, suffering no worries or anxieties. Indeed, he is smug as he revels in his exalted position.

Happiness may be, as Mrs. Foot says, an "intractable concept." Yet surely Fred is happy. Perhaps later in life he won't be. Or perhaps he will. He may come to the end of his days as happy as he is now. I presume his case provides a reason why God is supposed to have created hell, for if Fred suffers no punishment in the next world, he may escape punishment altogether. And believing in that prospect is yet another reason he is happy.

NOTE

1. *Moral Dilemmas* (Oxford: Clarendon Press, 2002), p. 35.

B. *The Unhappy Immoralist*

JEFFRIE G. MURPHY

All that you've just noted merely confirms my belief . . . that if we are to talk philosophy to any purpose, language must be re-made from the ground up.——*Doctor Glas*, HJALMAR SÖDERBERG

When presenting his version of the ancient and well-known challenge that the Sophists long ago posed to Socrates, Professor Cahn seems to be assuming at the outset—and asking us to grant—that the man he describes *is* happy. But such an assumption begs the whole question at issue here.

In both *Republic* and *Gorgias*, Plato has Socrates argue that the immoral man—even a tyrant with great power—may of course be happy as the ignorant world understands happiness but will not be happy as this concept will be truly understood by the wise philosopher.

Professor Cahn dismisses this as verbal "sleight-of-hand," but I think that such dismissal is hasty. Plato is trying to advance our philosophical understanding by making a conceptual or linguistic claim—no doubt a revisionary one—and surely not all such claims are merely useless verbal tricks. As I read Plato, he (like Philippa Foot) is suggesting that full human happiness is to be understood as the satisfaction one takes in having a personality wherein all elements required for a fully realized human life are harmoniously integrated. The immoralist lacks some of these attributes—integrity, moral emotions, and the capacity for true friendships, for example. Given what he lacks, it can be granted that he may indeed be happy in some limited way—e.g., enjoying a great deal of pleasure—while insisting that he cannot be happy in the full sense.

As a matter of common language, of course, many people do not use the word "happiness" in this rich sense but tend to mean by it something like "has a whole lot of fun." Because of this, the Greek word *eudaimonia*, which in the past was generally translated as "happiness," is now often rendered as "flourishing" to avoid confusion. But some are not so quick to give up the older and deeper usage:

> [Realizing how little the clergyman cared about his wife's health or even his own] I began to think that Markel and his Cyrenäics are right: people care nothing for happiness, they look only for pleasure. They seek pleasure even flat in the face of their own happiness. (*Doctor Glas* again)

Some of the spirit of Plato and Socrates is to be found in Kierkegaard's *Purity of Heart is to Will One Thing*—where he seeks to expose the conflicts and deficiencies present in the "double-minded" person who does not organize his life around the moral good, a person whom Kierkegaard regards as self-deceived if he thinks of himself as truly happy. Kierkegaard argues for this with a blending of conceptual and psychological claims—claims about the nature of those desires he calls "temporal." The person who wills only in pursuit of temporal rather than eternal (i.e., ethico-religious) desires will, he maintains, ultimately fall into boredom and despair since the objects of these desires are vulnerable to the vicissitudes of fate and fortune and carry only temporary satisfaction. The apparent happiness of the person in bondage to temporal desires will be momentary and will mask what is in fact that person's desperate attempt to generate and satisfy new desires as the old ones become boring or their objects pass away. Kierkegaard, in *Either/Or*, calls this boredom avoidance strategy "the rotation of crops." The person who lives solely for temporal values will, according to Kierkegaard, remain in his deficient state unless he experiences and listens to the moral emotions of regret and remorse—those "emissaries from eternity" that call us to our full humanity.

Is Professor Cahn's "happy immoralist" captured by Kierkegaard's diagnosis? I think that he is. He does, after all, "relish praise," "bask in renown," and smugly "revel in his exalted position." This suggests that, like the tyrant discussed by Plato, he is attached to temporal values that are *vulnerable*—e.g., dependent on the responses of others. Since these are ultimately out of his control, must he not consciously feel or repress *fear*—a fear that may not be compatible with happiness? Cahn admits that there may be a future time when his immoralist becomes unhappy, and I am inclined to think that the immoralist's conscious or repressed realization of this possibility would at the very least pose a serious obstacle to his being fully happy now. And is happiness simply a matter of *now* anyway? Perhaps, as Aristotle sometimes suggests, happiness is better understood as an attribute, not of a present moment of one's life, but of a whole life—the wisdom in the ancient Greek saying that we should call no man happy until he is dead. Finally, if there is any truth in the idea that love and friendship are among the constituents of the happiest of human lives, must not the immoralist's nature—his inability to make and honor binding commitments—forever foreclose these goods to him?

There is no doubt that Plato's and Kierkegaard's understanding of happiness does not capture everyone's understanding of the concept, and thus it must be admitted that some conceptual or linguistic revision is going on here —just as Socrates was engaged in such revision when he made the revolutionary suggestion (*Apology*) that a good person cannot be harmed because harm (*kakon*), when properly understood, will be understood as loss of moral integrity and not as personal pain or disgrace. And if this was "sleight-of-hand," it strikes me that our concept of morality—indeed our civilization— was enriched by it. Professor Cahn's attempt to undermine the Platonic happiness tradition with his story of "the happy immoralist" thus strikes me as no more successful than an attempt to refute Socrates's claim about a good man's insulation from harm by finding a good man and hitting him in the head with a baseball bat. Doctor Glas's friend certainly overstated the case when he said that philosophy requires that language be remade from the ground up, but it is true, I think, that conceptual or linguistic revision can sometimes enlarge and deepen our moral understanding—perhaps bringing to consciousness something that was latent all along.

To sum up: When I think of the man described by Professor Cahn, I find that I *pity* him—pity him because, with Plato, I think that he is punished simply by being the kind of person that he is. But why would I pity him if I thought that he was truly happy?

C. A Challenge to Morality

STEVEN M. CAHN

Why have so many philosophers, past and present, been loath to admit even the possibility of a happy immoralist? I believe they rightly regard the concept as a threat to morality. For the greater the divergence between morality and happiness, the greater the loss of motivation to choose the moral path.

Most of us, fortunately, have moral compunctions. But when our moral values and our happiness conflict, what are we to do? Those who doubt that such a situation can ever arise should consider the following example inspired by the plot of Woody Allen's thought-provoking movie, *Crimes and Misdemeanors*.

Suppose a happily married, highly respected physician makes the mistake of embarking on an affair with an unmarried airline stewardess. When he tries to break off this relationship, she threatens to expose his adultery, thus wrecking his marriage and career.

All he has worked for his entire life is at risk. He knows that if the affair is revealed, his wife will divorce him, his children will reject him, and the members of his community will no longer support his medical practice. Instead of being the object of people's admiration, he will be viewed with scorn. In short, his life will be shattered.

As the stewardess is about to take the steps that will destroy him, he confides in his brother, who has connections to the criminal underworld. The brother offers to help him by arranging for the stewardess to be murdered without any danger that the crime will be traced to either the physician or his brother.

Should the physician consent to the killing? Doing so is clearly immoral, but, if all goes as planned, he will avoid calamity.

Assume that the physician agrees to the murder, and that when it is carried out and the police investigate, they attribute it to a drifter who eventually dies of alcoholism, and the case is closed. The physician's life goes on without further complications from the matter, and years later he is honored at a testimonial dinner where, accompanied by his loving wife and adoring children, he accepts the effusive gratitude of the community for his lifetime of service. He is a happy man, taking pride in both the affection of his family and the admiration of his patients and friends.

Even those who might take issue with my claim that the physician is happy would agree that he is happier than he would have been had his life been destroyed. So his immorality enhanced his happiness. But then the feared question arises: What persuasive reasons, if any, can be offered to demonstrate that in securing his own happiness the physician acted unwisely? Here is a serious challenge to morality, of a sort we may face quite frequently in our lives, although usually the stakes are less momentous. How we decide tells us not only about morality and happiness but also about the sort of persons we choose to be.

D. A Further Challenge

Steven M. Cahn

For those who find farfetched the case of the adulterous physician, I offer the following fictional but realistic story from the world of academia.

*   *   *

TWO LIVES

Joan earned a doctoral degree from a first-rate university and sought appointment to a tenure-track position in which she could teach and pursue her research. Unfortunately, she received no offers and was about to accept non-academic employment when an unexpected call came inviting her for an interview at a highly attractive school. During her visit she was told by the Dean that the job was hers, subject to one condition: she was expected to teach a particular course each year in which numerous varsity athletes would enroll, and she would be required to award them all passing grades even if their work was in every respect unsatisfactory. Only the Dean would know of this special arrangement.

Joan rejected the position on moral grounds and continued trying to obtain a suitable opportunity in academic life. Never again, however, was she offered a faculty position, and she was forced to pursue a career path that gave her little satisfaction. Her potential as a teacher went unfulfilled, and her planned research was left undone. Throughout her life she remained embittered.

Kate also earned a doctoral degree from a first-rate university and sought appointment to a tenure-track position in which she could teach and pursue her research. She, too, received no offers and reluctantly was about to accept non-academic employment, when an unexpected call came inviting her for an interview at the same school that Joan had visited. The Dean made Kate the identical offer that had been made to Joan. After weighing her options, Kate accepted the appointment, even though she recognized that doing so would require her to act unethically.

Kate went on to a highly successful academic career, became a popular teacher and renowned researcher, moved to one of the nation's most prestigious universities, and enjoyed all the perquisites attendant to her membership on that school's renowned faculty. When on rare occasions she recalled the conditions of her initial appointment, she viewed the actions she had taken as an unfortunate but necessary step on her path to a wonderful life.

*   *   *

Joan acted morally but lived unhappily ever after, while Kate acted immorally but lived happily ever after. So, I leave you with this dilemma: which of the two was the wiser?

HAPPINESS AND MORALITY

Christine Vitrano

Christine Vitrano, coeditor of this volume, teaches philosophy at Brooklyn College, City University of New York. She argues against the view that happiness and morality are equivalent, viewing them instead as independent dimensions of a person's life.

A prominent tradition in moral philosophy amalgamates happiness and morality, denying the possibility of their independent occurrence. According to this view, one achieves a good life by being ethical and thereby attaining happiness. I shall argue to the contrary that morality and happiness are independent dimensions of a person's life, that neither implies the other, and that while being ethical may enhance the chances for happiness, merely appearing to be ethical may prove even more effective.

1. THE CONFLATION OF HAPPINESS AND MORALITY

Richard Taylor describes happiness as "having achieved fulfillment or having been blessed with the highest personal good" which is "the great good that is the object of the moral life, the kind of good that normally takes the better part of a lifetime to attain."[1] He denies that feeling satisfaction with one's life is sufficient for happiness, arguing that "genuine happiness is found through the exercise of creative intelligence."[2]

Taylor rejects the view that we ourselves are in the best position to judge our happiness. As he explains, "If someone seems to himself or herself to be happy, perhaps he or she really is happy after all. But one can see how shallow this is by asking whether one would really wish to *be* that other person. It is hard to see why not, if that other person is believed to be truly happy. But we know, in fact, that such persons are not; they only seem so to themselves, largely because they are unwilling to admit their own folly."[3]

On Taylor's view, my wanting (or not wanting) to be another person provides a test to determine whether that person is happy. I believe this criterion is unsatisfactory. If I do not share your penchant for chocolate ice cream, I might not wish to be you (while you are eating chocolate ice cream). However, my not wanting to be you implies nothing about the quality of your experience or your mental state; it has no bearing on the question of whether *you* are happy while eating your ice cream. My wanting or not wanting to be someone else reflects my values and preferences but says nothing about the quality of that person's life.

Furthermore, I might not want to be you because I have a moral objection to the cause of your happiness. For instance, you may derive pleasure from eating a juicy steak, but I might not want to be you because I am a vegetarian opposed to eating meat. That I object to the source of your satisfaction does not detract from any happiness *you* might experience when you eat steak. Would I deny your experience of fear on the grounds that I do not find your particular situation scary? Would I deny your hunger because I believe you have eaten enough? Obviously, what I feel (or what I suppose I would feel if I were in your shoes) has no bearing on your state of mind. The same reasoning applies to happiness. I cannot deny another person's feeling of satisfaction just because I would not be satisfied if I were that person.

Taylor's view fails to capture the way "happiness" is ordinarily used, as meaning "satisfaction with one's life." Although some people's happiness may be caused by "the exercise of creative intelligence," others may find happiness in the display of athletic talents, the development of social skills, or whatever. Why redefine the word "happiness" in an effort to make a philosophical point? Doing so only misleads those who continue to use the word in its ordinary sense.

Taylor's motivation for denying that satisfaction alone is sufficient for happiness derives from his identification of happiness with the good life. He maintains the Aristotelian thesis that happiness is the greatest good, the goal towards which all people strive. If we equate happiness with achieving the good life and then identify happiness with satisfaction, we would imply that we could achieve the good life by doing whatever satisfied us, which might include immoral activities. Taylor avoids this contradictory conclusion by refusing to identify happiness with satisfaction, thus deviating from ordinary usage and rendering his theory unhelpful. Rather than adopting this special sense of happiness, I believe we should reject his conflation of happiness and the good life. We can thereby accept the immoralist's happiness without thereby committing ourselves to that person's values.

Julia Annas offers a view of happiness that commits a related error. She begins by correctly noting that what she terms the "subjectivity" of modern theories of happiness (happiness as satisfaction) marks the great divide between ancient and modern views. Instead of identifying happiness with virtuous activity, the modern notion places no restriction on the cause of a person's happiness. She finds, however, that this notion is formed from "a variety of incompatible sources," resulting in a concept of happiness that "contains several different and incompatible elements."[4]

Annas cites the following example to support her claim that our modern conception of happiness is not entirely subjective. Her colleague asked the students in his class about their ideas of a happy life. They wished for such high-priced possessions as a large house, expensive car, and so forth. He then invited the class to imagine that a rich relative had died, leaving them the financial resources to acquire all they desired. "Would these holdings make you happy?" he asked his class. They replied in the negative.[5]

Annas argues that this response indicates that the modern notion of happiness is not merely a matter of getting what you want, but "also contained the idea of living a certain sort of life, of being active rather than a passive recipient of money and other stuff."[6] She believes our modern concept of happiness is tied to the ideas of activity and achievement, and the students' response implies that "my happiness must involve my living a good life."[7] She rejects a subjective understanding of happiness, because it "leaves out some important and more objective elements which our reflection has uncovered."[8]

I agree that happiness often results from fulfilling goals. Yet whether goals are sought or achieved does not always determine who is happy. For example, some may be happy only if they win tennis tournaments; others may find happiness simply playing tennis with their friends, regardless of who wins.

Furthermore, I believe she misinterprets the students' responses. Rather than indicating something profound about the nature of happiness, their replies indicate what would give *them* satisfaction. They might wish to acquire luxuries only by working hard toward a goal, but others would be pleased to receive the luxuries regardless of their source. Do winners of a lottery regret that they didn't work hard for the money? Annas has thus mistaken a common component of much happiness for the essence of happiness itself.

To see this point more clearly, consider the example of Mary, who has had many notable accomplishments but is never satisfied because she is her own harshest critic. She constantly dwells on what she has failed to accomplish, never appreciating her numerous successes. Her negative outlook motivates her to work harder and achieve more, but she remains unhappy.

The case of Mary demonstrates that we can have a successful life in which we achieve goals while failing to be happy, because our expectations are too high, or we do not appreciate the value of what we have done. The example also highlights why being happy implies nothing about the value of our accomplishments. We may experience satisfaction because we are deceived, lack moral qualms, or have taken certain drugs. Many of us would not want to achieve happiness in these ways, but that choice is a reflection of our own values and does not reveal the nature of happiness.

2. MORALITY OR THE APPEARANCE OF MORALITY?

Although happiness and morality are conceptually independent, an empirical correlation exists between a person's moral character and happiness. Because most of us desire to develop and sustain relationships with others who will be more likely to react positively to us if we are kind and trustworthy, being moral enhances our potential for happiness. Alternatively, a person's nastiness and treachery will win few friends.

I am not denying the possibility of the happy tyrant, the happy hermit, or the happy immoralist; however, most of us rely on the good will of others in order to be happy. Psychologists studying happiness have found a positive correlation between people's social contacts (including family and friends) and the level of satisfaction with their lives. As the psychologist Michael Argyle notes, "In many studies [social relationships] come out as the greatest single source of happiness." Because having a social network is for most people an important source of happiness, almost all of us have an interest in being viewed favorably by others. Acting immorally might result in short-term gains but in the longer run will besmirch our reputations.

While no controversy surrounds the recognition of an empirical connection between a person's moral character and happiness, a crucial issue often overlooked is whether the benefit to us derives from our being moral or merely appearing to be moral. The virtuous person is bound by moral obligations and so is unable to capitalize on opportunities to increase happiness through immoral actions. The person who merely appears to be virtuous will enjoy exactly the same advantages in reputation gained by someone who actually is virtuous, but will be able to exploit situations in which immorality enhances happiness. Thus what is crucial for maximal happiness is not being moral but appearing to be moral.

To develop this point more fully, consider these four cases: (1) a moral person who appears to be moral; (2) an immoral person who appears to be moral; (3) a moral person who appears to be immoral; (4) an immoral person who appears to be immoral.

Case (4) is worst for the subject. The blatant immoralist may be able to achieve some short-term gains but once recognized as immoral will be unlikely to be happy, because immoral actions will lead at least to social disapproval, if not a jail term.

Case (3), a moral person who appears to be immoral, is almost as bad for promoting happiness. Although the subject can take pride in knowing that she is acting morally, she will nevertheless suffer all the negative consequences associated with the blatant immoralist. Consider the example of an attorney who, believing that justice requires all those accused of crimes to have competent counsel, agrees to defend a terrorist accused of a murderous bombing, The attorney has no sympathy whatever for the deadly attack but does her best in the interest of her client. The public fails to appreciate her position and views her as a terrorist-sympathizer. Threats are made against her and her family, and she is eventually forced to give up her practice and move to another locale. She has acted morally and may receive some personal satisfaction from having taken a courageous stand, but because the public views her actions as immoral, she has impaired her happiness, just as she would have had she acted immorally.

Case (1), a moral person who appears to be moral, offers a commonly accepted model for achieving happiness but still has drawbacks. In those circumstances in which happiness depends on acting immorally, the moral person will be forced to sacrifice happiness for the sake of morality. Do such circumstances actually arise? Only those in the grip of an unrealistic philosophical theory would deny the possibility.

Consider the example of Anne, who is invited to go to a concert that takes place at the same time her sister is moving into a new apartment. Anne had promised to help her sister move, but the band is Anne's favorite, and this appearance is their last engagement before they break up. Anne does not want to miss this once-in-a-lifetime opportunity, but her sister would be greatly upset if Anne broke her promise. What should she do?

As a virtuous person she has no choice but to honor her commitment, thus missing an opportunity that would bring her happiness. If, however, she were not virtuous, she might fabricate a compelling excuse and achieve greater happiness. Some might suppose that Anne's lie would in some way bring her unhappiness, but that assumption, while perhaps comforting, is unwarranted. We could tell a story about how Anne's breaking her promise worked out badly for her and her sister, but we could equally easily tell a story about how the lie worked out well for both of them.

Sometimes the path of morality leads to misery. For example, someone may stop his car to help a stranger fix a flat tire, only to be hit by an oncoming truck. The whistle blower may as a result of telling the truth be fired, while the politician who refuses to vote against conscience may thereby forfeit a realistic chance for reelection. In all such cases the individual's happiness is lost as a result of adhering to moral standards.

In case (2), however, an immoral person who appears to be moral, the subject possesses all the advantages of a reputation for being moral while avoiding the disadvantages of always acting as morality dictates. Such an individual retains the option of acting immorally, whenever greater happiness would result. Admittedly, the person does take a significant risk, because exposure might bring ruin, but by striving to develop a reputation for being moral, and acting immorally only when the payoff is huge and the chances of being caught are small, the crafty immoralist may find more happiness than anyone else.

But is such an approach to life realistic? Consider the words of the French maxim writer La Rochefoucauld, a keen observer of human nature: "Very clever men pretend all their lives to condemn trickery so that, at a crucial moment and for a large stake, they may indulge in it."[9] Should we suppose that such unethical behavior invariably leads to unhappiness? I find no convincing evidence to support that contention.

3. CONCLUSION

Once we recognize the independence of happiness and morality, we open the door to the dreaded question: Why be moral? If we acknowledge that the desire for happiness can come into conflict with acting morally, and that to pursue one's own happiness is rational, we are forced to acknowledge that sometimes acting immorally could be rational.

Faced with this conclusion, many philosophers have been tempted to deny that morality and happiness can conflict, a position that flies in the face of ordinary language or common experience. Another strategy to defuse the problem is to focus on cases of extreme depravity and then make the obvious point that such behavior is less preferable than adherence to conventional morality. The more realistic choice that confronts each person, however, is not whether to choose unmitigated evils but whether to do wrong when such action offers a plausible path to happiness. In the end, as we face critical decisions in what may be highly tempting circumstances, we are, as Sartre wrote, "alone, with no excuses."

NOTES

1. Richard Taylor, *Virtue Ethics* (Amherst, NY: Prometheus Books, 2002), p. 111.

2. Ibid., p. 121.

3. Ibid., p. 109.

4. Julia Annas, "Virtue and Eudaimonism." *Social Philosophy and Policy* 15 (1998): pp. 53, 54.

5. Julia Annas, "Should Virtue Make You Happy?" *Aepiron* 35 (2003): pp. 18–19.

6. Ibid. pp. 18–19.

7. Ibid., p. 19.

8. Ibid., p. 19.

9. *The Maxims of La Rochefoucauld*, trans. Louis Kronenberger (New York: Random House, 1959), No. 124.

CPSIA information can be obtained
at www.ICGtesting.com
Printed in the USA
BVOW09s0721140218
508079BV00002B/5/P